ANCIENT LIVES

An Introduction to
Method and Theory in Archaeology

Brian Fagan

University of California, Santa Barbara

Prentice Hall, Upper Saddle River, NJ 07458

Fagan, Brian M.
    Ancient lives : an introduction to archaeology / Brian Fagan.
        p.   cm.
    Includes bibliographical references and index.
    ISBN 0-321-04790-7
    1. Archaeology.   2. Antiquities.   3. Excavations (Archaeology)
I. Title.
CC165.F24   1999
930.1—dc21   99-24685
                                                                   CIP

Editorial director: Laura Pearson
Publisher: Nancy Roberts
Managing editor: Sharon Chambliss
Editorial/production supervision and
    interior design: York Production Services
AVP/Director of production and manufacturing: Barbara Kittle
Manufacturing manager: Nick Sklitsis
Prepress and manufacturing buyer: Benjamin D. Smith
Marketing manager: Christopher De John
Cover design: Joseph Sengotta

This book was set in 10/12 ITC Garamond Light by York Production Services
and was printed and bound by The Press of Ohio.
The cover was printed by The Press of Ohio.

© 2000 by The Lindbriar Corporation
Published by Prentice-Hall, Inc.
Upper Saddle River, New Jersey 07458

Printed in the United States of America
10   9   8   7   6   5   4   3   2   1

ISBN 0-321-04790-7

Prentice-Hall International (UK) Limited, *London*
Prentice-Hall of Australia Pty. Limited, *Sydney*
Prentice-Hall Canada Inc., *Toronto*
Prentice-Hall Hispanoamericana, S.A., *Mexico*
Prentice-Hall of India Private Limited, *New Delhi*
Prentice-Hall of Japan, Inc., *Tokyo*
Pearson Education Asia Pte. Ltd., *Singapore*
Editora Prentice-Hall do Brasil, Ltda., *Rio de Janeiro*

For
Carol Ellick
with affection and because she rescued me from writer's block

CONTENTS

Chapter 4   How Did Cultures Change?   91

PART IV
RECONSTRUCTING PAST LIVES

PART V
INTERACTIONS

PART VI
RESOURCES

PREFACE

In the absence of History, the spade becomes

no mean historian.

WILLIAM A. MILES, *THE DEVEREL BARROW* (1826)

Everywhere we turn, the past is around us, setting precedent for our own lives, threatening us, providing cautionary tales or encouragement for the future. We marvel at the achievement of the ancient Egyptians in building the Great Pyramids, gasp in amazement at the magnificent wealth of the Moche Lords of Sipán on the other side of the world in Peru, and stand in awe in the shadow of the sacred buildings that tower over the city of Teotihuacán in highland Mexico. Sometimes we feel like Hernán Cortés and his conquistadors, who gazed down on the gleaming Aztec capital in the midst of the Valley of Mexico in 1519 and likened it to an enchanted vision. So vivid were the memories that conquistador Bernal Diaz remembered every detail when he wrote his account of the Spanish Conquest of Mexico a half century later while in his seventies. "All that we saw is now vanished," he wrote of a native American world entering historical oblivion.

A century ago, we knew little of the remoter human past, of what scientists now call "prehistory." We knew that humans had lived alongside long-extinct animals such as the saber-toothed tiger, and that archaic human beings had flourished in Europe long before modern humans. Austen Henry Layard, Heinrich Schliemann, and John Lloyd Stephens had revealed long-forgotten ancient civilizations such as those of the Assyrians and Maya and the Homeric city, Troy. But our predecessors had no idea how long humans had been on earth. They knew little of the broad sweep of human prehistory from its beginnings on the African savanna. Today, we know that humankind separated from nonhuman primates at least 4 million years ago and that the first toolmaking people lived 2.5 million years ago. The latest archaeological and genetic researches date the origins of modern humans, ourselves, to about 150,000 years ago and show that we are all descended from a common African stock. We can trace our remote ancestors across the Old World and into the Americas during, and immediately after, the late Ice Age. We know the origins of farming and animal domestication go back before 8500 B.C. in southwestern Asia and at least 5,000 years in the Americas. The archaeological discoveries of the past century have uncovered cities and entire ancient landscapes and painted remarkable portraits of preindustrial civilizations in many parts of the world. Thanks to close cooperation with historians, archaeologists have reconstructed minute details of early Colonial settlements, medieval cities, and the great diversity of eighteenth-century American settlements. Archaeologists have even studied railroad stations, factories, and other buildings of the Industrial Revolution as well as modern garbage dumps.

Over the past century, archaeology has turned from a largely amateur pursuit into a highly sophisticated, multidisciplinary science that studies every aspect of the 2.5 million years of human experience. As such, it is the only science that can study human biological and cultural change over enormously long periods of time.

Modern archaeology is a highly specialized discipline, which relies on all kinds of high-technology approaches and also on not so hi-tech methods to study an enormous range of ancient human behavior—everything from prehistoric diets to long-vanished religious beliefs and individual medical histories. There is an endless fascination in exploring the byways of scientific archaeology, but this book is concerned with the basics, with the most fundamental principles, methods, and theoretical approaches. *Ancient Lives* is a wide-ranging introduction to archaeological method and theory designed for the complete beginner.

THE PHILOSOPHY BEHIND *ANCIENT LIVES*

Writing a textbook such as *Ancient Lives* is a constant exercise in compromise and making decisions as to what to include and what to omit. There are several excellent comprehensive method and theory textbooks on the market (listed at the end of Chapter 1), which offer more extended coverage of the material in this book. *Ancient Lives* is designed as a first book in archaeology, which seeks to engage the reader in a complex enterprise, to explore some of the dimensions of archaeological method and theory at a fundamental level.

From the beginning, I made unashamed use of my own long fieldwork and laboratory experience, of years of visiting other archaeologists' excavations and surveys, to give a sometimes unavoidably arid subject matter greater immediacy. At the same time, I decided from the beginning to make this an international book, which draws on methods and sites from all parts of the world. Archaeology is a global enterprise, not just something carried out in Britain, North America, and Mexico. Thus, the beginner should enjoy archaeology in all its diversity of field experience and intellectual problems.

Ancient Lives makes use of examples from the Americas, from Africa, Europe, and all parts of Asia, from the earliest archaeological sites in the world and even from modern urban trash deposits. There are numerous examples of good applications of archaeological method and theory, so it has been hard to choose the best ones. One school of thought urges the use of the latest examples from brand-new research. Another feels that one should balance male and female archaeologists equally in the examples, without, apparently, any concern for the significance of the site or the methods. I have chosen to mix three ingredients: important sites and case studies, many of them several generations old, which are still outstanding and well-known instances of archaeological research; examples from different parts of the world; and new discoveries. There are many familiar sites and discoveries (Olduvai Gorge, the tomb of Tutankhamun, and so on) that transcend the narrow interests of individual teachers and students. They are used without apology here. After all, the best-known and most spectacular sites are those that often stick in the mind, even if they were excavated several generations ago.

Archaeology has witnessed constant theoretical ferment over the past half century, some of it inspired, some of it downright nonsense. The theoretical debates continue, many of them arcane and of little concern to the beginner. For this reason, this book espouses no particular theoretical bias, both because a wide range of instructors and students will use this book, and also because individual teachers can easily use the general summaries here and give their classes their own perspectives on the tidal currents of archaeological theory.

By the book's very nature, the discussions of many issues in these pages are cursory. I have erred on the side of overstatement, on the grounds that such excesses can easily be corrected in class or later courses. Best to get the point across, then qualify it rather than to wallow in a mishmash of "probablies" or "perhapses"!

Ancient Lives is written for people who want to know more about archaeology, not necessarily with a view to becoming a professional archaeologist (although I tell you how to do that), but so that you can carry some knowledge of the remote past and how we study it with you in later life. As you will discover, the future of the past depends on responsible stewardship of the finite archives of archaeology for future generations by archaeologists and society as a whole.

I have a modest ambition with this text. If this book leaves you with a lifetime interest in archaeology, enough background knowledge to understand the reasoning behind archaeological stories in such popular journals as *National Geographic* magazine, and respect for archaeologists and the achievements of our forebears, then its job is done.

COVERAGE AND SPECIAL FEATURES

Ancient Lives makes no attempt to be a comprehensive survey of method and theory in archaeology, but focuses on general issues at the expense of irrelevant or more specialized detail.

Coverage

This book covers all aspects of scientific archaeology, but pays particular attention to the following:

- Archaeological ethics, stewardship, and conservation of the past (Chapters 1, 2, and 13). These issues are frequently neglected in beginning archaeology courses, but are fundamental to the survival of the discipline.
- Alternative perspectives on the past and on time (Chapters 1 and 3) and important issues for Native Americans and other indigenous peoples.
- The people of the past and the study of human diversity, including gender and ethnicity (Chapter 11).
- The study of ancient religious beliefs and other cultural intangibles, a fascinating and rapidly expanding direction in the field (Chapter 12).
- Career opportunities in archaeology and living with the past on a day-by-day basis (Chapter 13).

Inevitably, compromises in subject matter had to be made. *Ancient Lives* does not provide much coverage of the history of archaeology, nor of cultural resource management (CRM, although I mention it and its career possibilities frequently), nor of archaeological theory. All these topics are more appropriately taught in greater detail in more advanced undergraduate courses. So are the minute details of archaeological survey, remote sensing, excavation, and artifact analysis. In all cases, I give examples of books or articles that provide more information on these important topics. The fact that something is not covered in these pages does not mean that it is unimportant.

Special Features

- A jargon-free, easy-to-read style.
- Comprehensive glossaries of technical terms and also sites and cultures, to amplify formal definitions given at intervals in the text in boldface, for terms, and italics, for sites and cultures.
- Boxes that describe key methods such as radiocarbon dating or geographic information systems.
- Unique, truly global coverage of archaeology, reflected in examples from all parts of the world.
- Guides to further reading at the end of each chapter to direct the reader to more specialized literature or more comprehensive coverage. This text does not have a full bibliography, as the guides to further reading at the end of each chapter contain such resources to fulfill this need.
- A brief guide to Web resources, included at the end of Chapter 1. This provides access to the cyberworld of archaeology, which is expanding rapidly. I have elected to keep this guide simple, because Web sites change constantly. Luckily, there are important key Web sites such as ArchNet, which provide up-to-date links to all kinds of archaeological resources. It is easy to list individual Web sites, but the information may be out of date before the book appears in print. Better to give a central resource, as a beginning point for your research.

- A feature unique to this book: "What Happened in Prehistory," a brief account of world prehistory from human origins to the beginnings of civilization which provides background for the many sites and cultures mentioned in the book.
- A comprehensive illustration program designed to amplify the text.

Welcome to the fascinating world of archaeology!

ANCILLARY MATERIALS

The ancillary materials that accompany this textbook have been carefully created to enhance the topics being discussed.

Instructor's Manual with Tests For each chapter in the text, this manual provides a detailed outline, list of objectives, discussion questions, classroom activities, and additional resources. The test bank includes multiple choice, true-false, and essay questions for each chapter.

Prentice Hall Custom Test This computerized test item file is a test generator designed to allow the creation of personalized exams. It is available in Windows and Macintosh formats.

Companion Web Site In tandem with the text, students and professors can now take full advantage of the World Wide Web to enrich their study of archaeology. The Fagan Web Site correlates the text with related material available on the Internet. Features of the web site include chapter objectives and study questions, as well as links to interesting material and information from other sites on the Web that can reinforce and enhance the content of each chapter. **Address:** *http://www.prenhall.com/fagan*

Anthropology on the Internet: A Prentice Hall Guide, 1999–2000 This guide introduces students to the origin and innovations behind the Internet and provides clear strategies for navigating the complexity of the Internet and World Wide Web. Exercises within and at the end of the chapters allow students to practice searching for the myriad of resources available to the student of anthropology. This 96-page supplementary book is free to students when shrinkwrapped as a package with *Ancient Lives: An Introduction to Method and Theory in Archaeology.*

ACKNOWLEDGMENTS

This book originated in discussions with my colleague and friend Mitch Allen, who suggested this approach to a method and theory text. I am grateful for his perceptions and encouragement. Alan McClare, Priscilla McGeehon of Addison Wesley Longman, and Nancy Roberts of Prentice Hall put their enthusiasm and long experience behind this project from the beginning. I am grateful to Gretchen Miller and the production staff at York Production Services for their efficiency and many kindnesses. Mira Schachne was responsible for the photographic research.

My thanks, too, to the following reviewers, who criticized the proposal and drafts of the text:

Diane Gifford-Gonzalez, University of California, Santa Cruz
Neel Smith, College of the Holy Cross
Elliot M. Abrams, Ohio University
Steve Collins, Kansas City, Kansas, Community College
John S. Henderson, Cornell University
George Milner, Pennsylvania State University
Michael J. O'Brien, University of Missouri
Silvia Tomaskova, University of Texas, Austin
John W. Hoopes, University of Kansas

A book like this is only as good as its readers. I welcome comments and corrections from instructors and students alike: c/o Department of Anthropology, University of California, Santa Barbara, CA 93106, or by e-mail: brian@brianfagan.com. Rest assured your comments will be taken seriously and that they will be acknowledged.

Brian M. Fagan

AUTHOR'S NOTE

- Dates before 10,000 years ago are expressed in years Before Present (B.P.)
- Dates after 10,000 years ago are expressed in years Before Christ (B.C.) or anno domini (A.D.).

Another common convention is B.C.E./C.E. (Before Common Era/Common Era), which is not employed in this book. By scientific convention, "present" is A.D. 1950.

Please note that all radiocarbon dates and potassium-argon dates should be understood to have a plus and minus factor that is omitted from this book in the interests of clarity. They are statistical estimates. Where possible, radiocarbon dates have been calibrated with tree-ring chronologies, which adds a substantial element of accuracy (see Chapter 5). For calibration of radiocarbon dates, see Stuiver et al., 1998.

Measurements.   All measurements are given in miles, yards, feet, and inches, with metric equivalents.

WHAT HAPPENED IN PREHISTORY?

Ancient Lives describes the basic methods and theoretical approaches of scientific archaeology. In so doing, we use numerous examples from the entire 2.5-million-year time span of the human past. While the historical sites described in these pages are probably familiar to most readers, I felt there was value in providing a short summary of human prehistory as a framework for the method and theory chapters which follow. This is, at best, a cursory story. Readers are referred to the books listed at the end of this essay for more information. (For an outline chronology, see Chronological Table.)

HUMAN ORIGINS AND EARLY PREHISTORY

In 1871, Charles Darwin, the Victorian biologist who is the father of modern evolutionary theory, hypothesized that humanity originated in Africa. He based his argument on the great diversity of ape forms south of the Sahara Desert and on the close anatomical relationships between humans and such living primates as the chimpanzee. A century and a quarter later, we know that Darwin was correct and that humanity did indeed evolve in tropical Africa.

Staggering advances in multidisciplinary research have changed our perceptions of human origins dramatically since 1959, when Louis and Mary Leakey announced the discovery of a robustly built hominid at Olduvai Gorge in Tanzania, East Africa (for definitions of terms used in this essay, see the glossary). At the time, the entire span of the human past was thought to encompass a mere quarter of a million years. Soon the hominid-bearing levels at Olduvai were potassium-dated to over 1.75 million years ago. Today, we know the first toolmaking humans appeared in East Africa at least 2.5 million years ago, while earlier hominid ancestors flourished on the savanna woodlands of the region as early as 4 million years before present.

The critical behavioral changes that separated humans from nonhuman primates developed over several million years, among them a shift to bipedal (two-footed) posture, significant increases in brain size and communication skills, and the appearance of hands capable of making and manipulating simple tools. These changes took place during a period of gradual global cooling, which culminated in the dramatic climatic shifts of the Ice Age. By 3 million years ago, a wide variety of hominids inhabited tropical Africa, among them the direct ancestors of the first human beings. The very first humanly manufactured artifacts (see the discussion of culture in Chapter 2) came into use about 2.5 million years ago: they were little more than sharp-edged flakes knocked from lava cobbles and used for butchering animals and other tasks

	Old World	The Americas
A.D. 1500	European Age of Discovery	Spanish Conquest of Aztecs and the Inca
	Renaissance	Columbus
	Medieval Times	Aztecs
		Toltecs
		Mississippian Anasazi
	Han civilization in China	Maya civilization
A.D. 1	Roman Empire	Moche state
	Unification of China (221 B.C.)	Moundbuilder cultures (North America)
	Mycenaean civilization	
	Minoan civilization	Chavin
	Shang civilization (China)	Olmec
	Harappan civilization	Village farmers
3000 B.C.	Ancient Egyptian and Sumerian civilization (metallurgy and writing)	Maize agriculture?
5000 B.C.	Euxine Lake disaster	
10,000 B.P.	Origins of food production	Paleo-Indian and Archaic cultures
	Great diversity of increasingly complex forager societies	First settlement of the Americas?
20,000	First European art tradition	
	First settlement of Australia	
	Modern humans in Europe	
50,000		
	European Neanderthals	
	Modern humans in southwestern Asia	
100,000	First modern humans in Africa	
250,000 B.P.	Archaic *Homo Sapiens*	
	Fire domesticated	
	Homo erectus radiates out of Africa	
1–9 million B.P.		
2.5 million B.P.	*Homo habilis* and other hominids First toolmaking	

(see Chapter 8). We know little of the behavior of these earliest humans, although laboratory studies of broken animal bones strongly suggest that they scavenged much of their meat from predator kills. At the same time, they relied heavily on wild plant foods, as have most hunter-gatherers ever since.

The earliest hominids flourished and evolved in sub-Saharan Africa. At the time, the rest of the world was still uninhabited. Around 2 million years ago, more-advanced humans with larger brains and more humanlike limbs evolved out of earlier hominid populations. About this time, too, humans tamed fire, which became a potent tool for adapting to much cooler environments. This was the moment at which humanity foraged its way across the Sahara Desert and into Asia and then Europe, adapting to a wide variety of tropical and temperate environments. This radiation of archaic humans, grouped generically under the label *Homo erectus,* may have taken place about 1.9 million years ago, or somewhat later, as part of a general movement of many mammal forms out of Africa into other parts of the world.

Three-quarters of a million years ago, the human population of the Old World was probably no more than a few tens of thousands of people, living in small family bands in temperate and tropical environments. By this time, the world had entered a seesaw-like pattern of alternating glacial and interglacial periods, oscillating between cooler and warmer conditions in such a way that global climate has been in a state of transition for 75 percent of the past 730,000 years. Our archaic ancestors adapted successfully to these dramatic long- and shorter-term shifts with brilliant opportunism. By 400,000 years ago, European hunters at Schoningen, Germany, were using long wooden spears to pursue even large and formidable game, while a simple and highly effective stone technology based on choppers and axes evolved slowly into much more sophisticated and specialized tool kits.

THE ORIGINS AND SPREAD OF MODERN HUMANS

Between 750,000 and 200,000 years ago, human biological and cultural evolution continued at a slow pace, as *Homo erectus* evolved gradually into more modern forms, toward ourselves, *Homo sapiens sapiens.* Most famous among these early *Homo sapiens* forms are the Neanderthals of Europe and central and southwestern Asia, who appeared over 200,000 years ago and adapted successfully to the extreme temperatures of the late Ice Age.

A vast anatomical and cultural chasm separates *Homo sapiens sapiens* from its more archaic *Homo sapiens* predecessors. We are the "wise people," capable of fluent speech and intelligent reasoning, brilliant innovators with the ability to adapt successfully to every extreme environment on earth. Great controversy surrounds our origins, with scientists divided into two broad camps. One school of thought believes that modern humans evolved separately in different parts of the world more or less simultaneously. However, most experts, including molecular biologists, think that our direct ancestors evolved out of more archaic human populations in tropical Africa between 150,000 and 200,000 years ago. They base their argument on a scatter of human fossil finds south of the Sahara Desert and on mitochondrial DNA, inherited through the female line, which places our ultimate roots in Africa.

Fully modern humans appeared in Africa well before 100,000 years ago, then foraged their way across the Sahara Desert during a period of increased rainfall that turned much of the desert into semiarid grasslands. By about 90,000 years ago, anatomically modern people were living in southwestern Asia alongside more archaic Neanderthal populations. Soon afterward, the moderns may also have moved into southern, then southeastern Asia: We do not know. But some 40,000 years passed before modern humans spread northward and westward into the colder environments of late–Ice Age Europe and Eurasia. But this time, our ancestors had developed much more sophisticated tool kits based on blade technology, which, like the modern-day Swiss Army knife, formed a basis for many more specialized artifacts such as knives, spear points, and chisel-like tools that could be used to cut and shape bone and antler.

Between 40,000 and 15,000 years ago, modern humans settled in every corner of the world. As the Cro-Magnons, they replaced European and Eurasian Neanderthal populations, developing an elaborate tool kit that enabled them to adapt to a highly changeable, often intensely cold environment. These are the people who produced the magnificent cave paintings and engravings of western Europe. By 40,000 years ago, perhaps earlier, small hunter-gatherer populations had crossed open water to New Guinea and Australia. Ten thousand years later, they had settled on the Solomon Islands and other relatively close southwestern Pacific Islands. The settlement of the offshore Pacific Islands did not take place until the development of root agriculture and outrigger canoes took settlers to the offshore islands of Melanesia and Polynesia nearly 30,000 years later.

FIRST SETTLEMENT OF THE AMERICAS

By 20,000 years ago, human beings had penetrated far into northern latitudes, onto the frigid steppe-tundra of central Asia, to Siberia's Lake Baikal, and perhaps into extreme northeastern Siberia. But the Americas were still virgin continents, joined to Siberia by a low-lying land bridge during the late Ice Age, when sea levels were about 300 feet (91 m) lower than today.

The first settlement of the Americas remains one of the great mysteries of archaeology. Everyone agrees that the ultimate ancestry of the Native Americans lies in northeast Asia, and perhaps China, but there is little agreement as to when or how the first settlers arrived in the New World. There are a few unsubstantiated claims for settlement before 20,000 years ago, perhaps even as early as 40,000 years before present. Unfortunately, none of the sites purported to document such early settlement stand up to close scientific scrutiny. Nor is there evidence for human occupation of the inhospitable reaches of northeastern Siberia before some 15,000 to 18,000 years ago. Most archaeologists believe that the first Americans arrived, either crossing the land bridge or perhaps by canoe along the frigid coastline during the very late Ice Age or immediately thereafter, perhaps as early as 15,000 years ago.

The earliest well-documented human settlement in Alaska dates to just before 9000 B.C., but there are also sites of that age, and even slightly earlier, much further south. No one knows, too, how the first human settlers moved from Alaska into the heart of the Americas. Perhaps they traveled southward along the coastline along now-submerged shores or overland, as the great ice sheets that once mantled northern North America retreated at the end of the Ice Age. We do know, however, that hunter-gatherer populations were scattered throughout the Americas by 10,500 B.C., well adapted to every kind of environment from open plains to tropical rainforest. From these early populations developed the great diversity of later Native American societies that were the direct ancestors of the much more elaborate indigenous societies of later times.

THE ORIGINS OF FOOD PRODUCTION

Since 15,000 years ago, the endless cycle of global climate change moved into another warming mode. The great ice sheets that had covered northern Europe and North America receded rapidly. World sea levels rose closer to modern levels. Global warming brought major shifts in rainfall patterns and vegetation. Birch and oak forests replaced open plains in Europe. The Sahara again supported dry grassland. Birch forests populated much of Canada. Hundreds of animal species large and small became extinct in the face of global warming, among them the long-haired arctic elephant (the mammoth) and the mastodon. Human societies everywhere adapted to radically different environments, many of them turning to intensive exploitation of small game, fish and sea mammals, and plant foods of every kind. Many groups settled at the boundaries of several ecological zones, or by estuaries, lakes, or sea coasts, where they could exploit diverse food resources and stay in one place for much of the year. In these resource-rich areas, local populations rose considerably and the landscape filled up, to the point when each group had its own territory, and there was sometimes competition for valuable food supplies. By about 10,000 years ago, demographers believe, the Old World was close to the limits of its ability to support growing human forager populations, even in favorable environments.

Post–Ice Age global warming did not proceed steadily, but in stops and starts. The mechanisms that drive long- or short-term climatic change are still a mystery, but they are closely connected to changes in the complex interactions between the atmosphere and the ocean, including the circulation of warm water from the tropics to northern latitudes and the downwelling of salt to the ocean floor in the North Atlantic. Whatever the causes of the change, the past 15,000 years have been marked by some dramatic millennium- and centuries-long climatic shifts, among them the famous "Little Ice Age" which caused regular famines in Europe between A.D. 1300 and 1850. But the most dramatic of these shifts occurred between 11,000 and 10,000 B.C., when the world suddenly returned to near-glacial conditions during the so-called Younger Dryas event (named after a polar shrub, see Chapter 5).

Early Food Production in the Old World

The Younger Dryas saw advancing glaciers in northern Europe and North America, while bringing severe drought to southwestern Asia. This drought had catastrophic effects on the sedentary forager populations clustered in favorable environments such as the Euphrates and Jordan river valleys, and elsewhere between Turkey and southern Iraq. Within a few generations, many of these societies turned to the cultivation of wild cereal grasses as a way of supplementing wild plant foods. Only a few generations passed before wild wheat and barley became domesticated crops and agriculture replaced plant foraging as a staple of human existence. At about the same time, some groups also domesticated wild goats and sheep, also pigs, and later cattle. By 8000 B.C., farming societies were widespread throughout southwestern Asia. Agriculture also began in Egypt's Nile Valley at about the same time, but the exact date is still unknown.

The new economies were brilliantly successful and spread rapidly through the eastern Mediterranean world and around the shores of the Euxine Lake (now the Black Sea), which was then a freshwater lake separated from the Mediterranean Sea by a huge natural earthen bank which crossed what is now the Bosporus between Turkey and Bulgaria. Farmers lived in Greece and southeastern Europe by 6000 B.C. Some five centuries later, the rising Mediterranean burst through the Bosporus and flooded the Euxine Lake in a natural disaster that unfolded over a few weeks, causing the new Black Sea to become brackish and rise hundreds of feet, displacing the many agricultural societies on its shores. The flooding of the Black Sea must have caused massive disruption and population movements away from the inundated areas, accelerating the spread of farming peoples northwestward into temperate Europe, where agriculture was well established by 5000 to 4500 B.C.

Food production did not develop in one region alone. Rice cultivation developed in southern China, along the Yangtze River, by at least 6500 B.C. and probably earlier, and cereal agriculture in the north by 6000 B.C. As in southwestern Asia, the new economies were a logical response to growing population densities and unpredictable climatic shifts.

In southwestern Asia, south Asia, and China, food production provided the economic foundation for the world's earliest preindustrial civilizations.

Early Farmers in the Americas

When Europeans arrived in the Americas in the fifteenth century A.D., they marveled at the expertise of Native Americans with cereal and root crops. The native Andeans domesticated hundreds of potato forms, while maize was the staff of life for millions of farmers between tropical South America and Canada's St. Lawrence Valley in northeastern North America.

Despite intensive research, we still know little of the origins of food production in the Americas. Thanks to AMS (accelerated mass spectrometry) radiocarbon dating (see Chapter 3) and generations of botanical research, we know that maize was domesticated from a wild grass named teosinte somewhere in south-central Mexico, at least as early as 3000 B.C., and probably earlier. Maize, as well as other crops such as beans, spread rapidly in various strains—into lowland and highland South America by at least 1000 B.C., and into the southwestern United States by 1500 B.C. The first domestication of the potato took place in the highland Andes at least as early as 2500 B.C., along with other staples, such as quinoa.

Maize agriculture spread widely among North American forager societies that were preadapted to food production by millennia of intensive hunting and gathering, often in densely populated environments such as the river valleys and lakes of the Midwest and Southeast. Some of these people were already cultivating native plants such as goosefoot and squashes many centuries before maize and bean agriculture became established among them.

As in the Old World, the new economies spread rapidly from their points of origin. By the time Europeans arrived in the fifteenth century A.D., Native Americans were exploiting hundreds of domesticated plants in every environment where agriculture was feasible. In many areas, such as the highland Andes, growing populations tested the limits of maize and other crops by planting them at ever higher altitudes and by breeding cold- and drought-resistant strains. It is no coincidence that many Native American crops are now staples of the modern global economy. At the same time, the Native Americans domesticated few animals other than the alpaca, dog, llama, and turkey, for they lacked the potentially domesticable animals that abounded in the Old World.

Only 2,000 years or so after the domestication of plants, Native American societies in Mesoamerica and the Andean region developed much more complex societies, and soon thereafter, the first indigenous New World civilizations.

THE FIRST CIVILIZATIONS IN THE OLD WORLD

Five thousand years after farming began in southwestern Asia, the first literate, urban civilizations developed almost simultaneously in southern Mesopotamia and along the Nile River. Their roots lay among increasingly complex farming societies which had become increasingly interdependent and centralized. Numerous innovations accompanied the emergence of the first civilizations—intensified agriculture, often relying on irrigation; metallurgy; the sailing ship; and writing among them.

The origins of state-organized societies (civilizations, see Chapter 4) is one of the most hotly debated issues in archaeology, for we still lack a definitive explanation of how civilization began. The most plausible scenario combines fast-rising population densities and increased competition for economic and political power with environmental changes which included a stabilization of global sea levels at modern levels. The complex economic, political, and social changes to civilization have been likened to a game of ancient Monopoly that pitted chief against chief in fast-moving diplomatic and economic games where the strongest and most decisive leaders survived. You can see the process along the Nile River, where increasingly large and more powerful riverside states competed with one another over many centuries. Eventually, powerful rulers in Upper (southern) Egypt conquered the states of the fertile delta region in the north and created a unified kingdom in about 3100 B.C. under a pharaoh (king) named Menes. Over the next few centuries, his successors created a powerful religious ideology and royal culture that turned the pharaoh into a divine ruler with supreme powers on earth. Egypt's conservative, yet surprisingly flexible, civilization endured for nearly 3,000 years as a preindustrial society that created the pyramids and nurtured some of the greatest rulers in history.

The route to civilization in Mesopotamia involved similar complex processes of environmental, political, and social change in a lowland environment where powerful cities became a patchwork of small city-states which competed one with another over water rights, trade routes, and land. The Sumerian civilization, a patchwork of competing city-states such as Eridu, Ur, and Uruk, was only rarely unified into a large entity until the third millennium B.C., when the rulers of Ur patched together a civilization that unified, at least nominally, a mosaic of smaller states from the Mediterranean coast to the Persian Gulf. Successive civilizations rose from the disintegration of Sumerian society after 2500 B.C., when Akkadians based in Babylon to the north created a new empire in southern Mesopotamia, followed in turn by the Assyrians of the first millennium B.C.

By this time, the civilizations of the eastern Mediterranean world were linked by increasingly close economic ties, to the point that some scholars have written of this as the first "world economic system," perhaps a somewhat grandiose term for a vast region between India and mainland Greece linked by land and oceangoing trade routes which handled goods and commodities of every kind (for trade, see Chapter 11). By 2600 B.C., Sumerian monarchs boasted of ships from distant Meluhha that docked at their ports. Meluhha was probably the Indus Valley in what is now northwestern Pakistan where the indigenous Harappan civilization developed before 2000 B.C. This was a loosely connected riverine civilization with numerous large towns and several large cities, among them Harappa and Mohenjodaro. Harappa traded regularly with Mesopotamia on such a scale that it had its own script and systems of weights and measures; it disintegrated about 1700 B.C. A few centuries later, the center of gravity of early Indian civilization moved eastward into the Ganges River valley, where the great Mauryan civilization flourished in the first millennium B.C.

The Greek mainland and Aegean islands nurtured their own distinctive civilizations, which developed from many centuries of long-distance trade in olive oil, wine, timber, and other commodities. Crete's Minoan civilization prospered off of far-flung trade routes that linked the Aegean with the eastern Mediterranean and the Nile Valley. Egyptian inscriptions and paintings show Minoan traders at the pharaoh's court as early as 1600 B.C., while the famous *Uluburun* shipwreck off the southern Turkish coast in 1310 B.C. chronicles the astounding wealth of foreign trade at the time (see Chapter 11). After 1450 B.C., the Mycenaeans ruled both the Greek mainland and Crete, strengthening their ties with the powerful Hittite civilization in what is now Turkey, the Assyrians in Mesopotamia, and the Egyptians. This prosperous, highly competitive world collapsed in political turmoil about 1200 B.C. for reasons that are still little understood. The first millennium B.C. saw the rise and fall of the Persian empire and of Alexander the Great's vast domains, the glories of classical Greece, and then, finally, the rise of the Roman Empire, which dominated the Western world from before the time of Christ until the Dark Ages.

As Egyptian and Mesopotamian civilizations appeared in the west, more complex societies developed in northern and southern China. By 2500 B.C., these "Lungshan" cultures enjoyed highly centralized, elaborate social organization and were developing into highly competitive and much larger political units. By about 2000 B.C., Chinese history enters an era of legend with a basis in fact, with the competing Xia, Shang, and Zhou dynasties of the Huang Ho (Yellow) River. Between 1766 and 1100 B.C., the Shang civilization dominated the north, to be succeeded by the Zhou dynasty, which in turn gave way to a historical jigsaw puzzle of warring states which were finally unified by the ruthless and despotic Emperor Shihuangdi in 221 B.C. The emperor is famous for his lavish and still unexcavated royal tomb, guarded by a regiment of spectacular terra-cotta soldiers.

By the time of Christ, Greek sea captains had discovered the secrets of the monsoon winds of the Indian Ocean, which allowed a sailing vessel to sail to India and back with favorable winds within 12 months. Within a few centuries, the Roman world was linked to India and, indirectly, with the Han empire in distant China. The Mediterranean and Asian worlds became interconnected with economic and diplomatic ties that endured until Portuguese explorer Vasco da Gama sailed around Africa's Cape of Good Hope direct to India along the monsoon route in A.D. 1497. His voyage took place as the European Age of Discovery brought Columbus to the Indies and other explorers to the Pacific and southeast Asia.

EARLY AMERICAN CIVILIZATIONS

The indigenous civilizations of the Americas developed a brilliant complexity, with many resemblances in general characteristics and organization to preindustrial states in the Old World.

Mesoamerican Civilization

In 1519, when Spanish conquistador Hernán Cortés and his motley band of followers gazed down on the glittering Aztec capital, Tenochtitlán, in the heart of the Valley of Mexico, they were astounded by the gleaming temples and palaces that could be seen from miles away. They marveled at the vast market, larger than that in Constantinople, attended by as many as 20,000 people a day. More than 250,000 Aztecs lived in or around Tenochtitlán, which was, at the time, one of the largest cities in the world. Within two years, the Aztec capital was a pile of smoking ruins after months of bitter fighting. Soon, the dazzling Aztec civilization was just a memory.

The Aztec empire developed out of more than 2,500 years of Mesoamerican civilization. The architecture of the Aztec capital, cosmology, religious beliefs, and their institutions of kingship had deep roots in earlier, much-revered civilizations.

Mesoamerican civilization developed from ancient village roots, but the religious beliefs and institutions of the Olmec people of the Veracruz lowlands were of paramount importance after 1500 B.C. The Olmec developed their religious ideology and distinctive art style from farmers' beliefs, which involved both shamanism and a profound belief in the power of the elusive, fierce jaguar. By 1200 B.C., their religious beliefs and the art style that accompanied them were widespread throughout lowland and highland Mesoamerica. Massive, brooding figures of Olmec rulers (see Figure 12.5) give an impression of immense shamanistic power, of individuals who traveled freely between the material and spiritual worlds, which is always a feature of Mesoamerican civilization. The Olmec had still little-known equivalents in other parts of the lowlands and highlands, but their influence on later Mesoamerican civilizations was enormous.

As the Olmec flourished, Maya civilization developed out of village cultures in the Yucatán lowlands. Some small ceremonial centers were flourishing by 1500 B.C. A thousand years later, the first large Preclassic Maya cities rose in the southern Yucatán, among them Nakbé and El Mirador, places where kingship became a formal institution and Maya lords became powerful rulers who presided over ever changing city-states. By A.D. 100, the Classic Maya civilization was well under way, as a jigsaw puzzle of city-states large and small competed ferociously with one another for political power, trade monopolies, and prestige. The Maya developed their own indigenous script, whose decipherment is one of the great scientific triumphs of the twentieth century. This decipherment has allowed us to reconstruct not only the complex Maya calendar (see Chapter 3), but many details of their political history and cosmology.

Classic Maya civilization flourished in the southern lowlands until the ninth century. The four largest city-states—Calakmul, Copán, Palenque, and Tikal—were all ruled by long-lived dynasties of authoritative lords. Meanwhile, the great city of Teotihuacán rose to prominence in the highlands. This was a city of more than 120,000 people and a trading and religious center of enormous power. From 200 B.C. to A.D. 750, Teotihuacán was the dominant presence on the highlands, ruled by increasingly militaristic rulers who traded with the city of Monte Albán in the Valley of Oaxaca and with the Maya, who were strongly influenced by the city's militaristic beliefs. In about A.D. 750, Teotihuacán abruptly collapsed, leaving a political vacuum in the highlands. In the eighth century, Maya civilization collapsed in the southern highlands, probably as a result of stress brought about by drought, environmental degradation, and internal social disorder. The dense urban populations scattered, but Maya civilization endured and flourished in the northern Yucatán until the arrival of the Spanish in 1517.

In the highlands, several centuries passed before the Toltec civilization emerged as a new, dominant force in the Valley of Mexico, only to implode in A.D. 1200, probably as a result of fierce external and internal rivalries. The Aztecs arrived in the valley soon afterward as obscure nomads entering a political environment of vicious competition between well-established city-states. With brilliant diplomatic and military skill, the Aztecs became mercenaries, then conquerors. By 1425, they were masters of the Valley of Mexico and in the midst of expanding their empire, which extended from the Gulf of Mexico to the Pacific Ocean and from Guatemala to northern Mexico, when the Spaniards gazed on Tenochtitlán in 1519. The Aztecs held their domains together by force and harsh tribute assessments. Inevitably, many vassal cities joined the newcomers as a way of overthrowing the hated Aztec masters, only to suffer a different form of bondage after the Spanish Conquest.

Andean Civilization

Andean civilization also developed from ancient village roots. It was to encompass the vast Inca empire, overthrown by Spaniard Francisco Pizarro in the early 1530s. At the time, as many as 6 million people lived under Inca rule, part of Tawantinsuyu, "the Land of the Four Quarters," which extended from Chile and Bolivia in the south to Ecuador in the north and encompassed the Andes highlands, some Amazonian rainforest, and the arid Pacific coast.

The origins of Andean civilization may be associated with the intensive exploitation of anchovies and other coastal fish, which flourished in the cold Humboldt Current, which flows close to the arid Pacific shoreline. This bounty, when combined with intensive agriculture in irrigated coastal river valleys, provided ample food surpluses for complex societies centered on increasingly elaborate ceremonial centers. By 900 B.C., a distinctive Andean religious ideology had appeared at Chavín de Huantar in the foothills and spread widely through the entire region along trade routes that linked highlands and lowlands.

The first millennium A.D. saw the development of two poles of Andean civilization. The first was centered on Peru's north coast, river valley societies that traded cotton, textiles, and marine products such as fishmeal with the highlands. The Moche state, which flourished for much of the early and mid-first millennium A.D., enjoyed great wealth, as its leaders organized elaborate intervalley canals and irrigation systems. North coast civilization was volatile and vulnerable to drought and catastrophic El Niño floods. By 1100, the Chimu state dominated the region, only to be overthrown by Inca conquerors in the fourteenth century.

The southern pole of Andean civilization was centered around the shores of Lake Titicaca and dominated by Pukara, and especially the city of Tiwanaku, which reached the height of its powers in the first millennium A.D. before collapsing in about A.D. 1000. The highland plains around Lake Titicaca were conquered early by the Inca, who began aggressive campaigns of conquest to expand their domains after 1438. The Inca empire was at its maximum extent when Spanish conquistadors brought smallpox and destruction to the Andean world in the 1530s.

The conquest of the Aztec and Inca empires was part of the final chapter of prehistory, which saw Western civilization expand to every corner of the world and the creation of the first truly global economy. But the great diversity of humankind in the modern world serves to remind us of our common roots in the remote past, a past reconstructed in large part by archaeology, the only scientific discipline that studies and explains human cultural evolution over long periods of time.

FURTHER READING

Three widely read college texts provide more specifics on human prehistory and are available in most academic libraries:

Fagan, Brian. 2001. *People of the Earth: An Introduction to World Prehistory.* 10th ed. Upper Saddle River, NJ: Prentice Hall.

Price, Douglas, Gary Feinman. 1996. *Images of the Past.* 2nd ed. Mountain View, CA: Mayfield.

Wenke, Robert. 2000. *Patterns in Prehistory.* 3rd ed. New York: Oxford University Press.

PART I

INTRODUCING ARCHAEOLOGY

*The very air you breathe, unchanged
through the centuries, you share with those
who laid the mummy to its rest. Time is
annihilated by little intimate details such as
these, and you feel an intruder.*

HOWARD CARTER ON TUTANKHAMUN'S TOMB, 1923.

CHAPTER 1
What Is Archaeology?

Wall painting of a bull from Lascaux Cave, France. c. 15,000 years ago. (Source: Peter H. Buckley/Pearson Education/PH College.)

CHAPTER OUTLINE

The priests supervised the hasty digging of a vast pit in the royal cemetery at *Ur* in what is now southern Iraq over a few days in 2100 B.C. Dozens of workers carried basketloads of earth up a lengthening ramp and dumped their loads to one side. Next, in the bottom of the hole, a few masons built a stone burial chamber with a vaulted brick roof. A small procession of high officials carried the royal corpse into the empty sepulcher and laid the dead man out in all his finery. They arranged food offerings alongside the bier in gold and silver bowls. Then the dead man's closest personal attendants knelt silently by their master. They swallowed poison and accompanied the prince into eternity. The walled-up chamber stood at the back of the empty pit, where the priests presided over a lavish funeral feast.

A long line of soldiers, courtiers, and male and female servants filed into the mat-filled burial pit. Everyone wore their finest robes, most brilliant uniforms, and badges of rank. Each courtier, soldier, or servant carried a small clay cup brimming with poison. The musicians bore their lyres. The royal charioteers drove the ox-drawn wagons down the ramp to their assigned place in the bottom of the great hole. Grooms calmed the restless animals as the drivers held the reins (Figure 1.1). Everyone lined up in their proper places in order of precedence. Music played. A small detachment of soldiers guarded the top of the ramp with watchful eyes. At a quiet signal, everyone in the pit raised their clay cups to their lips and swallowed poison. Then they lay down to die, each in his or her correct place. As the bodies twitched, then lay still, a few men slipped into the pit and killed the oxen with quick blows. The royal court had embarked on its long journey to the afterlife.

FIGURE 1.1 Reconstruction of a royal funeral at Sumerian Ur, as recorded by Sir Leonard Woolley. *(Courtesy of the Trustees of the British Museum.)*

The priests covered the grave pit with earth and a mudbrick structure before filling the hole and access ramp with layers of clay. A sacrificial victim marked each stratum until the royal sepulcher reached ground level.

Archaeology is the stuff dreams are made of—buried treasure, gold-laden pharaohs, the romance of long-lost civilizations. Many people think of **archaeologists** as romantic adventurers, like the film world's Indiana Jones. Cartoonists often depict us as eccentric scholars in solar helmets digging up inscribed tablets in the shadow of great pyramids. Popular legend would have us be absent-minded professors, so deeply absorbed in ancient times that we care little for the realities of modern life. Some discoveries, such as the royal cemetery at Ur, do indeed foster visions of adventure and romance.

British archaeologist Sir Leonard Woolley reconstructed the Ur funeral from brilliant archaeological excavations made in 1926; it was a layer of skeletons that seemed to be lying on a golden carpet. Woolley worked miracles of discovery under very harsh conditions. He excavated with only a handful of fellow experts and employed hundreds of workers. When the going got tough, he would hire a Euphrates River boatman to sing rhythmic boating songs with a lilting beat. Woolley cleared 2,000 commoners' graves and 16 royal burials in four years, using paintbrushes and knives to clean each skeleton. He lifted a queen's head with its elaborate wiglike headdress in one piece after smothering the skull in liquid paraffin oil. Nearby, he noticed a hole in the soil, poured plaster-of-paris down it, and recovered the cast of the wooden sound box of a royal lyre. Woolley recon-

FIGURE 1.2   A famous ornament from the Royal Cemetery at Ur, called by Leonard Woolley "Ram in the thicket." The wood figure was covered with gold leaf and lapis lazuli: The belly was covered in silver leaf and the fleece in shell. *(Courtesy of the University Museum, University of Pennsylvania.)*

structed a magnificent figure of a goat from tiny fragments (Figure 1.2). He called the cemetery excavation "a jigsaw in three dimensions" and wrote of the sacrificial victims: "A blaze of colour with the crimson coats, the silver, and the gold; clearly these people were not wretched slaves killed as oxen might be killed, but persons held in honour, wearing their robes of office . . ." (Woolley 1982, 123).

Woolley's excavations captivated the world three-quarters of a century ago. Archaeology has come a long way since then, turning from spectacular discoveries to slow-moving teamwork in often far-from-dramatic sites. However, the complex detective work accomplished by today's archaeologists, which teases out minor details of the past, has a fascination that rivals Ur's royal cemetery.

Chapter 1 introduces archaeology, describes how it began and what archaeologists do, and discusses the importance of the discipline in today's world.

HOW ARCHAEOLOGY BEGAN

The first archaeologists were adventurers and casual collectors, anxious for fame and fortune, or simply looking for new artifacts for their private collections. The practice of aristocratic gentlemen taking grand tours of Mediterranean lands was common as early as the seventeenth century. By the early nineteenth century, many British landowners were trenching into ancient burial mounds for funeral urns and skeletons (Figure 1.3). They would celebrate their discov-

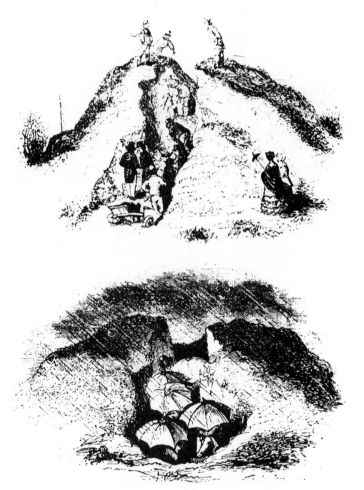

FIGURE 1.3 Burial mound excavation, nineteenth-century style, as depicted in *Gentleman's Magazine*, 1840. "Eight barrows were examined . . . . Most of them contained skeletons, more or less entire, with the remains of weapons in iron, bosses of shields, urns, beads, brooches, armlets, bones, amulets, and occasionally more vessels."

eries with fine dinners, toasting their friends with ancient clay vessels. At the same time, looters and tomb robbers descended on Egypt, seeking mummies, statues, and other precious ancient Egyptian artifacts. Giovanni Battista Belzoni (1778–1822), a circus strongman turned treasure hunter, ransacked tombs and temples along the Nile during 1816 to 1819. One of his specialties was collecting mummies. He scrambled into rocky clefts crammed with mummies: "surrounded by bodies, by heaps of mummies in all directions . . . The Arabs with the candles or torches in their hands, naked and covered with dust themselves resembled living mummies" (Belzoni 1820, 157). On one occasion he sat on a mummy by mistake and sank down in a crushed mass of bones, dried skin, and dry bandages. Belzoni eventually fled Egypt under threat of death. Those were the days when archaeologists settled their differences with guns.

The Discovery of Early Civilizations

A hundred and fifty years ago, you could find an ancient civilization in a month. Englishman Austen Henry Layard and Frenchman Emile Botta did just that in the 1840s. They dug into vast city mounds at *Khorsabad* and *Nineveh* in northern Iraq and unearthed the shadowy Assyrian civilization mentioned in the Old Testament. Layard tunneled into ancient Nineveh, following the walls of palace rooms adorned with magnificent reliefs of conquering armies, a royal lion hunt, and exotic gods. He transported his finds down the Tigris River on wooden rafts supported by inflated goatskins (Figure 1.4). His

FIGURE 1.4   Englishman Austen Henry Layard floated his Assyrian finds from Nineveh down the Tigris River on wooden rafts supported by inflated goatskins. Once the rafts reached the Persian Gulf, the skins were deflated, loaded on donkeys, and packed upstream. The wood was sold for a handsome profit. The Assyrians themselves had used similar river vessels. *(Courtesy of the Courthauld Institute of Art, London.)*

DISCOVERY

Austen Henry Layard at Nineveh

Austen Henry Layard was the consummate adventurer, who arrived in Mesopotamia in 1840 while riding from England to India. He became obsessed with the ancient city mounds of Nineveh and Nimrud. After a brief and hectic interlude as a diplomat and secret agent, Layard trenched into Nimrud on the banks of the Tigris River. He unearthed two Assyrian royal palaces in a month, then moved to Nineveh where he dug hundreds of yards of tunnels deep into King Ashurbanipal's palace. When his workers uncovered a room full of inscribed clay tablets, Layard casually shoveled them into baskets and shipped them back to London. Layard himself had no idea that this remarkable archive would prove to be the most important of all his discoveries. This was rough and ready excavation on a grand scale. Layard presided over his men like a monarch, throwing feasts, settling quarrels, even performing marriages. He employed hundreds of workers to tunnel into the palaces and to search for spectacular finds, working in temperatures of over 110°F. When he uncovered King Sennacherib's "Palace Without Rival," built in about 700 B.C., he uncovered the palace gateway, over 14 feet (4.2 m) wide, paved with great limestone slabs and guarded by human-headed bulls. The huge slabs still bore the ruts of Sennacherib's chariot wheels.

Layard was an accomplished writer, whose bestselling *Nineveh and Its Remains* (1849) is still in print today. He gave up archaeology in 1852, became a member of parliament, then a diplomat.

excavations also uncovered the royal library of Assyrian King Ashurbanipal (883–859 B.C.), which contained an account of an ancient flood in southern Iraq remarkably like that mentioned in Genesis. (See Discovery box above.)

American travel writer John Lloyd Stephens and artist Frederick Catherwood revealed the spectacular Maya civilization of Mexico, Guatemala, and Honduras in 1839. They visited *Copán, Palenque, Uxmal,* and other hitherto forgotten ancient cities, captivating an enormous audience with their adventures in the rainforest and with lyrical descriptions and pictures of an ancient society shrouded in tropical vegetation (Figure 1.5). Stephens laid the foundation for all subsequent research on ancient Maya civilization by declaring that the cities he visited were built by the ancestors of the modern inhabitants of the region. Like Layard, he was a bestselling author, whose books are still in print.

The Origins of Humankind

While Layard and others searched for ancient civilizations, the publication of biologist Charles Darwin's *Origin of Species* in 1859 caused a complete rethinking of human origins. For centuries, Christian teaching had proclaimed the story of the Creation in Genesis, Chapter 1, the literal historical truth.

FIGURE 1.5 John Lloyd Stephens examines a temple at Palenque in the Maya lowlands.

Sixteenth-century Archbishop James Ussher of Armagh in northern Ireland used the genealogies in the Old Testament to calculate the date of the Creation to be 4004 B.C., allowing a mere 6,000 years for all of human existence. However, repeated discoveries of the bones of long-extinct animals within the same geological levels as humanly made stone tools hinted at a much greater antiquity for humankind.

While Creationists argued for a series of worlds, each destroyed by divinely inspired catastrophic floods, stratigraphic geologists showed how the earth had formed through natural geological processes such as rainfall, earthquakes, and wind action. Darwin developed a theoretical framework that provided an explanation for why extinct animals and humans coexisted far earlier than the 6,000 years of the Creationists.

Meanwhile, generations of archaeologists had puzzled over crudely made stone axes found in the same geological strata as the bones of long-extinct animals such as the European elephant. In the 1840s, Frenchman Jacques Boucher de Perthes announced the discovery of stone axes and elephant bones in the gravels of the Somme River in northern France, and British geologists dug into caves in southwestern England looking for similar associations. As Charles Darwin published his famous *Origin of Species*, most scientists were skeptical. Wrote archaeologist John Evans in a letter: "Think of their finding flint axes and arrowheads at Abbeville in conjunction with bones of elephants and rhinoceroses forty feet below the surface in a bed of drift [gravel] . . . I can hardly believe it" (Evans, J. 1943, 222). Evans and geologist Joseph Prestwich inspected Perthes's discoveries in person. John Evans himself pulled an ax out of the same level as an elephant bone and was convinced the two were the same age. As a result of their report to the Royal Society of London, the scientific establishment rejected biblical chronologies for human origins and accepted the notion of a much earlier antiquity of humankind.

The Origins of Scientific Archaeology

Scientific archaeology began in the 1870s, just as the compelling and highly controversial German businessman-turned-archaeologist Heinrich Schliemann dug into Homeric Troy in 1871. Schliemann employed hundreds of men and engineers who had dug Egypt's Suez Canal to supervise and work in his enormous trenches. But, as Schliemann announced his sensational discoveries, Alexander Conze and other German archaeologists worked on sites such as *Olympia, Greece*, site of the ancient Olympic Games, with architects and stone masons. Their concern was more for knowledge and conservation than for spectacular discoveries. They turned excavation from treasure hunting into a careful process of recording the past with an architect always present on-site.

Far away in southern England, a Victorian military man with a passion for the history of weapons, General Augustus Lane Fox Pitt-Rivers (1827–1900), inherited millions and spent years excavating burial mounds and earthworks on his Cranborne Chase estates in southern England. Between 1880 and 1900, the general dug several prehistoric and Roman burial mounds, forts, and earthworks totally, observing details of their construction and layering (Figure 1.6). Not for the general the hasty trenches and casual looting favored by many of his contemporaries. He recorded the position of every find, described even the smallest objects minutely, and published his finds in four lavishly printed volumes. Pitt-Rivers believed that thorough recording of even minor details was vital for later investigators who might be seeking answers to questions unimagined in his day. His reports and photographs complete with workmen standing rigidly at attention to give the scale are of priceless value to modern-day researchers. Pitt-Rivers was ahead of his time. Only in the 1920s did a later generation of archaeologists adopt, refine, and point his excavation methods in the direction of the high standards of today (see Chapter 7).

By 1910, excavation methods in Egypt and the eastern Mediterranean had improved, in the hands of such scholars as Egyptologist Flinders Petrie; Arthur Evans, the excavator of Crete's *Minoan civilization*; and Leonard Woolley, who excavated the Hittite city of *Carchemish* on the Euphrates. However, archaeology was still considered an adventurous pursuit, more suitable for men than women. But two women broke the mold. Archaeological traveler Gertrude Bell traveled across the Syrian desert and deep into Saudi Arabia in the early years of this century, when women rarely became archaeologists

FIGURE 1.6 General Lane Fox Pitt-River's excavations at Wor Barrow in southern Britain were an astonishing example of early scientific excavation.

and never traveled alone in desert lands. Harriet Hawes, refused permission to dig in mainland Greece, crossed to Crete and went searching for sites on a mule. Working almost alone with her Cretan workers, she excavated *Gournia*, a small Minoan town on Crete's north coast.

The 1920s and 1930s saw dramatic discoveries in Egypt and Mesopotamia. Two Englishmen, Howard Carter and Lord Carnarvon, discovered the undisturbed tomb of the Egyptian pharaoh Tutankhamun in 1922, the greatest archaeological discovery of all time (Figure 1.7). It took Carter eight years to clear the tomb in a brilliant feat of on-site conservation under very tough working conditions. Leonard Woolley's Ur project, which lasted from 1922 to 1934, was one of the last heroic excavations that employed a small army of workers. His royal cemetery finds rivaled those from Egypt, but his methods were rough-and-ready by modern standards. Regrettably, his notes are too incomplete for modern scholars to verify his reconstruction of the royal funerals.

The 1930s saw the first attempts to reconstruct ancient environments, to place human settlements in their natural settings. However, the biggest change has come since World War II, when scientific archaeology has come of age. The invention of radiocarbon dating in the late 1940s (see Chapter 3), a host of new scientific methods, the impact of the computer with its ability to organize enormous quantities of raw data, and an explosion in the number of

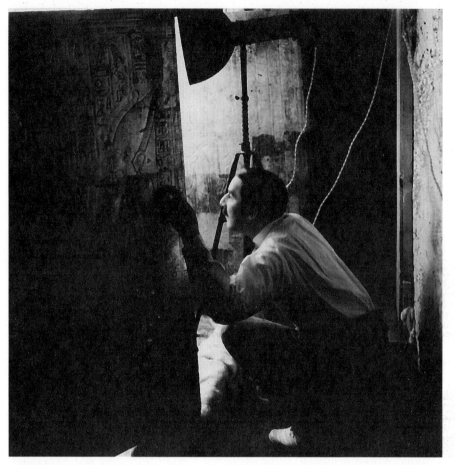

FIGURE 1.7 Howard Carter examining one of the nested golden shrines of the pharaoh Tutankhamun. *(Courtesy of the Metropolitan Museum of Fine Art, New York.)*

archaeologists has revolutionized a once relatively unsophisticated discipline and turned it into an important global science.

Leonard Woolley explored Ur with a tiny group of trained excavators, men and women immortalized by detective writer Agatha Christie in her classic *Murder in Mesopotamia*. (She later married Max Mallowan, one of the archaeologists on Woolley's staff who worked on the royal burials.) Woolley's late-twentieth-century successors move a fraction of the dirt in six times the amount of time. They would not dream of going into the field without a close-knit team of specialists, everyone from botanists to zoologists, and they study the site in the context of its natural environment. At the same time, new theoretical approaches have transformed the ways we look at the human past (see Chapter 4). Within the last 50 years, archaeology has changed from a basically descriptive science into a sophisticated way of interpreting culture change over 2.5 million years of the human past.

ARCHAEOLOGY

Archaeology is the scientific study of ancient human behavior based on the surviving material remains of the past. British archaeologist Stuart Piggott once described archaeology somewhat cynically as "the science of rubbish." In a way, he is right, for archaeology uses artifacts, food remains, and other objects to study ancient human behavior from its beginnings in East Africa more than 2.5 million years ago up to modern times. Our insights into ancient behavior come from building theories and then applying scientific methods and theoretical concepts in studying the material remains of past human cultures.

Archaeologists study ancient human behavior over an immensely long period of time. Their excavations and field surveys discover entire societies that flourished thousands, even hundreds of thousands, of years before Egyptian and Mesopotamian scribes developed writing systems some 5,000 years ago. However, the reconstructions and interpretations of the past come from surviving material things, which resulted from ancient human behavior. As we shall see in Chapter 2, some materials last much longer than others. Stone and fired-clay vessels are nearly indestructible; wood, skin, metals, and bone are much more perishable. Thus, any picture of life in the remote past is likely to be very one-sided, often based on row after row of stone tools or painted pot fragments recovered from dated sites. The archaeologist is like a detective fitting together an incomplete collection of clues to give a general impression and explanation of ancient culture and society. Imagine for a moment taking two spark plugs, a fragment of a beer can, a needle, a bicycle chain, and a candleholder and trying to reconstruct the culture of the people who made those diverse objects on the basis of those objects alone!

This is exactly what archaeologists do all the time, often with seemingly inconsequential finds. Some years ago, at the Royal Ontario Museum, Canada, archaeologist Victoria Badler of the University of Toronto was sorting storage jars from an ancient trading post at *Godin Tepe* in central western Iran. She noticed a dark stain on the interior of one of the vessels and wondered if it was a residue from the liquid that once filled the jar. Patrick McGovern and Rudoph Michel of the University Museum at the University of Pennsylvania isolated the organic constituents of the stain with boiling acetone and analyzed them by infrared spectroscopy. The absorption bands from the sample coincided almost exactly with those of tartaric acid, which is contained in wine. The 5,500-year-old Godin Tepe wine residue is the oldest known in the world. This chance discovery has triggered major research into the history of wine trading in the eastern Mediterranean world.

Some people think archaeology is little more than an assortment of techniques, such as accurate recording, excavation, and increasingly sophisticated laboratory techniques. They are wrong, for modern archaeology involves far more than just gathering finds from the earth and describing them. As we shall see later in this chapter, archaeologists, whatever their expertise, balance practical excavation and field survey with description of the finds and theoretical interpretation.

WHAT DO ARCHAEOLOGISTS DO?

What, then, do archaeologists do? We are certainly more than the pith-helmeted professors beloved by cartoonists. As recently as the 1940s, you would have been correct to assume that most archaeologists spent their time in the field engaged in excavation and surveys. A half-century ago, there were only a few hundred archaeologists throughout the world. Archaeology was still an academic village, where everyone knew everyone else (and where the gossip was ferocious and sometimes vicious!). Before World War II, most archaeological excavations focused on Europe, southwestern Asia (the Near East), and North America. Today, there are archaeologists working in every corner of the globe, in Australia and on the Pacific Islands, in China and Siberia, in tropical Africa, Latin America, and the high arctic. No one knows how many archaeologists there are worldwide, but the number must be near 10,000, most of them relative newcomers to the field. To give an example: In 1960, there were only about 12 professional archaeologists in the whole of Africa south of the Sahara Desert. Now there are nearly 100 in South Africa alone. Archaeology has turned from a village into a diverse, global community, concerned not with narrow historical issues but with the study of a truly global past. At the same time, our discipline has become a profession as much as an academic pursuit.

The change began after World War II, as archaeologists became concerned about the wholesale destruction of archaeological sites with no effort being made to investigate them first. "Salvage archaeology" was born, notably with the UNESCO (United Nations Educational, Scientific, and Cultural Organization)–sponsored international effort to find archaeological sites in the vast area of the Nile Valley to be flooded by the Aswan Dam, and with the Glen Canyon Dam project in Utah. The realization that archaeological sites were vanishing rapidly in the face of looters and industrial development, and also by deep plowing and mining, led to a stream of federal and state legislation from the 1960s through 1980s protecting the past. Archaeology itself changed character in Europe and North America, as pure academic research gave way to field and laboratory research aimed at assessing and preserving the past, and also mitigating the effects of construction and other activities. Such **Cultural Resource Management (CRM)** is a type of archaeology concerned with the management and assessment of the significance of cultural resources such as archaeological sites. It is now the dominant activity in North American archaeology. (See Doing Archaeology box on p. 15.)

The shift toward CRM is mirrored in employment figures. In the 1960s, nearly all archaeologists were university or college professors or worked in museums. In a recent study of American archaeologists, Melinda Zeder (1998) of the Smithsonian Institution has chronicled a dramatic shift in archaeological employment. Now only 35 percent of American archaeologists are academics; 8 percent labor in museums; and 23 percent work for federal, state, or local government, many in purely administrative functions. The fastest-growing segment of archaeological employment is in the private sector. In

DOING ARCHAEOLOGY

A Short Guide To (Some of) the Diversity of Archaeologists

Prehistoric archaeologists (prehistorians) study prehistoric times, from the time of the earliest human beings to the frontiers of written history. The numerous specialties within prehistoric archaeology include **paleoanthropology**, experts on the culture and artifacts of the earliest humans, authorities on stone technology, art, and hunter-gatherers. There are specialists in the prehistory of the Old and New Worlds, Europe, the American Southwest, and many other regions.

Classical archaeologists study the remains of the great classical civilizations of Greece and Rome (Figure 1.8). While many classical archaeologists study art and architecture, others study the same kinds of economic, settlement, and social issues that interest prehistorians.

Biblical archaeologists are experts on a variety of ethnic groups living in what is now Israel, Lebanon, and Syria. They attempt to link accounts in biblical and Canaanite literature with archaeological data.

Egyptologists, Mayanists, and *Assyriologists* are among the many specialist archaeologists who work on specific civilizations or time periods. Such specialties require unusual skills, for example, a knowledge of Egyptian hieroglyphs.

Historical archaeologists work on archaeological sites and problems from periods in which written records exist. They excavate medieval cities such as Winchester and York, in England, study Colonial American settlements, Spanish missions, and nineteenth-century frontier forts in the American West. **Historical archaeology** (sometimes called text-aided archaeology) is concerned mainly with the study of ancient material culture, for artifacts and technology tell us much about the diversity of ancient societies (see Chapter 11).

Underwater archaeologists study ancient sites and shipwrecks on the seabed and on lake beds, and even under the rapids in Minnesota streams where fur traders once capsized and lost canoe loads of trade goods. **Underwater archaeology** uses diving technology, but its objectives are identical to those of archaeology on land—to reconstruct and interpret past cultures, as well as ancient seafaring cultures (see the Uluburun shipwreck in Chapter 11).

Industrial archaeologists study buildings and other structures of the Industrial Revolution such as Victorian factories.

Apart from area specialists, there are experts in all manner of archaeological methods, including archaeobotanists, who study ancient food remains; lithic technologists, who are experts on stone technology; and **zooarchaeologists**, specialists in ancient animal bones.

FIGURE 1.8 The Parthenon on the Acropolis, Athens, Greece. *(Courtesy of George Holton, Photo Researchers.)*

1997, 18 percent of all American archaeologists worked for private consulting firms engaged in environmental monitoring and cultural resource management. The figure is still climbing.

The Zeder study shows that archaeology is changing rapidly from a purely academic discipline into a profession with strong roots in both government and private business. This is because the past is under siege from industrial civilization in the forms of deep plowing and mining, industrial development, road construction, and the inexorable expansion of huge cities—to say nothing of looters and pothunters, who think nothing of ravaging sites for valuable finds they can sell. Increasingly, archaeologists are managers rather than professors, supervising a precious and rapidly vanishing resource: the human past. The pith-helmeted professor of yesteryear is the cultural resource manager of today. An image further removed from Indiana Jones is hard to envision.

Archaeology is now a discipline and profession of specialists, often of dauntingly obscure topics. During the course of my career, I have worked with prehistorians and Egyptologists, and historical and underwater archaeologists, to mention only a few relatively broad specialties. But I have also collaborated with experts on ancient Egyptian wine, cultural resource management, Ice Age earthworms, southern African mice, reindeer teeth growth rings, and eighteenth-century Colonial American gardens! All this without mentioning the many federal and state government archaeologists and private sector specialists who have crossed my path.

WHY IS ARCHAEOLOGY IMPORTANT?

Archaeology exercises a curious fascination. Cavepeople, golden pharaohs, lost cities hiding in swirling mist: The fantasies abound. So do spectacular discoveries, such as the Moche Lords of *Sipán*, Peru, found intact in an adobe platform where they were buried in A.D. 400 with all their gold and silver regalia (Figure 1.9). Finds like Sipán or Ötzi the Ice Man, a Bronze Age traveler found deep-frozen high in the Italian Alps (see Figure 11.2), are indeed fascinating, even romantic, discoveries. Such scientific treasure troves appeal to the explorer and adventurer in us and bring the past to life in dramatic ways.

Few modern-day discoveries rival the excitement caused by three French cave explorers when they entered a 30-inch (80-cm)- wide cavity in the wall of a gorge in the Ardèche Mountains of southeastern France on December 18, 1994. Eliette Deschamps, Jean-Marie Chauvet, and Christian Hillaire squeezed through the narrow opening. They felt a draft flowing from a blocked duct, pulled out the boulders that blocked it, and saw a vast chamber 12 feet (3 m) below them. Using a rope ladder, they descended into a network of chambers adorned with natural calcite columns. Calcified cave bear bones and teeth lay on the floor, on which shallow depressions marked where the long-extinct beasts had hibernated. Suddenly, Deschamps cried out in surprise. Her lamp shone on a small mammoth figure painted on the wall. The explorers moved deeper into the chamber and came across more paintings—positive and neg-

FIGURE 1.9 Reconstruction of a Moche Lord of Sipán dressed in ceremonial regalia. *(Courtesy of the Fowler Museum of Cultural History, UCLA.)*

ative hand imprints and figures of cave lions and mammoths, one with a circle of dots emerging from its muzzle. As they gazed at the paintings, the three explorers felt as if time was abolished, as if the artists had left the cave only a few moments earlier. "The artists' souls surrounded us. We felt we could feel their presence" (Chauvet, Deschamps, and Hillaire 1996, 42).

The *Grotte de Chauvet*, named after one of the discoverers, lay undisturbed since the late Ice Age. Hearths on the floor looked as if they had been used the day before. The explorers found an extraordinary frieze of black wild horses and oxen and two woolly rhinoceroses facing one another. One 30-foot (10-m)-long frieze of black figures depicted lionesses, rhinoceroses, bison, and mammoths. Far to the right stood a human figure wearing a bison-head mask, perhaps the shaman supervising the immense frieze. Radiocarbon tests reveal that Grotte de Chauvet was visited repeatedly between about 31,000 and 24,000 years ago, one of the earliest painted caves in the world.

Mysteries of the Past

Chauvet's Ice Age animals caused an international sensation, like Tutankhamun's tomb and Ötzi the Ice Man. But the fascination with archaeology is much wider, for the past is redolent with unsolved mysteries and unexplained phenomena. You have only to watch fantasy movies on TV, which cover such hoary old favorites as the search for Noah's Ark, the curse of the pharaohs (made especially realistic in a memorable performance by Boris Karloff as a hyperactive mummy in a movie of the 1930s), or the lost continent of Atlantis. Such fantasy stories are little more than pseudoarchaeology, no more historical fact than the Indiana Jones adventure movies. (See Doing Archaeology box below.) More legitimate archaeological puzzles, such as how the ancient Egyptians built the pyramids, or why the Anasazi people

DOING ARCHAEOLOGY

Pseudoarchaeology, or You Too Can Be an Armchair Indiana Jones!

Take a few intrepid adventurers in an ancient sailing vessel, some startlingly new religious cult, a handful of pyramids, lots of gold, and exotic civilizations swirling in ever parting mists and you have the irresistible ingredients for an epic "archaeological" tale. Pseudoarchaeology is all the rage in a world where many people are fascinated by adventure, escapism, and space fiction. A distinctive literary genre tells compelling tales of a long-lost past. For instance, British journalist Graham Hancock has claimed that a great civilization flourished under Antarctic ice 12,000 years ago. (Of course, its magnificent cities are buried under deep ice sheets, so we cannot excavate them!) Colonists spread to all parts of the world from this Antarctic home, colonizing such well-known sites as *Tiwanaku* in the Bolivian highlands and building the Sphinx by the banks of the Nile. Hancock weaves an ingenious story by piecing together all manner of controversial geological observations and isolated archaeological finds. He waves aside the obvious archaeologist's reaction, which asks where traces of these ancient colonies

and civilizations are to be found. Hancock fervently believes in his far-fetched theory, and being a good popular writer, he has managed to piece together a best-selling book which reads like a "whodunit" written by an amateur sleuth.

Pseudoarchaeology appeals to people who are impatient with the deliberate pace of science and like to believe "there is always a faint possibility that . . . ." Some of these "cult archaeologies" show all the symptoms of becoming personality cults, even religious movements. The theories espoused by the leaders become articles of faith, the object of personal conversion. They are attempts to give meaning to being human and are often steeped in symbolism and religious activity. Almost invariably the cultists dismiss archaeologists as "elitists" or "scientific fuddy-duddies" because they reject wild theories that are unsupported by scientifically gathered evidence.

This book describes the science of archaeology, which, ironically, can be more interesting than the best fantasy tales.

of *Chaco Canyon*, New Mexico, built roadways leading to nowhere, intrigue much wider audiences than merely archaeologists. Today, archaeology is as much a part of popular culture as football or the automobile. Thousands of people read archaeology books for entertainment, join archaeological societies, and flock to popular lectures on the past.

The Powerful Lure of the Past

Armchair archaeology is one thing; to experience the sites and objects of the past firsthand is another. The monuments of antiquity cast an irresistible spell. The jetliner and the package tour have made archaeological tourism big business. Fifty years ago only the wealthy and privileged could take a tour up the Nile, visit classical Greek temples, and explore Maya civilization. Now package tours can take you to Egypt, to the Parthenon (Figure 1.8), and to *Teotihuacán*, Mexico (see Figure 10.10). The immense Pyramids of *Giza* in Egypt (see Figure 2.6), and the prodigious labor that built them; the white columns of the Temple of Poseidon at *Sounion*, Greece, touched with pink by the setting sun; the ruins at the Maya city of Tikal bathed in the full moon's light—as sights alone, these overwhelm the senses.

I once sat in the great classical amphitheater at *Epidauros*, Greece, on a spring evening as the setting sun turned the world a pale pink. As I sat high above the stage, a small group of German tourists gathered around their learned guide. He sent them to the stall seats, stood at center, and recited evocative stanzas from Euripides' play *Ion*. The ancient verses rolled and resonated through the still air. For a moment, I shut my eyes and imagined the theater crowded with a festive audience, incense wafting on the spring air; the stanzas gripping everyone's attention with electric tension, then pathos. . . . The guide's voice ceased. A deep silence fell and the magic of Epidauros' acoustics faded.

Visiting the past can be a deeply moving experience—the north wind blowing across *Hadrian's Wall* in northern England on a winter's day with a promise of snow, or a muggy afternoon at *Moundville*, Alabama, when the air stands still and the thatched huts and imposing mounds come alive in your mind with fresh color, with the smell of wood smoke, the cries of children, and barking of dogs.

You can get the same emotional connection the first time you see Pharaoh Tutankhamun's golden mask or a giant *Olmec* head with snarling face from lowland Mexico (see Figure 12.5), which lifts us to a realm where achievement endures and perceptions seem of a higher order. Even humble artifacts such as a stone chopper or a finely made clay pot can evoke emotions of wonder and insight. Years ago, I turned a 2-million-year-old, jagged-edged chopper end for end in my hands. Suddenly, I realized from the flake scars that the ancient maker had been left-handed. . . . I felt a sudden bond with the past.

There are moments when the remote past reaches out to us, comforting, encouraging, offering precedent for human existence. We marvel at the achievements of the ancients, at their awesome legacy to all humankind.

Archaeology and Human Diversity

Archaeology's unique ability lies in its capacity to reach back over the millennia, to reconstruct and explain the cultures and lifeways of unimaginably ancient societies as they changed over many centuries and thousands of years. Why did some societies vanish without trace, while others developed agriculture or highly complex urban civilizations? Who first tamed fire or invented the plow? How did bronze and iron smelting change the course of human history? Archaeology is fascinating because it enables us not only to study the most remote human origins, but also the ever changing biological and cultural diversity of humankind.

We live in a complex world of almost bewildering human diversity. We can land people on the moon, send space probes to Mars, establish our position in the midst of tropical rainforests within inches, and build computers of mind-numbing speed and complexity. Yet our collective understanding of human diversity and our ability to collaborate with others from different cultural backgrounds and cultural heritages remains at an elementary level. We tend to fear diversity, people who are different from us, who speak alien languages or look at the world with cultural perspectives that differ from our own. We fear diversity because of apprehension, sometimes bigotry, but all too often on account of plain ignorance. Archaeology is one of the major educational weapons in the fight against such ignorance.

The most important lesson about diversity that archaeology teaches us is that we are all descended from what Harvard University biologist Stephen J. Gould once called "a common African twig." As long ago as 1871, the great Victorian biologist Charles Darwin of *Origin of Species* fame theorized that humanity originated in Africa, because this was where the greatest variety of apes dwelt. Today, we know he was right. More controversially, thanks to DNA studies and archaeological finds, we also suspect that our own direct ancestors, *Homo sapiens sapiens*, originated on the same continent, then spread out of Africa replacing much older human populations. Most important of all, both archaeology and DNA studies have shown that the relationships among all modern humans are closer than they are different. Above all, we are all humans with the identical abilities to conceptualize and shape our world, to make inventions, to love and hate, and to adapt to any environment on earth. We just happen to do it in different ways.

The great Finnish paleontologist Bjørn Kurtén put it well: "Imagine a dinner table set for a thousand guests, in which each man is sitting between his own father and his own son. At one end of the table might be a French Nobel laureate in a white tie and tails, and with the Legion of Honor on his breast, and at the other end a Cro-Magnon man dressed in animal skins and with a necklace of cave-bear teeth. Yet each one would be able to converse with his neighbors on his left and right, who would either be his father or his son. So the distance from then to now is not really great" (Kurtén 1986, 61).

Archaeology studies diversity at its very beginnings, millennia before our intermingled industrial world changed forever by the massive population movements of the nineteenth and twentieth centuries. We seek answers to fundamental questions. Why are we biologically and culturally diverse? In what ways are we similar or different? When did the great diversity of humankind first come into being, and why? As we have seen, we have good reason to believe that we modern humans originated in tropical Africa, then spread throughout the world during the late Ice Age, after 100,000 years ago. This complex set of population movements and cultural changes was perhaps the seminal development of early human history. From it stemmed not only the brilliant biological and cultural diversity of modern humankind, but art and religious life, agriculture and animal domestication, village life and urban civilization—the very roots of our own diverse and complex world.

Archaeology provides a constant reminder of our common, and recent, biological and cultural heritage in a world where racism is commonplace.

Human artifacts are excellent barometers, not only of ancient behavior, but of cultural diversity as well. Early historic American society was very much more diverse than we often realize (see Chapter 11). Archaeologist Kathleen Deagan has excavated the site of *Fort Mose* in Florida, the first free African-American community in North America (Figure 1.10). This tiny hamlet of some

FIGURE 1.10
Reconstruction of the Fort Mose site, near St. Augustine, Florida. (*Courtesy of the Florida State Museum, University of Florida, Gainesville.*)

37 families, 2 miles (3.2 km) from Spanish St. Augustine on the Atlantic coast, was founded in 1738 and occupied until the Spanish abandoned Florida in 1763. In its heyday, the settlement of 22 thatched houses, a church, guard-houses, and a well lay behind earthen fortifications. Many of the inhabitants were of West African origin and used not only African artifacts, but objects of English, Native American, and Spanish origin. Eventually, Deagan and her researchers hope to use the artifacts to decipher what cultural elements were important in the lives of the inhabitants.

Archaeology as a Political Tool

Rulers and governments have used the past to justify the present since civi-lization began. The Sumerians, who created the world's first urban civiliza-tion between the Euphrates and Tigris Rivers in southern Iraq, created a heroic past personified by the Epic of Gilgamesh, a legendary ruler who ruled before a mythic flood that frightened even the gods. When the waters subsided, they restored kingship to earth at the city of Kish, where recorded history began.

The past has always served the present, for every society manufactures history. The Aztecs of highland Mexico were an obscure farming society in A.D. 1200. Only three centuries later, from a dazzling capital, Tenochtitlán, in the Valley of Mexico, they ruled over all of *Mesoamerica*, that area of Central America where indigenous civilizations arose, an area straddling much of highland and lowland Mexico, Guatemala, Belize, and Honduras. In 1426, a powerful official named Tlacaelel became the right-hand man to a series of fifteenth-century Aztec rulers in highland Mexico. He prevailed on his mas-ters to burn all earlier historical records of other cities in the valley. In their place, he concocted a convincing rags-to-riches story, which recounted the Aztecs' mercurial rise from obscurity to become masters of Mexico, as the chosen people of Huitzilopochtli, the Sun God himself. The new history was blatant political propaganda that justified a century of militant imperialism, which made the Aztecs the rulers of a vast empire.

No one can look back at the past objectively. We all bring our individual cultural biases to the study of history and archaeology, for we tend to look at past developments and events through the blinkered eyes of our own value system and society. Thus, any archaeological interpretation of the past is a form of narrative, which, by the nature of its evidence, is both a scientific and political/literary enterprise. As part of this enterprise, **archaeological theory** aims to explain the past as well as describe it.

Archaeology is peculiarly vulnerable to political misuse, because it deals with ancient societies and events that are little known, even from archaeo-logical sources. Most people who use the past for nationalistic or political ends are searching for a glorious past, a simple story that justifies their own political agenda. The Nazis unashamedly used archaeology before World War II to propagate notions of a true "Nordic" race in ancient Europe. In the for-mer Yugoslavia, the past has become a prize in endless political squabbles that go back centuries. Construction and ownership of a real or imagined past and its monuments serves as a vital political resource when seeking to sway public opinion. Such archaeologies are rarely based on scholarly standards of logic and evidence. Most, at best, stretch historical facts to their breaking points and promote bigotry, nationalism, and chicanery.

On the other side of the coin, archaeology, with its long time perspectives, has added entire new chapters to human history in areas of the world where written records extend back little more than a century. In parts of Central Africa, for example, the first documentary history begins with the establishment of Colonial rule in about 1890, with only a few Victorian explorers' accounts dating from earlier decades. The primary goal of archaeology in much of Africa is to write unwritten history as a way of fostering national identity, not from archives and documents, but from long-abandoned villages and rubbish heaps, the material remains of the past.

Archaeology and Economic Development

Bone-chilling cold descended on the high plains around Lake Titicaca, Bolivia, that night. White frost covered the dry hillsides, where local farmers planted their potatoes in thin soil. Many families watched all night as their growing potatoes withered and turned brown before their eyes. As dawn spread, they wandered through their ruined fields, glancing down at a thin white blanket of warm air covering some experimental plots on the plain below. They had watched suspiciously as the archaeologists had dug across long-abandoned ancient fields in the lowlands, then had given one of their neighbors seed potatoes to plant in a replica of such a field. He piled up layers of gravel, clay, and soil, then dug shallow irrigation canals alongside the raised fields. The green shoots of the new potatoes grew far higher than those on the arid slopes. As the temperature dropped below freezing, a white cloud of warm air formed above the raised fields, hiding them from view. Now the warming sun dispersed the white blanket, revealing lush, green potato plants, their leaves only slightly browned by frost.

After months of ground survey, excavation, and controlled farming experiments, archaeologists had rediscovered the forgotten genius of ancient Andean farmers for the benefit of their descendants. The ancestors had used water to protect their crops against frost with such success that they supported the glittering city of Tiwanaku and its powerful kingdom for more than five centuries. Today, more than fifteen hundred modern farmers have rediscovered the benefits of raised fields. Dozens of nearby communities clamor for training in ancient agriculture.

Archaeology shows how the traditional system has many advantages—high crop yields, no need for fertilizer, and much reduced risks of frost or flood damage. Furthermore, high yields can be obtained with local labor, local crops, and no expensive outside capital. At last count, nearly 2,125 acres (860 hectares) had been rehabilitated and many more fields are planned.

The Lake Titicaca raised-field experiments have been so successful that archaeologists are now actively involved in several other such projects in the

Americas. Governments are now slowly discovering something archaeologists have known for a long time. The ancients knew their environments intimately, exploited them efficiently without expensive twentieth-century technology. There is nothing wrong with their oft-forgotten ways of cultivating the soil, raising several crops a year, or of successful animal husbandry. Industrial-scale agriculture is not the universal answer to the world's food crisis.

University of Arizona archaeologist William Rathje has applied archaeological methods to the study of modern garbage dumps in Tucson and other American cities for a long time. He has found that bags of abandoned household garbage never lie, for six-packs of beer and liquor bottles are more eloquent testimony to a family's drinking habits than any questionnaire that denies heavy beer consumption. Rathje's long-term research has revealed fascinating differences between the wasteful discard habits of many lower-income families, while the wealthy are often more careful to consume leftovers. It's very easy to trivialize such research as being of more use to catfood companies than to archaeologists, but "garbagology" has much to tell us about the discard habits of modern industrial society. There are also important theoretical lessons for archaeologists investigating the middens of ancient Rome, Nineveh, or Thebes.

WHO NEEDS THE PAST?

> There is not yet one person, one animal, bird, fish, crab, tree, rock, hollow, canyon, meadow, forest. Only the sky alone is there; the face of the earth is not clear. Only the sea alone is pooled under all the sky; there is nothing whatsoever gathered together. . . . Whatever is that might be is simply not there: only the pooled water, only the calm sea, kept at rest under the sky. . . . (Tedlock 1996, 64).

The Maya *Popol Vuh*, a book of counsel, tells the story of the creation, recounts the deeds of gods and kings in a brilliant celebration of the Quiché Maya past. Sometimes called the Maya Bible, the impact of its creation myth is as powerful as that in the Book of Genesis.

All societies have an interest in the past. It is always around them, haunting, mystifying, tantalizing, sometimes offering potential lessons for the present and future. The past is important because social life unfolds through time, embedded within a framework of cultural expectations and values. In the high Arctic, Inuit preserve their traditional attitudes, skills, and coping mechanisms in some of the harshest environments on earth. They do this by incorporating the lessons of the past into the present. In many societies, the ancestors are the guardians of the land, which symbolizes present, past, and future. Westerners have an intense scientific interest in the past, partly borne of curiosity, but also out of a need for historical identity. There are many reasons to attempt to preserve an accurate record of the past. Nobody, least of all archaeologists, should assume that they are uniquely privileged in their interest in the remains of the past.

We have no monopoly on history. Many non-Western societies do not perceive themselves as living in a changeless world. They make a fundamental distinction between the recent past, which lies within living memory, and the more remote past which came before that. For instance, the Australian Aborigine groups living in northeast Queensland distinguish between *kuma*, the span of events witnessed by living people; *anthantnama*, a long time ago; and *yilamu*, the period of the creation. Furthermore, many societies also accept that there was cultural change in the past. In India, Hindu traditions of history speak of early people who lived without domesticated animals and plants. The Hadza hunter-gatherers of East Africa tell of their homeland's first inhabitants as being giants without fire or tools. These paradigms of the past take many forms, some with mythic creators of culture, usually primordial ancestors, deities, or animals establishing contemporary social customs and the familiar landscape, others with a more remote, discontinuous heroic era such as that of the Greeks, which allowed such writers as the playwright Aeschylus to evaluate contemporary behavior.

Most human societies of the past were nonliterate, which means that they transmitted knowledge and history orally, by word of mouth. The Aztec oral histories, partially set down after the Spanish Conquest in the sixteenth century A.D., are an excellent example of history transmitted by word of mouth. They were recited according to a well-defined narrative plot, which focused on great men, key events such as the dedication of the sun god Huitzilopochtli's temple in the Aztec capital in 1487, and the histories of favored groups. In these, as in other oral histories, there were formulas and themes, which formed the central ingredients of a story which varied considerably from one speaker to the next, even if the essential content was the same. Many oral histories are mixtures of factual data and parables which communicate moral and political values. But to those who hear them, they are publicly sanctioned history, performed before a critical group, and subject to the critical evaluation of an audience who may have heard the same stories before.

Oral traditions are hard to use scientifically, as their antiquity is difficult to establish. In some cases, in Australia, for example, there are instances where oral histories and archaeology coincide in general terms. For example, the traditions speak of the arrival of the first people from overseas, of flooding of coastal areas after the Ice Age, and of the hunting of giant marsupials (pouched animals like the kangaroo). So, Australia's past can be said to come from two sources: archaeological data and oral traditions. In some instances, the archaeologists and indigenous people have shared interests and come together, to identify sacred and historic places, often to ensure they are preserved, even if the two groups disagree significantly on the "significance" of a particular location (for instance, where archaeology finds no buildings or artifacts, yet the local people consider it a "sacred place").

But, all too often, archaeologists and local communities have different interests in the past. To archaeologists, the past is scientific data to be studied with all the rigor of modern science. To local people, the past is often

SITE

Inyan Ceyaka Atonwan, Minnesota

Inyan Ceyaka Atonwan, (Dakota: "Village at the Rapids," or the Little Rapids site) lies on the Minnesota River about 45 miles (72 km) southwest of Minneapolis. The settlement was occupied by Eastern Dakota people between the early and middle 1800s and lay close to a trading post at Fort Snelling, where artist Captain Seth Eastman sketched and painted an invaluable record of the local Native Americans. Archaeologist Janet Spector excavated the site during 1980 to 1982 and used artifacts from the excavation to identify different men's and women's activities in the village. As she wrote her report, she worried whether she as a non–Native American could do Native American-centered work. In 1985, she made contact with the local Dakota, one of whom was related through his mother to a man named Mazomani, who was a prominent member of the Little Rapids community in the early 1800s. They visited the site, then began a collaborative project between Dakota and archaeologists, combining oral history with archaeology, written records with modern-day experiences of the local people.

In 1980, Spector found a small antler handle for an iron awl used for perforating leather. Red ocher–filled dots adorned the handle, which she learned from his-torical sources recorded important accomplishments of the owner. She felt certain it had belonged to a woman, since they are responsible for hide work among the Dakota. Mazomani had a daughter named Mazaokiyewin ("Woman Who Talks to Iron"), who was a skillful leather worker. In her book *What This Awl Means* (1993), Spector tells Mazaokiyewin's life story and constructs a scenario for the loss of the awl just as it was worn out. She later presented her narrative to Mazaokiyewin's descendants, a story of a once vibrant place reconstructed by a skillful mediation between past and present, archaeology, oral tradition, and Native Americans' relationships with their history. The Inyan Ceyaka Atonwan project is research that mediates conflicting perspectives on the past. Spector writes: "I still find myself wishing for a time machine. I dream of spending time just one day at Little Rapids with some members of our project . . . and some of the nineteenth century figures linked to Inyan Ceyaka Atonwan. . . . I can visualize the day, but it is difficult to picture how we would communicate, given the distances between us" (1993, 129).

What archaeologist, at one time or another, has not wished for a similar time machine? Therein lies the frustration and fascination of archaeology.

highly personalized and the property of the ancestors. Such histories are valid alternative versions of history, which deserve respect and understanding, for they play a vital role in the creation and reaffirmation of cultural identity. And, they raise a fundamental question, which lies behind many Native American objections to archaeological research. What do archaeologists have to offer a cultural group which already has a valid version of its own history? Why should they be permitted to dig up the burial sites of the ancestors or other settlements and sacred places under the guise of studying what is, to the people, a known history? It is a question that archaeologists have barely begun to address. We should never forget that alternative, and often compelling, accounts of ancient times exist, and they play an important role in helping minority groups and others to maintain their traditional heritage as it existed before the arrival of the Westerner. (See Site box on p. 26.)

In Chapter 2, we describe the goals of archaeology, the process of archaeological research, and some of the basic principles of the discipline.

SUMMARY

Archaeology began over 150 years ago as a search for lost civilizations and artifacts. Since then, it has developed into a sophisticated, multidisciplinary way of studying human behavior in the past. Archaeologists use the material remains of the past to study this behavior. Archaeology is a unique way of studying culture change over long periods of time. It has an important role to play in the modern world, for it teaches important lessons about human diversity and is a form of serious entertainment which gives us an appreciation of the common cultural heritage of humankind. Data from excavations and surveys can sometimes provide important information on ancient economic practices that can be used today. Despite archaeology's unique perspective on culture change, archaeologists do not have a monopoly on describing and interpreting the past and must respect traditional histories. There are many types of archaeologists, including prehistorians, historical archaeologists, and scholars who work with classical civilizations, biblical and underwater sites, and in a variety of technical specialties.

KEY TERMS

Archaeology

Archaeological theory

Archaeologists

Classical archaeologists

Cultural Resource
    Management (CRM)

Historical archaeology

Oral traditions

Paleoanthropology

Prehistory (prehistorian)

Underwater archaeology

Zooarchaeologists

GUIDE TO FURTHER READING

Bahn, Paul. 1996. *The Cambridge Illustrated History of Archaeology*. Cambridge, England: Cambridge University Press.

An excellent summary of the history of archaeological discovery in all parts of the world. Lavishly illustrated.

Fagan, Brian M. 1996. *In the Beginning*. 9th ed. New York: Addison Wesley Longman.

A comprehensive survey of archaeological method and theory from a global perspective with examples from many areas.

Fagan, Brian M., ed. 1996. *The Oxford Companion to Archaeology*. New York: Oxford University Press.

Everything you have ever wanted to know about archaeology within the pages of a single reference book, with entries written by over 300 archaeologists.

———, ed. 1997. *Eyewitness to Discovery*. New York: Oxford University Press.

An anthology of firsthand accounts of archaeological discoveries ranging from Victorian adventurers to modern scientists.

Renfrew, Colin, and Paul Bahn. 2000. *Archaeology: Theories, Methods, and Practice.* 3rd ed. London: Thames and Hudson.

A lavishly illustrated introduction to archaeology for more-advanced readers. Authoritative, with many examples.

Spector, Janet. 1993. *What This Awl Means*. St Paul, MN: Minnesota Historical Society.

Spector's short essay on the Little Rapids site is a classic of contemporary archaeology.

Zeder, Marilyn. 1998. *The American Archaeologist: A Profile*. Walnut Creek, CA: AltaMira Press.

Zeder's authoritative study of the American archaeologist bristles with statistics and basic information, but gives a telling portrait of archaeology as a career.

THE WORLD WIDE WEB

The World Wide Web is becoming another medium of communication for archaeologists, like everyone else. This is a confusing universe for those unfamiliar with the Web, especially since so much is changing all the time. However, the major Web sites are here to stay and offer links to other important locations. Everything operates with Uniform Resource Locators (URLs), some of which we list here.

The Virtual Library for archaeology worldwide is ArchNet at http://www.spirit.lib.uconn.edu/archaeology/html. This is both geographically and subject-matter-based, covering everything from the archaeology of Australia to method and theory and site tours. There are also listings of academic departments, museums, and other archaeological organizations, even of journals. ArchNet is an extraordinary resource, which does not claim to be comprehensive, but it covers a huge range of topics. The European equivalent is ARGE, the Archaeological Resource Guide for Europe: http://www.bham.ac.uk/ARGE. This also lists areas and subjects and is multilingual. Both ArchNet and ARGE have links to virtually any kind of archaeology you are looking for.

Here's a selection of other useful Web sites, but please realize that Web pages and addresses change all the time, so this information may already be out of date. Many departments of anthropology and archaeology have Web sites, which you can access through ArchNet. For information on archaeology in southwestern Asia and the eastern Mediterranean, go to http://www.argonet.co.uk/education/diggings. *Internet Archaeology* is an international Web-based periodical for professionals, complete with a discussion list: http://intarch.ac.uk/. Even this book has a Web page! And you can contact the author at brian@brianfagan.com if you have questions.

Culture and the Archaeological Record

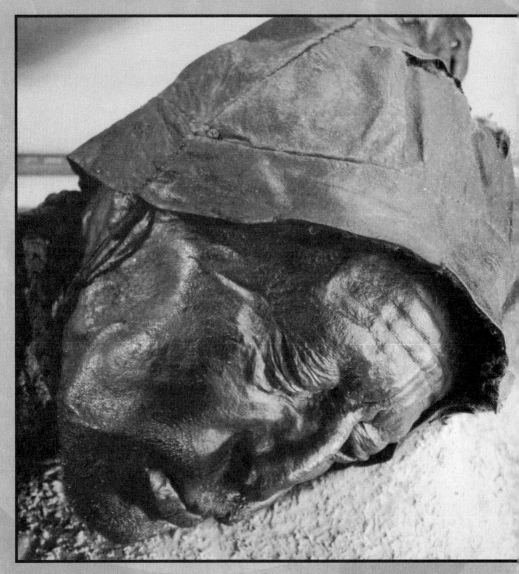

Tollund Man, Denmark, c. 100 B.C. (Source: Werner Forman Archive. Silkeborg Museum, Denmark. Art Resource, NY.)

CHAPTER OUTLINE

In 7000 B.C., a small group of foragers camped in a sandy clearing near *Meer* in northern Belgium. One day, someone walked away from camp, sat down on a convenient boulder, and made some stone tools, using some carefully prepared flakes and lumps of flint he or she had brought along. A short time later, a second artisan sat down on the same boulder. He or she had also brought along a prepared flint cobble, struck off some blanks, and made some borers. Later, the same two stone workers used their finished tools to bore and groove some bone. When they finished, they left the debris from their work lying around the boulder.

When Belgian archaeologist David Cahen excavated the site 9,000 years later, all he found were some scatters of stone debris. He plotted the clusters and painstakingly refitted the stone flakes onto their original stone cobbles. After months of work, he reconstructed the stone workers' activities and showed that the second one was left-handed.

A greater contrast in research with Austen Henry Layard's large-scale diggings at Nineveh is hard to imagine.

Chapter 2 describes the goals of archaeology and the basic processes of archaeological research that lead to remarkable studies like Cahen's. It also defines what is meant by the "archaeological record" and discusses the all-important issue of archaeological context in time and space.

THE GOALS OF ARCHAEOLOGY

The archaeologist has one primary and overriding priority: to preserve and conserve the material remains of the past for future generations. Archaeological sites and their contents are a unique record of our forebears in every part of the world. Unlike trees, this archive of the past, the archaeological record, is finite. Once disturbed or excavated, the record is gone forever. Conserving this priceless asset is our greatest responsibility to the past, whether professional archaeologists or laypeople.[1]

All archaeological research has three important goals, each of which builds on the others.

Constructing Culture History

Culture history is an approach to archaeology which assumes that artifacts can be used to build up generalized pictures of human culture in time and space, and that these can be interpreted. Culture history is the record of the human past described and classified in a context of time and space, which describes the past through time and in space across the changing ancient landscape. In other words, it answers the fundamental question: What happened where and when?

Culture history relies on careful excavation, detailed classifications of finds of all kinds, and accurate sequences of human cultures defined through time and by spatial distribution.

Until the 1950s, culture history dominated archaeological research. For example, during the 1930s, teams of archaeologists surveyed major river valleys in the southeastern United States in advance of dam construction. They found hundreds of archaeological sites, which they dated using sequences of stone tool and pottery forms. These now-classic surveys tell us a great deal about what happened in these river valleys and when, but they tell us little about the ways in which the various river valley societies lived or why they became more complex and took up maize agriculture over the past 2,000 years.

Culture history is the vital first stage of all archaeological research. You cannot examine more detailed questions until you have a clear idea what happened in a region and when. In many parts of the world, for example, Southeast Asia, archaeological research has hardly begun. Many archaeologists working in Cambodia or Thailand still have a primary concern for culture history. This focus will change once the basic framework of the past is in place.

The basic principles of culture history are described in Chapters 3 and 4.

---

[1]Ethics are all-important in archaeology. In this chapter I have set a series of statements about ethical principles in italics, so they stand out.

Reconstructing Ancient Lifeways

Archaeology is also the study of ancient human behavior, of people, not their artifacts. Stone tools, **potsherds,** iron weapons, houses, and other material remains are indeed the raw materials for classifying the past, but we should never forget they were made by people—men and women, adults and children, members of different households, communities, and societies. Logically, then, our second major goal is the reconstruction of how people made their living, the study of ancient lifeways.

The word *lifeways* covers many human activities, everything from hunting and plant gathering to agriculture, interactions between individuals and groups, social organization, and religious beliefs. Some of archaeology's most ingenious detective work reconstructs these activities, which, for convenience, can be grouped into broad categories.

Subsistence   How people make their living or acquire food is studied by using fragmentary animal bones, seeds, and other surviving evidence for ancient human diet and **subsistence** activities (Chapter 9).

Environmental Modeling   Subsistence activities depend heavily on a society's relationship with the natural environment. This means that studying ancient subsistence goes hand in hand with reconstruction of changing prehistoric environments (see Chapter 5).

Human Interactions   People act out their lives at many levels: as individuals, as men, women, and children; as members of families, communities, and cultures. They may be divine rulers, merchants, artisans, common farmers, or slaves. Reconstructing lifeways means examining evidence for changing sex roles, assessing the importance of social ranking within societies, reconstructing the complex mechanisms by which people exchanged exotic raw materials or precious artifacts over enormous distances.

Much cutting-edge research revolves around "people" questions, especially such issues as changing gender roles and the distinctive activities of inconspicuous and often historically anonymous minorities in large cities. We identify people from their artifacts, which are the products of cultural traditions handed down over many generations (see Chapter 11).

For instance, the great city of Teotihuacán in the Valley of Mexico attracted traders from every corner of the Mesoamerican world. The Teotihuacános ran a vast urban market which attracted people from all over the Mexican highlands and lowlands to trade everything from gold dust to tropical bird feathers. So lucrative and essential were some of these trading activities that the city authorities allowed foreigners from the distant Veracruz lowlands and valley of Oaxaca to live in their own compounds in Teotihuacán. We know this because the distinctive clay vessels characteristic of these two areas have come to light in several of the city's neighborhoods (Chapter 11). (See Discovery box on p. 33.)

DISCOVERY

The Folsom Bison Kill Site, New Mexico

One fine spring morning in 1908, cowboy George McJunkin rode slowly along the edge of a dry gully near the small town of Folsom, New Mexico. He was casting over the range for a lost cow. When he looked down, he saw some sun-bleached bones projecting from the soil. McJunkin dismounted and pried at the bones with his knife. A sharp stone fragment came loose in his hands, somewhat like the stone spear points he had seen lying on the ground on the ranch. The bones were much larger than those of a cow. McJunkin puzzled over his finds and took them back to the ranch house, where they lay around for 17 years. But in 1925, they ended up on the desk of Jesse Figgins, director of the Colorado Museum of Natural History, one of the few paleontologists in the west. He identified the bones as those of a long-extinct bison that had roamed the plains at the end of the Ice Age. But the stone point was another matter. Was it associated with the extinct bison or a much later artifact? In 1926, Figgins dug into the Folsom arroyo and recovered more bison bones and stone tools, including a spear point directly associated with bison fragments. He cut out the associated point and bone in a lump of soil to show his colleagues, but they were skeptical. Few experts believed Native Americans had lived in the Americas for more than a few thousand years. Figgins returned to Folsom a year later, inviting several colleagues to observe his excavations. Archaeologist Frank Roberts arrived just as Figgins was brushing the soil away from a projectile point still embedded between two of the ribs of a bison skeleton. He realized that this was definitive proof for ancient Native Americans living in North America perhaps as early as 10,000 years ago.

Social Organization and Religious Beliefs   Archaeologists are increasingly concerned with such intangibles as social organization and religious beliefs. Of course, we can never hope to capture the transitory events of the past, such as the fleeting ecstasy of a shaman's trance or a colorful dance performed in a plaza at Teotihuacán. However, artifacts, art styles, even entire temples and cities, are mirrors of the intangible, allowing us a fleeting glance into the social and spiritual worlds of ancient societies (see Chapter 12).

Explaining Cultural Change

Archaeology is a search for both facts and explanations. The third major objective of archaeology is to study and explain processes of cultural change (see Chapter 4). Such research attacks fundamental questions: After tens of thousands of years of hunting and plant gathering, why did people living over a huge area of southwestern Asia change over to agriculture before 9000 B.C.? What caused Maya civilization in the southern Mesoamerican lowlands, with its huge cities and powerful lords, to collapse in A.D. 900? Why did no one settle the offshore islands of the Pacific until about 3,000 years ago?

Studying **cultural process** is among the most challenging of all archaeological research. In Chapter 4, we describe some of the complex theoretical models which attempt to reconstruct such major developments as the origins of agriculture and the development of complex, urban civilizations. In recent years, archaeological theory has moved in new directions away from the study of changing cultural systems to new perspectives where researchers focus more and more on the role of people as individuals and members of small groups in causing cultural change.

The three main objectives of archaeology flow one into the other. A study of ancient lifeways depends on precise culture history, while an explanation of cultural processes requires large quantities of culture historical, environmental, and lifeway data to be meaningful.

THE PROCESS OF ARCHAEOLOGICAL RESEARCH

All archaeologists have an ethical responsibility to carry out their research according to established scientific procedures. Our research methods, however refined, destroy the archive of the past for future generations. This activity must include both full publication of the results of the work and proper conservation and storage of the finds.

In other words, the ethics of archaeology demand a process of rigorous and well-planned research (Figure 2.1).

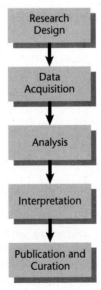

FIGURE 2.1 The process of archaeological research.

I vividly remember my first solo excavation, on a 1,000-year-old farming village in Central Africa. My field training was rudimentary at best: a few digs in Britain where you learned the basics as you worked as a student laborer. Now I was to dig on my own, a long way from anywhere with six unskilled laborers and an occupation mound 1/4 mile (400 m) long and 10 feet (3 m) deep in front of me (Figure 2.2). The only advice I received was to dig into the highest point, on the grounds that it would yield the longest occupation sequence. I had no formal research plan or any idea what I would find. In any event, my first trench did indeed find the deepest occupation in the village. But I made many mistakes and destroyed a lot of valuable artifacts and other finds before I found my scientific feet. Many years later, I shudder at the casual way in which I first went digging. It was irresponsible and ethically wrong both on my part and on the part of those who sent me into the field. (See Doing Archaeology box on p. 36.)

Any time you disturb an archaeological site, you are effectively destroying it. Unlike physics or chemistry, you cannot replicate your experiment again and again. As archaeologist Kent Flannery once remarked, we are the only scientists who murder our informants in the course of our research. As a result, every archaeological survey, every excavation, each laboratory project unfolds according to a carefully formulated, but flexible research plan.

FIGURE 2.2 General view of the excavations at Isamu Pati mound in southern Zambia.

DOING ARCHAEOLOGY

An Archaeologist's Ethical Responsibilities

Professional archaeologists live by multiple formal and informal codes of ethics that govern the ways in which they go about their business. The Society for American Archaeology's code is simple and to the point. It expects professional archaeologists to do the following:

• Practice and promote the stewardship of the archaeological record for the benefit of all people.
• Consult effectively with all groups affected by their work.
• Avoid activities that enhance the commercial value of archaeological objects that are not readily available for scientific study or cared for in public institutions.
• Educate the public in the importance of their findings and enhance public understanding of the past.
• Publish their findings in a widely accessible form.
• Preserve their collections, records, and reports properly, as part of a permanent record of the past for future generations. They must also allow other archaeologists access to their research materials without any legal or other compelling restrictions.
• Never undertake research without adequate training, experience, and facilities to complete the task at hand.

The process of archaeological research unfolds in five general stages, as follows.

Research Design

The formulation of a **research design** is the most important part of any archaeological project large or small. Such a design is the formal blueprint developed for any type of archaeological investigation which lays out the goals of the inquiry and the steps and methods to be taken to meet them. Preparing the design begins with the acquisition of as much background information about the site or area to be investigated. What previous research unfolded there? What collections and publications provide a starting point for you? What environmental and topographic data is on hand? Above all, you formulate initial questions and develop general theoretical models that will frame the research. (More specifics on research designs are in chapters 6 and 7.) Your research design also spells out the strategies you will follow to test your hypotheses and meet the objectives of the research. Of course these change as the fieldwork unfolds, but they provide a vital framework for the entire inquiry.

In the case of my African village, I read up on everything known about the people and that kind of site (which was almost nothing, in fact). Then I began to formulate the questions that my excavation would investigate. I also raised funds for the excavation, acquired permission from the landowner and relevant government agencies to excavate, and assembled the necessary equipment and staff to carry out the work.

The ethics of archaeology require that you work closely with the people affected by your work, be they landowners, native peoples, or government agencies.

Data Acquisition

Now it is time to go into the field for your survey or excavation, depending on the nature of your project. Data acquisition may take a few days, several weeks, months, or years, depending on the scope of the project. Dozens of archaeologists have collaborated on a long-term, multiyear investigation of the famous Maya city of Copán, Honduras (Figure 2.3). The complex projects there include a major investigation of the main ceremonial complex, where tunnels have revealed pyramids built by successive rulers stacked one upon the other between A.D. 400 and 800 (Chapter 7). Another large-scale project has surveyed the hinterland of the city and chronicled major changes in settlement in the Copán Valley over many centuries (Chapter 10). At the other end of the spectrum, a single archaeologist may spend a day surveying and excavating a scatter of 5,000-year-old stone tools on a one-acre (0.4 ha) building site in the Chicago suburbs.

FIGURE 2.3   Artist Tatiana Proskouriakoff's reconstruction of the central precincts of the Maya city at Copán, Honduras. *(Courtesy the Peabody Museum, Harvard University.)*

Whether excavation or field survey, data acquisition is a process of observation and recording information, in which meticulous records combined with the finds, whether artifacts such as potsherds or broken animal bones or house foundations, provide the data sets for the next stage: analysis.

Analysis

Data analysis is the most fundamental of archaeological tasks, the classification and description of everything recovered from the field. The **analysis** of artifacts and food remains is described in chapters 8 and 9. However, in these days when many researchers try to excavate as little undisturbed archaeological deposit as possible, many projects are pure laboratory undertakings. Often, modern experts work with notes left by their predecessors. For example, Smithsonian Institute anthropologist John Harrington spent a lifetime studying the customs and language of the few surviving Chumash Indians of southern California in the early 1920s. Harrington was a packrat who assembled an extraordinary database on vanished Chumash culture, which he recorded on file cards, in notebooks, and on isolated slips of paper in Chumash, English, and Spanish. Harrington's unpublished notes lay in government offices all over the country when he died in 1961. They provide a priceless archive of a culture that effectively became extinct in the nineteenth century. Using Harrington's notes, anthropologists Thomas Blackburn and Travis Hudson succeeded in building a replica of a Chumash planked canoe. At the same time, they became archaeological Sherlock Holmeses in an attempt to track down hundreds of Chumash artifacts looted and collected over a century ago.

Blackburn and Hudson found that some Chumash artifacts girdled the world. William Blackmore, a wealthy businessman, acquired many Chumash artifacts in the late nineteenth century. He donated his collections to the Salisbury Museum, a local organization in southern England. After his death in 1929, the museum disposed of the collection, with the archaeological finds going to the British Museum in London. Henry Beasley, a private collector, purchased the ethnographic artifacts. Upon his death, they ended up in museums in Cambridge, Liverpool, and London. Blackburn and Hudson tracked down Chumash baskets, stone tools, and weapons in Oxford, England; Edinburgh, Scotland; Ghent, Belgium; Göteborg and Stockholm, Sweden; Helsinki, Finland; and St. Petersburg, Russia. The two scholars documented an international archive of Chumash culture, which amplified Harrington's firsthand observations and archaeological excavations.

Interpretation

At this important stage in the process, the researcher pulls together all the data and tests the propositions in the research design. The **interpretation** represents the conclusions drawn from the data in the context of the theoretical model developed, then modified, as the project unfolded. In the case of my African village, I assembled all the chronological and stratigraphic information, the artifact analyses with their information on changing pottery styles and the subsistence data, then wrote a detailed interpretation of the site. As part of the process of explanation, I argued that changes in pottery styles toward globular pots and a rapid increase in percentages of cattle bones were signs of an economic shift toward cattle herding and milk consumption in about A.D. 1000—at the very end of the occupation.

Publication and Curation

Most important of all, the researcher ends by publishing the results of the project in full. Many CRM excavations are covered by contracts and requirements dictated by legally mandated compliances. The completion of a formal report is part of that contract. However, whether academic or contract-driven, full reporting in a form accessible to everyone is essential, for any excavation is destruction. Final publication, whether an elaborate monograph or a paper in a scientific journal, is the only permanent record of a now-vanished archive. As part of the publication process, the collections, basic data, photographs and drawings, and field notes should be archived in a proper curation facility, as they are part of the permanent record, to be consulted by future researchers.

One of the great scandals of archaeology is the lax way in which many fieldworkers shrug off their ethical responsibilities to publish their results. Many of the world's most important and extensively excavated sites are virtually unpublished, often because their excavators have continued digging elsewhere instead of fulfilling their basic archaeological responsibilities. Unfortunately, it's a reality of archaeological life that we receive more credit for making interesting discoveries than for the ethical behavior of writing them up! The great Egyptologist Flinders Petrie, who was a fanatic for prompt publication, put it so well as long ago as 1904: "I look forward to the production of a series of volumes, each of which will be incapable of being altogether superseded, and which will remain for decades to come—perhaps centuries—as the sources of facts and references on their subject" (Petrie 1904, 135). A glowing example of full publication is the monograph on the Abu Hureyra farming village in Syria, written over many years by Andrew Moore and his research team, listed at the end of this chapter.

An archaeologist's primary responsibility is to publish a complete record of his or her research accessible to all.

Finally, the excavator is responsible for depositing the finds and site records in a suitable or legally designated repository for proper curation.

Whatever their research designs or the sites they excavate, all archaeologists study the material remains of ancient human culture.

CULTURE

An intensely hot, windy day on the shores of Lake Turkana, East Africa, 2.5 million years ago: a small group of **hominids** (members of the family Hominidae, represented today by one species, *Homo*) runs up a dry streambed, carrying the bloody limbs of a recently killed antelope stolen from a lion kill. The females clasp their young to their bosoms and then set them on the ground under a shady thorn tree, protected from the wind. They join the males in cutting up the fresh meat with sharp-edged stone tools, which were flakes struck from lumps of lava carried to this place weeks before. The small band eats quickly, always alert for lurking predators, breaking bones with stone lumps, sucking succulent marrow from the limb bones. They throw stones at hovering vultures, then drop the cleaned bones and stone tools as they move away to climb trees as the sun sets.

Two and a half million years ago, these toolmaking hominids numbered but a few thousand, scattered over an enormous area of open grassland in eastern and southern Africa. They were unlike any other animals on earth, for they used manufactured stone tools to butcher animals and dig up roots.

Humans are unique. We are the only animals which use our **culture** as our primary means of adapting to our natural environment. It is our adaptive system. Biological evolution has protected the polar bear from arctic cold with dense fur and has given the duck webbed feet for swimming. Only humans make layered, tailored clothes and igloos in the Arctic and live with minimal clothing under light, thatched shelters in the tropics. We use our culture as a buffer between ourselves and the environment, a buffer that became more and more elaborate through the long millennia of the past. We are now so detached from our environment that removal of our cultural buffer would render us almost helpless and probably lead to our extinction in a short time.

Archaeologists, as anthropologists, study ancient human cultures. Few concepts in **anthropology** have generated as much controversy as culture. The great Victorian anthropologist Sir Edward Tylor (1872, 2) wrote one of the best definitions for this concept: "That complex whole which includes knowledge, belief, art, morals, law, custom, and any other capabilities and habits acquired by man as a member of society." To Tylor's words archaeologists would add the statement that culture is our primary means of adapting to our environment. Tylor's definition, and all other such formulations, agree on one important point: Culture and human behavior are shared ideas a group of people may hold.

Human cultures are made up of human behavior and its results; they obviously consist of complex and constantly interacting variables. Human culture is never static and is always adjusting to both internal and external change, whether environmental, technological, or social.

Culture can be subdivided in all sorts of ways—into language, economics, technology, religion, political or social organizations, and art, to mention only a few categories. But human culture as a whole is a complex, structured organization in which all the categories shape one another. All cultures are made up of myriad tangible and intangible traits, which result from complex adaptations to a wide range of ecological, societal, and cultural factors.

We transmit much of human culture from generation to generation by sophisticated communication systems: by word of mouth and oral tradition, by practical example, and sometimes in writing. Culture's transmittability allows us to forge ceaseless and complex adaptations to aid survival and help rapid cultural change take place, as happened, for example, when Western explorers and settlers came in contact with non-Western societies during the European Age of Discovery. Within two or three generations after the first European contacts in 1768–1769, Tahitian society changed rapidly as a result of connections with Western culture. At first local chiefs tolerated missionaries as they perceived them as political advantages, owing to missionaries' access to firearms. Within a half-century, Tahitian culture was transformed by Christianity, and not necessarily for the better, as traditional customs and beliefs went underground and many people suffered from grinding poverty.

We all live within a culture of some kind, and every culture is qualified by a label, such as "middle-class American," "Inuit," or "Maya." The qualification conjures up characteristic attributes or behavior patterns typical of those associated with the cultural label. One attribute of a middle-class American might be the enjoyment of hamburgers or an enthusiasm for football; of the Inuit, the kayak or skin boat; of the elite members of Maya society, elaborate cities and intricate **hieroglyphs,** which are an ancient writing featuring picture or ideographic symbols. Every culture has its individuality and recognizable style, which shape its political and judicial institutions and its morals.

Unfortunately, cultural labels often become simplistic and sometimes demeaning stereotypes, such as that of the Native Americans as "feathered braves," or of the French as romantic, consummate lovers. Cultural reality is much more complex and often deeply challenging for an outsider to penetrate and comprehend.

For working purposes, archaeologists often think of culture as possessing three components:

- The individual's own version of his or her culture, the diversified individual behavior that makes up the myriad strains of a culture. Individual decisions play a vital role in changing even elaborate cultures.
- Shared culture, the elements of a culture shared by everyone. These can include cultural activities such as human sacrifice, warfare, or any other shared human activity, as well as the body of rules and prescriptions that make up the sum of the culture. Language is critical to this sharing, so is the cultural system.
- The cultural system, the system of behavior in which every individual participates. The individual not only shares the cultural system with other members of society but also takes an active part in it.

You can think of culture as either a blend of shared traits or a system that permits a society to interact with its environment. To do anything more than just study sequences of ancient human cultures, archaeologists have to view culture as a group of complex, interacting components. These components remain static unless you define the processes that operate the system.

Archaeologists are deeply involved with the study of cultural process, the processes by which ancient human societies changed through time.

CULTURAL SYSTEMS

The notion of **cultural systems** has come into use in archaeology purely as a general concept to help us understand the ever changing relationship between human cultures and the environment. This perspective views culture and its environment as a number of linked systems in which change occurs through a series of minor, interconnected variations in one or more of these systems (see Chapter 4). Systems thinking considers, for example, an Eskimo cultural system as part of a much larger Arctic ecosystem. The cultural system itself is made up of dozens of subsystems: an economic subsystem, a political subsystem, and many others. Let us say that the climate changes suddenly. The Eskimo now switch from caribou hunting to fishing and sealing. The change triggers all sorts of linked shifts, not only in the economic subsystem but in the technological and social subsystems as well. A cultural system is in a constant state of adjustment within itself and with the ecosystem of which it is a part. The concept of cultural systems is derived from general systems theory, a body of theoretical concepts formulated in the 1960s as a means of searching for general relationships in the empirical world (see Chapter 4).

Clearly, no one element in any cultural system is the primary cause of change; instead, a complex range of factors—rainfall, vegetation, technology, social restrictions, population density—interact and react to changes in any element in the system. It follows, then, that human culture, from the ecologist's viewpoint, is merely one element in the ecosystem, a mechanism of behavior whereby people adapt to an environment.

The notion of cultural systems is a useful conceptual framework, provided you do not take it too far and apply it like a rigid, mechanistic formula. We should never forget that our forebears were human beings like ourselves, who made decisions as individuals and as groups, as friends, enemies, neighbors, lords, or commoners. This makes it impossible to apply universal rules of cultural behavior to humanity. Furthermore, many of the interacting components of culture are highly perishable. So far, no one has been able to dig up an unwritten language. Archaeologists have to work with the tangible remains of human activity that still survive in the ground. But these surviving remains are radically affected by intangible aspects of human culture. (See Site box on p. 43.) The archaeologist thus faces much greater limitations in research than the ethnographer, who works with living societies and can talk to individuals in that society.

CULTURAL PROCESS

The word *process* implies a patterned sequence of events that leads from one state of affairs to another. This patterned sequence is determined by a decision-making process that sets the order of events. A 40-foot (12-m) sailing yacht starts as a pile of materials—wood, aluminum, copper, bronze—

SITE

The 'Ain Ghazal Figurines

Studying ancient religious beliefs using material remains is among the hardest challenges for an archaeologist. Fortunately, the occasional remarkable discovery yields compelling evidence for the intangible. The 'Ain Ghazal village in Jordan was a flourishing community of cereal farmers and goat herders before 7500 B.C. The site was discovered during roadworks on the edge of modern-day Amman. The excavations yielded well-planned dwellings, even the toe bones of goats with scarring caused by the tethering ropes used in their pens. But the most remarkable 'Ain Ghazal discovery came in 1974, when archaeologists Gary Rollefson and Alan Simmons discovered a cache of badly fractured, plaster human figures in the early farming settlement. The figures date to about 7000 B.C. They look like department store mannequins with square, stylized torsos supporting lifelike shoulders and long necks with heads that bore calm, expres-

sive faces. The incised eyes, inlaid with bitumen, stare into space in an almost eerie fashion (Figure 2.4). Some figures had two heads, as if they memorialized a husband and wife or dual deities. No one knows exactly what the figures were used for, but there is good reason to believe they were revered ancestor figures in farming societies with close ties to the land, which was farmed by the same families for many generations. Rollefson and Simmons believe the figures may once have worn garments, perhaps cloaks or ceremonial gowns, which covered their torsos and nonexistent arms. Headdresses or long scarves may have adorned their heads. Whether ancestors, gods, or just prominent individuals, the 'Ain Ghazal figurines once commemorated powerful but intangible beliefs that have long vanished into oblivion. They offer a good example of the challenge facing archaeologists studying ancient human beliefs.

FIGURE 2.4 'Ain Ghazal figurines. *(Courtesy of the Sackler Gallery, Washington D.C., and the Jordanian Department of Antiquities.)*

and then a patterned sequence of manufacturing events turns the materials into a gleaming new ship. As we have seen, archaeology is a process, too. It involves designing the research project, formulating the hypothesis from prior research, collecting and interpreting new data to test the hypothesis, and finally, publishing the results. Of course, the process of change is usually not so conscious.

We should distinguish between a *condition* and a *process*. Conditions are events that force people to make decisions about how to deal with new situations. As such, they are distinct from the actual process of decision making—the mechanisms that lead to any kind of change. For example, occasional strong El Niño episodes devastate the arid Peruvian coast with torrential rains and catastrophic floods. One such event in the twelfth century A.D. caused catastrophic damage to the Chimu state, which ruled much of Peru's North Coast at the time. The Chimu barely managed to survive the onslaught of floodwaters (more on El Niño in Chapter 5).

In contrast, process is the actual process of change itself. Cultural process is the succession of processes by which human cultures changed through time, studied by a variety of models such as **processual archaeology,** which is the study of the process of culture change by looking at the complex relationships which lead to such change. In archaeology, the study of cultural process involves identification of the factors that were responsible for the direction and nature of change within cultural systems.

Processual archaeology is analysis of the relationships among variables that could lead to cultural change. These possible conditions are then tested against actual archaeological data, sometimes in a systems theory context.

THE ARCHIVES OF THE PAST: THE ARCHAEOLOGICAL RECORD

The foragers came in early fall, just as the acorns and pistachios ripened. They camped on a small ridge close to the river, at the foot of a low cliff, with a fine view of the surrounding floodplain. While the men erected small brush shelters, the women collected wild grass seeds from the edges of a nearby swamp where a meander of the stream had left a shallow lake. They returned to camp with laden baskets, lit fires, and pounded the seeds for the evening meal. As the sun went down, some of the men stalked deer from the nearby forest who came down to the water each evening to drink. Dogs barked, children shouted and played, families sat by the fires in the gathering dark. The same daily routine unfolded for several weeks as each family spent its days in the forest gathering thousands of ripe acorns and nuts for the winter ahead. But, as the days shortened and the leaves fell, the band moved on to a more permanent and better-sheltered winter camp upstream.

The abandoned shelters slowly collapsed under the weight of rain and winter snow. Small mudflows covered the hearths where families once sat. Within a few years, the small camp was invisible, the brush dwellings rotted away. A few discarded wooden artifacts had also vanished. Only a scatter of broken stone tools, some fractured deer bones, and thousands of minute seeds survived, buried under several inches of soil.

The soil weathered, centuries and millennia passed, and a dense woodland grew up where the foragers once lived. Then, European farmers came and cleared the trees, sinking their horse-drawn plows into the fertile soil. The plow blades cut through an ancient hearth, bringing some stone tools and charcoal to the surface of the plowed field. By chance, an archaeologist walks across the field, searching for artifacts and traces of human occupation. The ancient camp, once alive with living people, becomes an archaeological site—part of the archives of the past.

Archaeological data like this consist of any material remains of human activity. They are recognized by the archaeologist as significant evidence and all are collected and recorded as part of the research. Data are different from facts, which are simply bits of observable information about objects, conditions, and so on. Such data result from two processes.

The first is human behavior, the result of human activity. A hunter-gatherer **band** decides on a location for a temporary camp. The people gather building materials, be they sticks and grass, sod, or mammoth bones, then build dwellings and occupy them. Eventually, they abandon their houses, perhaps destroying them in the process. The archaeologist reconstructs the camp and the activities that unfolded there from the surviving material remains, discovered after centuries or millennia; this is what we call the **archaeological record,** a generic name for traces of ancient human behavior, reflected by a more or less continuous distribution of artifacts over the earth's surface, in highly variable densities.

Human behavior is the first step in the formation of the archaeological record. But what happens when people abandon their camps, bury the dead, and move elsewhere? The collapsed brush shelters, a scatter of stone tools, the remains of a meal are of no further use to their owners. All manner of humanly caused (cultural) and natural (noncultural) **transformational processes** then come into play as time passes. Such transformation processes (sometimes called site transformation processes) are continuous, dynamic, and unique cultural or noncultural processes that affect archaeological sites after their abandonment. The bodies of the buried dead decay; toppled shelters rot away in the sun. Perhaps a nearby lake rises and covers the abandoned settlement with fine silt. Windblown sand may accumulate over stone **artifacts,** the objects manufactured or modified by the humans. Another completely different society may come and build a farming village on the same spot or simply pick up and reuse the stone artifacts left by their ancient predecessors. Transformational processes vary from one location to another, for the archaeologist's data is always biased and incomplete, altered by a variety of such processes, which can affect the state of preservation of artifacts and other finds. For example, World Wars I and II destroyed thousands of archaeological sites, whereas wet conditions in northern European swamps preserve even 3,000-year-old corpses in perfect condition.

Archaeological data results from human behavior and transformation processes and makes up the archaeological record. The archaeological record is a finite and precious record of the human past, an archive of all our pasts, whether kings, queens, merchants, nobles, or commoners. Our archives are not dusty files, letters, or microfilms, but archaeological sites, artifacts, **ecofacts** (a term sometimes used to refer to food remains, such as animal bones, seeds, and other finds, which throw light on human activities), food remains—all the material remains of ancient human behavior. A scatter of broken bones, a ruined house, a gold mask, or a vast temple plaza—all are part of the archaeological record. All the elements in this enormous archive, the common cultural heritage of all humankind, have a context in time and space. Once destroyed, an archaeological site can never be replaced. Once disturbed, the context of an artifact, or any form of human behavior, is gone forever. The archaeological record is perishable, irreplaceable, and vanishing daily before our eyes.

The archaeological record can include unusually high densities of artifacts or other traces of human activity, which are subsumed under the term **site,** any place where objects, features, or other traces of human behavior are found. A site can range from a small camp to a city, from a quarry to a tiny scatter of stone artifacts. It can be defined by its function, such as a cemetery. (See Doing Archaeology box on p. 47.)

CONTEXT

Archaeologists have an ethical responsibility not to collect artifacts or buy and sell them for profit. They are students of the past, and, as such, have a responsibility to acquire information, not artifacts wrenched from their context in time and space.

I remember once examining a superb Mimbres painted bowl from the American Southwest (for an example, see Figure 8.12). The funerary vessel depicted a man fishing and had clearly come from a grave. Unfortunately, an anonymous looter plundered the burial, scattered the bones, and carried away the bowl, which he sold to the highest bidder. I admired the superb artistry of the painter, but the bowl was useless as archaeological data, for we had no information as to where it came from or about its precise age and cultural associations.

Ancient artifacts are not just objects to be displayed like paintings or sculpture. They came from precise contexts in time and space. Archaeological data do not consist of artifacts, features, structures, and ecofacts alone. They also consist of the **context,** the exact position of these finds in time and space.

The thin line of the 1,000-year-old cattle dung–covered hut floor appeared in the bottom of the trench, a hard, semicircular patch of fire-baked clay lined on its outer side with the charred bases of wall posts. We removed the overlying, ashy soil with slow care, using trowels, then paintbrushes to ease the **matrix** off the long-abandoned floor surface. The matrix is the physical substance that surrounds an archaeological find. It can be gravel, sand, mud, or

DOING ARCHAEOLOGY

Archaeological Sites

Archaeological sites can be classified by their artifact content and by the patterning of such finds within them. Here are the most common categories.

Living or habitation sites are the most important sites, for they are the places where people have lived and carried out a multitude of activities. The artifacts in living sites reflect domestic activities, such as food preparation and toolmaking. Dwellings are normally present. The temporary camps of California fisherfolk are living sites, as are Stone Age rock shelters, Southwestern pueblos, and Mesopotamian city mounds. Such **structures,** houses, granaries, temples, and other buildings, can be identified from standing remains, patterns of postholes, and other features in the ground. Habitation sites of any complexity are associated with other sites that reflect specialized needs, such as agricultural systems, cemeteries, and temporary camps. Often these sites contain many **features,** artifacts and artifact associations that cannot be removed intact from the ground, such as postholes and ditches.

Kill sites are places where prehistoric people killed game and camped around the carcasses while butchering the meat. They are relatively common on the American Great Plains. For example, archaeologist Joe Ben Wheat excavated the Olsen-Chubbock kill site of about 6000 B.C. (see Chapter 9). He was even able to determine the direction of the wind on the day of the game drive!

Ceremonial sites are those devoted primarily to religious and ritual observances. Some formed part of much larger communities. The Mesopotamian **ziggurat** (temple mound) of 3000 B.C. dominated its mother city. Mesoamerican cities such as Teotihuacán boasted imposing pyramid temples and open plazas surrounded by acres of crowded urban apartment compounds. Other famous ceremonial sites, such as *Stonehenge* in England (Figure 2.5), are

FIGURE 2.5 Stonehenge. *(Source: Superstock, Inc.)*

(Continued)

DOING ARCHAEOLOGY

Archaeological Sites *(Continued)*

isolated monuments. Ceremonial artifacts, such as stingray spines used in mutilation rituals, and statuary may be associated with sacred sites.

Burial sites include both cemeteries and isolated tombs. People have been burying their dead since at least 50,000 years ago and have often taken enormous pains to prepare them for the afterlife. Perhaps the most famous burial sites of all are the Pyramids of Giza in Egypt (Figure 2.6). Royal sepulchers, such as that of the Egyptian pharaoh Tutankhamun, absorbed the energies of hundreds of people in their preparation. Many burials are associated with special grave furniture, jewelry, and ornaments of rank.

Trading and quarry sites are locations where specialized activities took place. The special tools needed for mining obsidian, copper, and other metals identify quarry sites. Trading sites are identified by large quantities of exotic trade objects and by their strategic position near major cities. The Assyrian market that flourished outside the Hittite city of *Kanesh,* Turkey, in 1900 B.C. is one of these.

Art sites, which abound in southwestern France, southern Africa, Australia, California, and other areas, are identified by engravings and paintings on the walls of caves and rock shelters.

FIGURE 2.6 The Pyramids of Giza, Egypt. *(Courtesy of Odyssey, Chicago. Photograph by Robert Freerck.)*

water, or, in this case, ashy soil. Most archaeological matrices are of natural origin—passing time and external phenomena, such as wind and rainfall, create them. However, some, such as burial mounds, are of human origin. Three large boulders appeared in the soil. I brushed them off, exposing a patch of charcoal between them, also a broken ox jaw and the broken fragments of a small clay pot. The exposed floor was about 10 feet (3 m) across, with the hearth set near the center of the house. Before we lifted the hearth, artifacts, and hut floor, I recorded the **provenance** (or provenience) by measuring the exact position of every find and feature three-dimensionally, tying our measurements into a site grid linked in turn to the map of the area. I remember thinking as we took up the boulders that, in and of themselves, they were just three large stones. Taken together, plotted in relationship to the charcoal and artifacts, they told a story of long-forgotten household behavior. The finds had a context.

However, context is far more than just a find spot, a position in time and space. How, for example, did the find get to its position and what has happened to it since its original users abandoned it? Three general factors can affect context:

- The manufacture and use of the object, house, or other find by its original owners. For instance, the builders may have oriented a dwelling to a southwestern exposure to achieve maximum warmth from afternoon sun. Why is this important? Because archaeologists study not just houses, but the behavior that affected every aspect of their building and use.
- Ancient human behavior. Some discoveries, such as royal burials or caches of artifacts, were deliberately buried under the ground by ancient people; others vanished as a result of natural phenomena. Dilapidated houses that have been abandoned are slowly covered by blowing sand or rotting vegetation. Others vanish in natural disasters. The Roman city of *Herculaneum* in Italy, however, was buried quickly by a catastrophic eruption of Vesuvius in August of the year A.D. 79.
- What happened to the find after its abandonment or use? Was, for example, a 2,000-year-old burial from a burial mound in the Midwest disturbed by later interments in the same mound?

To add to the complication, you can come across both **primary contexts** (the original context of an archaeological find, undisturbed by any factor, human or natural, since it was deposited by the people involved with it) and **secondary contexts** (the context of a find whose original position has been disturbed by later activity). In A.D. 43, a Roman legion attacked a strongly fortified native British hill fort at *Maiden Castle* in southern England. The legion attacked the weakest point of the defenses at the eastern end, advancing under a hail of slingshots and arrows. Protected by their long, hide shields, the Roman soldiers fired iron-tipped arrows at the defenders atop the wooden palisades. As the attackers advanced, an arrow felled a tribesman in his tracks. The iron head penetrated his spine, killing him instantly (Figure 2.7). The Romans sacked and burned the fort, then retreated to their camp a short distance away. Under cover of darkness, the defenders crept back to the ramparts and buried their dead in

FIGURE 2.7
A Roman iron arrow-head lodged in a battle casualty's spine, Maiden Castle, England. *(Courtesy English Heritage.)*

shallow graves. One of those buried was the casualty with the arrow in his spine. Over 1,900 years later, archaeologist Mortimer Wheeler uncovered the burial in its *primary context,* curled up, fetuslike in his hastily dug sepulcher.

Secondary contexts can occur when a group allows the dead to remain exposed until the corpse has decomposed, then buries the bones in a bundle in a communal burial chamber, like a British Stone Age long barrow or in a Hopewell mound in the Ohio Valley. Secondary context also refers to burials deposited in the same place at a later date. For example, in 500 B.C., a group of Chumash Indians camped by a rocky peninsula on the south side of Santa Cruz Island off southern California. Their ancestors had collected shellfish and hunted sea mammals at this location for untold generations. They camped for several days, nursing a sick man. After he died, they buried his body in the large shell heap downwind of their camp and moved away. Fifty years later, another group visited the same spot and buried two children in the same mound. As they dug their graves into a corner of the original sepulcher, they disturbed the bones of the long-forgotten ancestor. When archaeologists uncovered the burials centuries later, they referred to the later interments as secondary burials.

Secondary contexts are common occurrences. For example, the tomb robbers who entered the sepulcher of Egyptian pharaoh Tutankhamun soon after his interment in 1342 B.C. searched frantically for gold and precious oils. They scattered other items of grave furniture into secondary contexts before being frightened away. In still other instances, finds can be shifted by the natural forces of wind and weather. Many of the Stone Age tools found in European river gravels have been transported by floodwaters to locations far from their original place of deposition. All these disturbed finds are in secondary contexts.

TIME AND SPACE

Every human artifact has a provenance in time and space. The provenance in time can range from a radiocarbon date of 1,400 ± 60 years before the present for a Maya temple to a precise reading of A.D. 1623 for a historic building in a Colonial village in Virginia. Frequently, it can simply be an exact position in an archaeological site whose general age is known. Provenance in space is based, finally, on associations between tools and other items that were results of human behavior in a culture. Provenance is determined by applying two fundamental archaeological principles: the principle of association and the principle of superposition.

The Law of Association

The Empress Dowager Dou lay in a rock-cut sepulcher in central China. The wife of Prince Liu Sheng, elder brother of Emperor Wu-di, died in about 103 B.C. She was buried in a tomb over 170 feet (51 m) long, dug by hand by hundreds of laborers. She lay in a central chamber with wooden walls and tiled roof, once hung with finely embroidered curtains. Dou Wan lay in a magnificent jade suit sewn together with gold thread. Han Emperors and their nobles believed in Taoist magical traditions, which taught that jade prevented body decay. All that remained was a jumble of jade plaques and gold thread. Her bones had vanished. A gilt-bronze lamp modeled in the form of a young serving girl watched over the corpse (Figure 2.8). The

FIGURE 2.8 The Dowager Dou's lamp. *(Source: The Metropolitan Museum of Art, on loan from the People's Republic of China. Photograph by Wang Yugui, Cultural Relics Bureau, Bejing.)*

serving girl is kneeling, a lamp in her hands. Both the lamp and its shade are adjustable, so that the direction and intensity of its rays could be changed at will. The direct **association** between the corpse and the lamp make it certain that the lamp belonged to Dowager Dou, especially since it bears the inscription "Lamp of the Palace of Eternal Trust." The Dowager's grandmother lived in a residence of that name, so Chinese archaeologists believe the lamp may have been a wedding gift from the grandmother to her granddaughter.

The archaeological principle of association (Figure 2.9) came into play in Dou Wan's sepulcher. Danish archaeologist J. J. A. Worsaae used this principle when excavating dozens of prehistoric burials in northern Europe as long ago as the 1840s. Worsaee wrote (1843, 247):

> The objects accompanying a human burial are in most cases things that were in use at the same time. When certain artifact types are found together in grave association after grave association, and when more evolved forms of the same tools are found in association with other burials, then the associations provide some basis for dividing the burials into different chronological groups on the basis of association and artifact styles.

This principle, sometimes called the law of association, is one of the foundations of all archaeological research. In 1859, association linked the bones of long-extinct animals in river gravels with humanly made stone axes found in the same levels. This discovery provided indisputable evidence for a very ancient humanity. The association showed that humans and such beasts had lived on earth at the same time, hundreds of thousands of years earlier than the mere 6,000 years suggested by the biblical Creation. The Meer stoneworkers described at the beginning of this chapter are known to us because of Daniel Cahen's meticulous plotting of hundreds of stone chips around the associated boulders where they sat. Association is a barometer of ancient human behavior, recorded in the intricate patterns of artifacts, food remains, and other finds in the soil.

The Law of Superposition

Archaeologist Alfred Kidder dug into the deep **middens** at Pecos Pueblo, New Mexico, in 1915. The pueblo had flourished four hundred years before, when the first Spanish conquistadors arrived in the Southwest in 1540. Kidder trenched into the historic levels, then dug through deep occupation horizons until he reached sterile bedrock. His huge trenches yielded over 750 burials in sealed graves with groups of pots and thousands of painted potsherds, whose designs changed considerably as he dug deeper into the ash and occupation debris. Alfred Kidder worked from the historic known back into the prehistoric unknown, using graves and potsherds to develop a long sequence of Pueblo culture, with the oldest at the base and the most recent at the top of the middens.

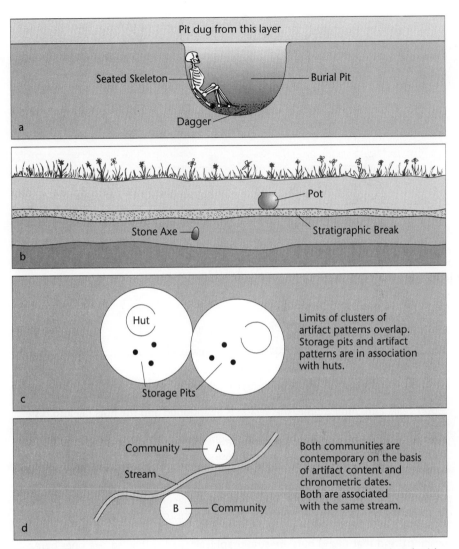

FIGURE 2.9 The law of association in archaeology: (a) a skeleton associated with a dagger; (b) a pot and a stone ax, separated by a stratigraphic break, which are not in association; (c) two contemporary household clusters associated with each other; (d) an association of communities that are contemporary.

Kidder used a fundamental principle of archaeology, the law of **superposition,** which comes from stratigraphic geology (Figure 2.10). The principle of superposition states that the geological layers of the earth are stratified one upon another, like the layers of a cake. Cliffs by the seashore and quarries are easily accessible examples. Obviously, any object found in the lowermost levels, whether a stone or something humanly made, was deposited there before the upper levels were accumulated. In other words, the lower

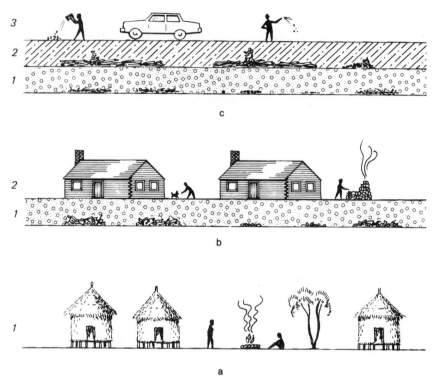

FIGURE 2.10 The principle of superposition: (a) a flourishing farming village 5,000 years ago. After a time, the village is abandoned and the huts fall into disrepair. The ruins are covered by accumulating earth and vegetation. (b) After an interval, a second village is built on the same site, with different architectural styles. This village, in turn, is abandoned; the houses collapse into piles of rubble and are covered by accumulating earth. (c) Twentieth-century people park their cars on top of both village sites and drop litter and coins that, when uncovered, reveal to the archaeologist that the top layer is modern. An archaeologist digging this site would find that the modern layer is underlain by two prehistoric occupation levels, that square houses were in use in the upper of the two, which is the later (law of superposition), and that round huts are stratigraphically earlier than square ones here. Therefore, village 1 is earlier than village 2, but when either was occupied or how many years separate village 1 from 2 cannot be known without further data.

strata are earlier than the upper strata. The same principle applies to archaeological sites. The order of deposition of tools, houses, and other finds in the layers of a site can be dated relative to the layers by their association with the stratum in which they are found. But it should be noted that archaeological finds can become jumbled in archaeological layers for all manner of reasons, among them human activities.

The basis of all scientific archaeological excavation is the accurately observed and carefully recorded stratigraphic profile, or **stratigraphy** (Chapter 7).

PRESERVATION CONDITIONS

He lay on his left side in a crouched position, a serene expression on his face, his eyes tightly closed. He wore a pointed skin cap and a hide belt—nothing else except for a cord knotted tightly around his neck. Twelve to 24 hours before his death, he had eaten a gruel of barley, linseed, and several wild grasses and weeds. *Tollund* Man was choked or hanged about 2,000 years ago, then laid to rest in a Danish bog, where peat-cutters found his well-preserved body in 1950 (Figure 2.11).

The archive of the past comes down to us in the form of a frustratingly incomplete archaeological record, consisting for the most part of an endless array of stone tools, potsherds, and more durable, artifacts such as grindstones and lava hammers. The sharp edges of stone choppers fabricated more than 2 million years ago may be as sharp as the day they were made, but such inorganic objects tell us little about their makers, beyond details of their technology.

FIGURE 2.11   The head of Tollund Man. *(Courtesy of the National Museum, Copenhagen, Denmark.)*

Just occasionally, though, the veil lifts when favorable preservation conditions bring us organic objects made of once-living substances, such as wood, leather, bone, or cotton. We know a great deal about Tollund Man, the manner of his death, his health, and his diet simply because his corpse survived under waterlogged conditions. Peat bogs, damp lake beds, and other wet sites can preserve wood and plant remains in near-perfect condition. So can ultradry climates, such as that of Egypt: witness the well-preserved tomb of pharaoh Tutankhamun. Both Arctic cold, in which permafrost literally refrigerates archaeological sites, and volcanic ash offer unusual opportunities to explore past societies. Following are four examples of truly exceptional preservation, which show the potential for spectacular discoveries.

Waterlogged Sites: Ozette, Washington

For more than 2,500 years, the ancestors of modern-day Makah Indians hunted whales and other sea mammals from a village at *Ozette,* on Washington's Olympia Peninsula. About 200 years ago, a sudden mudslide buried much of the village of cedar plank houses. Liquid mud cascaded over the dwellings, preserving their contents as the inhabitants abandoned them. Archaeologist Richard Daugherty of Washington State University used high-pressure hoses and fine sprays to tease the still-waterlogged soil from the remains of four perfectly preserved cedar log houses. The wet muck that had engulfed the houses had mantled them in a dense, wet blanket that preserved everything except flesh, feathers, and skins. One house was 69 feet long and 46 feet wide (21 by 14 m). There were separate hearths and cooking platforms. Low walls and hanging mats served as partitions. More than 40,000 artifacts came from the excavations, including conical rain hats made of spruce root fibers, baskets, wooden boxes, wooden bowls still impregnated with seal oil, mats, fishhooks, bows and arrows, even fragments of looms (see Figure 2.12).

The Ozette site is a classic example of how much can be recovered from a waterlogged archaeological site. Ozette is important in other ways, too, for the ancestors of the Makah Indians who lived there flourished along the coast for more than 2,500 years. Archaeology extended their known cultural heritage back far into the remote past.

Dry Sites: Chinchorro Mummies, Northern Chile

Two thousand years before the ancient Egyptians started mummifying their dead, the *Chinchorro culture* of northern Chile and southern Peru had developed its own mummification techniques. The Chinchorro were hunter-gatherers who subsisted off the rich Pacific inshore fisheries and local patches of wild plant foods in one of the driest environments on earth. They settled in permanent villages and buried their dead in cemeteries, where the corpses survive in near-perfect condition in the arid climate. Beginning in about 5000 B.C., the people dismembered the dead, skinned and eviscerated them, then

FIGURE 2.12 A whale fin carved from cedar wood and inlaid with more than 700 sea otter teeth, excavated at Ozette, Washington. The teeth at the base are set in the design of a mythical bird with a whale in its talons. *(Courtesy of the Department of Anthropology, Washington State University, Pullman, Washington.)*

packed the bodies with plant material and reinforced them with sticks. Later, they made neat incisions in the bodies for removing organs, then sewed them together with human hair and cactus spines. They attached wigs of human hair to the skulls like helmets, using red-painted ash paste, and they often painted the faces of the mummies black. The mummies were displayed and cared for, then eventually wrapped in shrouds of woven reeds and buried in shallow graves, sometimes in family groups of six or more.

The bone chemistry and bowel contents of the Chinchorro mummies reveal a diet rich in seafood and also evidence of tapeworm infestations and auditory exostoses, perhaps caused by diving for shellfish in deep, cold water.

Cold Conditions: The Nevado Ampato Mummy, Peru

Freezing conditions in an arctic environment or at high altitudes can literally dry out or refrigerate a corpse and preserve the finest of raiment. Anthropologist Johan Reinhard and his Peruvian assistant Miguel Zarate found the mummy bundle of a young girl at an altitude of 20,700 feet (6210 m) in the Peruvian Andes. The 14-year-old Inca girl died as a sacrificial victim five centuries ago and was buried on a summit ridge of the sacred *Nevado Ampato* mountain (Figure 2.13). Her well-preserved body was wrapped in a rough outer garment, then a brown-and-white-striped cloth. Underneath, she wore a finely woven dress and shawl fastened with a silver pin. Her feet bore leather moccasins, but her head was bare. She may originally have worn a fanlike feather headdress, which was dislodged when the summit ridge collapsed and her mummy bundle fell down a slope. CT (computerized topography) scans of her skull revealed fractures by the maiden's right eye. She

FIGURE 2.13 The Nevado Ampatu mummy, an Inca sacrificial victim buried high in the southern Andes Mountains of Peru. *(Source: Stephen Alvarez/NGS Image Collection.)*

died from a massive hemorrhage resulting from a swift blow to the head. Blood from the wound pushed her brain to one side of her skull.

Volcanic Ash: Cerén, El Salvador

Everyone has heard of Roman *Herculaneum* and *Pompeii,* flourishing towns buried by a massive eruption of Mount Vesuvius in A.D. 79. The smothering ash even preserved body casts of fleeing victims. Similarly, in the sixth century B.C., at Cerén in El Salvador, a volcanic eruption in a nearby river buried a small Maya village without warning. The people had eaten their evening meal but had not yet gone to bed. Upon the eruption, they abandoned their homes and possessions and fled for their lives. Payson Sheets and a multidisciplinary research team have recovered entire buildings, outlying structures, and their contents exactly where they were dropped. He found that each household had a building for eating, sleeping, and other activities, also a separate kitchen and storehouse (Figure 12.14). Substantial thatched roofs projected beyond the walls, providing covered walkways and places for proc-

FIGURE 2.14 Reconstruction drawing of Maya houses at Cerén, El Salvador.

essing grain and for storage. Sheets unearthed rows of young maize plants that had attained the height usual for August at this location, as well as herbs and other plants, each in their own mound of soil.

The Cerén excavations reveal Maya farmers going about their daily business, the men working in the fields and making obsidian tools, the women weaving cotton garments, making agave rope and twine, and fashioning clay vessels. Theirs was a life dictated by the passage of the seasons, by wet and dry months, by the cyclical demands of planting and harvest. By chance, the volcanic ash rained down just after supper, so their artifacts, including bowls smeared with food, preserve a chronicle of life at the end of a farmer's day. We even know the Cerén people kept sharp knives out of harm's way in the rafters of their houses.

Such well-preserved finds as Cerén or Ozette are few and far between, but they show the enormous potential for minute reconstruction of the past from wet sites and other exceptional locations. For the most part, however, the archaeologist works with an archaeological record that is a thing of shreds and patches, where preservation conditions militate against detailed portraits of ancient cultures.

SUMMARY

Chapter 2 discusses the fundamental principles of archaeology. Archaeologists have a primary responsibility to conserve the past for future generations. Archaeology's other goals are to construct culture history, reconstruct ancient lifeways, and to study processes of cultural change. The process of archaeological research begins with a research design, then proceeds to data collection, analysis, interpretation, and publication of the results. Archaeologists study ancient cultures, with culture being, in part, the shared ideas that human societies hold. Culture is also our primary way of adapting to our environment. Many archaeologists think of human cultures as cultural systems made up of many interacting subsystems, these cultures being part of much larger ecosystems. The study of cultural process involves interpreting the ways in which cultures change over long periods of time. The archaeological record comprises the material remains of human behavior, a finite archive of the past which has a context in time and space. Chapter 2 defines some of the components of the archaeological record and the widely differing preservation conditions that can affect our knowledge of the past. It makes the fundamental point that all archaeological finds have a context in time and space, defined by the laws of association and superposition.

KEY TERMS

Analysis
Anthropology
Archaeological data
Archaeological record
Artifact
Association
Band
Context
Cultural process
Cultural system
Culture
Culture history
Ecofact
Feature
Hieroglyphs
Hominid

Interpretation
Matrix
Midden
Potsherd
Primary context
Processual archaeology
Provenance (provenience)
Research design
Secondary context
Site
Stratigraphy
Structure
Subsistence
Superposition
Transformational processes
Ziggurat

GUIDE TO FURTHER READING

Deetz, James. 1967. *Invitation to Archaeology*. Garden City, NY: Natural History Press.
    A classic and informal exposition on basic archaeological concepts that has rarely been bettered.
Hester, Thomas R., Harry J. Shafer, and Kenneth L. Feder. 1997. *Field Methods in Archaeology*. 2nd ed. Mountain View, CA: Mayfield.
    A survey of archaeological fieldwork with important sections on the process of research and the goals of archaeology.
Moore, Andrew. 1998. *Village on the Euphrates*. New York: Oxford University Press.
    An exemplary monograph on an early farming village that applies the basic principles of archaeology admirably.
Renfrew, Colin, and Paul Bahn. 2000. *Archaeology: Theories, Methods, Practice*. 3rd ed. New York: Thames and Hudson.
    A comprehensive handbook of archaeological method and theory, with lavish illustrations.
Schiffer, Michael B. 1997. *Site Formation Processes of the Archaeological Record*. 2nd ed. Salt Lake City, UT: University of Utah Press.

Sheets, Payson. 1992. *The Cerén Site*. New York: Harcourt Brace Jovanovich.
    A short case study of this important Maya village buried by volcanic ash. Ideal for readers unfamiliar with archaeological methods.
Willey, Gordon R., and P. Phillips. 1958. *Method and Theory in American Archaeology*. Chicago: University of Chicago Press.
    This classic essay on culture history in North American archaeology is still a fundamental source on such topics as culture and culture history.

CHAPTER 3
How Old Is It?

Ancient Egyptian nobles and servants ride in long Nile boats during a fishing expedition. Tomb of Menna, Thebes. Menna was a high official during the reign of pharaoh Tuthmosis IV (1400–1391 B.C.), responsible for tallying harvests and temple tithes. (Source: Menna with Family Fishing and Fowling, Tomb of Menna. The Metropolitan Museum of Art. All Rights Reserved, The Metropolitan Museum of Art. 30.4.48.)

CHAPTER OUTLINE

Time—our lives depend on it. We live from day to day according to tight schedules: class times, doctors' appointments, flight departures, and tax deadlines. The hours of the day are the framework of our daily lives, of our jobs, and leisure time. Not for us the broad sweep of changing seasons or days measured by sunrise and sunset. We depend on the clock to guide us through the day, to regulate our lives. I write these words at precisely 8:23 A.M., and I could have obtained a reading for the exact moment when I wrote the numeral 8 if I wished; modern Westerners are obsessed with the passage and measurement of time.

All of us have a perspective on times past as well. My earliest memory is of balloons on my second birthday. I have continual memory from about age eight. My parents saw Queen Victoria in her extreme old age, driving in a carriage in central London in 1898. The collective family history encompasses the twentieth century—about a hundred years. My earlier sense of history comes from family ancestry, the history of my community, of our nation, of all humankind. Like all Westerners, I think of the human past in linear terms, as a long, albeit branching, line which began over 4 million years ago among the first hominids to live on the East African savanna.

How do we know that humans originated 4 million years before present? Chapter 3 describes the ways in which archaeologists study time and date the past.

CYCLICAL AND LINEAR TIME

Westerners think of the passage of the human past as occurring along a straight, if branching, highway of time. The great nineteenth-century German statesman Otto von Bismarck called this the "stream of time," upon which all human societies ride through good times and bad. The analogy is apt, if you think of time in a linear fashion, as archaeologists do. They use a variety of chronological methods to date the long millennia of the remote past.

An unfolding, linear past is not the only way of conceptualizing ancient times. Many societies, ancient and modern, think of time as a cyclical phenomenon, or sometimes as a combination of the linear and the cyclical. The cyclical perspective stems from the passage of the seasons and of heavenly bodies, from the close relationships between foragers and village farmers and their natural environments. It is also based on the eternal realities of human life: fertility and birth, life, growth, and death. The endlessly repeating seasons of planting and harvest, of game movements or salmon runs, and of ripening wild foods governed human existence in deeply significant ways. The ancient Maya developed an elaborate cyclical calendar of interlocking secular and religious calendars to measure the passage of the seasons and to regulate religious ceremonies.

But we should not assume that societies with cyclical views of time did not have linear chronologies as well. The celebrated Maya "Long Count" was a linear chronology, which formed an integral part of the close relationship between Maya rulers and the cosmos. The ancient Egyptians developed a linear chronology for administrative purposes. But, in general, societies develop linear chronologies only when they need them. For example, Western societies use linear time to regulate times of prayer, to control the working day, and for airline schedules. It is hard to generalize, but societies with centralized political systems tend to use the reigns of chiefs or kings as signposts along a linear time scale. For instance, the history of the rulers of the state of Benin in West Africa shows a significant shift in the interpretation of time. Before the fourteenth century A.D., Benin history is essentially mythological, with inaccurate chronology and a variable number of kings. But with the founding of the Yoruba dynasty, the deeds and reigns of every *oba* (king) are remembered in detail with chronological accuracy right down to modern times.

RELATIVE CHRONOLOGY

Archaeologists refer to two types of chronology:

- **Relative chronology,** which establishes chronological relationships between sites and cultures
- **Absolute chronology** (sometimes called chronometric chronology), which refers to dates in years

My aged tortoiseshell cat has just come into my study. Bulging with breakfast, she gives me a plaintive miaow and looks for a patch of sunlight on the carpet. She spots one, just where I have laid down a pile of important papers. Thump! With a sigh, she settles down right on top of the documents and passes out blissfully as I write. Time passes and I realize that I need one of the articles in the pile under my faithful beast. I debate whether to have a cup of coffee and procrastinate, or to disturb her, knowing there will be angry

DISCOVERY

Human Sacrifice at Teotihuacán, Mexico

Teotihuacán, on the edge of the Valley of Mexico, grew from a series of small villages into a huge metropolis with over 200,000 inhabitants by A.D. 650 (see Figure 6.10). A vast ceremonial complex dominated by the Pyramids of the Sun and Moon formed the core of the city, but little is known of the builders or of the rituals once celebrated there. In 1998, a team of American and Mexican archaeologists headed by Saburo Sugiyama excavated into the heart of the Pyramid of the Moon, where they unearthed four stratified substructures and a human burial dated to about A.D. 150. The grave contained more than 150 artifacts surrounding a male skeleton: clay vessels, jade artifacts, figurines, fine obsidian (volcanic glass) blades, and jadeite ear ornaments. The skeletons of several hawks and a jaguar, perhaps buried alive in their cages, lay nearby.

At first Sugiyama and his colleagues thought they had unearthed the burial of a noble. But the man's hands were bound behind his back and he lay at the edge of what is obviously a much larger burial complex. They believe that he was a sacrificial victim, killed as part of a ceremony to dedicate either a ruler or an important structure. Sugiyama believes that more burials await discovery deeper in the pyramid, including, perhaps, the undisturbed sepulcher of one of Teotihuacán's rulers. Such a discovery would be of the highest importance, as nothing is known of the great city's powerful rulers.

claws. In the end, writing deadlines prevail. I gently elevate the cat and slip the papers out from under her. She protests half-heartedly and settles down again, as I congratulate myself on escaping grievous injury. . . .

The case of the cat and the papers is a classic example of stratigraphy in action. Consider the sequence of events. I sit at my computer, consult some documents, then lay them to the side on the floor. This is the first event in the sequence. Some time later, the second event takes place: The cat settles on the publications and goes to sleep. More time passes. I need an article in the pile, lift the cat, and remove the papers. This third event is followed by the final act of this stirring drama, as the cat settles down again. An outside observer could use the law of superposition (Chapter 2) to reconstruct the sequence of events from the earliest (the dropping of papers on the floor) to the latest (the cat settling down again). However, while the observer can establish the sequence of events relative to one another in time, he or she cannot tell how long a span of time passed between each one. Nor can he or she know the age of the various objects in the pile. For instance, a document compiled in 1970 might lie in a folder under another one containing a letter written 10 years earlier.

Relative chronology is a foundation of all archaeological research, a time scale established by either stratigraphic observation or by placing artifacts in chronological order. As we saw in Chapter 2, stratigraphic observation is based on the law of superposition, which states that, in general, the earliest layers lay below later ones. Many ancient settlements, such as long-occupied caves and rock shelters or huge city mounds in southwestern Asia, can contain literally dozens of occupation levels, sometimes separated by layers of sterile soil. (See Discovery box on p. 65.)

Stratigraphy and Relative Chronology

Stratigraphic observation can sometimes yield remarkably long cultural sequences, which can be dated by radiocarbon and other methods. (See Site box below.)

Koster's stratigraphy was much less complex than that of ancient cities, where people lived in houses for a generation or more, then knocked them down and rebuilt on the same spot. They lost beads and ornaments, trampling them into the earth. They laid new floors, a layer of tile or a few centimeters of liquid cattle dung, over earlier living surfaces. Buildings crumbled, floods may have demolished structures, or fire consumed entire city blocks. People dug graves and storage pits, resurfaced streets, enlarged temples and open plazas. The archaeologist's relative chronology comes from deciphering these kinds of chronological jigsaw puzzles. I once spent two weeks excavating a two-foot (0.6-m) section cut through a Stone Age camp site, where at least five temporary occupations could be seen in the wall of the trench. Unfortunately, we could not separate them, or their artifacts, horizontally.

 SITE

Koster, Illinois

Few archaeological sites have such exceptional stratigraphy as the well-known Koster site in the Midwest's Illinois River Valley, where human occupations are separated by sterile layers from before 7500 B.C. right into the past millennium. Stuart Struever and James Brown isolated 14 stratified occupation levels in their large-scale excavations (see Figure 7.2). These provide an extraordinary chronicle of human exploitation of the river valley environment from about 7500 B.C. to A.D. 1200. The excavators were able to isolate different occupations and expose large areas of them, starting with transitory *Paleo-Indian* visitors, then a seasonal camp covering about 0.75 acre (0.3 ha) with temporary dwellings built in about 6500 B.C. They traced repeated visits by an extended family group of about 25 people to the same site over many centuries, perhaps timed to exploit rich fall nut harvests. Between 5600 and 5000 B.C., a large permanent camp with longhouses covered in hides or mats came into use; the inhabitants focused on a narrow spectrum of abundant foods throughout much of the year. By 3900 B.C., people lived at Koster year-round in a village covering 5 acres (2 ha). The excavations identified at least six houses with sunken earthen floors, whose inhabitants lived off fish from backwater lakes and fall nut harvests. Koster was abandoned in about 2800 B.C., then reoccupied briefly about 800 years later. The Koster excavations yielded a treasure trove of chronological information, which has provided a framework for studying major changes in Native American society over many thousands of years.

The law of association also comes into play, for the artifacts, food remains, and other finds that come from different occupation layers are as vital as the stratigraphy itself. Each layer in a settlement, however massive or however thin, has its associated artifacts, the objects that archaeologists use as chronological indicators and evidence of cultural change. Stratigraphic observation is rarely straightforward. Some key questions are never far from the observer's mind: Was the site occupied continuously? Was the sequence interrupted by a natural catastrophe such as a flood, or was it abandoned then reoccupied generations later? Far more is involved than merely observing different layers. Basically, the excavator has to reconstruct both the natural and cultural transformations that have affected the site since it was abandoned.

Cultural transformations are those resulting from human behavior. For example, occupants of a later village may dig rubbish pits or graves into earlier levels. Cattle penned on the site may disturb underlying strata with their hooves. People may cultivate the rich soils of an abandoned village and thus disturb the stratigraphic layers. The possibilities are endless.

Natural transformations result from natural phenomena, such as the volcanic eruption that buried Roman Pompeii in A.D. 79, or the earthquake that devastated another Roman town, *Kourion* on Cyprus, in A.D. 365. In the case of the Kourion quake, excavator David Soren was able to use historical records to identify the exact moment of the earth movement. The orientation of collapsed roof tiles gave him the general direction of the epicenter, which lay to the southwest of the town in deep water (see Figure 10.4). Both Roman Herculaneum and Pompeii have yielded graphic evidence of the awful destruction wrought by the sudden ash clouds, including casts of fleeing people frantically trying to escape the ash and fumes (Figure 3.1). In these cases, volcanic ash has sealed a precise moment in time, providing unique opportunities for observing life in a city at a single period.

Mudslides, floods, wind storms, and sand dunes can seal off occupation layers from later horizons. At the other end of the spectrum, burrowing animals can tunnel through soft ash layers and transform beautifully stratified layers into confused mazes. I remember once throwing out about half the contents of a deep trench through 500 years of human occupation because the entire deposit was riddled with rabbit burrows. Potsherds from the lowermost levels lay on the surface, while material from much higher up had slipped deep into the occupation layers. All we could do was start again in a less-disturbed part of the site.

Relative chronology depends on precise, and thorough, observation and interpretation. (There's more on stratigraphic observation in Chapter 8.)

Artifacts and Relative Chronology

Manufactured artifacts of all kinds are the fundamental data archaeologists use to study past human behavior. Artifacts are reflections of ancient human behavior, so it follows that they change as peoples' technologies, lifeways, and other activities shift over the millennia. Consider, for a moment, the

FIGURE 3.1 Cast of a beggar outside the Nucerian Gate at Pompeii who was felled by suffocating volcanic ash falling on the town, A.D. *79. (Courtesy of Werner Forman/Art Resource.)*

simple, sharp-edged flake knives used by our earliest ancestors 2.5 million years ago (see Figure 8.4). Modern-day experiments have shown that such artifacts were highly effective for slicing through fresh meat and butchering animals. Compare such tools with the highly sophisticated supercomputers used by banks and credit card companies today. In the final analysis, you could argue that one evolved from the other, but millions upon millions of minor technological and behavioral changes took place along the way as the simple artifacts of yesteryear branched into more and more sophisticated tools for all kinds of specialized purposes. Most changes were small, sometimes almost imperceptible: a more efficient method for edge sharpening a stone tool; changes in the lip angle or decoration on a clay bowl, which lead ultimately to an entirely different vessel; new alloys such as tin added to copper to make much tougher bronze. Such cumulative changes are an excellent way of establishing relative chronologies, a point demonstrated more than a century ago by British archaeologist John Evans (Figure 3.2).

In the 1880s and 1890s, a remarkable Egyptologist named Flinders Petrie unearthed hundreds of shallow graves in desert cemeteries at *Diospolis Parva* close to the Nile River. The graves were for villagers who farmed along the river many centuries before the first pharaoh, Menes, unified Egypt into a

FIGURE 3.2 How artifacts change through time. Nineteenth-century scholar John Evans showed how a British coin originated in a naturalistic coin of King Philip II of Macedon in southeastern Europe. Evans traced the changing style of this coin, known as a *stater,* as it spread across Europe.

single state in about 3100 B.C. Historical dates in Egypt went back to Menes, but then petered out. Petrie's "Predynastic" burial subjects wore few ornaments, but lay with groups of jars, pots, and bowls. Flinders Petrie had an eye for smaller objects. He hit on the brilliant idea of using the groups of clay vessels from the graves to place the graves in chronological order, by arranging the pots so that their stylistic differences reflected gradual design changes. The jar handles were especially informative, for they changed over time from mere ledgelike appendages to more decorative and functional handles before they degenerated into little more than painted lines. Petrie spent months dividing the grave lots into no less than 50 stages, which he called "sequence dates." His stages started with SD30, for he rightly assumed he had not found the earliest Predynastic pottery. SD80 linked the cemeteries to dynastic Egypt in about 3100 B.C.

Flinders Petrie's sequence dates provided an admirable way of placing Predynastic burials and sites throughout the Nile Valley into *relative* chronological order. Over half a century passed before anyone could provide calendar year dates for Predynastic Egyptian cultures with radiocarbon dates.

The Diospolis Parva graves provided one of the first instances where artifacts provided a reliable relative chronology. American archaeologist Alfred Kidder used much the same approach as Petrie at Pecos Pueblo, New Mexico, when he developed the first relative chronology of Southwestern pottery. Indeed, he was strongly influenced by Egyptologists' methods after a study tour of Egypt early in his career. Kidder excavated deep middens at Pecos, digging down from historical layers with dated pottery styles into much earlier horizons with entirely different ceramic styles. At the same time, he uncovered hundreds of graves where skeletons lay associated with painted pottery. By comparing the potsherds from the stratified layers with groups of vessels from the graves, Kidder was able to reconstruct a 2,000-year sequence of evolving Pueblo Indian culture, by working back from the present into the past. His Pecos observations, albeit much refined, are still a foundation for the relative chronology of much of the Southwest.

Sequence dating is now known as **seriation,** a technique for ordering artifacts by their morphology, which has achieved a high degree of sophistication since the 1920s. **Frequency seriation** employs percentages of artifacts and their features to develop cultural sequences.

We live in a world of whirlwind fashions. Automobiles acquire fins. A few years later, fins are gone and rounded contours are the rage. Whitewall tires are all the fashion; a decade later you never see them. Minivans replace station wagons; then sport utility vehicles reign supreme. The miniskirt suddenly descends to midcalf or even the ankle before rising to new flared heights. Fashions of all kinds are volatile and ever changing, including CDs in the top 40 or the colors of glass beads traded in remote African villages. In contrast, Stone Age handaxes took hundreds of thousands of years to assume more sophisticated shapes. All these changes, dizzyingly fast or mind-numbingly slow, have one thing in common—at some period in time, they enjoyed a brief, or long, moment of maximum popularity. All artifact seriations start with this assumption.

Back in the 1960s, two historical archaeologists, Edwin Dethlefsen and James Deetz, set out to document this assumption against known historical data. They chose dated New England Colonial gravestones from Stoneham, Massachusetts, for this purpose. Three decorative styles came into fashion at different times—death's heads, cherubs, and urn and willow motifs. Dethlefsen and Deetz recorded the percentages of the three motifs at nine-year intervals from 1720 to 1829. They found that the death's head was universally popular until 1760, when it began to give way to the cherub. Cherubs enjoyed high fashion until 1820, when they suddenly went out of favor as the urn and willow became the style of the day. When they plotted the percentages as horizontal bar graphs (Figure 3.3), they acquired a series of profiles, which looked very much like an old-fashioned battleship seen from above with its thick belt of armor amidships. The battleship curves of the Stoneham gravestones followed one upon the other with almost perfect symmetry. This classic and oft-quoted example of changing artifacts illustrates the principle perfectly.

The so-called battleship curve frequency seriation method is widely used in American archaeology. Let us say you have nine excavated archaeological sites, each containing different percentages of different pottery forms. You classify the vessels from each location into three distinct types, each with characteristic decoration, calculating the percentages of each in every site. Next, you apply the battleship curve principle, placing the sites in order by placing the horizontally arranged percentage bars in order (Figure 3.4). This gives you a relative chronology for the sites. Then, later on, you excavate two more settlements, where, again, you calculate the percentages of decorated pots. On the assumption that closely similar artifacts were made at

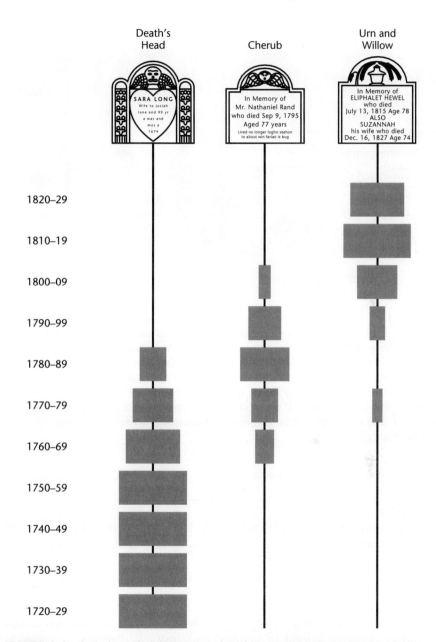

FIGURE 3.3   Seriation. The changing styles of New England gravestones, from Stoneham, Massachusetts, between A.D. 1720 and 1829, seriated in three styles. Notice how each style rises to a peak of maximum popularity and then declines as another comes into fashion. The cherub style shows the classic battleship curve. Each horizontal bar represents the percentage of a gravestone type at that date; for example, between 1720 and 1729, death's heads were at 100 percent. *(Courtesy of James Deetz, University of Virginia.)*

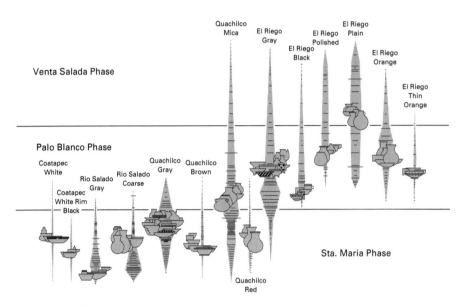

FIGURE 3.4 Seriation of pottery styles from the Tehuacán Valley, Mexico, showing many sites ordered into a single sequence. Richard MacNeish classified the different pottery types at each site, then placed them in chronological order on the basis of stratigraphic observations and periods of maximum popularity for each pottery type represented. Here the battleship curve principle is used to develop a sequence of changing pottery forms, each site being "fitted" into the sequence on the basis of the percentage of each pottery type represented. *(Courtesy of Richard MacNeish and the Peabody Foundation for Archaeological Research, Andover, Massachusetts.)*

approximately the same time at all sites within a restricted order, you can fit these new percentages into your master sequence and obtain a relative date for the extra sites.

Figure 3.4 shows a classic example of pottery seriation combined with stratigraphic observation from Mexico's Tehuacán Valley, famous for its evidence of early maize farming. Archaeologist Richard MacNeish worked before radiocarbon dating was a highly refined dating method. He had excavated or surface-collected dozens of stratified and unstratified sites and needed to develop a relative chronology based on changing pottery styles. He used a combination of stratigraphy and seriation of many distinctive pottery types to place three stages of Tehuacán culture in a relative chronology. Notice that MacNeish used no absolute dates to develop this sequence (which has subsequently been confirmed by radiocarbon dating).

Artifact seriation has obvious limitations and obviously works best when pottery types or other tool forms change predictably over a long period of time. Today's seriators use sophisticated statistical methods to produce the seriation and to test the validity of their conclusions. Relative chronology is comparatively straightforward compared with actual dating in calendar years.

ABSOLUTE DATING

"The first question is about dinosaurs, the second asks how old it is!" An old archaeologist friend welcomes visitors to his excavations, but finds their questions repetitive, especially in a society fascinated by dinosaurs. "Why are we so obsessed with dates?" he asks, and with good reason. I suspect it comes from the fascination of handling artifacts that were used centuries or thousands of years ago. I'll never forget the first time I handled a 50,000-year-old Neanderthal skull from a cave in southwestern France. The feeling of handling the head of someone who had lived in the Ice Age gave me an evocative thrill I shall always remember.

Many of our most fundamental questions about the past involve chronology. How old is this stone ax? Are these villages contemporary? When was this woman buried? More effort has gone into inventing methods of dating the past than into almost any other aspect of archaeology.

The landscape of the human experience stretches back more than two and a half million years into the past. Relative dating allows us to people this landscape with a myriad of long- and short-lived human cultures, ordered in local, regional, and continentwide sequences. The relatively dated past is like a branching tree, but a tree whose branches and limbs have never grown evenly or sprouted at the same time. Relative dating allows us to erect the tree, to plot its boughs and twigs in reasonably accurate order. We have a sense of a changing landscape, but no perspective of passing years. Without absolute dates, we do not know when humanity originated, when specific cultures began and ended, or how fast they changed. Nor do we have any inkling of when different major developments, such as the changeover from hunting and gathering to farming, took place in the Americas as opposed to southwestern Asia, or in China relative to tropical Africa. Absolute chronology is essential if we are to measure the rates of cultural change over long and short periods of time.

Dates in calendar years are the force that causes the stationary body of the past to come alive in the archaeologist's hands. Extremely precise tree-ring dates from the American Southwest tell the story of a prolonged drought cycle that affected the Anasazi people (the Ancient Ones) in the twelfth century, perhaps causing them to disperse from large pueblos into small villages. Radiocarbon dates calibrated with tree rings from Abu Hureyra, Syria, tell us that people switched from foraging to farming within a remarkably short time, perhaps a few generations. We now know that urban civilizations developed first in Egypt and Mesopotamia in about 3100 B.C., by 2000 B.C. in northern China, and in Central and South America shortly thereafter.

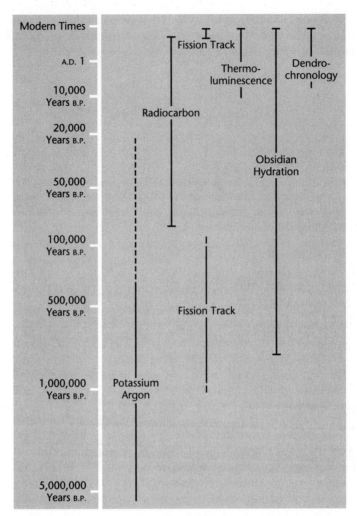

FIGURE 3.5 Major chronological methods used to date the human past.
(Courtesy of Bruce D. Smith, Smithsonian Institution, Washington D.C.)

Figure 3.5 shows the chronological span of the major absolute dating methods used to date the immense span of the human past. Let us now work our way back into the remote past, as we examine these major methods.

Historical Records, Calendars, and Objects of Known Age

Everyone learns the dates of major events in recent history in elementary school: the date of the Declaration of Independence (A.D. 1776), or the year when Roman general Julius Caesar landed in Britain (55 B.C.). Such years are landmarks which anchor the formation of modern nations, recorded in many documents. Unfortunately, however, written history has a short time span of only about 5,000 years; therefore, it is useful for dating sites and artifacts from about 3000 B.C. to the present.

Historical Documents   In 1290 B.C., the Egyptian king Seti I inscribed a king list on the walls of his temple at *Abydos* by the Nile River. His scribes recorded the names of 75 royal ancestors. His successor Rameses II ordered his own scribes to prepare yet another complete list of rulers, which survives as the so-called Turin Canon. This remarkable document appears to contain the list of every pharaoh from Rameses back to Menes, the first ruler of a unified Egypt in about 3100 B.C. The scribes who compiled the two king lists were less concerned with chronology than with making a political statement about the long continuity and stability of Egyptian civilization since the remotest past. Today, both the Seti list and the Turin document provide Egyptologists with a priceless record of the chronology of ancient Egyptian civilization.

Writing began in Mesopotamia and Egypt sometime just before 3000 B.C. At first, simple clay tokens and other marking systems recorded increasingly complex dealings between people living at some distance from one another. Eventually, the tokens became picture representations and then written scripts such as Sumerian **cuneiform** (Greek; *cuneus* = "wedge"), with its wedgelike symbols punched into wet clay, and Egyptian hieroglyphs. The earliest written records were little more than merchants' transactions and accounts, but early scribes soon widened their activities. Sumerian and Egyptian literature includes epics; love poetry; legal, political, and religious documents; and even school texts. By 2500 B.C., ancient scripts provide valuable chronological information.

Historical records provide dates for early eastern Mediterranean civilizations, for Chinese states after 2000 B.C., and for Europe after the Roman occupation just before Christ. However, document-based history only came to parts of tropical Africa and Asia in the late nineteenth century A.D. In the Americas, the Maya developed a complex written script just over 2,000 years ago and also an intricate calendar system that provides an accurate chronology for major events in later Mesoamerican history. Written sources for Native American societies elsewhere begin with European expansion after the fifteenth century.

Thus, documents provide accurate dates for only a tiny span of human history, most of it concentrated in the Mediterranean and east Asian worlds. We know the precise date when the Pilgrims settled Plymouth Plantation in Massachusetts and when galleons from the battered Spanish Armada foundered on the angry rocks of western Ireland. But history covers but the blink of a chronological eye in the larger landscape of a two-and-a-half-million-year-old past.

Calendars   People maintain calendars for many reasons—to commemorate the dates when rulers ascended to their thrones, to time important festivals, or to mark the passage of the seasons. Few ancient societies developed calendars as elaborate as those of the ancient Mesoamericans. The Maya calendar is justly famous. Once used to regulate the agricultural and religious years, the gear-wheel of intersecting sacred and secular calendars organized every aspect of Maya life in repeating cycles (Figure 3.6). At the same time, their

FIGURE 3.6 The Maya calendar comprised two interlocking cyclical calendars, which are illustrated here like two gear wheels of different size. The *tzolkin* of 260 days *(left)* was a sacred calendar and combination of 13 numbers and 20 day names. The *haab (right)* was a 365-day cycle that consisted of 18 "months" of 20 days each and one short 5-day "month." This was a farming calendar based on a cyclical time scale, which repeated itself every 52 years, 18,980 days, after which the name and number combinations repeated themselves.

priests maintained a linear calendar known as the Long Count, recorded on stone uprights. Experts have linked this to the Christian calendar and placed its span to be between 3114 B.C. and A.D. 909, although it lasted in places until the Spanish conquest of the sixteenth century. Much of this time scale unfolded before the Maya themselves lived in organized states, but their unique calendar provides a useful check on the dates of cities such as Copán, Palenque, and Tikal.

Like written documents, ancient calendars cover relatively short time brackets within the past 5000 years. Nevertheless, they are invaluable for detailed studies of such topics as Aztec or Egyptian civilization.

Objects of Known Age   We have already discussed cross-dating, where objects of known age such as Roman coins or Chinese porcelain can be used to date archaeological sites hundreds, if not thousands, of miles away from their point of origin. Sir Arthur Evans, who discovered Minoan civilization on the island of Crete in 1900, established the chronology of the Bronze Age Palace of *Knossos,* home of the legendary King Minos, using cross-dating in reverse. He developed an elaborate relative chronology of Minoan painted pottery at the palace, then consulted Egyptologists, who showed him examples of precisely similar vessels excavated from Egyptian sites dating to before 1500 B.C. Evans anchored Minoan chronology with these historical links, which resulted from an active trade in timber, olive oil, and other commodities between Crete and the Nile Valley (Figure 3.7).

FIGURE 3.7   The Palace of Knossos, Crete. *(Courtesy of Hirmir Verlag, Munich.)*

Historical archaeologists make extensive use of European ceramics of all kinds to date early Colonial sites in North America. Many colonists smoked tobacco in cheap clay pipes that broke easily. Thousands of pipes were manufactured, imported, broken, then thrown away each year, but the designs changed gradually over the decades. Not only the bowl but the length of the stem and diameter of the hole changed between A.D. 1620 and 1800. Historical documents and museum specimens allow researchers to date changing pipe styles and, thus, historic sites, with remarkable precision.

By the nineteenth century, the range of datable objects becomes enormous, thanks to more abundant documentation, mass production, and government patent records. Glass bottles, caps and openers, barbed wire, firearm components, uniform buttons, even horseshoes and iron nails—all are reliable chronological indicators. Bottles, buckets, and horseshoes may be the disrespected artifacts of archaeology, but they can be priceless chronological indicators. Objects of known historical age extend back about 5,000 years into the past.

Cross-Dating

Cross-dating uses objects of known historical age to date archaeological sites found far from the known objects' place of origin. This dating method is useful for a chronological span from 3000 B.C. to the present. Such objects as Chinese porcelain, Roman glass, cotton and flax fabrics, bronze daggers, and Greek amphorae traveled far from their homelands in the Old World. European coins and medals sometimes passed deep into the American interior along well-established trade routes, too. Such objects provide chronological horizons for dating hitherto undated pottery styles and other artifacts in remote areas such as, for example, western Europe during the Iron Age, after 3,000 years ago.

A classic example of cross-dating comes from Central Africa. Back in 1929, British archaeologist Gertrude Caton-Thompson traveled to the *Great Zimbabwe* ruins in southern Africa by oxcart and motor car. Torrential rain had flooded out low river bridges, so she had to walk the final few miles. She found herself confronted by a first-rate archaeological mystery. Great Zimbabwe was a complex of free-standing stone ruins clustered below a low hill where the ancient builders had erected stone-walled enclosures high above the valley floor (Figure 3.8).

The high granite walls of the oval-shaped Great Enclosure, adorned with a chevron pattern and an enigmatic conical tower, dwarfed the diminutive Caton-Thompson, who had never seen anything like them before. Great Zimbabwe was such a unique and sophisticated structure that early European archaeologists who ransacked the buildings for treasure refused to believe they were built by black Africans. By the time Caton-Thompson arrived, the white settlers firmly believed Zimbabwe was the work of long-vanished Phoenician settlers from Mediterranean lands. No African could build such structures, they argued. Passionate and racist writers bombarded the new-

FIGURE 3.8 The Great
Enclosure at Great
Zimbabwe, Central Africa.
*(Source: Tom Nebbia/Aspect
Picture Library Ltd.)*

comer with letters arguing that exotic civilizations, even the biblical Queen
of Sheba, were the builders of Great Zimbabwe.

Caton-Thompson promptly filed her fan mail in a folder labeled "Insane."
She searched for patches of undisturbed occupation deposit missed by earlier excavators and sunk carefully placed stratigraphic trenches in the hilltop
enclosures and in the Great Enclosure. Almost at once, she discovered fragments of imported Chinese porcelain, which had reached Zimbabwe in the
hands of traders from the distant Indian Ocean coast. From her research
in Egypt and elsewhere, she knew that experts could date Chinese porcelain
within remarkably narrow chronological limits in their places of origin. She
sent the porcelain to London's Victoria and Albert Museum, where specialists in Chinese artifacts assigned her imported potsherds to the Ming Dynasty,
specifically to the fourteenth and early fifteenth centuries A.D.

The Chinese porcelain provided Caton-Thompson with a solid cross-date
from China to Africa, thereby placing the heyday of Great Zimbabwe between
A.D. 1350 and 1450. She concluded that indigenous Africans built the stone
structures centuries after the Queen of Sheba and the Phoenicians had passed
into history. While radiocarbon dates have refined Caton-Thompson's
chronology, no scientist has subsequently challenged her cross-dating.

Cross-dating is also effective when you can date a single long cultural
sequence comprised of numerous archaeological sites using seriated artifacts,
then date the same sites and artifact forms with blocks of tree-ring or radiocarbon dates. You can then extrapolate the master chronology to nearby sites
in the same region by seriating distinctive artifact types and matching them
to the master sequence. Richard MacNeish used this approach with great success in Mexico's Tehuacán Valley, as have many other researchers in North
America. Kidder's Pecos sequence provided a broad framework for many
later excavations on pueblo sites throughout the northern Southwest and
wider afield, where radiocarbon dates and especially tree rings subsequently
provided an absolute chronology for the region.

Obsidian Hydration

Obsidian is a natural glass formed by volcanic activity, which was often used by the ancients for sharp-edged tools, mirrors, and ornaments. A freshly exposed obsidian surface will absorb water from its surroundings, forming a measurable hydration layer that is invisible to the human eye. The thickness of the hydration layer can be used to develop absolute and relative chronologies for all time periods, but little is known still about the effects of temperature changes and chemical compositions of soil on hydration. Obsidian hydration has been used successfully in widespread archaeological surveys around the Maya city at Copán, Honduras (see Chapters 6 and 10).

Tree-Ring Chronology

Everyone is familiar with tree rings—concentric circles, each circle representing annual growth—visible in the cross section of a felled tree's trunk. All trees form such rings, but they are better defined when the tree grows in an environment with well-marked seasons (winter and summer temperatures or dry and wet months). In about 1913, Arizona astronomer A. E. Douglass started counting tree rings as a way of dating sunspot activity. He soon realized the potential of **dendrochronology,** a method of using the tree rings to date ancient Southwestern pueblos. At first he developed two tree-ring sequences, one based on slow-growing and long-lived sequoias and California bristlecone pines; the latter eventually provided a chronology of 8,200 years. His second sequence used ancient, long-dead trunks, many of them pueblo door lintels and beams. Douglass was unable to link his "floating" chronology of pueblo beams to his master sequence until 1929, when he located the missing few years in a beam from Show Low, Arizona. Since then, Southwestern archaeologists have enjoyed a remarkably accurate chronology so precise it can date not only entire pueblos but sometimes individual rooms within them. (See Doing Archaeology box on p. 81.)

Extremely accurate chronologies for Southwestern sites come from correlating a master tree-ring sequence from felled trees and dated structures with beams from Indian pueblos. The beams in many such structures have been used again and again, and thus some are very much older than the houses in which they were most recently used for support. The earliest tree rings obtained from such settlements date to the first century B.C., but most timbers were in use between A.D. 1000 and historic times.

In one classic example, Jeffrey Dean collected numerous samples from wooden beams at *Betatakin,* a cliff dwelling in northeastern Arizona dating to A.D. 1270. He used 292 samples to reconstruct the history of the cliff dwelling, room by room. He found that three room clusters were built in 1267, and a fourth was added a year later. In 1269, the inhabitants trimmed and stockpiled beams for later use. These were not actually used until 1275, when 10 more room clusters were added to Betatakin. Such intrasite datings are possible when a large number of samples can be found. Similar

DOING ARCHAEOLOGY

Principles of Tree-Ring Dating

Tree rings are formed by all trees, but especially those where seasonal changes in weather are marked, with either a wet and dry season or a definite alternation between summer and winter temperatures. As a rule, trees produce growth rings each year, formed by the cambium, or growth layer, lying between the wood and the bark. When the growing season starts, large cells are added to the wood. These cells develop thicker walls and become smaller as the growing season progresses; by the end of the growth season, cell production has ceased altogether. This process occurs every growing year, and a distinct line is formed between the wood of the previous season, with its small cells, and the wood of the next, with its new, large cells. The thickness of each ring may vary according to the tree's age and annual climatic variations; thick rings are characteristic of good growth years.

Weather variations within a circumscribed area tend to run in cycles. A decade of wet years may be followed by five dry decades. One season may break a 40-year rainfall record. These cycles of climate are reflected in patterns of thicker or thinner tree rings, which are repeated from tree to tree within a limited area. Dendrochronologists have invented sophisticated methods of correlating rings from different trees so they can build up long master sequences of rings from a number of trunks that may extend over many centuries.

Samples are normally collected by cutting a full cross section from an old beam no longer in a structure, by using a special core borer to obtain samples from beams still in a building, or by V-cutting exceptionally large logs. Delicate or brittle samples are impregnated with paraffin or coated with shellac before examination.

Once in the laboratory, the surface of the sample is leveled to a precise plane. Analyzing tree rings consists of recording individual ring series and then comparing them against other series. Comparisons can be made by eye or by plotting the rings on a uniform scale so that one series can be compared with another. The series so plotted can then be computer-matched with the master tree-ring chronology for the region (Figure 3.9).

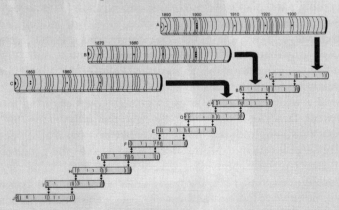

FIGURE 3.9 Building a tree-ring chronology: (A) a boring taken from a living tree after the 1939 growing season; (B–J) specimens taken from old houses and progressively older ruins. The ring patterns match and overlap back into prehistoric times.

research at *Walpi Pueblo,* a Hopi site in Arizona founded in A.D. 1400 and still inhabited today, proved the essential validity of Dean's methods, but also highlighted the difficulties of dating complex sites where beams are reused frequently, as when salvaged beams have been trimmed and reused.

Dendrochronology was once confined to the American Southwest, but is now widely used in many other parts of the world, including Alaska, Canada, parts of the eastern United States, England, Ireland, and continental Europe, and also the Aegean Islands and eastern Mediterranean. The Europeans have worked with oak trees with ages of 150 years or more to develop master chronologies for recent times. Using visual and statistical comparisons, they have managed to link living trees to dead specimens serving as church and farm-house beams and others found well preserved in bogs and waterlogged peats or prehistoric sites. The resulting tree-ring sequences go back at least 10,021 years in Germany and 7,289 years in Ireland. The Aegean Dendrochronology Project has developed a tree-ring sequence covering 6,000 of the last 8,500 years, which is leading to much more precise dates for the Minoan and Mycenaean civilizations than those suggested by cross-dating or radiocarbon readings. So precise are the master sequences, that an expert can date even short ring cycles to within a handful of years. Art historians even use tree rings to date the oak boards used by Dutch old masters as a means of authenticating paintings!

Tree-ring chronologies have far wider importance than merely dating the past. They can provide records of short-term climatic change in areas such as the American Southwest, where cycles of wetter and drier weather can cause radical changes in settlement patterns. Southwestern chronologies are accurate to within a year, a level of accuracy rarely achieved with archaeological chronologies anywhere. In recent years, the Laboratory of Tree Ring Research at the University of Arizona has undertaken a massive dendroclimatic study that has yielded a reconstruction of relative climatic variability in the Southwest from A.D. 680 to 1970. The same scientists, headed by Jeffrey Dean, are now producing the first quantitative reconstructions of annual and seasonal rainfall, and also of temperature, drought, and stream flow for the region. Such research is extremely complex, involving not only tree-ring sequences, but intricate mathematical expressions of the relationships between tree growth and such variables as rainfall, temperature, crop yields, and so on. These calculations yield statistical estimations of the fluctuations in these variables on an annual and seasonal basis.

By using a spatial grid of 27 long tree-ring sequences from throughout the Southwest, Dean and his colleagues have compiled maps that plot the different station values and their fluctuations like contour maps, one for each decade. This enables them to study such phenomena as the progress of what Dean calls the "Great Drought" of A.D. 1276 to 1299 from northeast to southwest across the region. In 1276, the beginnings of the drought appear in tree rings in the northwest. During the next 10 years, very dry conditions expand over the entire Southwest before improved rainfall arrives after 1299. This form of mapping allows close correlation of the vacation of large and small pueblos with short-term climatic fluctuations.

Radiocarbon Dating

In 1949, University of Chicago scientist Willard Libby revolutionized archaeology with the radiocarbon dating method of dating wood, bone, and other **organic materials** up to 40,000 years old. (See Doing Archaeology box below.) Libby's discovery was a direct offshoot of the development of the

DOING ARCHAEOLOGY

Principles of Radiocarbon Dating

The **radiocarbon dating** method is based on the fact that cosmic radiation produces neutrons that enter the earth's atmosphere and react with nitrogen. They produce carbon 14, a carbon isotope with eight rather than the usual six neutrons in the nucleus. With these additional neutrons, the nucleus is unstable and is subject to gradual radioactive decay. Willard Libby calculated that it took 5,568 years for half the carbon 14 in any sample to decay, its so-called **half-life.** (The half-life is now more accurately measured to be 5,730 years.) He found that the neutrons emitted radioactive particles when they left the nucleus, and he arrived at a method for counting the number of emissions in a gram of carbon.

Carbon 14 is believed to behave exactly like ordinary carbon from a chemical standpoint, and together with ordinary carbon it enters into the carbon dioxide of the atmosphere. The tempo of the process corresponds to the rates of supply and disintegration. Because living vegetation builds up its own organic matter through photosynthesis and by using atmospheric carbon dioxide, the proportion of radiocarbon present in it is equal to that in the atmosphere. As soon as an organism dies, no further radiocarbon is incorporated into it. The radiocarbon present in the dead organism will continue to disintegrate slowly, so that after 5,730 years only half the original amount will be left; after

about 11,100 years, only a quarter; and so on. Thus, if you measure the rate of disintegration of carbon 14 relative to nitrogen, you can get an idea of the age of the specimen being measured. The initial amount of radiocarbon in a sample is so small that the limit of detectability is soon reached. Samples older than 50,000 years contain only minuscule quantities of carbon 14.

A date received from a radiocarbondating laboratory is in this form: 3,621 ± 180 radiocarbon years before the present (B.P.). The figure 3,621 is the probable statistical age of the sample (in radiocarbon years) before the present. Notice that the sample reads in radiocarbon years, not calendar years. Corrections from tree rings must be applied to make this a chronometric date.

The radiocarbon age has the reading ± 180 attached to it. This is the **standard deviation,** an estimate of the amount of probable error. The figure 180 years is an estimate of the 360-year range within which the date falls. Statistical theory provides that there is a two out of three chance that the correct date is within the span of one standard deviation (3,441 and 3,801). If we double the deviation, chances are 19 out of 20 that the span (3,261 and 3,981) is correct. Most dates in this book are derived from carbon 14-dated samples and should be recognized for what they are—statistical approximations.

atomic bomb during World War II. At first, he tested his new method against organic objects of known historical age, such as Egyptian mummies, but he soon started dating archaeological sites occupied thousands of years earlier. Today, radiocarbon dating based on **accelerator mass spectrometry (AMS)** allows the dating of objects as tiny as a fleck of charcoal inside a tool socket or an individual seed from an early farming village. Thanks to AMS radiocarbon dating, we know that farming first began in southwestern Asia in about 8800 radiocarbon years B.C.—and we have the dated seeds to prove it. And calibrations based on tree rings, tropical corals, and other geological phenomena convert these radiocarbon ages into calendar chronologies.

Radiocarbon dating is the most widely used dating method for dating the past after 40,000 years ago until A.D. 1500 and provides a global radiocarbon chronology for world prehistory and the late Ice Age. This allows us to measure rates of cultural change in different regions of the world and to compare the chronology of such major developments as the first farming or the development of urban civilization in widely separated locations.

Libby made a false assumption when he originally formulated the radiocarbon method. He had argued that the concentration of radiocarbon in the atmosphere remained constant as time passed, so that prehistoric samples, when alive, would have contained the same amount of radiocarbon as living things today. In fact, changes in the strength of the earth's magnetic field and alterations in solar activity have considerably varied the concentration of radiocarbon in the atmosphere and in living things. For example, samples of 6,000 years ago were exposed to a much higher concentration than are living things today. It is possible, fortunately, to correct radiocarbon dates by using accurate dates from tree rings dating to between about 10,000 B.C. and A.D. 1950. The discrepancies between radiocarbon and calibrated dates are wide. Here is an example: A radiocarbon age of 1000 B.C. is a calibrated date of 1267 B.C. (standard deviations omitted here, see Figure 3.10). Radiocarbon dates around 10,000 B.C. may be as much as 2,000 years too young.

Earlier dates are still uncalibrated, but recently scientists have used a new, highly accurate technique based on the decay of uranium into thorium to date fossil coral near Barbados in the Caribbean. They compared these dates to radiocarbon results and found that radiocarbon dates between 10,000 and 25,000 years ago may be as much as 3,500 years too recent. The new coral researches, combined with ice core and deep sea core data, are beginning to provide calibrations back to 25,000 years ago, which is about 28,000 years ago in calibrated years.

In the early days of radiocarbon dating, the C14 laboratory required as much as a handful of charcoal or other organic material for a single date. I remember collecting dozens of plastic bags of charcoal from charred hut posts and hearths, which only gave us very general dates for different structures and occupation layers. Today, accelerator mass spectrometry (AMS) allows radiocarbon dating to be carried out by direct counting of carbon 14 atoms

Radiocarbon Age (Years A.D./B.C.)	Calibrated Age (in years) Tree-ring Calibrations
A.D. 1760	A.D. 1945
1505	1435
1000	1105
500	635
1	15
B.C. 505	B.C. 767
1007	1267
1507	1867
2007	2477
3005	3795
4005	4935
5005	5876
6050	7056
7001	8247
8007	9368
9062	9968

Uranium-Thorium and AMS Carbon 14 (Barbados) Calibrations

AMS Radiocarbon Dates	Uranium-Thorium Calibration
B.C. 7760	B.C. 9140
8270	10,310
9320	11,150
10,250	12,285
13,220	16,300
14,410	17,050
15,280	18,660
23,920	28,280

[increasing differences after 25,000 B.C. (calibrated)]
Calibrations based on tables in *Radiocarbon* 40 (3), Tucson, AZ, 1998. It should be stressed that these calibrations are provisional, statistically based, and subject to modification, especially before 7000 B.C.

FIGURE 3.10 A table of calibrated radiocarbon dates.

(Figure 3.11). Accelerator dating distinguishes between carbon 14 and carbon 12 and other ions through their mass and energy characteristics, requiring only tiny organic samples such as one single seed to do so. The samples needed are so small that it is possible, for example, to date an individual tree ring, a plant fragment, or an actual artifact. This has allowed archaeologists such as Bruce Smith and Andrew Moore to date single wheat or maize seed fragments, which, obviously, give far more accurate dates for such developments as the origins of agriculture than samples that reflect a whole occupation layer do.

Radiocarbon dates reach their outer limits around 40,000 years ago, which means they are useful for dating the all-important developments of the late Ice Age and more recent times. Earlier prehistory is far harder to date, because

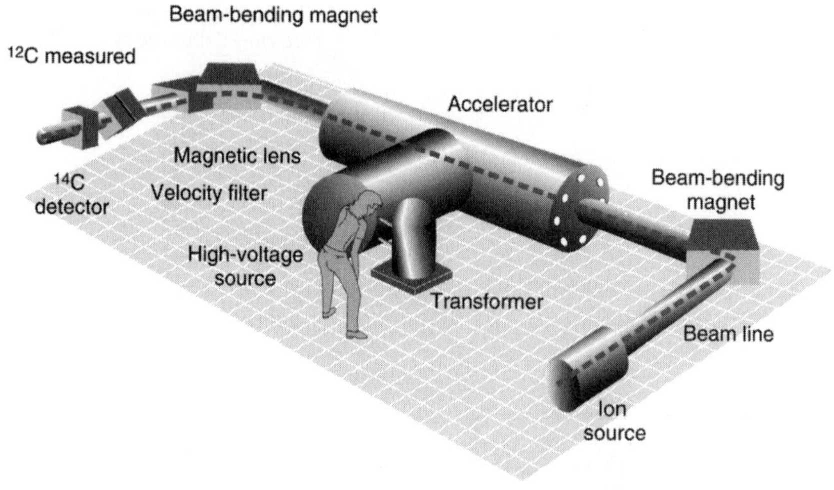

FIGURE 3.11 Accelerator mass spectrometry (AMS) radiocarbon dating. Ionized carbon atoms from the sample are first pulled in beam form toward the accelerator. As the beam passes through the first beam-bending magnet, lighter atoms turn more sharply than heavier ones. They move to the inside of the diverging beam, where a filter blocks the further progress of all charged particles except those of atomic mass 14. When the beam enters the accelerator, it is stripped of all molecules of mass 14 that might be indistinguishable from single carbon 14 atoms. The accelerator pushes the remaining ions through a second beam-bending magnet, filtering out more non–carbon 14 particles. Then the beam is focused before reaching an extremely sensitive detector that counts the number of remaining ions.

of the large periods of time involved and the lack of reliable dating methods that cover much of the Ice Age.

Potassium-Argon Dating

The only viable means of chronometrically dating the earliest archaeological sites is the **potassium-argon dating** method. Geologists use this radioactive counting technique to date the age of the earth from rocks as much as 2 billion years old and as recent as 50,000 years old. (See Doing Archaeology box on p. 87.)

Fortunately, many early human settlements in the Old World are found in volcanic areas, where such deposits as lava flows and tuffs are found in profusion. The first archaeological date obtained from this method came from Olduvai Gorge, Tanzania, where Louis and Mary Leakey found a robust Australopithecine skull, *Australopithecus boisei,* stone tools, and animal bones in a lake bed of unknown age. Lava samples from the site were dated to about 1.75 million years, doubling the then-assumed date for early humans. Stone flakes and chopping tools of undoubted human manufacture have come from *Koobi Fora* in northern Kenya, potassium-dated to about 2.6 million years, the earliest date for human artifacts. Still earlier ***Australopithecus*** fossils have been dated to about 4.5 million years ago by the same method at *Aramis* near the Hadar in Ethiopia. Recently, a team of Berkeley scientists have dated ***Homo erectus***–bearing levels at *Modjokerto* in southeast Asia to 1.8 million years using a new laser fusion technique.

Other Dating Methods

Accurate dating of the past remains one of the greatest challenges of archaeology, partly because of the enormous time scales involved, and also because

DOING ARCHAEOLOGY

Principles of Potassium-Argon Dating

Potassium (K) is one of the most abundant elements in the earth's crust and is present in nearly every mineral. In its natural form, potassium contains a small proportion of radioactive potassium 40 atoms. For every hundred potassium 40 atoms that decay, 11 become argon 40, an inactive gas that can easily escape from material by diffusion when lava and other igneous rocks are formed. As volcanic rock forms through crystallization, the concentration of argon 40 drops to almost nothing. But regular and reasonable decay of potassium 40 will continue, with a half-life of 1.3 billion years. It is possible, then, to measure with a spectrometer the concentration of argon 40 that has accumulated since the rock formed. Because many archaeological sites were occupied during a period when extensive volcanic activity occurred, especially in East Africa, it is possible to date them by associations of lava with human settlements.

Potassium-argon dates have been obtained from many igneous minerals, of which the most resistant to later argon diffusion are biotite, muscovite, and sanidine. Microscopic examination of the rock is essential to eliminate the possibility of contamination by recrystallization and other processes. The samples are processed by crushing the rock, concentrating it, and treating it with hydrofluoric acid to remove any atmospheric argon from the sample. The various gases are then removed from the sample, and the argon gas is isolated and subjected to mass spectrographic analysis. The age of the sample is then calculated using the argon 40 and potassium 40 content and a standard formula. The resulting date is quoted with a large standard deviation—for early Pleistocene sites, on the order of a quarter of a million years.

In recent years, computerized argon laser fusion has become the technique of choice. By steering a laser beam over a single irradiated grain of volcanic ash (feldspar), a potassium-argon specialist can date a lake bed layer or even a small scatter of tools and animal bones left by an early hominid. The grain glows white hot and gives up a gas, which is purified, then charged by an electron beam. A powerful magnet accelerates the charged gas and hurls it against a device which counts its argon atoms. By measuring the relative amounts of two isotopes of the element, researchers can calculate the amount of time which has elapsed since the lava cooled and the crystals formed.

each archaeological site is different and there are so many stratigraphic and other variables that affect the formation of archaeological deposits.

The specialist literature is full of quite well established and still experimental dating methods that are destined to become part of the archaeologist's regular tool kit or to vanish into scientific oblivion. Following are some of the more common dating methods.

Thermoluminescence (TL) Dating   This is based on the fact that every material on earth receives a low level of radiation from the radioactive elements in the environment. Many solid materials store small fractions of this energy, which accumulates steadily over time. When the solid is heated, the stored energy is released and emits light, a phenomenon called **thermoluminescence.** The age of the sample comprises the length of time since the object was heated to a very high temperature. TL dating has obvious applications for dating volcanic rocks and other geological formations, but can also be applied to humanly heated objects such as clay vessels, heat-treated stone artifacts, or fired bricks.

Samples are taken by crumbling an object such as a potsherd or by drilling tiny holes in it for core samples. The laboratory measures the natural TL of the object with an alpha radiation counter, the rate at which the sample has been obtaining radiation from the environment (by monitoring the location where it was found), and the amount of TL produced by known amounts of radiation. All this assumes that humanly manufactured objects have been heated to a sufficiently higher temperature originally, which is not always the case.

Thermoluminescence is claimed to have an accuracy of about ± 7 percent and is most commonly used to date pottery or clay-fired objects between 50 and about 20,000 years old. TL dates have also been applied to burnt flint and other silicious toolmaking materials found in Stone Age rock shelters and burials, such as Neanderthal graves in Israel, which date to more than 40,000 years ago. A related dating method uses laser technology to date the emissions from quartz and feldspar grains in archaeological layers. This optically stimulated luminescence (OSL) method can date sites in the 100- to 100,0000-year range and is claimed to date the first settlement of Australia to as early as 60,000 years ago.

TL sometimes provides absolute dates, but is more often used to produce relative readings that allow archaeologists to establish whether a clay vessel is actually of the same relative age as the known date of similar pots—a useful approach for unmasking forgeries. Although TL has been used to date such developments as the appearance of anatomically modern humans in southwestern Asia and early Australian colonization, most authorities agree that independent verification from radiocarbon or other approaches is advisable.

Electronic Spin Resonance (ESR)   This technique measures radiation-induced defects or the density of trapped electrons within a bone or shell sample without the need to heat them. This promising dating method is somewhat similar to TL and has the advantage of being nondestructive. It is especially effective on tooth enamel and also bone, allowing investigators to date fossil fragments up to about a million years old. ESR has important applications for the study of early human evolution and has already been used to date Neanderthal teeth in southwestern Asia.

Uranium Series Dating   This dating method measures the steady decay of uranium into various daughter elements inside any formation made up of calcium carbonates, such as limestone or cave stalactites. Since many early human groups made use of limestone caves and rock shelters, bones and artifacts embedded in calcium carbonate layers can sometimes be dated by this method, using techniques somewhat similar to those used in radiocarbon dating. Uranium series dating is still at an experimental stage in its development but is most effective when applied to sites between 50,000 and a million years old.

Fission Track Dating   Many minerals and natural glasses, such as obsidian, contain tiny quantities of uranium that undergo slow, spontaneous decay. The date of any mineral containing uranium can be obtained by measuring the amount of uranium in the sample. This is done by counting the fission tracks in the material, which are narrow trails of damage in the sample caused by fragmentation of massive, energy-charged particles. The older the sample, the more tracks it possesses. Volcanic rocks, such as are commonplace at Olduvai Gorge and other early human sites, are ideal for fission track dating. The volcanic level under the earliest hominid sites at Olduvai has been dated to 2.03 ± 0.28 million years, which agrees well with potassium-argon dates from the same location.

Accurate dating of the past is central to any study of cultural change, which is the main focus of the next chapter. Chapter 4 surveys some of the major theoretical approaches used to explain and interpret the archaeological record.

SUMMARY

Chapter 3 describes the ways in which archaeologists study time and date the past. We make a distinction between cyclical and linear time, and distinguish between absolute and relative chronology. Relative chronology is based on the law of superposition and provides a relative framework for the past. Such chronologies come from the observation of stratified layers in archaeological sites or from seriation, artifact ordering. Seriation relies on changing artifact styles to place different archaeological sites in the same region and the layers within them into chronological sequence. Absolute, or chronometric, dating methods assign specific or ranges of dates to sites and artifacts. Archaeologists use four major chronological methods to date the past in calendar years. Objects of known age come from historic times, which includes the past 5,000 years in some parts of the world. Prehistory is dated with tree-ring chronologies and by using radiocarbon and potassium-argon dating methods. Other absolute dating methods are still under development.

KEY TERMS

Absolute (chronometric) chronology
Accelerator mass spectrometry (AMS)
Australopithecus
Cross-dating
Cuneiform
Dendrochronology (tree-ring dating)
Electronic spin resonance (ESR) dating
Fission track dating
Frequency seriation
Half-life

Homo erectus
Obsidian
Organic materials
Potassium-argon dating
Radiocarbon dating
Relative chronology
Seriation
Standard deviation
Thermoluminescence (TL) dating
Uranium series dating

GUIDE TO FURTHER READING

Aitken, M. J. 1990. *Science-based Dating in Archaeology*. New York: Longman.
    An introduction to scientific dating methods for the general reader.
Deetz, James. 1967. *Invitation to Archaeology*. Garden City, NJ: Natural History Press.
    Deetz's little volume on the basics of archaeology is one of the best ever written. His discourse on seriation, complete with New England tombstones, is a classic.
Taylor, R. E., and Martin J. Aitken, eds. 1998. *Chronometric Dating in Archaeology*. New York: Plenum.
    Authoritative descriptions of the major dating methods used for earlier prehistory. For the more-advanced reader.
Taylor, R. E., A. Long, and R. S. Kra, eds. 1992. *Radiocarbon Dating after Four Decades: An Interdisciplinary Perspective*. New York: Springer-Verlag.
    Essays on radiocarbon dating that offer an excellent overview of this all-important dating method.
Wintle, Ann G. 1996. "Archaeologically-relevant Dating Techniques for the Next Century." *Journal of Archaeological Science* 23:123–138.
    An up-to-date survey of the current state of absolute dating methods in archaeology. The paper has a comprehensive bibliography.

How Did Cultures Change?

Olmec head. La Venta, Mexico. c. 1000 B.C. (Source: Adalberto Rios/PhotoDisc, Inc.)

I once excavated a deep, 1,000-year-old central African village, which occupied the same site for more than 400 years. The inhabitants had settled on a low ridge overlooking rolling woodland and open clearings, where their cattle had grazed. After four centuries of occupation, the settlement lay atop a mound of occupation debris more than 300 yards (91 m) across and 10 feet (3 m) deep. We dug through stratified hearths and collapsed houses, collected thousands of decorated potsherds and animal bone fragments. As far as we could tell from the stratigraphy, the village, a cluster of thatched huts and cattle enclosures surrounded by a thorn fence to keep out the lions which had abounded in the area until modern times, had been occupied more or less continuously.

The portrait of the village seemed simple, until I unpacked the pottery and animal bones back in the laboratory. After sorting the artifacts and recording the undecorated pot fragments, I laid out the decorated pieces from each layer on a large table. Startling differences caught my attention at once. The earliest inhabitants had used well-made, thick-walled pots adorned with coarse, stamped decoration. However, as time went on, the village potters changed their style. For three centuries, their vessels were rounder and thinner, with decoration confined to a single, cordlike band just below the lip. A thousand years ago, another change: Everyone started using baglike pots with out-turned rims, which could only have been used for carrying liquids.

While I puzzled over these remarkable changes, I turned my attention to the animal bones. Again, dramatic differences emerged over the centuries. The earliest villagers kept cattle and goats, but relied heavily on game meat. They hunted small antelope, which still flourish near the site, and occasionally also larger animals such as the kudu. However, as the centuries passed, the people began to rely more and more on cattle and goats, to the point that hunting became unimportant. Interestingly, the baglike pots of the upper layers coincided with a sudden increase in cattle bones.

A straightforward, long-occupied settlement turned out to be much more complex than I had imagined. How could I explain the changes in pottery styles and cattle herding over four centuries? Had different cultural groups settled at the site one after the other? Or did the sequence merely reflect a process of gradual cultural change among people who had lived in the same region for many generations and relied more and more on cattle? While I believe that the same people occupied the village for four centuries, I am still at a loss to explain how their culture changed so profoundly.

Chapter 4 looks at the ways in which archaeologists reconstruct and explain the past, starting with culture-historical methods and moving on to the explanation of cultural change.

CULTURE HISTORY

As we discussed in Chapter 2, culture history describes human cultures in the past and is based on the chronological and spatial ordering of archaeological data. Culture history depends on scientific observations of the archaeological record in time and space, on artifacts and other data from one or many sites.

Culture history is based on two fundamental principles:

- **Descriptive (inductive) research methods.** The development of generalizations about a research problem based on numerous specific observations
- **A normative view of culture.** An assumption that abstract rules govern what human societies consider normal behavior. This approach assumes that surviving artifacts display stylistic and other changes that represent the changing norms of human behavior over time. It also assumes considerable uniformity within a culture at any time.

The interpretation of culture-historical data depends on analogies from historical and ethnographic data. For instance, when excavating my African village, I found some heavily worn iron blades with short tangs. By comparing them with modern equivalents from the same area, I was able to show they were hoes used for turning the soil before planting.

Most archaeological interpretation begins with the culture-historical approach, for this provides the basic framework in time and space for studying culture change and explaining the past. In the final analysis, our knowledge of world prehistory comes from thousands of local cultural sequences reconstructed in time and space using descriptive and normative approaches. The result is an ever changing and accumulating synthesis of what happened in the human past that leads to generalizations based on the available data.

Constructing Culture History

Culture history construction proceeds in four broad steps, which build one upon the other to produce a synthesis of a segment of the past in time and space:

1. *Identification of a research area and site survey.* A preliminary stage in which the researcher identifies as many sites as possible and develops a provisional chronology based on seriations of surface artifacts.
2. *Excavation.* Carefully selected excavations designed to test the validity of the sequence and to refine and expand it as well. The digs may proceed at several sites and recover houses, even complete settlement layouts, but their primary concerns are always stratigraphic observing and recording of occupation layers and developing relative and absolute chronologies.
3. *Artifact analysis.* Laboratory analysis and classification of the data base of artifacts and structures as a means of refining preliminary classifications and chronologies put together before digging began.
4. *Synthesis.* Comparing and contrasting the cultural sequences from different sites into a broader synthesis, using such methods as seriation and cross-dating (Chapter 3). (See Discovery box on p. 95.)

Synthesis

The basis of all culture-historical reconstruction is the precise and carefully described site chronology. The synthesis of these chronologies beyond the narrow confines of a single site or local area involves repeating the same descriptive process at other sites, and also constantly refining the cultural sequence from the original excavations. The resulting synthesis is cumulative, for some new excavations may yield cultural materials that are not represented in the early digs. It is here that the techniques of seriation and cross-dating come into play. This is, of course, an entirely descriptive process that yields no explanations whatsoever.

In the case of my African village, I discovered about a dozen similar settlements within a 30-mile (50-km) radius. Were they all occupied at the same time? Did similar cultural changes unfold at all of them? Were some abandoned before others came into use? Unfortunately, we did not have the funds or the time to survey or excavate all the sites, but a colleague had excavated what

DISCOVERY

Hallucinogenic Plants in the Pecos River Valley, Texas

By no means do all archaeological discoveries come from excavations. The Pecos River valley of southwestern Texas has long been famous for its rock paintings, painted by hunter-gatherers over many millennia. The dating and interpretation of these paintings relies both on scientific excavation and AMS radiocarbon dating, and on ethnographic analogies from religious beliefs of modern Huichol Indians of nearby northern Mexico.

Archaeologists Carolyn Boyd and J. Philip Dering have studied anthropomorphic figures in the caves and rock shelters and believe they are depictions of shamans. The figures appear alongside paintings of deer impaled by arrows and spiny ovals attached to wooden staffs that closely resemble the seed pods of hallucinogenic jimson weed. Also, disk-shaped peyote cactus crowns appear in the same friezes, depicted as dots. Boyd and Dering point out that deer and the

hallucingenic peyote are linked in the religious beliefs of the modern-day Huichol Indians. Huichol shamans routinely hunt and shoot the peyote cacti with arrows, as if they were deer. Both jimson and peyote are used by the same shamans to access the spirit world in a tradition, that, to judge from AMS-dated seeds in nearby middens, began at least 4,000 years ago. If Boyd and Dering are right, then the human figures in the Pecos paintings represent ancient shamans and the plants they used to journey into the spiritual realm. Rock paintings from other areas, such as southern California, are also the work of shamans, who may have painted recollections of their hallucinogenic visions on cave walls after emerging from their trances. In both ancient and modern Native American societies, the boundaries between the living and spiritual worlds were and are blurred.

appeared to be a closely similar, but smaller, settlement about 10 miles (16 km) away. I sunk a small trench into this site to obtain larger pottery samples and seriated the two cultural sequences. Both radiocarbon dates and a "fit" between the two pottery series showed that the smaller site had been abandoned about a century before the inhabitants of my original site had developed a fashion for bag-shaped vessels and relied almost entirely on cattle for meat. I have no doubt that if we were to return to the area, we would be able to develop a highly detailed cultural sequence for this small area, with a stratified and seriated pottery series as precise as those Richard MacNeish developed for Mexico's Tehuacán Valley (Figure 3.4). However, this sequence would tell us absolutely nothing about the reasons *why* individual villages were occupied or abandoned, or *why* the cultures that lived there changed so much.

A Hierarchy of Archaeological Units

The database from the archaeological record comprises artifacts, structures, food remains, and other information. Artifacts and structures are the objects of primary interest to a culture historian, for they provide often sensitive barometers for correlating cultural sequences from many sites. All culture history depends on artifact classifications and on the grouping of artifact complexes into increasingly larger units that transcend space and time (for more on artifact classification, see Chapter 8). It is a site-oriented procedure, an exercise of classification in time and space that bears no resemblance to the large-scale regional surveys of ancient landscapes described in Chapter 10.

Archaeologists use a series of arbitrary time-space units to help in the process of culture-historical construction. This hierarchy of archaeological units developed in a somewhat haphazard fashion in the early days of archaeology, but was formalized into its present general form for the Americas by archaeologists Gordon Willey and Philip Phillips in 1958. Such units represent the combining of the formal content of a site (or sites) with its distribution in time and space. For instance, a deep cave in Missouri contains six occupation levels, each with its own distinctive artifact assemblages, which have been sorted into different types (Chapter 8). A dozen nearby sites have yielded examples of these comparable six layers. What arbitrary units can we use to compare these various sites and occupation levels with their different contents?

The hierarchy of archaeological units proceeds from artifacts and artifact assemblages (already defined in Chapter 2) to components and phases, then to regions and culture areas. (See Figure 4.1 and Doing Archaeology box on p. 98.)

DESCRIPTIVE MODELS OF CULTURAL CHANGE

Back at my African mound village, I completed the classification and analysis of thousands of potsherds, iron tools, and animal bone fragments. Four hundred years of significant cultural change measured by these finds lay in front of me on the laboratory table. The pottery styles changed from relatively coarse vessels to much finer wares, culminating in the globular vessels which accompanied a dramatic increase in cattle bones. Now the question of questions: How did these changes come about? From continuous culture change among people who settled in the same general area for four centuries? Or had successive groups arrived from outside and settled on an abandoned village site, where nitrogen-rich soils yielded nice crops of vegetables and other minor crops? At this point, I turned to five widely used descriptive models of cultural change: inevitable variation; cultural selection; and three classic processes of change—invention, diffusion, and migration.

Inevitable Variation

As people learn the basic behavioral patterns of their societies, inevitably some minor differences in learned behavior appear from generation to generation. Although minor in themselves, these differences accumulate over a

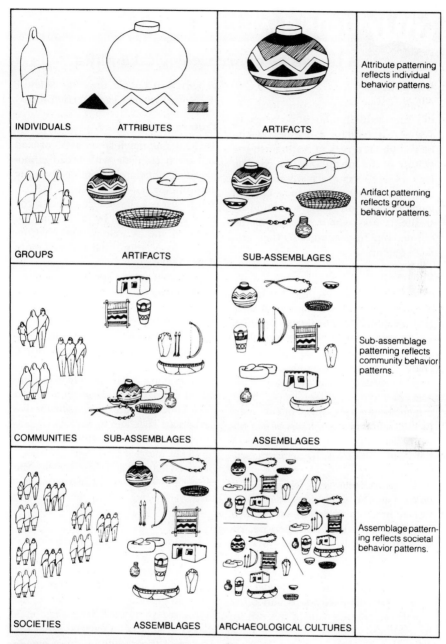

FIGURE 4.1   The hierarchy of archaeological units.

long period of time in a snowball effect called **inevitable variation.** For instance, about 1.9 million years ago, ancient Africans developed a crude form of stone hand ax, with rough edges and a crude point for butchering game and other uses (see Figure 8.10*b*). This highly effective multipurpose

DOING ARCHAEOLOGY

A Hierarchy of Archaeological Entities

Components

Components occur at one location, the physically bounded portions of a site that contain a distinct assemblage, which serves to distinguish the culture of the inhabitants of a particular land. For example, many rock shelters in southwestern France contain many occupation levels separated by sterile layers, which can be distinguished one from another by their artifact content.

Phases

Cultural units represented by similar components at different sites or at separate levels of the same site, although always within a well-defined chronological span. The assemblages of artifacts characteristic of a phase may be found over hundreds of square miles within the area covered by a local sequence. Phases can endure for a few years, or centuries, include numerous subphases or components, each dated to short periods of time with their own characteristic artifacts.

Many archaeologists use the term *culture* in the same sense as phase. Phases or cultures are usually named after a key site where characteristic artifacts are found. For example, the late–Ice Age Magdalenian culture of 16,000 years ago is named after the southwestern French rock shelter of La Madeleine, where the antler harpoons and other artifacts so characteristic of this culture were found.

Regions

Archaeological regions are normally defined by natural geographic boundaries and display some cultural homo-geneity, for example, the Ohio Valley or the Santa Barbara Channel, California.

Culture Areas

These define much larger areas of land and often coincide with broad ethnographic culture areas identified by early anthropologists. The North American Southwest is a classic example of a culture area, defined by a century of research and by cultural and environmental associations that endured more than 2,000 years.

Two other terms are in common use in the Americas.

Horizons

These link a number of phases in neighboring areas that have general cultural patterns in common. For instance, an all-embracing religious cult may transcend cultural boundaries and spread over enormous areas. The distinctive Chavín art style and its associated religious beliefs spread widely over the highland and lowland Andean region between 900 and 200 B.C.—whence the term *Early Horizon* in Peruvian prehistory.

Traditions

This term is used define artifact types, assemblages of tools, architectural styles, economic practices, or art styles that last much longer than one phase or even the duration of a horizon. For instance, the celebrated Arctic Small Tool Tradition of Alaska originated as early as 4000 B.C. The small tools made by these people were so effective that they continued in use right into modern times and became a foundation of recent Eskimo hunter-gatherer culture.

tool spread over much of Africa, Europe, and south Asia over the next million years. Hundreds of small, isolated forager bands used the same tool and developed hand axes to a high degree of refinement. By 150,000 to 100,000 years ago, inevitable variation among isolated populations produced great variations in hand ax design in Europe and Africa.

Cultural Selection

Cultural selection is somewhat akin to the well-known process of natural selection in biological evolution. Human societies accept and reject new ideas, whether technological, economic, or intangible, on the basis of whether they are advantageous to society as a whole. Like inevitable variation, cultural selection leads to cumulative cultural change and operates within the prevailing values of the society as a whole. For instance, the great civilizations of Mesopotamia and Mexico resulted from centuries of gradual social evolution, throughout which centralized political organization seemed advantageous.

Invention

We live in a world that honors inventors, people who think up truly new ideas that can change our lives. The electric lightbulb, the transistor, and the computer are three examples. An **invention** implies either the modifying of an old idea or series of ideas or the creation of a completely new concept either by accident or by intentional research. The atom was split after long and deliberate experimentation aimed at such an objective. Fire was probably tamed over 1.5 million years ago by accident. Inventions spread, and if they are sufficiently important, such as the plow, they spread rapidly and widely.

A century ago Victorian scientists believed that farming, metallurgy, and other major innovations were invented in only one place, then spread all over the world. But now that we understand the great importance of environment in the past, we have realized that many inventions were not the work of solitary geniuses but the result of complex, interacting pressures such as climatic change, rising population densities, and fundamental social change, which occurred in many places. For instance, agriculture was developed independently in southwestern Asia, southern China, Mesoamerica, and the Andes.

Diffusion

Inventions and ideas spread. **Diffusion** is the process by which new ideas or cultural traits spread from one person to another, or from one group to another, often over long distances. Back in the early twentieth century, British anatomist and amateur Egyptologist Elliot Grafton Smith, famous for his pioneering X rays of Egyptian mummies, became obsessed with sun worship along the Nile. He wrote a series of widely read books in which he proclaimed that Egyptian "Children of the Sun" voyaged all over the world from their Nile homeland, carrying the arts of civilization, pyramid building, and sun worship with them. Smith's simplistic theories and others of this ilk are long discredited, for the vast quantities of archaeological data from all parts of the world show his ideas to be ludicrous. However, diffusion is an important mechanism of cultural change, which is hard to identify from archaeological remains.

Had I wished to invoke diffusion as a factor in my mound village, I would have had to identify, say, a distinctive pottery type, which suddenly appeared at a highly specific moment in the 400-year sequence. This would be just the first step. I would then have had to identify similar potsherds in neighboring sites and those at a greater distance, then studied the site distribution and dated each occurrence of the sherds, so that I could identify not only the moment the vessels appeared at each site, but a chronological gradient for diffusion from a place of origin (see Figure 4.2). In any event, there were no clay vessel forms that were distinctive enough to warrant such an inquiry, and it is questionable whether I would have been able to identify the process of diffusion anyhow.

We know that ideas and technologies spread by word of mouth and from hand to hand, but this process is very hard to identify in specific terms in the archaeological record.

Migration

In 1947, Norwegian explorer and archaeologist Thor Heyerdahl electrified the world with a courageous voyage across the eastern Pacific from Peru to

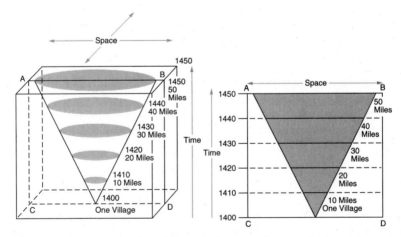

FIGURE 4.2 The cone effect of diffusion: the spread of a culture trait in space and time.

Polynesia in the balsa raft *Kon-Tiki,* a replica of an ancient Andean raft. Heyerdahl undertook his passage to prove that Peruvians colonized Polynesia in prehistoric times. His successful ocean journey showed that a balsa raft could reach Polynesia on the wings of the prevailing trade winds, but it certainly did not prove that ancient Peruvians migrated by sea to the heart of the Pacific. Fifty years of research since the voyage have not revealed a single Peruvian artifact anywhere in Polynesia. Few people accept Heyerdahl's theory today.

Migration, however, is the process of deliberate settlement, when entire populations, large or small, decide to move into a new area. Migration can be peaceful or the result of military invasion and conquest. For migration to be identified in the archaeological record, an archaeologist would need to find local sequences in which the phases show a complete disruption of earlier cultural patterns by an intrusive new phase with a completely new tool kit or lifeway, even if some earlier culture traits survived and were integrated into the new culture.

Classic examples of migration in prehistory abound, among them the first settlement of the Americas and Australia. Perhaps the best known is the colonization of Polynesia, not from the east, but from the west, by open-water voyagers in double-hulled canoes, starting about 3,000 years ago. The voyagers that colonized Tahiti, remote Easter Island, and Hawaii did so as acts of deliberate exploration and set out with intentions of returning. In this case, carefully excavated sites and radiocarbon dates document a process of colonization that proceeded over many centuries, identified by pottery styles with close relationships to those used on the western Pacific islands.

There are other types of migration, too. For instance, the Mexican city of Teotihuacán accepted entire colonies of merchants from the Valley of Oaxaca and other distant places because they were of economic advantage to the metropolis. Artisans and slaves would wander as unorganized migrants, as do seamen, accounting for the great, and often unsuspected diversity of many early cities, among them imperial Rome. Finally, there are the great warrior migrations of the past, such as those of eastern nomads in Europe and of the warlike Nguni tribes of South Africa, who raided and settled as far north as eastern Zambia.

Construction of culture history is a difficult and complex descriptive process that needs large quantities of well-dated finds to be effective. In the end, the changes in the cultural sequence at my African mound left me somewhat challenged. I concluded that the pottery style and economic changes were the result of cultural selection among people living in an environment ideal for cattle herding and subsistence agriculture. But I never took my investigation further, for the explanation of cultural process required far more complex models based on quite different approaches to archaeology which were not in existence when I published my excavations.

ANALOGY

The very first models of prehistoric times came from the pens of pioneer anthropologists such as Englishman Edward Tylor and American Lewis Morgan. Fervent believers in evolutionary doctrines, they thought of ancient and living human societies as involved continually in the process of acquiring ever greater complexity. They and their disciples felt comfortable in making direct comparisons between living societies such as the Eskimo of the Arctic and late–Ice Age peoples who lived in France 16,000 years ago, on the grounds that these groups were at the same stage of development and thus enjoyed close cultural similarities. Such comparisons, or analogies, to use the common archaeological term, have long been abandoned, as they are far too simplistic. Nevertheless, **analogy** plays a vital role in archaeology, for it infers that the relationships between various traces of human activity found in the archaeological record are similar to those of similar phenomena found among modern "primitive" peoples.

Archaeologists use analogy in several ways, but are always aware that they cannot explain the past simply with reference to the present, for to do so is to assume that nothing new has been learned by generations of people and that the past was the same, or not much different, from the present.

Historical analogies work from the known to the unknown, from living peoples with written records to their ancestors for whom we have no written records.

A classic example comes from Colonial Virginia. When Ivor Noël Hume excavated a small settlement of the early 1620s at *Martin's Hundred,* Virginia, he found some short strands of gold and silver wire in the cellar filling of one of the houses. Each was as thick as a sewing thread, the kind of wire used in the early seventeenth century for decorating clothing. Noël Hume turned to historical records for analogies. He found European paintings showing military captains wearing clothes adorned with gold and silver wire. He also located a resolution of the Virginia governor and his Council in 1621 forbidding "any but ye Council and heads of hundreds to wear gold in their cloaths" (Noël Hume 1982, 216). Using these, and other historical analogies, he was able to identify the owner of the house as William Harewood, a member of the Council and the head of Martin's Hundred.

Historical records also provide valuable analogies, when they describe the customs and societies of nonliterate cultures with which they came into contact. The Roman general Julius Caesar, who conquered Gaul (present-day France) left invaluable accounts of the warlike Gauls in his *Commentaries.* British navigator Captain James Cook's accounts of Tahitian society are an invaluable source of information about Polynesian culture at the time of European contact (Figure 4.3). However, the effectiveness of direct historical analogies such as these diminishes rapidly the further back in time you ven-

FIGURE 4.3   Tahitian war canoes depicted by John Webber, artist on Captain James Cook's first expedition, 1769.

ture, for human cultures everywhere change constantly in response to many factors.

Many archaeological analogies are at a simple level. For example, researchers working on the North American Plains have inferred that small, pointed pieces of stone were projectile points, because there are ethnographic records of people making small, pointed pieces of stone for spear and arrow tips. We have also found such objects embedded in the bones of both animals and people, so the general analogy is secure. Such analogies are obvious enough, but they are a far cry from claiming that both the ancient and modern societies used the projectile point in exactly the same way.

Functionalism is an important school of thought in anthropology, which argues that cultures are not made up of random selections of culture traits, but that such traits are integrated in various ways and influence each other in fairly predictable ways. This line of thinking appeals to archaeologists who think of cultures as systems of interacting subsystems in turn interacting with the ecosystem. Six thousand years ago, Great Basin people made widespread use of carefully fabricated fiber sandals, which survive in dry cave deposits (Figure 4.4). The function of these objects is obvious today, and they were also used in historic Great Basin societies. However, the functionalist approach fosters other questions, for example, were sandals made by men or women, by individuals of their own initiative or working in groups? We turn to the ethnographic literature and find that Australian Aborigines and the !Kung of the Kalahari Desert use sandals, which are usually made by women working alone or with one or two helpers. On this basis, we might now argue that Great Basin sandal making was a domestic task carried out by women. However, Pueblo men in the Southwest weave in special

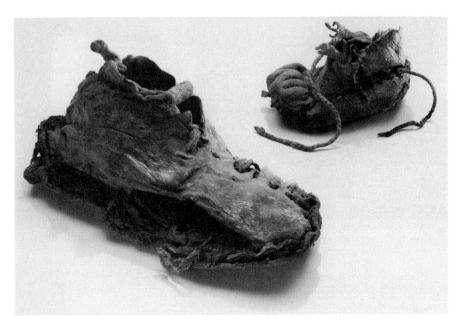

FIGURE 4.4 A perfectly preserved fiber sandal from *Hogup Cave,* Utah. *(Courtesy University of Utah Museum of Anthropology.)*

ceremonial rooms and because much ritual performed there reflects very ancient Pueblo Indian practices, we might be led to infer that Great Basin people did not regard weaving as a domestic task 6,000 years ago, so it must have been carried out by men. No matter which alternative we choose, we would not have much confidence in our choice. That is, we have not directly evaluated the data at hand.

Ethnographic analogy is only the first step in the inquiry. In the case of the Great Basin sandals, the archaeologists would take the two conflicting analogies back to the field. They would develop test implications to be tested against the archaeological data:

- If sandal making were a domestic task carried out by women, then one would expect to find the raw materials for sandal manufacture associated with tools that may represent womens' work, such as grinding stones for food preparation.
- If men made the sandals as a ritual activity, they would anticipate finding the same raw materials in different settings, perhaps in a special area of the occupation associated with known ceremonial artifacts such as dance rattles.

Such testing requires large quantities of data, sophisticated excavation and recording, and advanced analytical tools, including statistical tests. The ethnographic analogy provides the raw material for letting the present serve the past.

ETHNOARCHAEOLOGY AND EXPERIMENTATION

The present is alive and dynamic, the archaeological record of the past is static and has been ever since it ceased to be part of the culture that created it. To understand and explain the past, we must comprehend the relationship between static, material properties common to both past and present and the long-extinct dynamic properties of the past.

Ethnoarchaeology

Ethnoarchaeology is the study of living societies to aid in understanding and interpreting the archaeological record. By living in, say, an Australian Aborigine camp and observing the activities of its occupants, the archaeologist hopes to record archaeologically observable patterns, knowing what activities brought them into existence.

Ethnoarchaeology goes far beyond simple observations of artifact scatters or the surveying of recently excavated !Kung camp sites to record tool and animal bone patternings as a basis for interpreting far earlier sites. In fact, such research deals with the dynamic processes of human behavior in the modern world.

Since 1984, James O'Connell of the University of Utah has recorded more than 70 incidents of large mammal butchery by Hadza hunter-gatherers in East Africa (Figure 4.5). The Hadza hunt animals when they encounter them

FIGURE 4.5   Ethnoarchaeology among the Hadza. Recording details of a hunter's kill. *(Courtesy of Professor James O'Connell, Department of Anthropology, University of Utah at Salt Lake City.)*

and also ambush their prey from specially constructed blinds near water holes in the late dry season. They are very determined hunters, tracking wounded quarry for hours, even days. They also scavenge meat from predator kills at every opportunity. O'Connell records kill rates for a single camp of 70 to 80 large animals a year, or about 1 for 40 to 60 hunter-days of foraging, with scavenging accounting for about 10 to 15 percent of the total. The researchers were mainly interested in time allocation, food choice, and food-sharing activities, so they routinely recorded site location, distance from residential bases, method of acquiring the prey, carcass condition, details of the butchery, and the sexes and ages of the people involved. In addition, they collected comprehensive "archaeological" data from each location, when possible, including the positions of broken bones and abandoned artifacts.

The Hadza research casts serious doubt on many of the assumptions made by archaeologists about ancient hunter-gatherer kill sites. O'Connell's team found that 75 to 80 percent of the Hadza's large mammal prey were underrepresented in their bone samples, by virtue of the people's hunting and butchering practices. Most prehistoric kill sites have been excavated on a small scale, whereas many Hadza butchery sites occupy a large area, through which the hunters scatter the bones, often in the process of finding shade in which to work. Furthermore, the disarticulation of bones follows a similar pattern whether carnivores or humans are at work—the limbs first, then the backbone, with differences being more the result of individual animal anatomy than deliberate cultural choice.

In another famous ethnoarchaeological study, Lewis Binford studied caribou hunting among the Nunamiut Eskimo of Alaska in a research project that involved meticulous recording of butchery procedures and archaeological sites. He found the hunters behaved absolutely rationally in their exploitation of caribou in spring and fall, taking full account of the vagaries of the local environment and logistical considerations. They had an encyclopedic knowledge of caribou anatomy and were utterly pragmatic in their approach to hunting. All these factors resulted in a great variety of archaeological sites and profound differences in artifact frequencies between them. In other words, archaeology is about ancient human behavior, not changing percentages of artifacts and animal bones!

Experimental Archaeology

Controlled experiments with precise replicas of prehistoric artifacts and with ancient technologies offer fruitful sources of data for studying cultural dynamics. Such research began in the eighteenth century, when people tried to blow the spectacular bronze horns unearthed from peat bogs in Scandinavia and Britain. One ardent experimenter, Dr. Robert Ball of Dublin, Ireland, blew an Irish horn so hard that he was able to produce a deep bass note, that resembled a bull's bellow. Sadly, a later experiment with a trumpet caused him to burst a blood vessel, and he died several days later. Dr. Ball is the only recorded casualty of experimental archaeology, which has become an important part of interpretation by analogy.

Most **experimental archaeology** is confined to replicating ancient technologies, such as stone toolmaking, pot-making techniques, or traditional metallurgies. Louis Leakey, archaeologist of Olduvai Gorge fame, trained himself to become an expert fabricator of stone axes and other Stone Age tools. Another lithic expert, rancher Don Crabtree of Idaho, spent 40 years experimenting with the manufacture of North American Paleo-Indian projectile points. He managed to replicate the distinctive "flute" or thinning flake at the base of the well-known Clovis and Folsom points (see Figure 8.6). Crabtree also learned of descriptions by early Spanish friars of how Native American stoneworkers used chest punches to remove dozens of thin, parallel-sided blades from cylindrical pieces of obsidian (volcanic glass). When an eye surgeon carried out an operation on his vision, Crabtree specified obsidian blades to be used, which were sharper than the finest surgical steel!

Does the production of an exact replica mean, in fact, that modern experimentation has recovered the original technique. We can never be certain, but lithic experimentation is invaluable if combined with other analytical approaches, such as refitting flakes onto their original cores or edge wear analysis (see Chapter 8).

Experimental archaeology can rarely provide conclusive answers. It can merely provide material for careful analogies or insights into the methods and techniques possibly used in prehistory, since many of the behaviors involved in, say, prehistoric agriculture have left few traces in the archaeological record. All experimentation is undertaken under controlled conditions, using precisely the same raw materials and the same manufacturing techniques. For instance, it is no use conducting an experiment with a carefully replicated prehistoric plow without using plow-trained oxen. The loss of efficiency would be enormous.

Archaeology by experiment covers a wide range of activities, everything from controlled experiments at forest clearance with stone axes, to burning down replicas of ancient dwellings to duplicate foundations for comparison with ancient remains. At Butser in southern England, archaeologists have built an Iron Age village as part of a long-term experiment that explores every aspect of Iron Age life. The researchers grow prehistoric cereals using Iron Age technology, keep a selection of livestock that resembles prehistoric breeds, and even store grain underground in sealed pits for long periods without rotting.

Such types of long-term controlled experiments will give archaeologists objective data they need to understand the static archaeological record as studied in the dynamic present. They will help us evaluate our ideas about the past, and to answer the question of questions, not "what happened?" but "why?"

THE SCIENTIFIC METHOD IN ARCHAEOLOGY

Culture history and the mechanisms of culture change give us a global framework for the human past, defined in time and space. But how do archaeologists explain culture change in ancient times? Why did hunter-gatherers in

Syria's Euphrates Valley change over from foraging to agriculture 11,000 years ago? What caused widely separated human societies in different parts of the world to make the same changeover in later millennia? Why did some human societies develop into highly complex civilizations, while others flourished as simple village societies? These and many other questions about cultural processes have baffled archaeologists for generations. Today's complex theoretical models for explaining such developments as the origins of agriculture stem from more than a century of often-passionate debate about theories of culture change. They also result from an explosion of new scientific methods and from the now-routine use of computers to manipulate enormous amounts of raw archaeological data.

During the early 1960s, a young, University of Michigan–trained archaeologist named Lewis Binford wrote a series of papers about archaeological theory, which sent archaeology along a new theoretical track. Binford stressed the close links between archaeology and ethnography. He pointed out how science was a disciplined and carefully ordered search for knowledge, carried out in a systematic manner.

For more than a century, scientists have developed general procedures for acquiring data, known as the **scientific method.** The scientific method is a disciplined and carefully ordered approach to acquiring knowledge about the real world using deductive reasoning combined with continuous testing and retesting. The scientific method assumes that knowledge of the real world is both cumulative and subject to constant rechecking. For decades, Binford said, archaeologists had made inferences about archaeological data by simple **inductive reasoning,** using ethnographic knowledge of modern societies and experiments with such technologies as stone toolmaking as interpretative guides. Binford acknowledged these methods worked quite well much of time, but advocated a more explicitly scientific approach, based on **deductive reasoning.** (See Doing Archaeology box on p. 109.)

The scientific method advances archaeological knowledge not by proof, but by disproof, proposing the most adequate explanations for the moment. Every scientist knows that new and better explanations will come in the future. The key to the scientific method is the continuous self-correction that goes with the process of researching the past.

Lewis Binford's insistence on a more rigorous scientific approach to archaeology allowed researchers to link old data, new ideas, and fresh data. Binford himself challenged the assumption that because the archaeological record is incomplete, reliable interpretation of such intangibles as religious beliefs, or perishable components of ancient society and culture was impossible. He wrote (1968, 3): "Data relevant to most, if not all, of the components of past sociocultural systems are preserved in the archaeological record." Binford argued that the artifacts found in an archaeological site functioned at one time within a particular culture and society. Thus, they occur in meaningful patterns that are systematically related to economies, kinship

DOING ARCHAEOLOGY

Deductive and Inductive Reasoning

Science establishes facts about the natural world by observing objects, events, and phenomena. Archaeologists proceed by using both inductive and deductive reasoning in making their observations.

Inductive reasoning is a relatively simple process, which takes specific observations and makes a generalization from them. For example, I once found nearly 10,000 wild plant fragments in a 4,000-year-old Stone Age hunter-gatherer camp in Central Africa. More than 42 percent of them were from the *bauhinia* shrub. The *bauhinia* flowers from October to February. I learned from an anthropologist colleague that modern-day !Kung foragers of southern Africa's Kalahari, a few hundred miles away from my site, still eat many *bauhinia* fruit and roots. From these observations, I used the process of induction to hypothesize that the *bauhinia* was a preferred seasonal food in Central Africa for thousands of years.

Deductive reasoning, on the other hand, is based on developing specific hypotheses using induction, then testing them against archaeological data. Archaeologists form specific implications from the hypotheses. For example, anthropologist Julian Steward studied the Shoshonean foragers of the Great Basin in the western United States in the 1920s and 1930s. He formulated general hypotheses about the ways the Shoshoneans moved their settlements throughout the year. In the late 1960s, archaeologist David Hurst Thomas asked, "If the late prehistoric Shoshoneans behaved in the fashion suggested by Steward, how would the artifacts they used have fallen on the ground?" Thomas constructed more than 100 predictions based on Steward's original hypotheses. Next, he devised tests to verify or invalidate his predictions. He expected to find specific forms of artifacts associated with particular activities, such as hunting or plant collecting in seasonal archaeological sites where different activities were important. Then he collected the archaeological data needed for his tests in the field. Finally, Thomas tested each of his predictions against the field data and rejected about 25 percent of his original ones. The same data supported the remaining predictions and refined Steward's original hypotheses. Thus, each generation of fieldwork fine-tunes earlier hypotheses and provides more data to test them further.

systems, and other contexts in which they were used. The archaeologist's task is to devise methods for extracting this information from the archaeological record.

At the time, Binford's so-called new archaeology burst on the archaeological world like a thunderclap, offering hope for a giant leap forward. Nearly 40 years later, we can see that the "new" archaeology was not all that new. Binford actually combined a cry for more scientific rigor with a synthesis of several converging lines of thought, including systems theory, cultural ecology, and multilinear evolution. The result was a now widely used approach known as processual archaeology.

PROCESSUAL ARCHAEOLOGY

Processual archaeology, the study of the processes by which human societies changed in the past, developed in the 1960s from several converging streams of thinking and from some important archaeological discoveries. Three major elements make up this approach: systems theory and the notion of cultural systems, cultural ecology, and multilinear cultural evolution. Processual archaeology is effective because archaeologists now have the computer power to manage large amounts of data and to analyze them in a sophisticated, quantitative fashion.

General Systems Theory

During the late 1950s, archaeologists discovered **general systems theory,** a body of theoretical constructs that provides a way for looking for "general relationships" in the empirical world of science. Under this perspective, a system is a whole that functions by virtue of the interdependence of its parts. Thus, any organization, however simple or complex, can be studied as a system of interrelated concepts. Systems theory enjoys wide popularity in physics and other hard sciences, where relationships between parts of a system can be defined with great precision. It has obvious appeal to archaeologists, who study cultures made up of many interacting elements such as technology, social organization, and religious beliefs. Today, they often talk of cultural systems made up of dozens of interacting subsystems: an economic subsystem, a political subsystem, a social subsystem, and many others.

In Syria's Euphrates Valley, for example, the people of a small settlement now called Abu Hureyra lived on the borders of several environmental zones: the river floodplain, oak forests, and open grassland. For thousands of years, they exploited both fall nut harvests and the spring and autumn migrations of gazelle, small desert antelopes. About 9000 B.C., a severe drought cycle caused local nut-bearing forests to shrink and retreat far from the site. The people responded by foraging for wild grasses, then by planting their own cereals. Eventually, the foragers became farmers. The effect of the changeover from foraging to agriculture rippled through the entire cultural system, affecting architecture, social organization, technology, religious beliefs, and the entire human relationship to the natural environment. All the many and interacting components of the cultural system adjusted to changes in one another and in the ecosystem.

Cultural Ecology

Between the 1930s and 1950s, two scientific discoveries changed the way archaeologists looked at the past. The first was aerial photography, which became highly refined in World War II, and provided an overhead view of changing ancient landscapes (see Chapter 6). The second was the work of

Swedish botanist Lennart von Post, who used minute fossil tree pollens preserved in Scandinavian bogs to reconstruct the dramatic changes in northern European vegetation after the Ice Age (see Chapter 5). Subsequently, two archaeologists used these advances in innovative field research that changed the face of archaeology forever.

Harvard University archaeologist Gordon Willey spent several field seasons in the coastal Vírú River valley of Peru during the late 1940s. Using aerial photographs and maps, he walked most of the valley, recording hundreds of archaeological sites and studying the dramatic changes in human settlement as ever more complex farming societies developed in the region. The Vírú Valley project established settlement archaeology as a highly effective approach to studying the past (see Chapter 10).

In 1949, Cambridge University archaeologist Grahame Clark excavated a tiny, 10,000-year-old Stone Age hunter-gatherer site at *Star Carr* in northeastern England. Star Carr lies on the edge of a long-dried-up glacial lake in northeast England, close to the North Sea. From the beginning of the excavation, Grahame Clark and a team of carefully selected scientists from other disciplines deliberately studied the tiny site in the context of its ecosystem. Star Carr comprised a tiny platform of birch trees set in the midst of lakeside reeds (Figure 4.6). Pollen analyses showed how birch forest came down close to the water's edge, where the Star Carr people hunted red deer and elk. Radiocarbon dates on the birch wood in the site dated to about 8500 B.C., a

FIGURE 4.6   Birch trees felled to make a small platform by a small lake, Star Carr, England. *(Courtesy of Cambridge Museum of Archaeology and Ethnology, Cambridge University.)*

time when world sea levels were still much lower than today and much of the nearby North Sea was still dry land. The wet deposits preserved not only the birch platforms, but a canoe paddle, bark rolls, and red deer antler spearheads used for hunting and shallow-water fishing. By studying the many red deer antlers among the animal bones, Clark was able to show that Star Carr was visited on several occasions in late spring and early summer.

The Star Carr excavations were a sensation when they were published in 1954, causing archaeologists all over the world to realize the importance of studying sites within their natural settings. Recent researches have confirmed the essential correctness of Clark's conclusions, even if refined AMS radiocarbon dates and tree-ring chronologies have now dated Star Carr to before 9000 B.C. and have even isolated the inhabitants' irregular visits to the site.

Just as the Star Carr project ended in 1954, anthropologist Julian Steward of the University of Illinois developed the concept of **cultural ecology.** This, then-revolutionary approach argued that similar human adaptations may be found in widely separated cultures in similar environments. For example, the African !Kung, the Australian Aborigines, and Fuegian Indians of South America all lived in small bands, with kinship descent passing through the father. Their environments differed dramatically from desert to cold and rainy plains, yet the practical requirements of their hunter-gatherer lifeway and general adaptations were very similar. Steward also pointed out that no culture has ever achieved an adaptation that remained unchanged over any length of time, for environments change constantly. Cultural ecology views human cultures as subsystems interacting with other subsystems, all forming a total ecosystem with three major subsystems: human culture, the biotic community, and the physical environment.

Clark, Steward, and Willey each helped establish one of the foundations of modern archaeological theory: Archaeologists cannot study culture change without studying ancient cultures within the contexts of their changing environments.

Multilinear Cultural Evolution

A century ago, anthropologists thought that all human societies evolved in a ladderlike way. Simple hunter-gatherer groups such as the !Kung of southern Africa or the Tasmanians were on the bottom rung, village farmers were along the middle rungs, and modern industrial civilization was at the very pinnacle. This linear, or ladderlike, view of the past came from the then-new discipline of sociology, which thought of human societies in evolutionary terms, as the result of "progress" upward from crude savagery to sophisticated civilization. Fortunately, this simplistic and racist portrait of humanity soon vanished when scientists came to discover the full and astonishing diversity of humankind.

Julian Steward and University of Michigan anthropologist Leslie White were responsible for far more sophisticated formulations of human cultural evolution, which appeared in the 1940s and 1950s. They developed a new multilinear (many tracked) model of cultural evolution, which recognized that there were many evolutionary tracks, from simple to complex, with the differences resulting from the adaptations made by individual societies to widely differing environments.

Multilinear cultural evolution is best thought of as a bush with many branches and clusters of twigs expanding from a single trunk. This loosely formulated model is of vital importance because it brings together the notion of cultural systems and cultural ecology into a closely knit, highly flexible way of studying the processes of cultural change (Figure 4.7).

Processual archaeology has enjoyed considerable success, largely because it allows the study of complex relationships between culture change, subsistence, and environmental shifts. The combination of a systems and ecological approach allows us to examine the ways in which cultural systems function both internally and in relation to external factors such as the natural environment. Intricate to develop and apply, the processual approach frees us from simplistic explanations of such phenomena as the origins of the first civilizations. No longer can we claim that a single agent of change, for example, irrigation or diffusion, was responsible for, say, Maya civilization. The

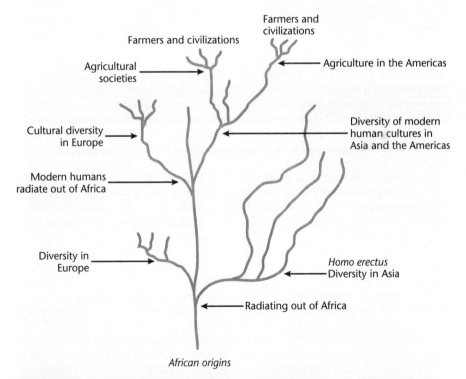

FIGURE 4.7 Multilinear cultural evolution is a bushlike concept. This grossly simplified diagram shows how many of the major developments in prehistory can be modeled as a bushlike development, with the main trunk originating in Africa, where humanity evolved.

processual approach focuses on the relationships between different components of a cultural system and also the system as a whole and its environment. (See Site box below.)

Processual archaeology with its systems approach is valuable as a way of studying general processes of human culture change. With cultural ecology and cultural systems at its core, this approach has emphasized environmental change, subsistence, and settlement (Chapters 5, 9, and 10).

SITE

Guilá Naquitz Cave, Mexico

Guilá Naquitz Cave in Mexico's Valley of Oaxaca was occupied sporadically by a tiny band of hunter-gatherers over a span of a few thousand years after 8750 B.C. Kent Flannery excavated the site in a classic instance of sophisticated processual archaeology (see Figure 2.1); he was searching for evidence of early maize and bean agriculture. He used the unspectacular finds of stone artifacts, animal bones, and seeds from the cave to reconstruct a portrait of changing adaptations in a high-risk environment. Flannery asked two questions: What was the strategy that led to the choice of the wild plants eaten by the inhabitants? And how did this strategy change when they began planting?

Archaeologist Robert Reynolds developed a computer model to approach these questions, starting with a hypothetical, and totally ignorant, band of five people who settle in the area. Over a long period of trial and error, they "learn" how to schedule the gathering of 11 major food plants over the year, in an environment with highly unpredictable rainfall. Experience passed from one generation to the next was vital, for this was the basis upon which they developed survival strategies that enabled them to endure hungry years. After many generations, the people developed strategies that ranked plant foods in order of size of harvest. The band became so efficient they achieved a stable performance level.

The plant food mix from the cave matched the simulated mix very well, showing a wide range of plant foods were used in wet years, a much narrower spectrum of higher-yielding species in dry. At first, the people deliberately planted wild beans in rare wet years, when they could afford the risk, in an attempt to extend the distributions of existing food plants. The strategy had so many advantages that they extended it to dry years as well. The simulation suggests bean cultivation near the cave allowed the people to collect more food and travel less. As the group gained experience with planting, so yields rose, and they placed ever more emphasis on cultivation as opposed to foraging. Eventually, their descendants became full-time farmers. When Reynolds added climatic change and population growth to his simulation, he found that unpredictable climatic fluctuations and population shifts were major factors that led to the shift to food production.

The computer simulation helped Flannery use an ecosystem model to interpret the Guilá Naquitz excavations. This model allows for people responding to changes in their ecosystem in several ways—for example, by reducing the search area for wild plants, then growing protein-rich beans.

THE ARCHAEOLOGY OF MIND

Inevitably, there has been a reaction against processual archaeology, cultural evolution, and systems approaches. Many critics of processual archaeology claim that it has dehumanized the past in a quest for anonymous, broad cultural processes. What about people?, they ask. How did the constant interactions between the individuals, households, communities, and diverse groups that made up ancient human societies affected culture change? What about religious beliefs, symbolism, ideology, and social organization?

These criticisms came from the context of a boisterous late-twentieth-century world. We live in fractious times, in societies riven by factional disputes, special interest groups, accusations of racism, and calls for political correctness. Inevitably, today's archaeologists look at the past with new, more individualistic eyes, peering beyond anonymous cultural processes to a past made up of people following widely diverse, and often controversial, agendas.

Postprocessual Archaeology

Postprocessual archaeology is a loosely defined term describing various, and often short-lived, schools of archaeological thought that focus on the roles of people and their involvement in culture change. However, there is no precise definition of postprocessual archaeology!

Postprocessual archaeologists argue that we can no longer interpret the past purely in terms of ecological, technological, and other material considerations. Culture is interactive, created by people as actors, who create, manipulate, and remake the world they live in. We are doing this ourselves in the rapidly changing industrial societies of today, where ethnic identity, gender roles, and social equality are constant issues in daily life. Surely, postprocessualists point out, the same kinds of behavior marked the diverse societies of the past and played a major role in the creation of civilizations and myriad societies large and small, simple and complex.

Processual archaeology uses multilinear cultural evolution theories with the widely held assumption that all human societies change, in the long term, from the simple to the more complex. Postprocessual schools of thought are more "horizontal" in their thinking. The thinking shifts constantly, but in general postprocessualists are more concerned with the *meaning* of ancient cultures and the diversity within them than with general, more "vertical" models of increasing cultural complexity, which emphasize individual power and social ranking.

Postprocessual archaeology contributes two important elements to our study of the past and is based on the long-held assumption that culture is interactive, the result of peoples' actions, whether individuals, groups, or entire societies. First, one cannot interpret culture change without examining the hitherto neglected perspectives of what have been called "the people without history," including women, ethnic minorities, and anonymous illiterate commoners.

Second, archaeologists, whatever their cultural or political affiliations, bring their own cultural biases to their interpretations of the past. In other words, there is no such thing as a totally dispassionate take on ancient societies. Many Westerners believe that science offers the broadest perspective on human history. Others consider the Old Testament the literal historical truth. Native Americans often discount scientific archaeology and prefer their own worldview. All archaeologists can do is be active mediators of the past.

Postprocessual archaeology, which developed after processual approaches, is concerned with the role of people in cultural change. All postprocessual archaeologists grapple with a fundamental question: Can one study the development of human consciousness, religious beliefs, and the whole spectrum of human behavior—human cognition—from the material remains of the past? The *Oxford English Dictionary* defines *cognition* as "the action or faculty of knowing taken in its widest sense, including sensation, perception, etc." Clearly, you ignore "human knowing," the "archaeology of mind" (cognitive archaeology), at your peril. Some archaeologists are trying to bring together the best of scientific, processual approaches with the more all-embracing, sometimes instinctual, methods of postprocessualists.

Cognitive-Processual Archaeology

The archaeology of mind includes all forms of archaeology that combine the scientific rigor of processual archaeology with data from many sources to study intangible human behavior.

Archaeologists Kent Flannery and Joyce Marcus (1993) consider the archaeology of mind to be the "study of all those aspects of ancient culture that are the product of the ancient mind." This includes cosmology, religion, ideology, iconography, and all forms of human intellectual and symbolic behavior. They believe that this form of **cognitive-processual archaeology** offers great promise when rigorous methods are applied to large data sets. To do otherwise, they write, causes archaeology to become "little more than speculation, a kind of bungee jump into the Land of Fantasy" (1993, 205).

Flannery and Marcus applied a rigorous cognitive-processual approach in the Valley of Oaxaca, Mexico, where they used ethnographic data, historical records, and archaeological finds to trace the appearance of a distinctive **ideology** that rationalized social inequality. An ideology is a product of society and politics, a body of doctrine, myth, and symbolism associated with a social movement, a class, or a group of individuals, often with reference to some political or cultural plan, along with the strategies for putting the doctrine into place. Flannery and Marcus excavated simple village communities dating from between 1400 and 1150 B.C., in which there was no apparent social ranking. Between 1150 and 850 B.C., the first depictions of supernatural ancestors appear, some representing the earth, others the sky in the form of lightning or a fire serpent. The new art appears at a time when the first signs of hereditary social rank appear in Oaxaca villages, identified from exotic artifacts clustered in some households. Then the great city of *Monte Albán* rose to power, ruled by a powerful Zapotec nobility (Figure 4.8). The art they commissioned to commemorate their power depicts sky and light-

FIGURE 4.8   The city of Monte Albán, Valley of Oaxaca, Mexico. *(Courtesy of Robert Harding.)*

ning, while earth and earthquake symbols fade into obscurity. Thus, careful analysis of artistic motifs and other finds chronicles a vital ideological shift which rationalized social inequality throughout Zapotec domains.

The archaeology of mind is at its most powerful when archaeologists can work with both historic documents and archaeological data. For instance, a half-century ago, archaeologists of Maya civilization (Mayanists) believed that Maya lords were peaceful astronomer-priests with a preoccupation with calendars. In one of the great triumphs of twentieth-century science, a group of scholars succeeded in deciphering the intricate Maya script. This decipherment revealed a far more complex Maya world, one of constant diplomatic activity, intense competition between different kingdoms, and endemic warfare. It seems the Maya lords were no peace-loving priests, but ambitious, power-hungry leaders obsessed with prestige and power. The intricate Maya glyphs with their tales of conquest and genealogical chronicles are a sobering reminder that we can never hope to unravel the full complexity of even the seeming simplest ancient societies without the help of written records. However, by combining the rigor of processual archaeology with the more people-oriented approaches of the archaeology of mind, we can sometimes achieve remarkable insights into the intangible forces that once drove human culture change.

The archaeology of mind will never be an easy undertaking. Pursuing the people of the past and their intangible behavior requires large data sets, excellent preservation, and sophisticated theoretical models. The pursuit is often frustrating and relies on a broad array of scientific methods from dozens of scientific disciplines, among them botany, nuclear physics, and zoology. Australian historian Inga Clendinnen, an expert on the Aztec civilization, cites *Moby Dick* when she likens archaeologists to the following:

Ahabs pursuing our great white whale. . . . We will never catch him. . . . It is our limitations of thought, of understandings, of imagination we test as we quarter these strange waters. And then we think we see a darkening in the deeper water, a sudden surge, the roll of a fluke—and then the heart-lifting glimpse of the great white shape, its whiteness throwing back its own particular light, there on the glimmering horizon (1991, 275).

SUMMARY

This chapter examines the ways in which archaeologists describe and explain the past. Culture history describes ancient human cultures in a context of time and space and is based on the normative view of culture and descriptive research methods. As part of this descriptive process, archaeologists use a hierarchy of arbitrary archaeological units, which proceed from artifacts and assemblages to components, phases, regions, and culture areas. Syntheses of culture history rely on descriptive models of culture change: inevitable variation, cultural selection, invention, diffusion, and migration. Culture-historical interpretation relies on analogy from historical and ethnographic sources, tested against archaeological data, with the aid of ethnoarchaeological and experimental research.

Explaining cultural change involves both processual and postprocessual approaches. Processual archaeology is a combination of systems approaches, cultural ecology, and multilinear evolution. Such approaches have been criticized for being too impersonal. Recent postprocessual approaches have focused on the study of people and intangibles such as religious beliefs using cognitive approaches that combine ethnographic and historical records with scientifically acquired archaeological data.

KEY TERMS

Analogy

Cognitive-processual archaeology

Components

Cultural ecology

Cultural selection

Culture areas

Deductive reasoning

Descriptive (inductive) research methods

Diffusion

Ethnoarchaeology

Experimental archaeology

Functionalism

General systems theory

Horizons

Ideology

Inductive reasoning

Inevitable variation

Invention

Migration

Multilinear cultural evolution

Normative view of culture

Phases

Postprocessual archaeology

Processual archaeology

Regions

Scientific method

Traditions

GUIDE TO FURTHER READING

Binford, Lewis R. 1978. *Nunamiut Ethnoarchaeology*. Orlando, FL: Academic Press.
     A descriptive monograph on Arctic caribou hunting that is a classic of ethnoarchaeology for the serious student.
———. 1983. *In Pursuit of the Past*. New York: Thames and Hudson.
     Binford describes his archaeological thinking for laypeople. It is a useful introduction to processual archaeology and ethnoarchaeology.
Coles, John M. 1973. *Archaeology by Experiment*. London: Heinemann.
     An introduction with many examples, mainly from the Old World.
Lyman, R. Lee, Michael O'Brien, and Robert Dunnell. 1996. *The Rise and Fall of Culture History*. New York: Plenum Press.
     A splendid analysis of culture history in American archaeology. Essential reading for advanced students.
Preucel, Robert W., and Ian Hodder, eds. 1997. *Contemporary Archaeology in Theory*. Oxford, England: Blackwell.
     A useful and comprehensive anthology of archaeological theory, which covers everything from processual archaeology to gender.
Renfrew, Colin, and others. 1983. "What Is Cognitive Archaeology?" *Cambridge Archaeological Journal* 3(2): 247–270.
     A series of essays on the emerging approach called cognitive archaeology. A thoughtful analysis of contemporary theory.
Willey, Gordon R., and Philip Phillips. 1958. *Method and Theory in American Archaeology*. Chicago: University of Chicago Press.
     Often described as the culture historian's bible, this is still the best book on the methods of the descriptive approach. Every professional archaeologist reads this book.

PART II

@

VANISHED WORLDS

*The earth spins around the sun; year is
added to year, century to century,
millennium to millennium. . . . For the dead
bison, time stopped ages ago; all processes
were suspended; the bison rests in a
changeless present, as fresh as when it froze
a thousand generations ago.*

BJORN KÜRTEN, *HOW TO DEEP-FREEZE A MAMMOTH*, 1986, 60.

CHAPTER 5
Ancient Environments

Easter Island Statues, South Pacific. c. A.D. 1400. (Source: George Holton/Photo Researchers, Inc.)

In 4500 B.C., a patch of woodland in northern England boasted mature oak, ash, and elm trees, interspersed with occasional patches of open grassland and swamp. In 3820 B.C., some foragers set fire to the forest to encourage fresh green shoots to feed the deer. Birch and bracken then appeared. About 30 years passed before the landscape was cleared even more. Judging from numerous charcoal fragments, fire swept through the undergrowth, leaving fine ash to fertilize the soil. Then wheat pollen and pollen of a cultivation weed named *Plantago lanceolata* appeared. Fifty years of wheat farming ensued. These years saw only two fires, one after six years, the other 19 years after that. Then, 70 years passed, during which agriculture ceased and the land stood vacant. Hazel, birch, and alder became more common and oak resurged as woodland rapidly gained ground.

This scenario of brief clearance, slash-and-burn agriculture, then abandonment and regeneration was repeated at thousands of locations in ancient Europe in the early years of Stone Age farming. Over a few centuries, the natural environment of mixed oak forest was transformed beyond recognition by gardens and domesticated animals. Until a few years ago, we could only have guessed at these environmental changes. Today, fine-grained pollen analysis and other highly sophisticated methods allow the reconstruction of even short-lived climatic and environmental changes in the remote past.

Archaeology is unique in its ability to study culture change over very long periods of time. By the same token, it is a multidisciplinary science that also studies human interactions with the natural environment over centuries and millennia. Chapter 5 describes some of the ways archaeologists study long- and short-term environmental change from a multidisciplinary perspective.

LONG- AND SHORT-TERM CLIMATIC CHANGE

Climatic change comes in many forms. The long cycles of cold and warm associated with the Ice Age occur on a millennial scale and have long-term effects on human existence. For example, the existence of a low-lying land bridge between Siberia and Alaska during much of the late Ice Age may have allowed humans to forage their way from Asia into the Americas before 15,000 years ago, but the actual formation of the shelf that linked the two continents would have taken many centuries and human generations. Short-term climatic change, such as the floods or droughts caused by El Niño episodes or the volcanic eruptions which dump ash into the atmosphere, are another matter. Memories of catastrophic famines and other results associated with such events would have endured for generations, for they had immediate impact on hundreds, if not thousands, of people. Throughout human history, people have developed strategies to deal with sudden climatic shifts, which bring drought, hunger, or unexpected food shortages. Humans have always been brilliant opportunists, capable of improvising solutions to unexpected problems caused by environmental change. Thus, environmental reconstruction and climatic change are two major concerns for archaeologists wherever they work.

GEOARCHAEOLOGY

Geoarchaeology, the study of archaeology using the methods and concepts of the earth sciences, plays a major role in reconstructing ancient environments, also long- and short-term climatic change. This is a far wider enterprise than geology and involves at least four major approaches:

- Geochemical, electromagnetic, and other remote-sensing devices to locate sites and environmental features (Chapter 6)
- Studies of site-formation processes and of the spatial contexts of archaeological sites (Chapters 3 and 10), a process that includes distinguishing humanly caused phenomena from natural features
- Reconstructing the ancient landscape by a variety of paleogeographic and biological methods, including pollen analysis
- Relative and chronometric dating of sites and their geological contexts

People are geomorphic agents, just like the wind. Accidentally or deliberately, they carry inorganic and organic materials to their homes. They remove rubbish, make tools, build houses, abandon tools. These mineral and organic materials are subjected to all manner of mechanical and biochemical processes while people live on site and after they abandon it. The controlling geomorphic system at a site, whatever its size, is made up not only of natural elements but of a vital cultural component as well. The geoarchaeologist is involved with archaeological investigations from the very beginning and deals not only with formation of sites and with the changes they underwent during occupation, but also with what happened to them after abandonment.

In the field, the geoarchaeologist is part of the multidisciplinary research team, recording stratigraphic profiles within the excavation and in special nearby pits to obtain information on soil sediment sequences. At the same time, he or she takes soil samples for pollen and sediment analyses and relates the site to its landscape by topographic survey. Working closely with survey archaeologists, geoarchaeologists locate sites and other cultural features in the natural landscape using aerial photographs, satellite images, and even geophysical prospecting on individual sites. As part of this process, they examine dozens of natural geological exposures, where they study the stratigraphic and sedimentary history of the entire region as a wider context for the sites found within it. The ultimate objective is to identify not only the microenvironment of the site but also that of the region as a whole—to establish ecological and spatial frameworks for the socioeconomic and settlement patterns that are revealed by archaeological excavations and surveys.

LONG-TERM CLIMATIC CHANGE: THE GREAT ICE AGE

About 1.8 million years ago, global cooling marked the beginning of the **Pleistocene** epoch, or the Great Ice Age. (The term **Quaternary** is commonly used to describe both the Pleistocene and the Holocene [postglacial times].) It was remarkable for dramatic swings in world climate. On numerous occasions during the Pleistocene, great ice sheets covered much of western Europe and North America, bringing arctic climates to vast areas of the Northern Hemisphere. Scientists have identified at least eight major glacial episodes over the past 730,000 years, alternating with shorter warm periods, when the world's climate was sometimes warmer than it is today. The general pattern is cyclical, with slow coolings culminating in a relatively short period of intense cold, followed by rapid warming. For 75 percent of the past three-quarters of a million years, the world's climate has been in transition from one extreme to another. We still live in the Ice Age, in a warm interglacial period. If the current scientific estimates are correct and humanly caused global warming does not interfere, we will probably begin to enter another cold phase in about 23,000 years.

No one knows exactly what causes the climatic fluctuations of the Ice Age, but they are connected with oscillations in the intensity of solar radiation and the trajectory of the earth around the sun. Such climatic changes are of great importance to archaeologists, for they form a long-term environmental backdrop for the early chapters of our past. Although almost no human beings lived on, or very close to, the great ice sheets that covered so much of the Northern Hemisphere, they did live in regions affected by geological phenomena associated with the ice sheets: coastal areas, lakes, and river floodplains. When human artifacts are found in direct association with

Pleistocene geological features of this type, it is sometimes possible to tie in archaeological sites with the relative chronology of Pleistocene events derived from geological strata. (See Discovery box below.)

Glacial Geology and Sea Levels

Ice Age glaciers and ice sheets formed in mountainous, high-latitude areas and on continental plains during the Pleistocene. Prolonged periods of arctic climate and abundant snowfall caused glaciers to form over enormous expanses of northern Europe, North America, and the alpine areas of France, Italy, and Switzerland. These alternated with shorter interglacial phases, when world climate was considerably warmer than it is today. Glacial geologists have identified the rubble deposits left by advancing and retreating ice sheets throughout the Northern Hemisphere. However, the processes of advance and retreat were so destructive of earlier deposits in most places that we only have a clear picture of the last two or three glacial advances.

Every ice sheet had a **periglacial** zone, an area affected by glacial climatic influences. For example, at the height of the late Ice Age some 20,000 years ago, the persistent glacial high-pressure zone centered over the north-

DISCOVERY

Akrotiri, Santorini, Greece

Only rarely do archaeologists find sites associated with direct evidence of ancient climatic or natural phenomena. A half-century ago, Greek archaeologist Spyridon Marinatos speculated that the flamboyant Minoan civilization of Crete was severely damaged by a huge volcanic eruption that blew the center of the island of Santorini (Thera), 62 miles (100 km) north, into space in about 1450 B.C. Few archaeologists agreed with his theory. Undeterred, Marinatos searched diligently for Minoan sites on Santorini but found that everything was buried under massive volcanic ash deposits. In 1967, he heard reports from farmers of masses of stones close underground in the fields around Akrotiri in the south of the island. So dense were the boulders that they could not plow their land. Marinatos began digging into places where the ground had collapsed between the subterranean masonry and promptly discovered the Greek Pompeii, an island town of 3500 years ago completely buried by pumice and ash when the volcano erupted. Akrotiri's houses were remarkably well preserved, their stone and timber walls often two stories high. Brilliant polychrome frescoes still adorned some of the rooms, depicting religious and military scenes, the island landscape, animals, and plants. Food storage jars still stood in the basements of the houses. But there was no trace of the inhabitants, who had fled when ominous subterranean rumblings began. The imported Minoan pottery at Akrotiri is at least 20 to 30 years earlier than that from the latest levels of Cretan villages, proving that Marinatos was wrong. The Santorini eruption did not destroy Minoan civilization.

ern ice sheet caused dry, frosty winds to blow over the periglacial regions of central Europe. The dry winds blew fine dust, known as **loess,** onto the huge, rolling plains of central and eastern Europe and Northern America (Figure 5.1).

About 18,000 years ago, a hunter-gatherer band lived on the edge of the shallow Dnepr Valley at *Mezhirich* in southern Ukraine. These people dug the floors of their semisubterranean dwellings into the soft loess soil, then roofed them with lattices of mammoth bones, using the enormous jaw bones to support the roofs. Once covered with sod, the domelike houses hugged the ground and offered excellent protection from the bitter cold winds of winter. Both radiocarbon dates and the stratified loess deposits date the Mezhirich site to within close chronological limits.

The ice sheets growing on land had effects beyond the formation of loess plains. The water that fell as snow to form the ice sheets and glaciers ultimately came from the oceans. When large areas in the northern latitudes were covered with ice, enormous quantities of water—enough to reduce the general level of the oceans by many yards, more than 295 feet (90 m) at the height of the last glaciation 18,000 years ago—were

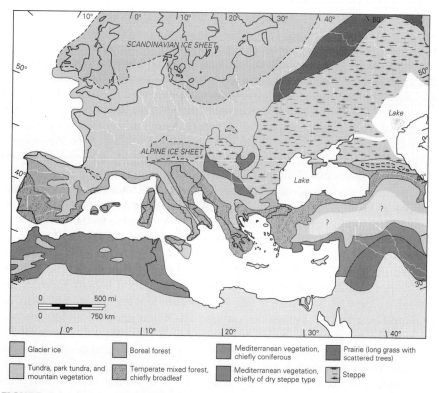

FIGURE 5.1 Europe during the height of the last Ice Age glaciation. *(After Butzer. Courtesy of Cambridge University Press.)*

immobilized on land. This **eustatic** effect was accompanied by an **isosta-tic** effect as well. The sheer deadweight of the massive ice sheets sank the loaded continental blocks of the land masses into the viscous underlying layers of the earth that lie some 6 miles (10 km) below the surface. In inter-glacial times, the world's sea levels rose sharply to levels higher than they are today. As the water levels retreated once again, they left their aban-doned beaches raised high above later sea levels, high and dry where geol-ogists can study them today.

Many prehistoric settlements that were occupied during periods of low sea levels are, of course, buried deep beneath the modern ocean waters. Numerous sites on ancient beaches have been found dating to times of higher sea levels. American archaeologist Richard Klein excavated a coastal cave at *Nelson's Bay* in Cape Province of South Africa that now overlooks the Indian Ocean. Large quantities of shellfish and other marine animals are found in the uppermost levels of the cave. But in the lower levels, occu-pied roughly 11,000 to 12,000 years ago, fish bones and other marine resources are very rare. Klein suspects that the seashore was many miles away at that time, for world sea levels were much lower during a long period of arctic climate in northern latitudes. Today the cave is only 50 yards (45 m) from the sea.

Deep-Sea and Ice Cores

Our knowledge of Ice Age climatic change comes from many sources, includ-ing geological strata, such as glacial deposits and ancient high beach levels, and fossil animal bones from environmentally sensitive mammals as large as elephants and as small as mice. Such approaches have long provided a crude outline of Ice Age glaciations. But in recent years the study of deep seabed samples and ice cores has revolutionized our understanding of the Pleistocene by providing long sequences of constantly changing Ice Age climates from deep below the ocean floor and the heart of the Greenland ice sheet.

The world's ocean floors are a priceless archive of ancient climatic change. Deep-sea cores produce long columns of ocean-floor sediments that include skeletons of small marine organisms that once lived close to the ocean's sur-face. The planktonic foraminifera (protozoa) found in deep-sea cores consist largely of calcium carbonate. When alive, their minute skeletons absorbed organic isotopes. The ratio of two of these isotopes—oxygen 16 and oxygen 18—varies as a result of evaporation. When evaporation is high, more of the lighter oxygen 16 is extracted from the ocean, leaving the plankton to be enriched by more of the heavier oxygen 18. When great ice sheets formed on land during glacial episodes, sea levels fell as moisture was drawn off for continental ice caps. During such periods, the world's oceans contained more oxygen 18 in proportion to oxygen 16, a ratio reflected in millions of foraminifera. A mass spectrometer is used to measure this ratio, which does not reflect ancient temperature changes but is merely a statement about the size of the oceans and about contemporary events on land.

You can confirm climatic fluctuations by using other lines of evidence as well, such as the changing frequencies of foraminifera and other groups of marine microfossils in the cores. By using statistical techniques, and assuming that relationships between different species and sea conditions have not changed, climatologists have been able to turn these frequencies into numerical estimates of sea surface temperatures and ocean salinity over the past few hundred thousand years and to produce a climatic profile of much of the Ice Age (Figure 5.2). These events have been fixed at key points by radiocarbon dates and by studies of paleomagnetism (ancient magnetism). The Matuyama-Brunhes magnetic reversal of 730,000 years ago (when the world's magnetic field suddenly reversed) is a key stratigraphic marker, which can be identified both in sea cores and in volcanic strata ashore, where it can be dated precisely with potassium-argon samples.

Deep-ice cores are the equivalent of seabed cores, but pose very different interpretive problems. Paleoclimatologists have drilled deep into Greenland ice, into the Antarctic ice sheet, and into mountain glaciers and ice caps in locations as widely separated as China and Peru. Many of the interpretive problems revolve around the complex process by which

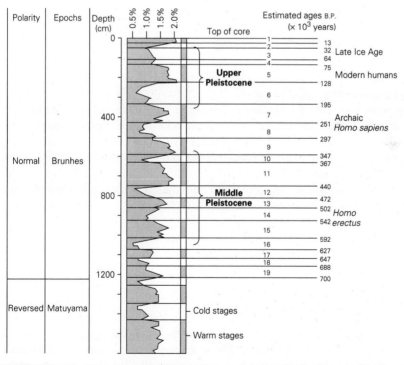

FIGURE 5.2 The deep-sea core that serves as the standard reference for the past 730,000 years comes from the Solomon Plateau in the southwestern Pacific Ocean. The Matuyama-Brunhes event occurs at a depth of 39.3 feet (11.9 m). Above it a sawtoothlike curve identifies at least eight complete glacial and interglacial cycles. *(After Neil Shackleton. Courtesy of Cambridge University Press.)*

annual snowfall layers are buried deeper and deeper in a glacier until they are finally compressed into ice. Scientists have had to learn the different textures characteristic of summer and winter ice, so they can assemble a long record of precipitation that goes back deep into geological time, as well as using more easily accessible records of temperature change, carbon dioxide, methane, and other chemical properties. Snowfall changes are especially important, for they can provide vital evidence on the rate of warming and cooling during sudden climatic changes. Researchers can now read ice cores like tree-ring samples, with very good resolution back for 12,000 years, and improving accuracy back to 40,000 years. Ice cores have been especially useful for studying not so much the long-term fluctuations of Ice Age climatic change, but the short-term episodes of warmer and colder conditions that occurred in the middle of glaciations, which had profound effects on humanity. For example, scientists now suspect that there were bursts of human activity in late–Ice Age western Europe about 35,000 and 25,000 years ago, when conditions were relatively warm for short periods of time.

Ice cores reveal complex climatic changes, among them long-term changes that result from the 100,000- and 23,000-year periodicities in the earth's orbit. They also provide evidence of medium-range shifts between 5,000 and 10,000 years in duration, and data of particular importance to archaeologists: still little understood, high-frequency climatic changes with periodicities of about 1,000 years. All three types of climatic change interact in the ice core record, which looks rather like a wave diagram of a radio playing three stations at once.

Research is still in its infancy, but some paleoclimatologists believe that changes in arctic climate may have triggered coupled changes elsewhere in the world, reflected in such phenomena as pollen records in Florida lakes, glacial records in the Andes, and ocean-bottom sediments in the Santa Barbara Channel, California.

Ice-core research is also providing convincing evidence of drought cycles and other climatic fluctuations during the Holocene (see the following section).

Ice and sea cores, combined with pollen analysis, have provided a broad framework for the Pleistocene, which is in wide use by archaeologists and worth summarizing here (see Figure 5.3).

The Pleistocene Framework

The Pleistocene began about 1.8 million years ago, during a long-term cooling trend in the world's oceans. These millennia were ones of constant climatic change. The Pleistocene is conventionally divided into three long subdivisions.

The *Lower Pleistocene* lasted from the beginning of the Ice Age until about 730,000 years ago. Deep-sea cores tell us that climatic fluctuations between warmer and colder regimes were still relatively minor. These were critical

Temperature ←Lower Higher→	Dates (B.P.)	Periods	Epochs	Subdivisions	European Glacials/ Interglacials	North American Glacials/Interglacials	Human Evolution	Prehistory	Three-Age System
	10,000	Holocene	Holocene	Holocene	Holocene	Holocene		Cities, agriculture Settlement of New World	Iron Age Bronze Age Neolithic Mesolithic
	118,000		Brunhes	Upper Pleistocene	Weichsel (Würm)	Wisconsin	*Homo sapiens sapiens* ←		Upper Paleolithic
	128,000	Quaternary			Eemian	Sangamon			
				Middle Pleistocene	Saale (Riss)	Illinoian			
			Pleistocene		Holstein	Yarmouth	*Homo sapiens* ←	Hunter-gatherers	Lower and Middle Paleolithic
	730,000		Matuyama	Lower Pleistocene	Elster (Mindel)	Kansan	*Homo erectus*		
		Tertiary	Olduvai Event						
Uncertain climate detail before 130,000 years ago	1,600,000		Pliocene				Early hominids and *Australopithecus*		

Note for the advanced reader and the instructor: Throughout this book I have used the glacial terminology applied to northern Europe in discussing the successive glaciations and interglacial periods in the Old World. This system follows Karl Butzer's definitive synthesis, *Environment and Archeology*, 3rd ed. 1974. Hawthorne, N.Y.: Aldine. Many still use Alpine names preferred in earlier literature, but I have chosen to reduce confusion and recognize that not everyone will agree. For the newcomers, here are the equivalent names. Alpine terms: Würm, Riss, and Mindel. Northern European terms: Weichsel, Saale, and Elster.

FIGURE 5.3   Provisional chronology and subdivisions of the Ice Age.

millennia, for it was during this long period that humans first spread from tropical regions in Africa to other regions, and then into temperate latitudes in Europe and Asia.

The *Middle Pleistocene* began with the Matuyama-Brunhes reversal in the earth's magnetic polarity about 730,000 years ago, a change that has been recognized geologically not only in deep-sea cores, but in volcanic rocks ashore, where it can be dated by potassium-argon samples.

Since then, there have been at least eight cold (glacial) and warm (interglacial) cycles, the last cycle ending about 12,000 years ago. (Strictly speaking, we are still in an interglacial today.) Typically, cold cycles have begun gradually, with vast continental ice sheets forming on land—in Scandinavia, on the Alps, and over the northern parts of North America (Figure 5.4). These expanded ice sheets locked up enormous quantities of water, causing world sea levels to fall by several hundred feet during glacial episodes. The geography of the world changed dramatically, and large continental shelves were opened up for human settlement. When a warming trend began, deglaciation occurred very rapidly and rising sea levels flooded low-lying coastal areas within a few millennia. During glacial maxima, glaciers covered a full one-third of the earth's land surface, while they were as extensive as they are today during interglacials.

Throughout the past 730,000 years, vegetational changes have mirrored climatic fluctuations. During glacial episodes, treeless arctic steppe and tundra covered much of Europe and parts of North America, but gave way to temperate forest during interglacials. In the tropics, Africa's Sahara Desert may have supported grassland during interglacials, but ice and desert landscape expanded dramatically during dry, cold spells.

The *Upper Pleistocene* stage began about 128,000 years ago, with the beginning of the last interglacial. This period lasted until about 118,000 years ago, when a slow cooling trend brought full glacial conditions to Europe and North America. This Würm glaciation, named after a river in the Alps, lasted until about 15,000 years ago, when there was a rapid return to more temperate conditions.

The Würm glaciation was a period of constantly fluctuating climatic change, with several episodes of more temperate climate in northern latitudes (Figure 5.4). It served as the backdrop for some of the most important developments in human prehistory, notably the spread of anatomically modern *Homo sapiens sapiens* from the tropics to all parts of the Old World and into the Americas. Between about 30,000 and 15,000 years ago, Northern Eurasia's climate was intensely cold, but highly variable. A series of Stone Age hunter-gatherer cultures evolved both on the open tundra of central Europe and Eurasia and in the sheltered river valleys of southwestern France and northern Spain, cultures famous for their fine antler and bone artifacts and exceptional artwork.

The world's geography was dramatically different 18,000 years ago during the last glacial maximum. These differences had a major impact on

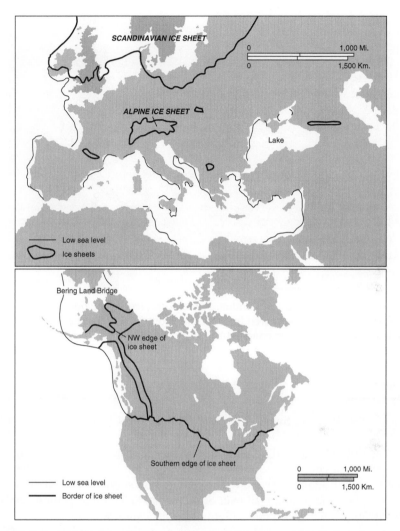

FIGURE 5.4   Distribution of major ice sheets in Europe and North America during the last Ice Age glaciation, and the extent of land exposed by low sea levels.

human prehistory—one could walk from Siberia to Alaska across a flat, low-lying plain, the Bering Land Bridge (Figure 5.5). This was the route by which humans first reached the Americas some time before 12,000 years ago. The low-lying coastal zones of Southeast Asia were far more extensive 15,000 years ago than they are now, and they supported a thriving population of Stone Age foragers. The fluctuating distributions of vegetational zones also affected the pattern of human settlement and the course of human history.

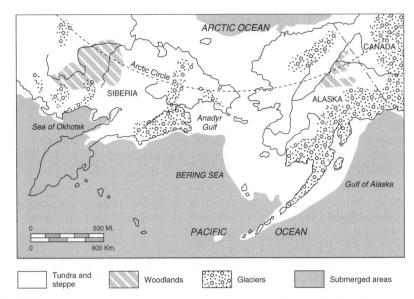

FIGURE 5.5 The Bering Land Bridge, as reconstructed by multidisciplinary research. Alaska finally separated from Siberia about 11,000 years ago as sea levels rose in response to warmer conditions.

POLLEN ANALYSIS

As long ago as 1916, Swedish botanist Lennart von Post used fossil pollen grains from such familiar trees as birches, oaks, and pines to develop a sequence of vegetational change for northern Europe after the Ice Age. He showed how arctic, treeless tundra gave way to birch forest, then mixed oak woodland in a dramatic sequence of change that survived in pollen samples from marshes and swamps all over Scandinavia. Since then, **pollen analysis (palynology)** has become a highly sophisticated way of studying both ancient environments and human impacts on natural vegetation. (See Doing Archaeology box on p. 135.)

Pollen analysis reconstructs ancient vegetational change and provides insights into the ways people adapted to shifting climatic conditions. For instance, palynology is providing new perceptions of Stone Age life at the height of the last glaciation in southwestern France, some 15,000 to 20,000 years ago (Figure 5.7, p. 136). This was, we are told, a period of extreme arctic cold, when Europe was in a deep freeze, and people subsisted off of arctic animals and took refuge in deep river valleys such as the Dordogne and the Vézère, where some of the earliest cave art in the world has been discovered. In fact, pollen grains from the rock shelters and open camps used by Stone Age hunter-gatherers of this period paint a very different picture of the late–Ice Age climate in this area. It is a portrait of a favored arctic environment in which the climate fluctuated constantly, with surprisingly temperate

DOING ARCHAEOLOGY

Pollen Analysis

The principle is simple. Large numbers of pollen grains are dispersed in the atmosphere and survive remarkably well if deposited in an unaerated geological horizon. The pollen grains can be identified microscopically (Figure 5.6) with great accuracy and can be used to reconstruct a picture of the vegetation, right down to humble grasses and weeds, that grew near the spot where the pollen grains are found.

Pollen analysis begins in the field. The botanist visits the excavation and collects a series of closely spaced pollen samples from the stratigraphic sections at the site. Back in the laboratory, the samples are examined under a very powerful microscope. The grains of each genus or species present are counted, and the resulting figures subjected to statistical analysis. These counts are then correlated with the stratigraphic layers of the excavation and data from natural vegetational sequences to provide a sequence of vegetational change for the site. Typically, this vegetational sequence lasts a few centuries or even millennia (Figure 5.7). It forms part of a much longer pollen sequence for the area that has been assembled from hun-

dreds of samples from many different sites. In northern Europe, for example, botanists have worked out a complicated series of vegetational time zones that cover the past 12,000 years. By comparing the pollen sequences from individual sites with the overall chronology, botanists can give a relative date for the site.

Palynology has obvious applications to prehistory, for sites are often found in swampy deposits where pollen is preserved, especially fishing or fowling camps and settlements near water. Isolated artifacts, or even human corpses (such as that of Tollund Man found in a Danish bog, see Figure 2.11), have also been discovered in these deposits; pollen is sometimes obtained from small peat lumps adhering to crevices in such finds. Thus, botanists can assign relative dates even to isolated finds that would otherwise remain undated.

Until recently, pollen analysts dealt in centuries. Now, thanks to much more refined methods and AMS radiocarbon dating, they can study even transitory episodes, such as the brief farming incident described at the beginning of this chapter. For example, dramatic declines

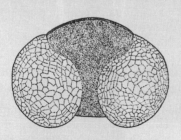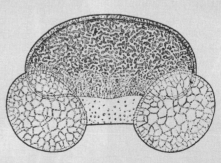

FIGURE 5.6 Pollen grains: spruce *(left)*, silver fir *(right)*. Both 340 times actual size.

(Continued)

DOING ARCHAEOLOGY

Pollen Analysis *(Continued)*

in forest tree pollens at many locations in Europe chronicle the first clearances made by farming cultures with almost decade-long accuracy—at a moment when characteristic cultivation weeds such as *Plantago lanceolata*, already mentioned, appear for the first time. In the United States, Southwestern archaeologists now have a regional pollen sequence that provides not only climatic information but also valuable facts about the functions of different pueblo rooms and different foods that were eaten by the inhabitants.

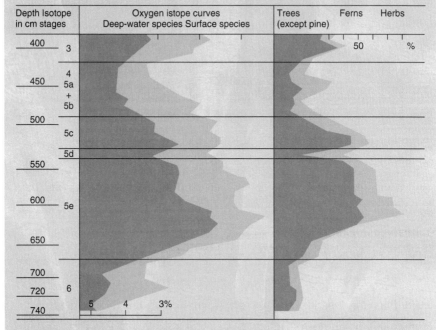

FIGURE 5.7 A long-term pollen sequence for the Ice Age from Spain *(right)* compared to oxygen-isotope curves taken from a deep-sea core in the nearby Bay of Biscay *(left)*, showing the close correlation between the two.

conditions, especially on the south-facing slopes of deep river valleys. Here, people used rock shelters that faced the winter sun, where snow melted earlier in the spring, within easy reach of key reindeer migration routes and of arctic game that wintered in the valleys. The vegetational cover was not treeless, as is commonly assumed, but included pine, birch, and sometimes deciduous trees, with lush summer meadows in the valleys.

The late Ice Age was a period of continual, and often dramatic, short- and long-term climatic change. Some of these changes lasted millennia, bringing intervals of near-modern conditions to temperate Europe interspersed with much colder winters. Other cold and warm snaps extended over a few centuries, causing human populations to adapt to dramatically new conditions. Just like today, there were much shorter climatic episodes, which endured for a year or more, bringing unusually warm summers, floods, droughts, and other short-term events.

HOLOCENE ENVIRONMENTAL RECONSTRUCTION

In 1931, a trawler working the North Sea's Leman and Ower Bank hauled up a lump of peat from a depth of 118 feet (36 m). The trawlermen cursed. Their nets snagged and tore on waterlogged wood and mud lumps as they probed for bottom fish. Wearily, they bent over to throw the dark fragment overboard, but the lump split open and a brown, barbed object fell on the deck with some peat still adhering to it. Fortunately for science, the skipper was intrigued and brought the find back to port with his catch.

News of the discovery came to the ears of a young Cambridge University archaeologist named Grahame Clark, a brilliant researcher who had just completed a doctoral dissertation on the Stone Age inhabitants of Britain at the end of the Ice Age. He identified the mysterious object as a finely made Stone Age deer antler spearhead, identical to similar specimens found on both sides of the North Sea.

Clark had traveled widely in Scandinavia where he studied the dramatic environmental changes in the far north after 15,000 years ago, when the great ice sheets of the north retreated, forming the Baltic Sea. How, he wondered, had human populations adapted to massive global warming? He knew that rising postglacial sea levels had flooded the southern North Sea, once a low-lying, marshy plain that joined Britain to the Continent and theorized boldly that Stone Age people had colonized southeastern England from lands across the North Sea. The Leman and Ower find confirmed his hypothesis, but he was even more interested in the damp peat adhering to the spearhead, which had the potential to yield priceless information about the buried land bridge. Clark handed over the precious artifact and its matrix to a young Cambridge botanist friend, Harry Godwin, one of the first British scientists to specialize in fossil pollen analysis. Godwin and his wife Margaret assigned the antler point peat to what pollen experts called the Boreal phase, a period when oak forests first spread northward into northern Europe.

The famous Leman and Ower spear point dramatizes the extraordinary changes in global climate since the Ice Age. With the rapid retreat of late–Ice Age glaciers 15,000 years ago, the world entered a period of profound environmental change, which saw the great ice sheets of northern latitudes melt and world sea levels rise to modern levels. Thus dawned the **Holocene** period (Greek *holos* means "recent"), which saw massive global warming, sudden cold episodes, periods of warmer climate than today, and the appearance of both food production and civilization, and also the Industrial

Revolution. Many people believe this warming has been continuous and is reflected in the record warm temperatures of today. In fact, the world's climate has fluctuated just as dramatically as it did during the late Ice Age. Recent research is revolutionizing our knowledge of these changes, which started new chapters in human history, overthrew civilizations, and caused widespread disruption.

We can identify Holocene climatic changes from ice cores, sedimentary records in caves, tree rings, and pollen samples with a chronological resolution that improves every year as analytical methods become ever more refined. For example, the famous Star Carr Stone Age forager camp in northeastern England has been dissected with the aid of highly refined pollen analysis, AMS radiocarbon dating, and minute studies of wood charcoals and soils. Researchers believe that the site was occupied repeatedly over about 350 years around 8500 B.C. The inhabitants burned the lakeside vegetation repeatedly, built a substantial wooden platform in the reeds as part of a much larger settlement on nearby dry land than was originally thought when the site was excavated in the late 1940s.

The onset of the Holocene coincided with a period when Stone Age foragers had occupied virtually all inhabitable parts of the Old World, except the offshore Pacific Islands. By this time, too, a tiny number of humans had probably foraged their way into the Americas. Wherever they flourished, the global population of the early Holocene had to adjust to radically new, and often very challenging, environmental conditions. Over a period of a mere 5,000 years, hundreds of familiar, large Ice Age animals such as the mammoth, Ice Age bison, and arctic rhinoceros became extinct. People turned to far more intensive exploitation of local environments. Many became specialized hunters, fisherfolk, or concentrated on plant foods to the virtual exclusion of all other resources. And some became farmers, changing the course of human history.

Centuries-Long Climatic Changes: The Younger Dryas and the Black Sea

At least three major cold episodes have cooled global temperatures since 11,000 years ago (Figure 5.8). The last of these was the so-called Little Ice Age, a global event of sometimes markedly colder conditions which lasted from A.D. 1400 to 1850. The earlier two of these cold intervals had major effects on the course of human history, which we can now assess thanks to new deep-sea core, ice-core, and pollen researches.

The Younger Dryas   This period lasted from 11,000 to 10,000 B.C. For some still little understood reason, global warming ceased abruptly, perhaps as a result of sudden changes in the warm water circulation in the Atlantic Ocean. Within a century or so, Europe again shivered under near–Ice Age conditions, as forests retreated and widespread drought affected areas such as southwestern Asia. This catastrophic drought after centuries of ample rainfall may have

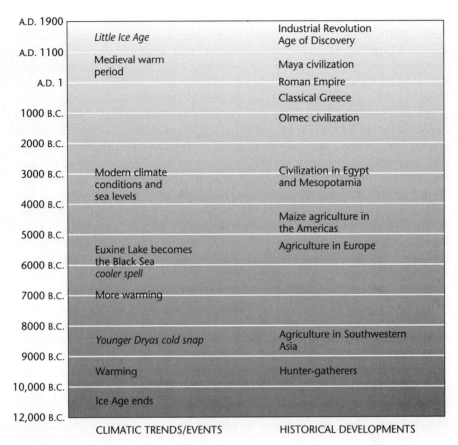

CLIMATIC TRENDS/EVENTS	HISTORICAL DEVELOPMENTS

FIGURE 5.8 Major climatic and historical events of the Holocene. (This is, of course, a gross simplification of reality.)

been a major factor in the appearance of agriculture and animal domestication in such areas as the Euphrates and Jordan River valleys, where dense forager populations had long subsisted off abundant food resources. What happened next has been documented by botanist Gordon Hillman with plant remains at the Abu Hureyra site (see Chapter 9). When the drought came, nut harvest yields plummeted, game populations crashed, and wild cereal grasses were unable to support a dense human population. So the foragers turned to cultivation to supplement their food supplies. Within a few generations, they became full-time farmers. The Younger Dryas–induced drought was not the only cause of the development of agriculture, but the sudden climate change was of great importance. The same economic shift was repeated at many locations and within a few centuries, agriculture was widespread throughout southwestern Asia. Thanks to accurate radiocarbon dating of individual seeds and pollen grains from freshwater lakes, Moore and his colleagues were able to tie the changeover to farming to the 1,000-year-long Younger Dryas.

The Black Sea This was an enormous freshwater lake (often called the Euxine Lake) isolated from the Mediterranean by a huge natural earthen levee in the Bosporus Valley between Turkey and Bulgaria during the early Holocene. Four centuries of colder conditions and drought again settled over Europe and southwestern Asia between 6200 and 5800 B.C. Many farmers abandoned long-established villages and settled near the great lake and other permanent water sources. Deep-sea cores and pollen diagrams chronicle what happened next as the climate warmed up again after 5800 B.C. Sea levels resumed their inexorable rise toward modern high levels. Salty Mediterranean waters climbed ever higher on the Bosporus levee. Then, in about 5500 B.C., the rising water breached the barrier. Torrents of saltwater cascaded into the Euxine Lake 500 feet (150 m) below. Within weeks, the great waterfall had carved a deep gully and formed the narrow strait that now links the Black Sea to the Mediterranean. The former lake not only became a saltwater sea, but rose sharply, flooding hundreds of agricultural settlements on its shores, perhaps with great loss of life. This long-forgotten event has recently been reconstructed from deep-sea cores taken in the Mediterranean and also in the Black Sea, which chronicle not only the cold episode and drought, but the sudden change in the now-drowned lake.

The Black Sea discoveries are so new that archaeologists still have to assess their full consequences. The flooding of the huge lake does coincide with the spread of farmers across temperate Europe from the Balkans. Some experts believe the environmental catastrophe and the spread of farming were connected, as people fled their once-fertile homelands.

Short-Term Climatic Change: El Niño

We look back at the past through shadowed mirrors, which become increasingly easy to use as we approach recent times. Our knowledge of Ice Age climatic change is necessarily on a grand scale, for, until recently, even ice cores did not attain the year-by-year resolution that is needed to track short-term shifts. Yet, such sudden changes are the most important of all to human populations, who have to adjust constantly to unusual weather conditions—to droughts and floods, extreme heat and cold. The Younger Dryas and Black Sea drought and flood are centuries-long events, which are considered short by geological and early prehistoric standards. It is only now that we are beginning to understand their profound impact on ancient societies. As research into these and other centuries-long events has intensified, so more scholars have paid increasing attention to violent, yearlong episodes such as monsoon failures, volcanic eruptions, and, most important of all, El Niños.

Identifying ancient short-term climatic change requires extremely precise and sophisticated environmental and climatic evidence, much of it obtained from ice cores, pollen diagrams, and tree rings. Ice cores, in particular, are revolutionizing our knowledge of ancient climatic shifts, for they are now achieving a resolution of five years or less, which really allows researchers to study drought cycles and major El Niño events of the past.

El Niños like those in 1982/1983 and 1997/1998 have grabbed world head-lines, and with good reason. Billions of dollars of damage resulted from drought and flood. California experienced record rains, Australia and north-east Brazil suffered through brutal drought, enormous wildfires devastated rainforests in southeast Asia and Mexico. Once thought to be a purely local phenomenon off the Peruvian coast, El Niños are now known to be global events, which ripple across the entire tropics as a result of a breakdown in the atmospheric and ocean circulation in the western Pacific. From the archae-ologist's point of view, El Niños are of compelling interest, for they had dras-tic effects on many early civilizations living in normally dry environments, where flooding may have wiped out years of irrigation agriculture in hours. Humanity was not that vulnerable to El Niños until people settled in perma-nent villages, then cities, when the realities of farming and growing popula-tion densities made it harder for them to move away from drought or flood (Figure 5.9).

A classic example of such vulnerability comes from the north coast of Peru, where the Moche civilization flourished around A.D. 400, ruled by pow-erful, authoritarian warrior-priests (see Figure 1.9). The Moche survived in one of the driest environments on earth by using elaborate irrigation schemes to harness spring runoff from the Andes in coastal river valleys. Everything depended on ample mountain floodwaters. When drought occurred, the Moche suffered.

The Quelccaya ice cap in the Cordillera Occidental of the southern Peruvian highlands lies in the same zone of seasonal rainfall as the moun-tains above Moche country. Two ice cores drilled in the summit of the ice cap in 1983 provide a record of variations in rainfall over 1,500 years, and, indirectly, an impression of the amount of runoff that would have reached lowland river valleys during cycles of wet and dry years. In the southern highlands, El Niño episodes have been tied to intense short-term droughts in the region, also on the nearby *altiplano*, the high-altitude plains around Lake Titicaca. The appearance of such drought events in the ice cores may reflect strong El Niño events in the remote past. However, it is more produc-tive to look at long-term dry and wet cycles.

The two ice cores, 508 and 537 feet (154.8 and 163.6 m) long, each yielded clear layering and annual dust layers that reflected the yearly cycle of wet and dry seasons, the latter bringing dust particles from the arid lands of the west to the high Andes: They are accurate to within about 20 years. The cores show clear indications of long-term rainfall variations. A short drought occurred between A.D. 534 and 540. Then, between A.D. 563 and 594, a three-decade drought cycle settled over the mountains and lowlands, with annual rainfall as much as 30 percent below normal. Abundant rainfall resumed in 602, giving way to another drought between A.D. 636 and 645.

The 30-year drought of A.D. 563 to 594 drastically reduced the amount of runoff reaching coastal communities. The effect of a 25 or 30 percent reduc-tion in the water supply would have been catastrophic, especially to farm-ers near the coast, well downstream from the mountains. Moche society

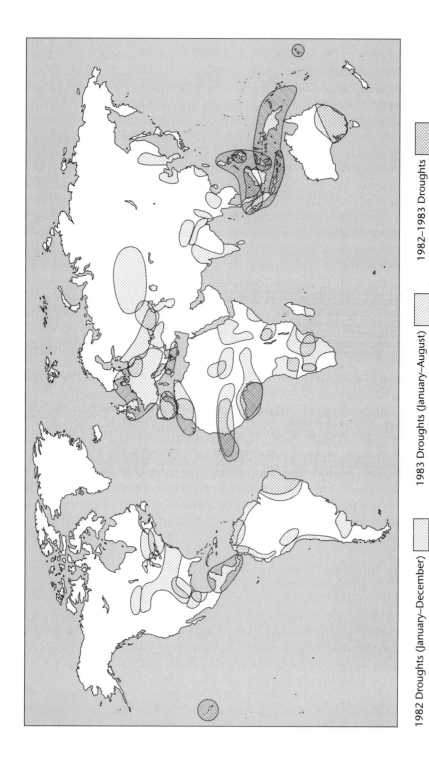

1982 Droughts (January–December) ▨   1983 Droughts (January–August) ▨   1982–1983 Droughts ▨

FIGURE 5.9 The worldwide effects of a strong El Niño, reconstructed on the basis of the 1982/1983 event. We can assume that generally similar effects were experienced over the past 5,000 years. *(Michael Glantz. Courtesy of Cambridge University Press.)*

apparently prospered until the mid sixth century's severe drought cycle. As the drought intensified, the diminished runoff barely watered the rich farming lands far downstream. Miles of laboriously maintained irrigation canals remained dry. Blowing sand cascaded into empty ditches. By the third or fourth year, as the drought lowered the water table far below normal, thousands of acres of farmland received so weak a river flow that unflushed salt accumulated in the soil. Crops withered. Fortunately, the coastal fisheries still provided ample fish meal—until a strong El Niño came along without warning, bringing warmer waters and torrential rains to the desert and mountains.

We do not know the exact years during the long drought when strong El Niños struck, but we can be certain that they did. We can also be sure they hit at a moment when Moche civilization was in crisis, grain supplies running low, irrigation systems sadly depleted, malnutrition widespread, and confidence in the rulers' divine powers much diminished. The warmer waters of the El Niño reduced anchovy harvests in many places, decimating a staple both of the coastal diet and highland trade. Torrential rains swamped the Andes and coastal plain. The dry riverbeds became raging torrents, carrying everything before them. Levees and canals overflowed and collapsed. The arduous labors of years vanished in a few weeks. Dozens of villages vanished under mud and debris as the farmers' cane and adobe houses collapsed and their occupants drowned. The floods polluted springs and streams, overwhelmed sanitation systems, and stripped thousands of acres of fertile soil. As the water receded and the rivers went down, typhoid and other epidemics swept through the valleys, wiping out entire communities and eroding fertile soils. Infant mortality soared.

The Moche's elaborate irrigation systems created an artificial landscape that supported dense farming populations in the midst of one of the driest deserts on earth, where farming would be impossible without technological ingenuity. The farmers were well aware of the hazards of droughts and El Niños, but technology and irrigation could not guarantee the survival of a highly centralized society driven as much by ideology as pragmatic concerns. There were limits to the climatic shifts Moche civilization could absorb. Ultimately, the Moche ran out of options and their civilization collapsed.

We do not know how long El Niños have oscillated across the globe, but they have descended on Peru for at least 5,000 years. A new generation of climatic researches from ice cores and other data show that short-term climatic shifts played a far more important role in the fate of early civilizations than once realized.

Tree Rings: Studying Southwestern Drought

Many ancient societies lived in environments with unpredictable rainfall, where agriculture was, at best, a chancy enterprise. The ancient peoples of the Southwestern United States farmed their semiarid environment with brilliant skill for more than 3,000 years, developing an extraordinary expertise at water management and plant breeding. One central philosophy of modern-day Pueblo Indian groups surrounds movement, the notion that people have to move to escape drought and survive. Until recently, archaeologists did not fully appreciate the importance of movement in Southwestern life and were at a loss to explain the sudden dispersal of the Anasazi people of Chaco Canyon and the Four Corners region in the twelfth and thirteenth centuries A.D. (See Doing Archaeology box on p. 145.)

The Anasazi dispersal can be better understood by dividing the relationship between climatic change and human behavior into three broad categories. Certain obvious stable elements in the Anasazi environment have not changed over the past 2,000 years, such as bedrock geology and climate type. Then there are low-frequency environmental changes—those that occur on cycles longer than a human generation of 25 years. Few people witnessed these changes during their lifetimes. Changes in hydrological conditions such as cycles of erosion and deposition along stream courses, fluctuations in water table levels in river floodplains, and changes in plant distributions transcend generations, but they could affect the environment drastically, especially in drought cycles.

Shorter-term, high-frequency changes were readily apparent to every Anasazi: year-to-year rainfall shifts, decade-long drought cycles, seasonal changes, and so on. Over the centuries, the Anasazi were probably barely aware of long-term change, because the present generation and its immediate ancestors experienced the same basic adaptation, which one could call a form of "stability." Cycles of drought, unusually heavy rains, and other high-frequency changes required temporary and flexible adjustments, such as farming more land, relying more heavily on wild plant foods, and, above all, movement across the terrain.

Such strategies worked well for centuries, as long as the Anasazi farmed their land at well below its carrying capacity. When the population increased to near carrying capacity, however, as it did at Chaco Canyon in the twelfth century, people became increasingly vulnerable to brief events such as El Niños or droughts, which could stretch the supportive capacity of a local environment within months, even weeks. Their vulnerability was even more extreme when long-term changes—such as a half-century or more of much drier conditions—descended on farming lands already pushed to their carrying limits. Under these circumstances, a yearlong drought or torrential rains could quickly destroy a local population's ability to support itself. So, the people dispersed into other areas, where there was ample soil and better water supplies. Without question, the Anasazi dispersed from Mesa Verde and Chaco Canyon because drought forced them to do so. Unlike the Moche in distant Peru, they had the flexibility to move away.

The coming decades will see a revolution in our understanding of ancient environments and short-term climatic change, as scientists acquire a closer knowledge both of climates in the past and of the still little known forces that drive the global weather machine. Like our predecessors, we still live in the Ice Age, which, some estimates calculate, will bring renewed

♛ DOING ARCHAEOLOGY

Climate Variability in the Ancient Southwest

Dendrochronologies for the Anasazi are now accurate to within a year, giving us the most precise time scale for any early human society anywhere. In recent years, the Laboratory of Tree-Ring Research at the University of Arizona has undertaken a massive dendroclimatic study that has yielded a reconstruction of relative climatic variability in the Southwest from A.D. 680 to 1970. The same scientists, headed by Jeffrey Dean, are now producing the first quantitative reconstructions of annual and seasonal rainfall, also of temperature, drought, and stream flow for the region. Such research involves not only tree-ring sequences but intricate mathematical expressions of the relationships between tree growth and such variables as rainfall, temperature, and crop yields. These calculations yield statistical estimations of the fluctuations in these variables on an annual and seasonal basis.

By using a spatial grid of 27 long tree-ring sequences from throughout the Southwest, Dean and his colleagues have compiled maps which plot the different station values and their fluctuations like contour maps, one for each decade. This enables them to study such phenomena as the progress of what Dean sometimes calls the "Great Drought" of A.D. 1276 to 1299 from northwest to southeast across the region. In 1276, the beginnings of the drought appear as negative standard deviations from average rainfall in the northwest, while the remainder of the region experiences above-average rainfall. During the next 10 years, very dry conditions expand over the entire Southwest before improved rainfall arrives after 1299. This form of mapping allows close correlation of vacated large and small pueblos with short-term climatic fluctuations (Figure 5.10).

When the research team looked at the entire period from A.D. 966 to 1988, they found that the tree-ring stations in the northwestern region accounted for no less than 60 percent of the rainfall variance. In contrast, stations in the southeastern part of the Southwest accounted for only 10 percent. This general configuration, which persisted for centuries, coincides with the modern distribution of seasonal rainfall in the Southwest: Predictable summer rainfall dominates the southeastern areas, while the northwest receives both winter and summer precipitation. Winter rains are much more uncertain. When the scientists examined this general rainfall pattern at 100-year intervals from 539 to 1988, they observed that it persisted most of the time, even though the boundary between the two zones moved backward and forward slightly.

But this long-term pattern broke down completely from A.D. 1250 to 1450, when a totally aberrant pattern prevailed in the northwest. The southeast remained stable, but there was major disruption elsewhere. For nearly two centuries, the relatively simple long-term pattern of summer and winter rains gave way to complex, unpredictable precipitation and severe droughts, especially on the Colorado Plateau. This change to an unstable pattern would have had a severe impact on Anasazi farmers, especially since it coincided with the Great Drought of A.D. 1250 to 1299.

(Continued)

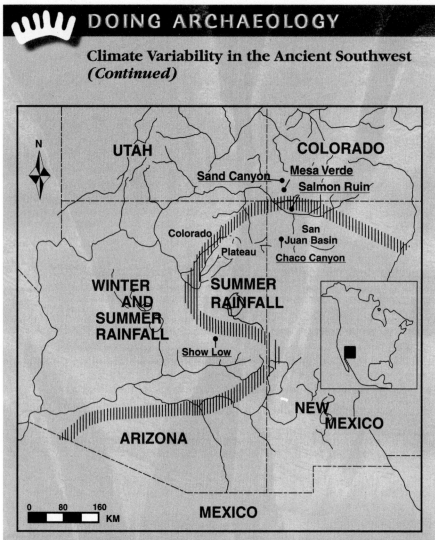

FIGURE 5.10 The climatic regimes of the American Southwest, showing the general configuration of rainfall across the region reconstructed with tree rings. The northwest receives both summer and winter rainfall, the southeast only predictable summer rainfall.

glacial conditions in about 23,000 years time. So it is hardly surprising that, like our forebears, we have had to adjust to constant short-term climatic changes. And, as humanly induced global warming accelerates, these changes may become more frequent and violent, spelling danger for an overpopulated world.

RECONSTRUCTING HUMANLY
CAUSED ENVIRONMENTAL CHANGE

One of the great myths of history proclaims that most preindustrial societies lived in exquisite ecological balance with their natural environments. While it is true that the imprint of a small forager group on the landscape is rarely catastrophic, many early societies used fire to burn off dead grass and stimulate new growth for game to feed on or to grow edible grasses, with long-term effects on the natural vegetation. However, the relationship between humans and their environments changed dramatically with the advent of agriculture and animal domestication.

Back in 1944, a Danish botanist named Johannes Iverson noticed that pollen diagrams from Scandinavian bogs showed a dramatic falloff in forest cover at about the time when farmers first settled in northern Europe. Simultaneously, pollen counts for grasses of all kinds rose rapidly. He also found evidence for *Plantago lanceolata*, a little-known weed that grows on cultivated fields. Iverson's discovery produced confirmation of the changes wrought by forest clearance. Herds of grazing animals can also change the landscape dramatically. Goats, for example, are voracious feeders, who can strip bushes and trees and tear out plants by their roots. Many archaeologists believe that the natural environment of southwestern Asia was stripped of much tree and natural grass cover by overgrazing a few centuries after animal domestication. (See Site box on p. 148.)

Like mollusks, beetles can provide remarkably precise information about the habitats in which they flourished. Many species feed off specific host plants, some of which grow as a result of human activity. There are, for example, distinct beetle forms associated with stored and decaying organic material such as human feces or food. When another British archaeologist, Francis Pryor, discovered an artificial platform of 1350 B.C. in the middle of waterlogged *Flag Fen* in eastern England, he was anxious to discover if the jumble of ancient timbers in the midst of the water included actual dwellings. Biologist Mark Robinson took core samples from organic sediments adjacent to the platform and from sealed layers on the structure itself. The beetles from the side samples were predominantly those that flourished in marsh habitats and in stagnant water. Robinson also found the remains of dung beetles, which feed on cattle droppings. The same species came from the platform itself, but no insects that typically feed on damp thatch, old straw, stored grain, or foul matter such as settlement refuse were found. Robinson concluded that there were no active human settlements within 164 feet (50 m) of any of his samples. He also believes the timbers became waterlogged rapidly, because they contained almost no woodworm beetles which feast off fresh, dry wood.

In the American Southwest, archaeologists now have a regional pollen sequence that provides not only climatic information but also valuable facts

SITE

Environmental Archaeology at Easton Down, England

Obtaining evidence of ancient landscapes requires careful excavation and sample collection, most often of the original land surfaces under burial mounds and earthworks. When archaeologist Alisdair Whittle excavated some test trenches into a burial mound at *Easton Down* in southern England, he exposed the original land surface, also the core of stacked turves, chalk, and topsoil under the mound, which gave him an unusual opportunity to obtain a portrait of the local vegetation in about 3200 B.C. First, he turned to pollen analysis. Small amounts of pollen grains from the land surface were predominantly from grasses, showing that no woodland grew close to the tumulus when it was built. A well-sealed section of the pre-mound soil yielded 11 mollusk samples, which chronicled a dramatic change from woodland to open grassland forms over a short period of time. Whittle located an ancient tree hollow under the mound, which, hardly surprisingly, contained woodland mollusks. A sudden increase in open-country mollusks followed, a change so rapid that human clearance of the land seems the only logical explanation. Interestingly, soil scientists found signs of lateral movement of the soil below the mound, which can have resulted only from cultivation before the mound was built.

Excavations such as Easton Down can only give us snapshots of the complex mosaic of cleared and uncleared land that characterizes any agricultural landscape. For example, mollusks and soil samples under the famous stone circles at Avebury, near Easton Down, tell us that the great temple of 2550 B.C. rose on long-established but little-grazed natural grassland close to a forest that had generated after being cleared for farming (see Figure 6.1).

This kind of environmental archaeology is now so precise that we can fix the exact seasons when monuments were built or buildings erected. For example, soil samples from carefully cut sod laid under the original ground surface of 130-foot (40-m) Silbury Hill, built in about 2200 B.C. close to Easton Down, show that the builders started work in the late summer, most likely after the harvest when people had time for construction work. We know this because the well-preserved sods contain ants and anthills. The ants were beginning to grow wings and fly away from their anthills, as they do in late summer.

about the functions of different pueblo rooms and different foods that were eaten by the inhabitants. Identifying cultural activities from pollen archaeological sites can be extremely tricky, for the tiny grains can be transported to a site in many ways—by wind, water, rodents, even by people bringing ripe fruit home. Sometimes, too, people will use surface soil from neighboring areas, complete with its pollen content, to make house floors. Some species such as the sunflower have heavy pollen that can cling to ripe fruit. Such factors are likely to contaminate the pollen samples from many sites, and unless researchers have other plant evidence, such as, say, squash rind or seeds, it becomes difficult to confirm the palynological data.

The most powerful reconstructions come from a combination of lines of evidence. The medieval town at Uppsala, Sweden, was burnt down in 1543, leaving a treasure trove of ecological data for archaeologists. A team of researchers studied the wood, mollusks, and plant remains, as well as the insects, which were among the most informative ecological finds. Magnus Hellqvist and Geoffrey Lemdahl identified 81 insect forms dating from the twelfth to fifteenth centuries, almost all of them were beetles found in a row of oak barrels. The beetles were varieties that flourished in moist habitats, open areas, and cultivated fields, suggesting the settlement of mainly farm buildings lay in an open landscape. Several of them were species that live in habitats in and around farm buildings, suggesting that towns such as Uppsala were more rural than urban. Some of the beetles do not occur as far north as Uppsala today, suggesting that summers were one or two degrees warmer than the 63°F (17°C) of modern times, which is not surprising, for the history of the town spans the end of the medieval warm period of A.D. 900 to 1300 as well as the subsequent Little Ice Age.

SUMMARY

The study of long- and short-term climatic and environmental change is of vital importance to archaeologists concerned with human societies' changing relationships with their surroundings. This chapter describes ways of studying such changes. Geoarchaeology is a multidisciplinary approach to the study of human adaptations that reconstructs ancient landscapes using such approaches as remote sensing and paleographic and biological methods, including pollen analysis. Deep-sea cores and ice drillings provide us with a broad framework of climatic change during the Pleistocene (Ice Age) era that chronicle at least nine glacial periods during the past 730,000 years. The Pleistocene itself is divided into three broad subdivisions, the last of which coincides with the spread of modern humans across the world from Africa. The Holocene covers postglacial times and witnessed not only global warming but at least three short periods of much colder conditions. The Younger Dryas brought drought and cold conditions and may have helped trigger the development of agriculture in southwestern Asia. The catastrophic flooding of the Black Sea lake in approximately 5500 B.C. by salt water from the Mediterranean caused major population movements in Europe. Short-term events such as El Niños and drought cycles are studied with the aid of ice cores, geological observations, and tree rings, methods which are achieving increasing precision. We are now beginning to realize that short-term climatic change played a vital role in the rise and fall of many human societies.

KEY TERMS

Eustatic

Geoarchaeology

Holocene

Isostatic

Loess

Periglacial

Pleistocene

Pollen analysis (palynology)

Quaternary

GUIDE TO FURTHER READING

Butzer, Karl. 1974. *Environment and Archaeology.* 3rd ed. Hawthorne, NY: Aldine.

————. 1982. *Archaeology as Human Ecology.* Cambridge: Cambridge University Press.
    Butzer's two books are still fundamental sources on geoarchaeology and environmental reconstruction, even if outdated in detail.

Fagan, Brian. 1999. *Floods, Famines, and Emperors: El Niño and the Fate of Civilizations.* New York: Basic Books.
    A popular account of the potential of climatic change for explaining culture change in the past.

Roberts, Neil. 1989. *The Holocene: An Environmental History.* Oxford: Blackwell.
    An excellent introduction to postglacial climate change for general readers.

PART III

@

DISCOVERY

I'd found that to say:"This was made three thousand years ago" now hardly stirred my sense of time at all. But I thought of it this way: the little head, wedged in that rubble, up against a ruined wall in this silent, sunny place in Egypt, had been lying there, face downwards, while Troy was burning; while Sennacherib was ransacking cities beyond his borders; on through the slow centuries, while the greatness of Athens came and went, and Christ lived out his days.... On and on through the years, until this hot afternoon when the brush and knife came nearer and nearer to it through the yielding rubble, until it stirred, dropped, and lay once again in a warm human hand.

ARCHAEOLOGIST MARY CHUBB, 1954, AFTER DISCOVERING
A SMALL FIGURINE AT EL-AMARNA, EGYPT, IN THE 1930S.

CHAPTER 6
Finding the Past

Ishtar Gate at Babylon. c. 580 B.C. (Source: Hirmer Fotoarchiv.)

In 1649, a gentleman antiquarian named John Aubrey galloped into the middle of the village of *Avebury* in southern England while hunting foxes (Figure 6.1). He found himself surrounded by a deep ditch and mysterious, weathered stones erected in a circle inside the earthwork. Aubrey was "wonderfully surprized at the sight of these vast stones, of which I had never heard before" and returned later to sketch and explore (Fagan 1998, 117). Today, the Avebury stone circles are one of the most famous archaeological sites in Europe.

Aubrey never excavated at Avebury, but he made the first survey of one of Britain's most remarkable sacred monuments. He speculated that it was built by ancient Britains, "who were, I suppose, two or three degrees less savage than the Americans."

Some archaeological sites, such as the Pyramids of Giza in Egypt or the stone circles at Stonehenge, 23 miles (37 km) south of Avebury (see Figures 2.5 and 2.6), are so conspicuous that they have never been "discovered" by archaeologists. Avebury was well known to local farmers in Aubrey's day, but he was the first person to draw the site to the attention of a wider scientific community. Earthworks, burial mounds, and entire cities are relatively easy to find, for they form an easily identified part of the modern landscape. But how do archaeologists locate inconspicuous Stone Age foraging camps, tiny early farming villages, and sites that appear to leave no traces on the surface whatsoever? This chapter describes how archaeologists find archaeological sites.

Until recently, people went into the field to find and excavate "important" sites, places where they were guaranteed a large number of artifacts. Today,

FIGURE 6.1 The great stone circle at Avebury, England. *(Courtesy of the Robert Harding Picture Library.)*

excavation is the strategy of last resort, as the archaeological record is vanishing rapidly in the face of modern industrial expansion. Archaeological survey has assumed much greater importance in recent years, as the focus of much research has turned away from the individual site to entire areas and regions. In part, also, this is because cultural resource management usually involves small- or large-scale field survey.

Modern archaeological survey methods are highly sophisticated and make use of high technology such as satellite imagery and ground-penetrating radar to amplify foot surveys and research on the ground. All of these approaches make up what is often called **nonintrusive archaeology,** field research without excavation that does not disturb the archaeological record.

FINDING ARCHAEOLOGICAL SITES

How do you find an archaeological site? Many archaeological sites can be spotted from a long distance away: the Parthenon in Athens, Stonehenge in southern Britain, the elaborate mounds and earthworks at *Cahokia* in southern Illinois (see Figure 7.19). My first survey experience was in the white chalk country of southern England, where farmers have tilled the soil for more than 6,000 years. But we were looking for much earlier human occupation—for Stone Age foragers, who had ranged over the area at least 2,000 years before that. They left few traces of their presence behind them, since

they were constantly on the move and had relatively few imperishable artifacts. We walked over acres of freshly plowed muddy fields, looking for telltale signs of human activity: fresh rabbit burrows with sharp-edged stone
tools thrown up in the debris, scatters of tiny stone arrow barbs on the plow
land. After three days, we had located one possible site. Discouraging, perhaps, but a reflection of the difficulties of finding archaeological sites.

Archaeological sites manifest themselves in many ways: in the form of
tells, which are mounds of occupation debris; middens, which are mounds
of food remains and occupation debris; or conspicuous caves or temples. But
many others are far less easily located, perhaps displaying no more than a
small scatter of stone tools or a patch of discolored soil. I once surveyed an
area on the banks of Uganda's Victoria Nile River where the archaeological
sites were nothing more than concentrations of white quartz arrow barbs,
scrapers, and flaking debris. Fortunately, the vegetation was low and we
could see the clusters of quartz fragments from some distance away. On
another occasion, I searched for ancient shell middens on the coasts of Santa
Cruz Island in southern California from a boat close inshore. We could spot
the middens from the stunted grass and light gray soil that marked them from
yards away. Still other sites leave no traces of their presence above the ground
and may come to light only when the subsoil is disturbed, such as the temple of Ehecatl-Quetzalcoatl, found during excavation of Mexico City's Metro
line (Figure 6.2).

FIGURE 6.2 Temple of the Aztec god Ecehatl-Quetzalcoatl unearthed during the
construction of the Mexico City Metro and exhibited in the Pino-Suarez station
forecourt. *(Courtesy of Lesley Newhart.)*

Finding archaeological sites is a matter of common sense and patience, of putting yourself into the mind's eye of the original inhabitants, who had good reasons to settle where they did. Every archaeologist has to develop a keen sense of landscape and a close familiarity with the local environment for then archaeological sites are easier to find.

CHANCE DISCOVERIES

Deep plowing, highway construction, strip-mining, and urban renewal are churning the world's soil like never before. (See Discovery box below.) In the course of such activities, countless archaeological sites have come to light, many of them destroyed, alas, before archaeologists learn of them. CRM archaeologists spend much of their time investigating accidental discoveries made in the course of such projects as airport expansion. Federal and state law in the United States now mandates archaeological investigations before construction or other disturbance begins on publically owned

DISCOVERY

African-American Burial Ground, New York

In 1991, the federal government planned to build a 34-story office building in the heart of Lower Manhattan, New York. The responsible agency, the General Services Administration (GSA), retained a team of archaeologists to study the cleared site. When they examined eighteenth-century city maps of the area, they found what surveyors of the day called a "Negro Burial Ground" had existed at this location. The experts assumed that the basements of nineteenth-century buildings had destroyed most of, if not all, the graves in the abandoned cemetery, so it was safe to proceed with construction. Six weeks before the contractors were due to move in, the GSA hired another group of archaeologists to check the lot in case one or two odd burials remained. Dozens of undisturbed burials appeared over the next two months. Four hundred twenty graves, often stacked one on top of the other, came from one small portion of the cemetery alone. Intense controversy exploded over the discovery, as New York's black community expressed outrage at the way in which the survey and excavations had been handled without consultation with African Americans. Eventually, the skeletons were handed over to biological anthropologist Michael Blakey of Howard University for study and eventual reburial.

Few archaeological discoveries are as controversial as the African Burial Ground, where much bitterness and political activity could have been avoided by more thorough field research well ahead of time. Nevertheless, this celebrated find highlights the great complexity of archaeological survey, especially in urban areas, where historical records and sites of all kinds form a tangled archive for the modern scholar. Extensive archaeological research is under way in many of the world's largest cities, among them Amsterdam, London, and San Francisco.

land and on private property if government funds are involved. Many cities and counties have similar regulations, designed to prevent the destruction of chance finds.

Nature sometimes uncovers sites for us, which may then be spotted by a sharp-eyed archaeologist looking for natural exposures of likely geological strata. Erosion, flooding, tidal waves, low lake levels, earthquakes, and wind action are just some of the processes that uncover the past. A massive earth movement over 100,000 years ago created Olduvai Gorge in Tanzania's rolling Serengeti Plains, exposing hundreds of feet of ancient lake beds dating to early in the Ice Age. In 1907, a German butterfly hunter named Wilhelm Kattwinkel literally fell into the gorge while chasing his quarry and found fossil animal bones in the lake beds. A quarter-century later, the famous paleoanthropologist Louis Leakey unearthed Stone Age axes at Olduvai, which is now famous for its early human occupations and fossils dating back at least 2 million years (Figure 6.3).

Many spectacular finds result from human activity. In June 1968, a detachment of China's People's Liberation Army on patrol among the barren hills near Man-Zh'ieng in central China stumbled on a subterranean burial chamber. They found themselves inside a vast rock-cut sepulcher, where their flashlights caught the glint of gold, silver, and jade. Bronze and clay pots stood in orderly rows. Fortunately, for science, the soldiers reported their find to the Academy of Sciences in Beijing, which had experts on-site in hours. They rapidly identified the tomb as that of Liu Sheng, a prominent Han nobleman, elder brother of the emperor, and governor of the Principality of Zhou-shan until his death in 113 B.C. A few days later, the tomb of Liu

FIGURE 6.3   Olduvai Gorge, Tanzania. *(Courtesy of the Institute of Human Origins, Arizona State University, Tempe, Arizona.)*

Sheng's wife Tou Wan came to light nearby. The Han emperors were the longest-lived dynasty of Chinese rulers, assuming power in 206 B.C. and reigning for 400 years. Han rulers developed the Great Silk Road across Central Asia and sent trading missions deep into Southeast Asia, making China a major power. The two tombs reflected the prestige and wealth of a man and woman at the pinnacle of Han society (see Figure 2.8). Both wore jade suits made of hundreds of thin plaques sewn together with gold wire (jade was associated with immortality).

I, myself, was involved in a spectacular accidental discovery in 1960, when workers building a water-pumping station in Central Africa's Middle Zambezi Valley uncovered some richly decorated human skeletons atop a low hill called *Ingombe Ilede* close to the river. Archaeologist James Chaplin excavated 11 graves from the hilltop under very difficult conditions as construction workers stood by. The burials were of young men in their twenties, who wore cotton raiment and fine bronze wire bangles on their arms and legs. One man in his late twenties was adorned with fine strings of 18-carat gold beads and thousands of imported glass beads. He was a skilled wire maker, for his tools lay close to his head, along with lengths of copper wire and cross-shaped ingots. He wore nine *Conus* shells, a seashell imported from the Indian Ocean coast 600 miles (965 km) away, each worth a fortune in elephant ivory or slaves as recently as the nineteenth century. I returned to the site some months later to carry out further excavations, which radiocarbon dated the richly decorated burials to about A.D. 1450, a time of active gold and ivory trading between the East African coast and the Zambezi Valley just before Portuguese explorers arrived in southeast Africa in 1497. Ingombe Ilede, an accidental discovery, has thrown much light on early trading in the depths of the African interior.

Sometimes, archaeologists have the opportunity to work alongside construction workers in the expectation that chance discoveries will come to light. The construction of Mexico City's 26-mile (42-km) Metro subway system yielded a wealth of archaeological material. Mexico City was built on the site of Tenochtitlán, the capital city of the Aztecs, destroyed by Spanish conquistador Hernan Cortés in 1521. Little remains on the surface today of the once-great city, but construction work yielded more than 40 tons of pottery, 380 burials, and even a small temple dedicated to the Aztec wind god Ehecatl, which was preserved on its original site in the Pino Suárez Metro station (Figure 6.2). The archaeologists on the project were authorized to stop tunneling if a find came to light, so many important chance discoveries were saved.

FIELD SURVEY

Famous archaeological sites such as the Parthenon have never been lost (see Figure 1.8). The Acropolis at Athens was remembered even when Athens itself had become an obscure medieval village. The temples of ancient

Egyptian Thebes were famous as long ago as Roman times and have never vanished from historical consciousness. Other sites, such as Homeric Troy, were celebrated in classical literature, but Troy's precise location at *Hissarlik* in northwestern Turkey only came to light with Heinrich Schliemann's excavations in 1871.

Of course, most of the world's archaeological sites are far less conspicuous than the Parthenon, and unlike Troy, they have no historical records to testify to their existence. The early antiquarians discovered sites primarily by locating burial mounds, stone structures, hill forts, and other conspicuous traces of prehistoric human works on the European landscape. The tells of the Near East, occupied by generation after generation of city dwellers, were easily recognized by early travelers, and the temples and monuments of ancient Egypt have attracted antiquarian and plunderer alike for many centuries. New World archaeological sites such as Teotihuacán were described by some of the first conquistadors. Maya sites were vividly cataloged by John Lloyd Stephens and Frederick Catherwood in the mid-nineteenth century (see Figure 1.5).

Site survey did not become a serious part of archaeology until field archaeologists began to realize that people had lived their lives against the background of an ever changing natural landscape, modified both by climatic and other ecological changes and by human activities. Most early archaeological survey sought individual sites for eventual excavation. But as archaeologists have grown more intent on studying variability in the archaeological record, they have come to deal with entire regions rather than individual sites. The objectives of survey also have partly shifted. Although archaeologists still search for sites to excavate, most do so within an entirely different theoretical framework. Also, a great deal of archaeological survey is now conducted as part of cultural resource management, which relies heavily both on electronic detection methods and careful fieldwork.

Today, **surface surveying** is one of the most important components of archaeological investigation, for it is concerned with the archaeological record of ancient settlement patterns, with ancient peoples' imprints on the land. Site survey seeks to identify ancient landscapes, which are far more than merely site dots or settlement patterns plotted on a map. A landscape is both material and symbolic, for every society has given meaning to its surroundings. For example, the Avebury stone circles never functioned in isolation. They were part of a much wider landscape and a complex relationship between living people, the forces of the spiritual world, the ancestors, and the environment. Landscapes are created by symbol and language and are the spatial and material manifestation of the relationships between humans and their environments. Archaeologists have only the material remains of such relationships to study, so many of them refer to **landscape signatures,** the material imprints left on the earth's surface by specific human groups. Archaeological sites and other signs of ancient human activity of all kinds are the surviving material remains of these imprints as they have changed and developed over centuries and millennia.

Under this approach, settlement sites are not the only landscape signatures. In recent years archaeologists have paid special attention to what they call **offsite areas,** places with a low density of artifacts. Some of these locations may not, indeed, qualify as sites. But such areas are of vital importance, especially when studying hunter-gatherers or herders, who enjoyed highly mobile lifeways and left few traces behind them. Offsite evidence can include scatters of artifacts, ancient plow marks, and even entire field systems that can only be spotted from telltale traces visible in aerial photographs. At *Céide Fields* in northwestern Ireland, described in Chapter 10, more than 5,000 acres (2,023 ha) of field systems dating to about 5000 B.C. are still preserved under peat, and they are as revealing about the society that created them as their houses and settlements (see Figure 10.1).

With all archaeological survey, the issue is not just site distributions, but the uses which ancient societies made of an ever changing landscape. Like experts on ancient scripts, we are in the decipherment business, but our "script" is a mosaic of sites and many other conspicuous, and inconspicuous, remains of human activity.

Approaches to Archaeological Survey

Most archaeological sites are discovered by careful field surveying and thorough examination of the countryside for both conspicuous and inconspicuous traces of the past. A survey can vary from searching a city lot for historic structures or a tiny river valley with a few rock shelters in its walls to a large-scale survey of an entire river basin or water-catchment area—a project that would take several years to complete. For all these, the theoretical ideal is the same: to recover all traces of ancient settlement in the survey area.

Many people make a fundamental distinction between two types of survey:

- **Reconnaissance survey** is just that, a preliminary examination of a survey area to identify major sites, to assess the potential, and to establish tentative site distributions. Reconnaissance survey also involves background research, such as examining archives if historical properties are involved, and acquiring general environmental information.
- **Intensive survey** is a systematic, detailed field survey that covers an entire area. It may include subsurface testing.

Most surveys are in the reconnaissance category, especially if large areas are involved. However, many CRM projects involve intensive survey of small areas such as a road corridor or a single city lot. (See Doing Archaeology box on p. 161.)

No surface survey, however thorough and however sophisticated its remote-sensing devices, will achieve complete coverage. The key to effective archaeological surveying lies in proper research designs and in rigorous sampling techniques to provide a reliable basis of probability for extending the findings of the survey from a sample zone to a wider region. A great deal depends, too, on the intensity of the survey in the field. The survey area can

Basic Types of Ground Survey

Michael Schiffer of the University of Arizona identifies four basic types of intensive ground survey:

1. *Conspicuous and accessible sites* are located by superficial survey, such as that by Catherwood and Stephens with Maya sites in the Yucatán in the 1840s (see Figure 1.5). The investigator visits only very conspicuous and accessible sites of great size and considerable fame.

2. *Relatively conspicuous sites* at accessible locations are studied in the next level of survey, assisted by local informants such as landowners. This approach was used frequently in the 1930s for the classic river basin surveys in the lower Mississippi Valley, when archaeologists worked on Depression-era survey projects. This approach, while effective, gives a rather narrow view of the archaeological sites in an area.

3. *Limited-area survey* involves door-to-door inquiries, supported by actual substantiation of claims that a site exists by checking the report on the ground. This type of survey, with its built-in system of verification, may yield more comprehensive information on sites. But it still does not give the most critical information of all, data on the ratios of one site type to another, nor does it assess the percentage of accessible sites that have been found.

4. *Intensive foot survey* is when a party of archaeologists covers an entire area by walking over it, perhaps with a set interval between members of the party. This is about the most rigorous method of survey, but it does work. When Paul Martin and Fred Plog surveyed 5.2 square miles (13.5 sq. km) of the Hay Hollow Valley in east-central Arizona in 1967, they supervised a team of eight people who walked back and forth over small portions of the area. Workers were 30 feet (9 m) from each other, their pathways carefully laid out with compass and stakes. Two hundred fifty sites were recorded by this survey, at the cost of 30 person-days per square mile. One would think every site would have been recorded. Yet two entirely new sites were discovered in the same area in 1969 and 1971: prehistoric irrigation canals were spotted by an expert on some aerial photographs, and some sandstone quarry sites were also found.

As we have said, the chances of any archaeological survey recording every site in even a small area are remote. Obviously, though, total survey of an area is desirable, and sometimes nearly total coverage can be achieved by combining remote sensing and ground survey. The excavators of the Roman town of *Wroxeter* in central England are surveying the topography of the now-vanished town using a combination of aerial photographs and ground survey. Volunteers are taking measurements every 33 feet (10 m) and combining their survey with systematic surface collections of potsherds and other finds (Figure 6.4).

FIGURE 6.4 Foot survey in the hinterland of Roman Wroxeter, England.

be traversed by automobile, horseback, mule, camel, bicycle, or—most effectively—foot. Footwork is important, for it enables the archaeologist to acquire an eye for topography and the relationships of human settlement to the landscape.

The most successful survey projects combine several approaches, which is the method used by the research teams who have surveyed the hinterland of the Maya city at Copán, Honduras, in recent years. William Sanders and his colleagues carried out a famous long-term archaeological survey of the Basin of Mexico in which they elected to try locating every site in the area over many seasons of fieldwork (see Chapter 10). At the end of the project, Sanders argued that this approach was far more effective than any sampling of the area, for it gave a much clearer picture of site variability on the ground. Undoubtedly he is right, if one has the time and the money. In these days of limited budgets and short-term archaeological contracts dictated by impending site destruction, the archaeologist has turned to both remote sensing and statistical sampling to achieve goals of the survey.

Sampling in Archaeological Survey

Very few archaeological surveys are limited to areas small enough that one can cover every corner of the survey area. Dictates of time and sheer economy and the demands of cultural resource management warrant the use of statistical sampling methods. Sampling techniques enable us to ensure a statistically reliable basis of archaeological data from which we can make generalizations about our research data, the assumption being that the sample observations are a mathematical representation of the whole.

Few modern archaeological surveys fail to make use of sampling, for archaeologists are only too aware that many site distributions reflect the distribution of archaeologists rather than an unbiased sampling of the archaeological record. This bias applies particularly in densely vegetated areas such as the Mesoamerican and Amazonian rainforests, where the cover is so thick that even new roads are in constant danger of being overgrown. It is no coincidence that most archaeological sites found in rainforests are near well-trodden roads and tracks. The early archaeologists located sites by following narrow paths through the forest cut by chicleros, local people who collected resin from forest trees and guided researchers to sites. Even today, archaeologists can pass right through the middle of a large site in the forest or within a few feet of a huge pyramid and see nothing. Some years ago, I visited the Maya center at *Naranjo* in Guatemala, only a few miles from the great city of Tikal. As we walked though the overgrown center of the huge site, all I could see were the earthen slopes of pyramids and platforms on either side, which vanished into the tree canopy. Without a plan in hand, I could never gain an overall impression of the site, which was mantled in dense forest.

Statistical sampling theory occupies an important place in archaeological research, and some statistical training is now integral to every professional's training. Sampling is an enormous and complex subject which cannot be discussed in detail here. But systematic and carefully controlled sampling of archaeological data is essential if we are to rely heavily, as we do, on statistical approaches in the reconstruction of past lifeways and cultural process. For example, if we are interested in past adaptations to environmental conditions, we must systematically sample many types of sites in each environmental zone, not merely those that look important or seem such as are likely to yield spectacular finds.

Archaeologists generally use probabilistic sampling, a means of relating small samples of data in mathematical ways to much larger populations. A classic example of such sampling is the public opinion poll, which uses a tiny sample, say 1,500 people, to draw more general conclusions on major political issues. In archaeology, probability sampling improves the chance that the conclusions reached on the basis of the sample are relatively reliable. The outcome depends, of course, on very carefully drawn research designs, knowledge of the structure of the sample population, and precisely defined sample units. (See Doing Archaeology box below.)

DOING ARCHAEOLOGY

Probability Sampling Schemes

Three basic probability sampling schemes are common in archaeological survey and excavation:

1. **Simple random sampling** determines the sample size and the area to be sampled, then randomly selects the number of units required with a table of random numbers, numbers being assigned to a grid drawn over the survey area or site. This approach treats all samples as absolutely equal, a useful approach when surveying an unknown area or site.

2. **Systematic random sampling** chooses one unit at random, then selects others at equal intervals from the first one. This is useful for studying artifact patterning on a surface site.

3. **Stratified sampling** is used when sample units are not uniform. The population is divided into separate groups, or strata, which reflect the observed range of variation in certain features, for example, ecological zones, occupation layers, artifact classes, and so on. Such units permit intensive sampling of some units and less-detailed work on others.

Random sampling is the most common sampling strategy used in survey and excavation.

Under ideal circumstances, probabilistic sampling makes for more precise comparisons between and within sites. However, field survey means dealing with such realities as patches of open and thickly vegetated terrain, uncooperative landowners, and urban sprawl. There is rarely a perfect world in the field, so the researcher has to watch carefully for bias in the data and select a sampling strategy that provides a truly representative sample of the total data universe.

REMOTE SENSING

To investigate the past without digging, without destruction of valuable sites, is one of the great archaeological dreams. Maybe the day will one day dawn when we can use highly sophisticated radar to "excavate" a site without disturbing the ground, but we are a long way from that scholarly nirvana at the moment. Nevertheless, nonintrusive archaeology, fieldwork without excavation, is a rapidly growing field, involving increasing use of **remote sensing,** technological ways of locating sites using aerial photography, satellite radar, and other devices. CRM archaeologists make sophisticated use of remote-sensing devices to locate sites and buried features when time is short and much ground has to be investigated.

Aerial Photography

Back in World War I, a handful of archaeologists served as airborne artillery reconnaissance observers on the Western Front and in Mesopotamia. As they gazed down at the trenches, they noticed and photographed outlines of Roman forts and ancient earthworks far below them, many of which were invisible on the ground. Since then, aerial photography has become a staple of archaeological survey. Thousands of hitherto unknown sites have come to light as a result, including entire Roman road systems in North Africa and completely plowed under earthworks that no longer can be seen at the surface. Huge archives of air photographs document well-studied areas such as the Avebury and Stonehenge regions of southern England; they were taken at all times of year, under different lighting conditions, in all weathers—at times of drought and with snow on the ground. Nevertheless, new photographs sometimes turn up additional sites, including a stone circle in the heart of the Avebury earthworks located during a long drought when the ground was exceptionally dry.

Aerial photographs are important archival sources for large-scale regional projects. The archaeologists studying the hinterland of the Roman town at Wroxeter near the Welsh border in central England have drawn on thousands of such pictures as a database of a formerly densely populated Roman landscape (see Figure 10.12).

Aerial photography gives an unrivaled overhead view of the past. Sites can be photographed obliquely or vertically, at different seasons or times of day, and from many directions. Some features, such as earthworks, pueblos, or stone circles, are easily visible. More often, however, the clues are more subtle and involve identifying telltale marks that are almost invisible on the ground.

Shadow Sites Many earthworks and other complex structures have been leveled by plow or erosion, but their reduced topography shows up clearly from the air. The rising or setting sun can cast long shadows, emphasizing the relief of almost-vanished banks or ditches, so that the features of the site stand out in the oblique light.

Crop and Soil Marks   These are found in areas where the subsoil is suitable for revealing differences in soil color and in the richness of crop growth on a particular soil. Such marks cannot be detected easily on the surface, but under favorable circumstances they can be seen clearly from the air. The principle on which the **crop mark** is based is that the growth and color of a crop are mainly determined by the amount of moisture the plant can derive from the soil and the subsoil (Figure 6.5). If the soil depth has been increased by digging features, such as pits and ditches, and then filling them in or by heaping up additional earth to form artificial banks or mounds, crops growing over such abandoned structures are tall and well nourished. The converse is true where topsoil has been removed and the infertile subsoil is near the surface or where impenetrable surfaces such as paved streets are below ground level and crops are stunted. Thus, a dark crop mark can be taken for a ditch or pit, and a lighter line will define a more substantial structure. **Soil marks** result from plowing soil from such features as banks and show up as a color lighter than that of the darker, deeper soil around them.

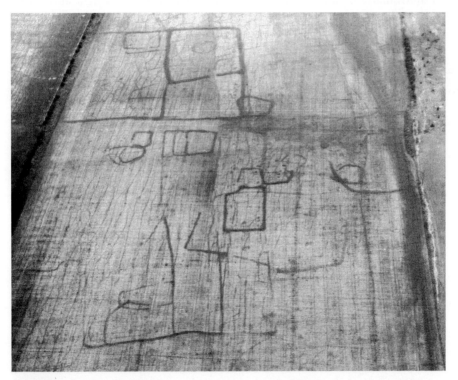

FIGURE 6.5   A crop mark of a series of enclosures at Thorpe in eastern England. Under favorable conditions such marks can be seen clearly from the air. *(Courtesy of the Cambridge University Air Photograph Collection.)*

Most aerial photographs are taken with black-and-white film, which gives definition superior to that of color and is much cheaper to buy and reproduce than color. The wide range of filters that can be used with black and white give the photographer great versatility in the field. Infrared film, which has three layers sensitized to green, red, and infrared, detects reflected solar radiation at the near end of the electromagnetic spectrum, some of which is invisible to the human eye. The different reflections from cultural and natural features are translated by the film into distinctive "false" colors. Bedrock comes up blue on infrared film, but strong grass growth on alluvial plains shows up bright red. Vigorous plant growth showing up red on infrared photographs has been used to track shallow subsurface water sources in the American Southwest where springs were used by ancient peoples.

Air photographs are vital tools for anyone surveying a well-defined region. In the late 1940s, in a pioneer application, Harvard University archaeologist Gordon Willey used a standard Peruvian Air Force photographic mosaic of cultivated valley bottoms and margins of the Virú Valley in northern coastal Peru to survey changing settlement patterns. Employing these photographs as the basis for a master site map of the valley, Willey was able to plot many archaeological features. Three hundred fifteen sites in the Virú Valley were located, many of them stone buildings, walls, or terraces that showed up quite well on the mosaics. Some much less conspicuous sites were also spotted, among them midden heaps without stone walls, refuse mounds that appeared as low hillocks on the photographs, and small pyramidal mounds of insignificant proportions. The aerial photographs enabled Willey and his team to pinpoint many sites before going out in the field. The result was the fascinating story of shifting settlement patterns in Virú over many thousands of years, a classic of its kind.

Willey later applied the same basic approach in the Copán Valley in Honduras, where he plotted distributions of outlying settlements that surrounded the great Maya city. During the 1980s, Pennsylvania State University researchers revised and expanded Willey's survey. They used aerial photographs as part of a long-term mapping project that covered 52 square miles (135 sq. km) of the valley. The survey resulted in the discovery of over 1,400 archaeological sites around Copán's urban core (for more on Copán, see Chapter 10).

Nonphotographic Methods

Archaeological sites can be detected from the air, even from space, by nonphotographic techniques as well. Aerial photography is the last of the "do-it-yourself" types of remote sensing, a technique whose cost is within the reach of even a modest archaeological expedition. Aerial sensor imagery, using aircraft, satellites, and even manned spacecraft, involves instrumentation that is astronomically expensive by archaeological standards. Thus, these exciting techniques are only occasionally used, and then only when the collaboration of NASA and interested experts can be enlisted.

Aircraft-Borne Sensor Imagery Aircraft-borne instrumentation of several types can be used to record images of the electromagnetic radiation that is reflected or emitted from the earth's surface. A multispectral scanner, for example, measures the radiance of the earth's surface along a scan line perpendicular to the aircraft's line of flight. A two-dimensional image is processed digitally. Multispectral scanners are ideal for mapping vegetation and for monitoring bodies of water when more complete data are needed than can be obtained from aerial photographs. Thermal infrared line scanners were originally used for military night survey but now have many applications in the environmental sciences. The line scanners have thermal devices that record an image on photographic film. The temperature data obtained from such scans are combined with aerial photographs to reveal tiny thermal patterns that may indicate different crop uses, the distribution of range animals, or variations in soil moisture and groundwater, both ancient and modern.

Sideways-Looking Airborne Radar (SLAR) This technique senses the terrain to either side of an aircraft's track. It does this by sending out long pulses of electromagnetic radiation. The radar then records the strength and time of the pulse return to detect objects and their range from the aircraft. SLAR has great potential for archaeology because it is not dependent on sunlight. The flying aircraft enables the observer to track the pulse lines in the form of images, no matter what obscures the ground. The SLAR images are normally interpreted visually, using radar mosaics or stereo pairs of images, as well as digital image processors. SLAR was originally used for oil exploration, geology, and geomorphology—applications that could justify its high cost. It is useful for mapping surface soil moisture distributions, something that has great potential for the study of ancient roads such as the ancient Silk Road between China and the West opened by Chinese Han emperors approximately 2,000 years ago.

SLAR can show where many changes in topography have taken place or where the subsoil of large sites has been disturbed. It can also be applied to underwater sites to locate wrecks on the seafloor. So far, applications of this exciting technology to the past have been few and far between, but experiments in the Mesoamerican lowlands have hinted that SLAR may be able to identify buildings beneath dense rainforest canopy. Scans of the Maya lowlands have shown that areas of wet-season swamp often have irregular grids of gray lines in them, multitudes of ladder, lattice, and curvilinear patterns. These have been compared to known ancient canal systems and represent long-forgotten large-scale irrigation schemes.

Surface investigations at *Pulltrouser Swamp* in northern Belize have shown that Maya farmers exploited the edges of seasonally flooded swamps between 200 B.C. and A.D. 850. A rising population of farmers brought under cultivation more than 740 acres (300 ha) of raised field plots, linked with interconnecting canals. These fields were hoed, mulched, and planted with maize, amaranth, and perhaps cotton.

The space shuttle *Columbia* used an imaging radar system to bounce radar signals off the surfaces of the world's major deserts in 1981. This experiment was designed to study the history of the earth's aridity, not archaeology, but it identified bedrock valleys in the limestone up to 20 feet (6 m) under over-lying sand sheets in the eastern Sahara Desert. Such identifications were possible because of the arid deposits. Wetter soils do not permit such deep access, for the water table blocks the radar eye completely. All remote sensing is useless unless checked on the ground, so a team of geologists, including archaeologist C. Vance Haynes of the University of Arizona, journeyed far into the desert to investigate the long-hidden water courses. About the only people to work this terrain were the British army in World War II and Egyptian oil companies. The oil companies kindly arranged for a skip loader to be transported into the desert. To Haynes's astonishment, the skip-loader trenches yielded some 200,000-year-old stone axes, dramatic and unexpected proof that early Stone Age hunter-gatherers had lived in the heart of the Sahara when the landscape was more hospitable than it is today. The Haynes find is of cardinal importance, for African archaeologists now believe that the Sahara was a vital catalyst in early human history that effectively sealed off both archaic and modern Africans from the rest of the Ice Age world for many millennia.

The most accurate space images of all are, of course, in the closely guarded hands of the military. Despite the veil of secrecy, some astonishingly clear black-and-white satellite photographs have proved a bounty to geologists who are expert in analyzing subtle tone, texture, and light reflections given off by rock formations on earth. Herein lies a remarkable bonus for archaeology, for potential hominid fossil beds in Ethiopia and other parts of East Africa can be detected from shuttle images. Only a few years ago, paleoanthropologists such as the Leakeys and Don Johanson could spend months on end combing hundreds of square miles of potentially fossil-bearing landscape just to locate promising deposits. Recently, John Fleagle of the State University of New York at Stony Brook used shuttle photographs to investigate fossil beds in the Fejeji region of the Ethiopian Rift Valley. He returned some months later with some 3.7-million-year-old hominid teeth from one of the earliest *Australopithecus* yet discovered. Ethiopian archaeologists are now using images from space to develop an inventory of potential fossil deposits in their country.

Space technology also allows scientists to explore remote and inaccessible parts of the world. The Arabian peninsula's Rub al Khali, the "Empty Quarter," is one of the most inhospitable desert regions on earth. Few archaeologists had ventured there until NASA scientists at the Jet Propulsion Laboratory used radar imagery from space to delineate hitherto invisible desert tracks where camels had traveled across the desolate landscape. The tracks converged on the long-vanished site of Shisur in Oman, the major center of the frankincense trade from 1000 B.C. to A.D. 400 and possibly the mythical "lost city" of *Ubar*.

Satellite Sensor Imagery   This method is well known for its military applications, but earth resources technology satellites, both manned and unmanned, have proved extremely valuable for environmental monitoring. The most famous of these satellites are the LANDSAT series, which scan the earth with readers that record the intensity of reflected light and infrared radiation from the earth's surface. The data from scanning operations are converted electronically into photographic images and from these into mosaic maps. Normally, however, these maps are taken at a scale of about 1:1,000,000, far too imprecise for anything but the most general archaeological surveys. The first LANDSAT images could detect features about 200 feet (61 m) wide. The pyramids and plazas of Teotihuacán in the Valley of Mexico might appear on such a map, but certainly not the types of minute archaeological distribution information that the average survey seeks. The latest images pick up features only 90 feet (27 m) wide, while the French SPOT satellites can work to within 60 feet (18 m). In their latest generations, both have great potential for archaeological use. Both are expensive, especially when complex imaging processing equipment is required. At a cost of up to $3,000 an image or more, only the most well-heeled researchers can make use of this revolutionary technology—and few archaeologists have access to this kind of money.

The LANDSAT imagery offers an integrated view of a large region and is made up of light reflected from many components of the earth: soil, vegetation, topography, and so on. Computer-enhanced LANDSAT images can be used to construct environmental cover maps of large survey regions that are a superb backdrop for both aerial and ground survey for archaeological resources.

Space-borne imaging radar is helping map the many sites around the great ceremonial center at *Angkor Wat* in Cambodia (Figures 6.6 and 6.7).

ASSESSING ARCHAEOLOGICAL SITES

In these days of wholesale destruction of archaeological sites through industrial activity, deep plowing, and illegal excavation, archaeologists do all they can to avoid disturbing subsurface levels. This, and the need for management of archaeological resources of all kinds, makes the assessment of archaeological sites a critical process. Assessment involves recording location, controlled surface collection and investigation, and, in some cases, subsurface detection using electronic and other methods.

Recording Sites

Studies of changing settlement distributions plotted against environmental data are now of major importance, as they provide significant information on changing human exploitation of the landscape (see Chapter 10). Thus,

FIGURE 6.6 A Spaceborne Imaging Radar C/X-band Synthetic Aperture Radar photograph of the city of Angkor, Cambodia, taken from the space shuttle *Endeavour* on September 30, 1994. The image shows an area about 34 by 53 miles (5 by 85 km). The principal complex, Angkor Wat, is the rectangle at lower right, surrounded by a dark line, which is a reservoir. Cambodia's great central lake, the Tonle Sap, lies at lower right. A network of ancient and modern roads can also be seen. The data from these images are being used to establish why the site was abandoned in the fifteenth century A.D. and to map the vast system of canals, reservoirs, and other works built during the city's heyday. *(Courtesy of Robert Harding, Jet Propulsion Laboratory, NASA, Pasadena.)*

FIGURE 6.7 Angkor Wat, Cambodia.

recording the precise geographic location of the archaeological phenomena revealed by a survey is a high priority. On a small-scale survey, site data come almost entirely from actual fieldwork. With larger regional investigations and extensive cultural resource management projects, especially in the western United States, remote sensing and geographic information systems are used to record and manage archaeological sites. Except for rainfall patterns, all the environmental information required for many surveys can be plotted with information obtained from aerial and satellite maps.

Although large archaeological sites such as road systems or major cities can be located on aerial photographs, very small phenomena such as scattered artifacts or cattle enclosures are generally impossible to find on even the most detailed maps. Aerial photographs can be used, however, to mark the locations of any archaeological occurrences once they have been located on the ground. It is not enough, however, just to plot a site on a good map and record its precise latitude, longitude, and map grid reference. Special forms are used to record the location of the site, as well as information about surface features, the landowner, potential threats to the site, and so on. Every site in the United States is given a name and a number. Sites in Santa Barbara County, California, for example, are given the prefix CA-SBa- and are numbered sequentially.

So many sites are now known in North America that most states and many large archaeological projects have set up computer data banks containing comprehensive information about site distributions and characteristics. Arkansas, for example, has a statewide computer bank that is in constant use for decisions on conservation and management.

Maps

Maps are a convenient way of storing large quantities of archaeological information. Mapping specialists, called cartographers, have developed many effective and dramatic ways of communicating information graphically, devices that are very useful inclusions in archaeological reports.

Topographic Maps   The distributions of archaeological sites are plotted on large-scale topographic maps that relate the ancient settlements to the basic features of the natural landscape (Figure 6.8, *left*). This master base map can be overlaid with plots that show vegetational cover—either prehistoric or modern—and soil types, and even prehistoric trade routes.

Planimetric Maps   These are commonly used to record details of archaeological sites. They relate different archaeological features to each other and contain no topographic information (Figure 6.8, *right*).

Site Plans   These are specially prepared maps made by archaeologists to record the horizontal provenance of artifacts, food residues, and features (see Figure 7.12). Site plans are keyed to topographic and other surveys from a carefully selected point (datum point), such as a survey beacon or a landmark

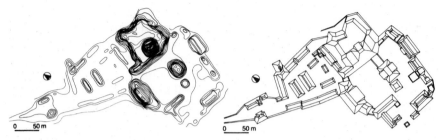

FIGURE 6.8 Examples of archaeological maps: a topographic map that shows the relationship between sites and the landscape *(left)*. A planimetric map showing the features of a site *(right)*. Both are of Nohmul, a Maya ceremonial center.

that appears on a large-scale map. This datum point provides a reference from which a grid of squares can be laid out over the area of the site, normally open-ended so that it can be extended to cover more ground if necessary. A site grid is critical for recording surface finds and during excavation for use in three-dimensional recording.

Geographic Information Systems (GIS)

More and more survey and site data are now entered into **Geographic Information Systems (GIS).** Computer-aided mapping came into being during the 1970s as a means of presenting cartographic information rapidly and accurately. Geographic Information Systems go beyond mapping. They are computer-aided systems for the collection, storage, retrieval, analysis, and presentation of spatial data of all kinds. GIS incorporates computer-aided mapping, computerized databases, and statistical packages, and is best thought of as a computer database with mapping capabilities. It also has the ability to generate new information based on the data within it. GIS is really a distinct technology, based on recent developments in cartography and many other disciplines, with enormous potential for the study of site distributions and spatial problems in archaeology, especially of artifacts, settlements, and cultures distributed over a landscape.

GIS data comes from digitizing maps and from remote-sensing devices such as LANDSAT satellites, as well as manual entries on a computer keyboard. Sophisticated software packages allow the acquisition, processing, analysis, and presentation of data of many kinds. From the archaeological perspective, GIS has the advantage of allowing the manipulation of large amounts of data, which is especially useful for solving complex settlement analysis problems (see Chapter 10). Satellites acquire environmental and topographic information; the archaeological data can be added to the same database. Analyses that once took years can be done in minutes, even seconds.

Until the advent of GIS, most archaeological surveys and settlement studies were confined to the site itself. Now the archaeologist can move away from the narrow confines of the site and examine, for example, the environmental potential of areas where no sites have been found—as a way of assessing the overall distribution of sites within the environment.

Vincent Gaffney and Zoran Stancic used GIS for a regional survey of the island of Hvar off the Adriatic coast (Figure 6.9). They created an environmental database for the island by covering it with a grid of 66-foot (20-m) square pixels (survey units), for a total of 3.8 million pixels. Then they entered modern data on elevation, soils, geology, and microclimate. In the field, they visited and recorded every known archaeological site on the island from early farming villages to post-Roman settlements, and then entered the data into a computer database. They then combined this database with the GIS data for a series of studies on the extent of site territories, analysis of land use within the same territories, and on the factors that affected site location. (For instance, they were able to show that Roman villas were located near good agricultural soils.) GIS also allows archaeologists to model different environmental scenarios and to study such problems as the ways in which different settlements controlled valuable land.

The Italian archaeologists responsible for conserving and studying Roman Pompeii, overwhelmed by an eruption of Vesuvius on August 24, A.D. 79, have used GIS technology to capture and interpret life in the town as it was 2,000 years ago, employing a computerized database of material excavated since 1862. They used an IBM computer to digitize archaeological maps and local terrain and to integrally link visual representations of the artifacts to both the detailed descriptions of each find from the city and to the locations in which they were found. The thousands of computerized pictures of specific artifacts are linked to the maps to provide detailed insights into individual houses, rooms, and walls, the places where the finds were excavated.

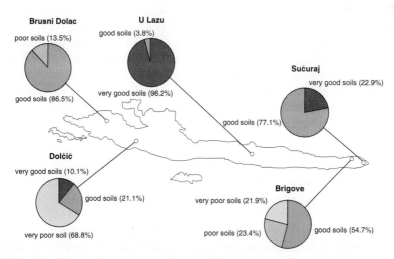

FIGURE 6.9 Roman sites on Hvar Island, with pie charts showing the proportions of soil types within catchment areas derived from GIS analysis. *(Courtesy of Vincent Gaffney, Birmingham University.)*

This "Neapolis" system, with its 50 gigabytes of detailed information about Pompeii, can be used to study such topics as the relationships between lifestyle and distribution of wealth, the spread of fashions and trends, or to correlate fresco motifs on house walls from one end of the town to the other. In this instance, GIS is used to understand relationships not readily perceived by the human mind, the myriad interconnections that tie works of art, buildings, and individual artifacts to an entire culture and community.

The most comprehensive North American GIS project is the National Archaeological Database, an on-line system that contains thousands of archaeological reports. Any archaeologist with a telephone or an electronic mail system can access the database, which also provides comprehensive site distribution information from many states and background environmental information through the Geographic Resources Analysis Support System administered by the National Park Service. You can also consult a bibliographic database.

GIS databases are assuming great importance in CRM projects of every kind, for they provide a convenient way of storing and integrating archaeological and environmental information that can be accessed by a large number of independent workers. Some of the most advanced GIS research is under way in England, where an international team of archaeologists is studying the Roman city of Wroxeter and its hinterland (see Chapter 10).

Assessment: Surface Investigations

The artifacts and other archaeological finds discovered on the surface of a site are a potentially vital source of information about the people who once lived there. Surface collecting has assumed great importance in archaeology because of cultural resource management projects, where time is short and investigation necessarily cursory. Obviously artifacts collected on the surface of any archaeological site provide a skewed view of what lies under the ground. Plows bring up material from the uppermost occupation layer, although isolated finds dug up by burrowing animals may provide clues as to what lies further beneath the ground. Nevertheless, surface collections can provide valuable information on site conditions, the former uses of the location, and the different periods of occupation such as are likely to be found there.

Surface collection has four objectives:

- To gather representative samples of artifacts from the surface of the site to establish the age of the area and the various periods of occupation
- To establish the types of activity that took place on the site.
- To gather information on the areas of the site that were most densely occupied and that might be most productive for either total or sample excavation
- To locate major structures that lie, for the most part, below the surface

Many archaeologists distrust surface collection, arguing that artifacts are easily destroyed on the surface and can be displaced from their original positions by many factors. But this viewpoint neglects a truth: All archaeological deposits, however deep, were once surface deposits, subject to many of the same destructive processes as those outcropping on the surface today.

Like buried deposits, surface levels contain abundant information about artifact patternings if one can separate cultural patterns from those caused by formation processes that have occurred since the site was abandoned. The same influences affect both surface and buried deposits: natural weathering, erosion, rainfall, and human activity for years, which may result in the pulverizing of potsherds, stone tools, and bone fragments. But surface data have two major advantages: They are a body of information that can be obtained on a regional scale, not site by site, and the cost of obtaining the data is but a fraction of that for excavation.

There are various ways of collecting artifacts from the surface of a site, but the process is always carefully controlled. Controlled surface collection sometimes involves meticulous recording of all finds, using a grid laid out over the surface of the site, an approach especially effective on plowed fields. Experiments have shown that even more than a century of cultivation will scatter artifacts over no more than a radius of 20 feet (6 m). This relatively small "halo" area makes total collection feasible, especially for small hunter-gatherer settlements.

When dealing with a well-known area or with sites containing distinctive artifacts, it is possible to collect only diagnostic artifacts, items such as potsherds, stone artifacts, or other characteristic finds that are easily classified and identified. These key finds may enable the archaeologist to assess what periods of occupation are represented at the site. Under these, and indeed all, circumstances, surface collections are carefully controlled, in such a way that the provenance of the finds is plotted on a map at the time of collection.

A common controlled surface collection method involves random sampling. Because total collection is impossible on sites of any size where surface finds are abundant, some type of sampling technique is used to obtain a valid random sample of the surface artifacts. One oft-used random-sampling approach involves laying out a grid of squares on the surface of the site and then collecting everything found in randomly selected units. Once such a "controlled collection" has been made, the rest of the site is covered for highly diagnostic artifacts. Rigorous sampling techniques are essential to obtain even a minimal sample of finds at the individual site level. Surface collection and sampling are often combined with small test-pit excavations to get preliminary data on stratigraphic information. Very small test trenches, called **shovel units,** and sampling with augers are methods commonly used for such testing.

Evidence of the activities of a region's inhabitants can be obtained from surface collections, but only when the relationship between remains found on the surface and those found below the ground is clearly understood.

Sometimes the surface finds may accurately reflect site content; at other times they may not. This problem is compounded not only by natural erosion and other factors but also by the depth of the occupation deposits on the site. Obviously, almost no finds from the lowest levels of a 30-foot (9-m)-deep village mound will lie on the surface today, unless erosion, human activity, or animal burrows bring deeply buried artifacts to the surface.

SITE SURVEY

Archaeological surveys are designed to solve specific research problems and find sites. Once sites are located, they are surveyed carefully, with these objectives in mind:

- To collect and record information on subsurface features, such as walls, buildings, and fortifications, traces of which may be detected on the surface. Such features may include ancient roads, agricultural systems, and earthworks, which are first detected from the air and then investigated on the ground.
- To collect and record information on artifacts and other finds lying on the surface of the site.
- To use both of these categories of data to test hypotheses about the age, significance, and function of the site.

(See Site box on p. 177 for an example of a site survey.)

Site survey has the great advantage of being much cheaper than excavation, provided that the methods used are based on explicit research designs. Many of the most exciting recent studies of cultural process and changing settlement patterns have depended heavily on archaeological survey and site survey. The large-scale field surveys around the Maya city of Copán have used remote sensing, field survey, and obsidian hydration dating to record changing settlement patterns before and during the collapse of Maya civilization. The data from the survey show a concentration of population in the urban core during the height of Classic Maya civilization, followed by a rapid, then slowing, dispersal into rural communities causing the environment to become overexploited at the time of the collapse (see Chapter 10).

SUBSURFACE DETECTION

Every archaeologist dreams about ways to explore sites without the labor of excavating them! Subsurface detection methods are new to archaeology, many of them originally developed for oil or geological prospecting. Most are expensive; some are very time-consuming. But their application can sometimes save many weeks of expensive excavation and, on occasion, aid in formulating an accurate research design before a dig begins.

Teotihuacán, Mexico

Site surveys can be as complex as those covering large areas. Perhaps the largest site survey project ever undertaken was the Teotihuacán Mapping Project directed by George Cowgill and René Millon. Teotihuacán lies northeast of Mexico City and is one of the great tourist attractions of the Americas (Figure 6.10). This great pre-Columbian city flourished from about 250 B.C. until A.D. 700. Up to 150,000 people lived in Teotihuacán at the peak of its prosperity. Huge pyramids and temples, giant plazas, and an enormous market formed the core of the well-organized and well-planned city. The houses of the priests and nobles lay along the main avenues; the artisans and common people lived in crowded compounds of apartments and courtyards.

Cowgill and Millon realized that the only effective way to study the city was to make a comprehensive map of all of the precincts; without it they would never have been able to study how Teotihuacán grew so huge. Fortunately, the streets and buildings lay close to the surface, unlike the vast city mounds of the Near East, where only excavation yields settlement information.

The mapping project began with a detailed ground survey, conducted with the aid of aerial photographs and large-scale survey maps. The field data were collected on 147 map data sheets of 500-meter squares at a scale of 1:2,000.

Intensive mapping and surface surveys, including surface collections of artifacts, were then conducted systematically within the 8-square-mile (20-sq.-km) limits of the ancient city defined by the preliminary survey. Ultimately, the architectural interpretations of the surface features within each 1,640-foot (500-m) square were overprinted on the base map of the site. These architectural interpretations were based on graphic data and surface data collected on special forms and through artifact collections, photographs, and drawings. Extensive use of sophisticated sampling techniques and quantitative methods was essential for successful completion of the map.

By the end of the project, more than 5,000 structures and activity areas had been recorded within the city limits. The Teotihuacán maps do not, of course, convey to us the incredible majesty of this remarkable city, but they do provide, for the first time, a comprehensive view of a teeming, multifaceted community with vast public buildings, plazas, and avenues; thousands of small apartments and courtyards, which formed individual households; and pottery, figurine, and obsidian workshops, among the many diverse structures in the city. The survey also revealed that the city had been expanded over the centuries according to a comprehensive master plan. (For more on Teotihuacán, see Chapter 10.)

FIGURE 6.10 Teotihuacán, Mexico, with the Avenue of the Dead bisecting the city. *(Courtesy of Lesley Newhart.)*

Nonmechanical Detection

Bowsing   In this low-tech, nonmechanical method, the surface of the site is thumped with a suitable heavy pounder. The earth resonates in different ways, so much so that a practiced ear can detect the distinctive sound of a buried ditch or a subsurface stone wall. Bowsing, more an art than a geophysical method, really works—with practice. I have used it on several occasions to detect buried walls.

The Auger, or Core Borer   This is a tool used to bore through subsurface deposits to find the depth and consistency of archaeological deposits lying beneath the surface. This technique has its value during an excavation, but it has the obvious disadvantage that the probe may destroy valuable artifacts. Augers were used quite successfully at the Ozette site in Washington to establish the depth of midden deposits. Some specialized augers are used to lift pollen samples. Augers with a camera attached to a periscope head are also used to investigate the interiors of Etruscan tombs. The periscope is inserted through a small hole in the roof of the tomb to inspect the interior. If the contents are undisturbed, excavation proceeds. But if tomb robbers have emptied the chamber, many hours of labor have been saved.

Mechanical Detection

Three types of mechanical detection are resistivity survey, magnetic survey, and pulse radar.

Resistivity Survey   The electrical resistivity of the soil provides some clues to subsurface features on archaeological sites. Different soils vary in their ability to conduct electricity, mainly because the deposits have moisture containing mineral salts in solution. For example, clay soils provide the least resistance to current flow, sandy soils much more. A **resistivity survey** meter can be used to measure the variations in the resistance of the ground to an electric current. Stone walls or hard pavements obviously retain less dampness than a deep pit filled with soft earth or a large ditch that has silted up. These differences can be measured accurately so that disturbed ground, stone walls, and other subsurface features can be detected by systematic survey. To survey a site, all that is needed is the meter, which is attached to four or five probes. A grid of strings is laid over the site, and the readings taken from the probes are plotted as contour lines. These show the areas of equal resistance and the presence of features such as ditches and walls. This method was, for example, employed to identify subsurface features at the Late Woodland and Early Historic Howorth-Nelson site in southwestern Pennsylvania.

Magnetic Survey   Magnetic location is used to find buried features such as iron objects, fired-clay furnaces, pottery kilns, hearths, and pits filled with rubbish or softer soil. The principle is simple: Any mass of clay heated to about 700°C and then cooled acquires a weak magnetism. Rocks, boulders, and soil will also acquire magnetism if iron oxides are present when they are heated. When the remanent magnetism of fired clay or other materials in a pit or similar feature is measured, it will give a reading different from that of the intensity of the earth's magnetic field normally obtained from undisturbed soils. The proton magnetometer is the instrument most commonly used to magnetically detect archaeological features. A site is surveyed by laying out 50-foot-square (15-sq.-m) units, each of them divided into a grid of 5-foot (1.5-m) squares. The measurement is taken with a staff, to which are attached two small bottles filled with water or alcohol enclosed in electric coils. The magnetic intensity is measured by recording the behavior of the protons in the hydrogen atoms in the bottle's contents. The magnetometer itself amplifies the weak signals from the electrical coils. Features are traced by taking closely spaced measurements over areas where anomalies in the magnetic readings are found. Computers record the field data and convert them into a display on a TV screen or a printout. Sophisticated software allows the operator to screen out nonarchaeological variations in soil magnetism.

Magnetic Detection   This method has been used successfully to record pits, walls, and other features in the middle of large forts or fortified towns, where total excavation of a site is clearly uneconomical. This method has been used widely in Europe and on Olmec pyramids at La Venta, Mexico, but it is subject to some error because of such modern features as barbed-wire fences, electric trains, and power cables.

Pulse Radar   The pulse induction meter applies pulses of magnetic field to the soil from a transmitter coil. This instrument is very sensitive to metals and can be used to find pottery and metal objects and graves containing such objects. A soil conductivity meter can be used to detect subsoil features by measuring changes in the conductivity of the soil. Anomalies spotted by the instrument can be plotted with good accuracy, and pits as small as 12 inches (30 cm) in diameter and 4 inches (10 cm) deep have been located. Individual metal objects can also be detected using this method, which holds great promise for the future.

The use of radar and other electronic devices is proliferating in archaeology. Ken Weeks and a team of fellow Egyptologists have embarked on a long-term project to map all of the royal tombs in Thebes's Valley of the Kings. They are using a hot-air balloon, X rays, and sonic detectors to map subterranean features and hidden chambers in royal tombs; they have recently located a large tomb which once housed Rameses II's sons.

The excavations at the Maya village of Cerén in San Salvador offer an instructive example of coordinated use of geophysical methods to locate subsurface features. The site was buried under up to 16 feet (5 m) of volcanic ash and was first located by a chance bulldozer cut. Obviously, it was uneconomical to bulldoze large areas, so Payson Sheets called in geophysicist Hartmut Spetzler, who analyzed the properties of the volcanic ash at Cerén, and of the adobe buildings buried beneath it. There were considerable differences in porosity and density between the ash and the adobe, so he recommended deploying a portable seismograph, a ground-penetrating radar, and a resistivity meter.

The survey started with the seismograph, which records shock waves passing through the earth. Instead of the usual dynamite, Sheets struck a steel plate set in the soil with a hammer, recording the resulting waves with a set of 12 sensitive microphones. Buried hut floors conducted shock waves faster than the surrounding ash, and the seismograph did indeed locate some structures, but, designed as it was for detecting huge geological anomalies, the results were somewhat haphazard. Sheets then turned to ground-penetrating radar, using an instrument developed for studying permafrost melting along the Alaska Oil Pipeline. Instead of attaching it to a pickup truck, he enlisted the services of an ox cart, which eliminated all background vibration. The ox cart driver simply drove slowly and steadily along a carefully marked straight line (Figure 6.11). The machine itself sent microwave energy deep into the soil and detected it as it was reflected back. The subsurface stratigraphy was recorded on special paper and revealed some strong reflectors, some of which turned out to be the clay surfaces of hut floors covered by ash.

Using a drill rig, Sheets then tested some of the anomalies. Some were the result of eroded and redeposited volcanic ash. Others were large structures, but the radar was unable to detect smaller features, although it may be able to do so when the data are digitized and the original ground surface is mapped.

FIGURE 6.11   Using an ox-cart-borne ground-penetrating radar unit on the Maya village at Cerén, San Salvador. *(Courtesy of Payson Sheets, University of Colorado, Boulder.)*

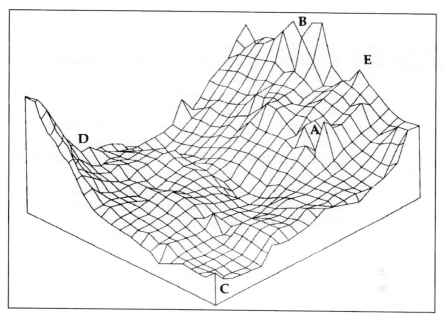

FIGURE 6.12 A three-dimensional computer plot of a resistivity survey at Cerén. The anomalies resulting from different electrical resistance show up as sharp peaks (A to E), of which A and B have been investigated and shown to be prehistoric structures. *(Courtesy of Payson Sheets, University of Colorado, Boulder.)*

Resistivity surveys over Cerén recorded the resistance of subsurface deposits to electricity. Sheets expected that house floors would conduct electricity better than the surrounding ash, for they are constructed of dense, fired clay. His researchers recorded measurements along a grid over the site and fed the data into a laptop computer. The three-dimensional software revealed interesting double-peaked anomalies, which, when tested with a drill rig, turned out to be large prehistoric structures (Figure 6.12).

Thus a combination of geophysical methods provided an effective and economic way to locate subsurface features at Cerén, at a fraction of what it would have cost to bulldoze away acres of ashy overburden.

SUMMARY

Archaeological survey is of great importance in archaeology, for it allows not only the discovery of sites, but the study of human occupation on a regional basis. Archaeological sites manifest themselves in many ways, such as in the form of mounds, middens, caves, and rock shelters. Many more are much less conspicuous and are located only by chance or by soil discolorations or surface finds. Ground survey ranges from general surveys leading to location of only the largest sites down to precise foot surveys aimed at covering an entire area in detail. In most cases, total survey is impracticable, and so archaeologists rely on sampling methods to obtain unbiased samples of the research area. A battery of new survey techniques involves aerial photography and remote sensing, including side-scan aerial radar and scanner imagery.

Site assessment involves mapping, controlled surface collection, and subsurface detection methods designed to assess the significance of the site without intrusive excavation. Controlled surface collection is designed to collect and record artifacts and other surface finds, to test hypotheses about the age, significance, and function of the site. Geographic Information Systems (GIS) technology offers great potential as a way of mapping archaeological data and analyzing it in a wider environmental context.

Subsurface features are often detected with subsurface radar, and also resistivity surveys, which measure the differences in electrical resistivity of the soil between disturbed and undisturbed areas. Proton magnetometers are used to locate iron objects, fired-clay furnaces, and other features.

KEY TERMS

Crop mark
Geographic Information Systems
  (GIS)
Intensive survey
Landscape signatures
Nonintrusive archaeology
Offsite area
Reconnaissance survey
Remote sensing

Resistivity survey
Shovel units
Simple random sampling
Soil mark
Stratified sampling
Surface surveying
Systemative random sampling
Tells

GUIDE TO FURTHER READING

Clark, Anthony. 1997. *Seeing Beneath the Soil*. London: Batsford.
    A basic description of remote-sensing methods with a European bias.
Gaffney, Vincent, and Zoran Stancic. 1991. *GIS Approaches to Regional Analysis: A Case Study of the Island of Hvar*. Ljubljana, Jugoslavia: Znanstveni institut Filozofske fakultete.
    An exemplary case study in the use of Geographic Information Systems in archaeology. It is also readable!
Hester, Thomas R., Harry J. Shafer, and Kenneth L. Feder, 1997. *Field Methods in Archaeology*. 7th ed. Mountain View, CA: Mayfield.
    A classic field manual aimed at American archaeologists, which contains much valuable information on field survey and remote sensing.
Millon, René. 1973. *The Teotihuacán Map: Urbanization at Teotihuacán, Mexico, vol. 1*. Austin: University of Texas Press.
    A prime example of a complicated survey and mapping project.
Mueller, James A., ed. 1975. *Sampling in Archaeology*. Tucson: University of Arizona Press.
    Useful essays on problems in field survey sampling, for the advanced reader.

Sanders, William T., Jeffrey R. Parsons, and Robert S. Santley. 1979. *The Basin of Mexico: Ecological Processes in the Evolution of a Civilization*. Orlando, FL: Academic Press,

The best description of a long-term survey project and of survey problems.
Weeks, Kent R. 1998. *The Lost Tomb*. New York: William Morrow.

A popular account of site survey and mapping in the Valley of Kings, which focuses on the tomb of Rameses II's sons. This is a marvelous example of the detective work that is modern-day Egyptology.

A useful Web site for remote sensing methods is http://www.ads.ahs .ac.uk/project/goodguides/gis.

CHAPTER 7
Digging Up the Past

1952 excavations in the scribes' quarter in the Sumerian city of Ur, Iraq. Scientists from the University of Chicago's Oriental Institute and the University of Pennsylvania Museum are excavating levels dating to the 20th century B.C., the heyday of the Third Dynasty kings. (Source: AP/Wide World Photos.)

184

Excavation! The very word conjures up images of magnificent pyramids and mysterious cities revealed by the spade. Indiana Jones and the spectacular discoveries of such nineteenth-century archaeologists as Austen Henry Layard in Mesopotamia and Heinrich Schliemann at Troy have cast the archaeologist as treasure hunter and adventurer, as a bold digger unafraid of danger and discomfort. Reality is very different, for modern-day excavation is a deliberate, usually slow-moving process of observation and recording, a search for information rather than spectacular discoveries. Nevertheless, archaeological excavation exercises a peculiar fascination, perhaps because of the lure of unexpected discoveries and sometimes spectacular finds. (See Discovery box on p. 186.) This chapter describes some of the basic principles of excavation.

DISCOVERY

The Dead Sea Scrolls

Mohammed Adh-Dhib had lost a goat that hot day in 1947. The young Bedouin teenager chased the errant beast as it skipped into the craggy hills near Qumran by the Dead Sea. The sun grew hotter, so he lay down under a rocky overhang to rest. His curiosity aroused by a small hole in the cliff face, he threw a stone into the opening. He heard it strike a clay vessel in the dark. He then pulled himself up to the hole and saw several cylindrical objects standing in rows. They were wide-necked jars. Next day, Mohammed returned with a friend. They examined the jars and found bundles of tarry rags and folds of smooth leather. Back in camp, they unrolled one roll and found that it stretched from one side of their tent to the other. Eventually, the roll and other finds ended up in the hands of a Christian cobbler, who thought he might use the leather for shoes. When he saw the writing on them, he took them to a Jerusalem convent and ransacked the Qumran caves in search of more scrolls. The first scholars to see the scroll realized it was a copy of the book of Isaiah in the Old Testament and of priceless value. Months of careful negotiations and detective work passed before the fragmentary Dead Sea Scrolls passed got into scholarly hands and years of research began.

The Dead Sea Scrolls are important religious texts, which bear witness to the historical environment in which Christianity first emerged. They were buried in a remote cave by the members of an austere Jewish community at Qumran in about A.D. 58, when Roman persecution made life impossible. The Scrolls soon became political symbols of immense value, now on view to tourists in Israel's Shrine of the Book. Their study and interpretation occupies dozens of experts to this day.

EXCAVATION IS DESTRUCTION

The excavations of yesteryear were often conducted on a large scale and with scant regard for minute detail. Today's excavator moves less earth in a month than Sir Leonard Woolley's Ur excavations shifted in a day (see Figure 1.1). Woolley went so far as to employ a Euphrates River boatman to sing rhythmic paddling songs as hundreds of men shoveled overburden from occupation levels. Not that every excavation was on such a scale. In the early 1930s, when Cambridge University archaeologist Dorothy Garrod excavated the ancient Stone Age caves at Mount Carmel in what was then Palestine, she employed a small crew, lived very simply, and operated on a shoestring budget, while unearthing some of the earliest anatomically modern humans in the world.

Academic excavations tend to be slower-moving than many digs, which form part of small- and large-scale CRM investigations. Here the archaeologist often makes use of earthmoving machinery to scrape off overburden and even to remove thin layers a few inches thick. There is an art to using a back-hoe or small bulldozer that comes with constant practice. In trained hands, such a machine can save hours of time and hundreds of dollars, freeing up trained diggers for delicate jobs such as uncovering house foundations or storage pits (Figure 7.1).

Until a generation ago, excavation was considered a primary objective of archaeological fieldwork. However, the destruction of the archaeological record has reached such epidemic proportions that excavation has now become a strategy of last resort. Every archaeologist knows that the record is finite, that once disturbed, archaeological context is gone forever. They never forget that *every excavation destroys part of the archaeological record*. Nonintrusive archaeology has become increasingly important in recent years, as regional studies have replaced site-oriented investigations as a primary thrust in archaeology. At the same time, excavation has become increasingly selective, both because of its high cost, and also because of a desire to leave part of a site intact for future generations to investigate.

Excavators shoulder a heavy responsibility, for they destroy the past on the one hand, yet record it in meticulous detail on the other. An archaeologist's excavation is only as good as the notes, computer records, photographs, and plans that reconstruct the dig when it is complete.

FIGURE 7.1   A CRM excavation uses earthmoving machinery to clear sterile over-burden. *(Source: Archeological Survey of Arkansas.)*

Every excavator has vital ethical responsibilities:

- To excavate only within the context of a specific research design
- To record the archaeological context of the finds and to make a complete record of the excavation
- To publish a permanent record of the results and to ensure that the notes, drawings, maps, plans, artifacts, and other finds are deposited in a facility that will preserve them permanently

One of the great scandals of archaeology concerns publication, for thousands of important archaeological sites around the world have never been reported on in full. Until they are, the information from the excavation is effectively lost forever. The problem is compounded by CRM investigations, many of which are carried out to satisfy legal, not necessarily archaeological, requirements. The reports from such fieldwork are often of restricted distribution and sometimes inaccessible to archaeologists as a whole. In recent years, efforts have been made to establish repositories for such documents, but the coverage is still incomplete.

What we know of the record of the human past from archaeology is based on what has been published about it, not necessarily on what has actually been discovered. So, if you become an archaeologist, please be sure to publish your work and add publicly to our knowledge of the past!

ORGANIZING ARCHAEOLOGICAL EXCAVATIONS

The twentieth century has witnessed the total transformation of archaeology, from treasure hunting and curiosity seeking to scientific investigation and problem-oriented excavation. Today's excavation is limited by ever rising costs, by the need to minimize damage to the archaeological record, and by the sheer complexity of the data that can now be recovered from a site. Some of the more elaborate sites are dug by teams of specialists with very little unskilled help. Others are staffed by volunteer laborers, interested amateurs, and students who gain practical experience in all aspects of excavation, from using a shovel to recording a complicated stratigraphic profile. Most CRM excavations involve teams of professional archaeologists and fieldworkers, who work together to complete a job according to contract guidelines and legal requirements within a finite amount of time. They are concerned as much with "compliance" with the law as they are with academic archaeological information—although many CRM archaeologists are first-rate scholars.

The director of a modern archaeological field expedition needs skills beyond those of a competent archaeologist. He or she also must be able to fill the roles of accountant, politician, doctor, mechanic, personnel manager, and even cook. On a large dig, though manual labor may not be the director's responsibility, logistic problems are compounded, and he or she will head a large excavation team of site supervisors, artists, photographers, and numerous minor functionaries. Above all, the field director has to be the leader of a multidisciplinary team of specialist fieldworkers.

Multidisciplinary Research Teams

Modern archaeology is so complex that all major excavation projects now require multidisciplinary teams of archaeologists, botanists, geologists, zoologists, and other specialists who work together on closely integrated research problems, such as the origins of food production. The team approach is particularly important where environmental problems are most pressing and where the excavations and research seek the relationships between human cultures and the rest of the ecosystem.

A good interdisciplinary or multidisciplinary study is based on an integrated research design bringing a closely supervised team of specialists together to test carefully formulated hypotheses against data collected by all of them. Notice that we say "data collected by all of them." An effective multidisciplinary archaeological team must be just that—a team whose combined findings are used to test specific hypotheses.

Multidisciplinary research teams have been employed with great success at early hominid sites in East Turkana, Kenya, where geologists provided the background environmental data; zoologists, the identifications and interpretations of fossil animals found in the sites; and archaeologists, the data on surviving cultural remains, while **physical anthropologists** studied the human remains found in the 2- to 2.5-million-year-old sites. This approach is logical, but it is rarely carried to its ultimate extreme, in which the experts would design their research together, share an integrated field mission, and communicate daily about their findings and research problems. One of the most successful of such excavations was conducted by Andrew Moore at the Abu Hureyra early farming village in Syria's Euphrates valley. This complex investigation, mentioned several times in these pages, involved the excavation of an occupation mound occupied from about 9000 B.C. for 3,000 years (see Chapter 9). Moore used the researches of a botanist to study the changing vegetation around the site and the shifting plant diet of the inhabitants, a zooarchaeologist to investigate the gazelle hunting at the site as well as the domesticated animals, and a biological anthropologist to study the human burials deposited in the occupation levels—to mention only a few specialists. The resulting final report is masterpiece of interdisciplinary reporting.

The criteria, then, for selecting members of multidisciplinary research teams include academic skills, the ability to communicate with people in other disciplines, highly specific specialist qualifications, and, above all, a willingness to work closely with a group of researchers who are committed to solving common problems. Such people are hard to find, and thus truly effective interdisciplinary research teams are few and far between. More loosely knit team approaches in which each member of a group pursues his or her own research but contributes to more general overall goals are far more common. In many CRM projects, multiple technical specialists contribute to the agenda of the research director as needed.

PLANNING AN EXCAVATION

Excavation is the culminating step in the investigation of an archaeological site. It recovers from the earth data obtainable in no other way. Like historical archives, the soil of an archaeological site is a document whose pages must be deciphered, translated, and interpreted before they can be used to write an accurate account of the past.

Excavation is destruction—the archaeological deposits so carefully dissected during any dig are destroyed forever and their contents removed. Here, again, there is a radical difference between archaeology and the sciences and history. A physical scientist can readily re-create the conditions for a basic experiment; the historian can return to the archives to reevaluate the complex events in, say, a politician's life. But all that we have after an excavation are the finds from the trenches, the untouched portions of the site, and the photographs, notes, and drawings that record the excavator's observations for posterity. Thus, accurate recording and observation are overwhelmingly vital in the day-to-day work of archaeologists, not only for the sake of accuracy in their own research but also because they are creating an archive of archaeological information that may be consulted by others.

Archaeological sites are nonrenewable resources. Thus, unfocused excavation is useless, for the manageable and significant observations are buried in a mass of irrelevant trivia. Any excavation must be conducted from a sound research design intended to solve specific and well-defined problems. Many investigators carry out a geomorphological survey of the site before excavation begins, the better to understand the ancient landscape and **site-formation processes** ahead of time. Alternatively, they use subsurface radar and other remote sensing devices to locate subsurface features ahead of time, as Payson Sheets did at Cerén (see Chapter 6).

RESEARCH DESIGNS

There was a time when archaeologists selected a site for excavation because it "looked good," or because dense concentrations of surface finds suggested that promising discoveries lay below the surface. Excavations are traditionally conducted on larger sites, on sites that look more productive, on sites threatened by development, or on those nearest to roads. These criteria bear no resemblance to the goal that is actually required, which is acquiring representative and unbiased data to answer a particular question—a problem whose limits are ultimately defined by available money and time. Unbiased data, which do not reflect the investigator's idiosyncrasies, can properly yield statistical estimates of the culture from which the samples were drawn. This kind of information requires explicit sampling procedures, to select a few sites from an area to excavate, and also to control reliability of the information by using probability and statistics.

Excavation costs are so great that problem-oriented digging is now the rule rather than the exception, with the laboratory work forming part of the continuing evaluation of the research problem. The large piles of finds and records accumulated at the end of even a small field season contain a bewildering array of interdigitating facts that the researcher must evaluate and reevaluate as inquiry proceeds—by constantly arranging propositions and hypotheses, correlating observations, and reevaluating interpretations of the archaeological evidence. Finds and plans are the basis of the researcher's strategy and affect fieldwork plans for the future, the basis for constant reevaluation of research objectives.

The need for sound planning and design is even more acute in ecological research in archaeology, in which archaeologists try to understand changes in human culture in relation to human environmental systems. Let us take the example of the Koster excavation in Illinois, one of the largest and most complex digs ever undertaken in North America.

The Koster Site

In the lower Illinois valley lies the Koster site, a deep accumulation of 26 ancient occupation layers extending from about 10,000 years ago to around A.D. 1100 to 1200 (Figure 7.2). The wealth of material at Koster first came to

FIGURE 7.2 The Koster excavations. *(Courtesy of D. Baston, Center for American Archaeology, Kampsville, Illinois.)*

light in 1968 and has been the subject of extremely large-scale excavation. The dig involved collaboration by three archaeologists and six specialists from other disciplines such as zoology and botany, as well as use of a computer laboratory. Even superficial examination of the site showed that a very careful research design was needed, both to maximize use of funds and to ensure adequate control of data. In developing the Koster research design, James Brown and Stuart Struever were well aware of the numerous, complex variables that had to be controlled and the need to define carefully their sampling procedure and the size of the collecting units.

They faced a number of formidable difficulties. Thirteen of the Koster cultural horizons are isolated from their neighbors by a zone of sterile slope wash soil, which makes it possible to treat each as a separate problem in excavation and analysis—as if it were an individual site—although, in fact, the 13 are stratified one above another. Because the whole site is more than 30 feet (9 m) deep, the logistical problems were formidable, as in all large-scale excavations. One possible strategy would have been to sink test pits, obtain samples from each level, and list diagnostic artifacts and cultural items. But this approach, though cheaper and commonly used, was quite inadequate to the systems model the excavators drew up to study the origins of cultivation in the area and cultural change in the lower Illinois valley. Large-scale excavations were needed to uncover each living surface so that the excavators could not only understand what the living zones within each occupation were like but also, after studying in detail the sequence of differences in activities, make statements about the processes of cultural change.

From the large scale of the excavations, Brown and Struever saw the need for immediate feedback from the data flow from the site during the excavation. Changes in the excavation method would no doubt be needed during the season's fieldwork to ensure that maximum information was obtained. To accomplish this flexibility, both excavation and data-gathering activities were combined into a data flow system to ensure feedback to the excavators that would be as close to instantaneous as possible. The categories of data—animal bones, artifacts, vegetable remains—were processed in the field, and the information from the analyses was then fed by remote-access terminal to a computer in Evanston, Illinois, many miles away. Pollen and soil samples were sent directly to specialist laboratories for analysis (Figure 7.3).

The effects of the data flow system are highly beneficial. The tiresome analysis of artifacts and food residues is completed on the site, and the data are available to the excavators in the field in a few days instead of months later, as is usual. The research design can be modified in the field at short notice, with ready consultation between the team members in the field. A combination of instant data retrieval; comprehensive and meticulous collecting methods involving, among other things, flotation methods (see Chapter 9); and a systems approach to both excavation strategy and research planning have made the Koster project an interesting example of effectively used research design in archaeology. Today, many excavators, especially on CRM projects, make use of the World Wide Web to record and transmit data.

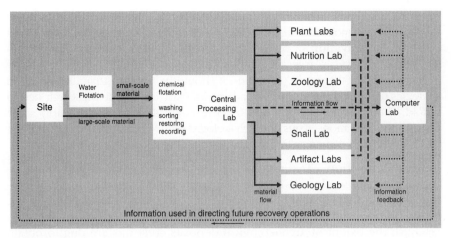

FIGURE 7.3   The data flow system at the Koster excavations.

In many projects, excavation is only part of the overall research design. As a method, it should be used sparingly, for the end result is always destruction of a site.

TYPES OF EXCAVATION

Archaeological excavation is designed to acquire as much raw data as possible with available financial and other resources. Its ultimate objective is to produce a three-dimensional record of an archaeological site, in which the various artifacts, structures, and other finds are placed in their correct provenance and context in time and space.

Total and Selective Excavation

Total excavation of a site has the advantage of being comprehensive, but it is expensive and is undesirable because it leaves none of the site intact for excavation at a later date with, perhaps, more advanced techniques. **Selective excavation** is much more common, especially on CRM projects, where time is often of the essence. Many sites are simply too large for total excavation and can only be tested selectively, using sampling methods or carefully placed trenches. Selective excavation is used to obtain stratigraphic and chronological data as well as samples of pottery, stone tools, and animal bones. From this evidence, the archaeologist can decide whether to undertake further excavation.

Vertical and Horizontal Excavation

Invariably, **vertical excavation** is selective digging, uncovering a limited area on a site for the purpose of recovering specific information. Most vertical excavations are probes of deep archaeological deposits, their real objective being to reveal the chronological sequence at a site. **Horizontal excavation** (sometimes called **area excavation** or block excavation) is used to expose contemporaneous settlement over a larger area and is the most commonly employed strategy in many parts of the world. However, it should be stressed that all excavation strategies are based on decisions made as an excavation and a research design unfold. The illustrations in this and other texts, for that matter, invariably show completed excavations. Thus, an archaeologist may legitimately switch from test pits to horizontal or vertical excavation, or back again, during even a short dig.

Vertical Excavation   **Test pits,** sometimes given the French name *sondages,* or even "telephone booths," are a frequently used form of vertical excavation. They consist of small trenches just large enough to accommodate one or two diggers and are designed to penetrate to the lower strata of a site to establish the extent of archaeological deposits. Test pits are dug to obtain samples of artifacts from lower layers, and this method may be supplemented by augers or borers.

Test pits are a preliminary to large-scale excavation, for the information they reveal is limited, at best. Some archaeologists will use them only outside the main area of a site, on the grounds that they will destroy critical strata otherwise. But carefully placed test pits can provide valuable insights into the stratigraphy and artifact content of a site before larger-scale excavation begins (Figure 7.4).

Figure 7.4   Test pits at the Maya city of Quirigua. *(Courtesy of the University Museum, University of Pennsylvania.)*

Test pits are also used to obtain samples from different areas of sites, such as shell middens, where dense concentrations of artifacts are found throughout the deposits. In such cases, test pits are excavated on a grid pattern, with the positioning of the pits being determined by statistical sampling or by a regular pattern such as alternate squares.

Vertical trenches are much larger, deeper cuttings used to establish such phenomena as sequences of building operations, histories of complex earthworks, and long cultural sequences in deep caves (Figure 7.5).

Vertical trenches have been widely used to excavate early village sites such as Abu Hureyra in southwest Asia. They may also be used to obtain a cross section of a site threatened by destruction or to examine outlying structures near a village or a cemetery that has been dug on a large scale. Vertical excavations of this kind are almost always dug in the expectation that the most important information to come from them will be the record of layers in the walls of the trenches and the finds from them. But clearly, the amount of information to be obtained from such cuttings is of limited value compared to that from a larger excavation.

Horizontal Excavation   Horizontal, or area (block), excavation is done on a much larger scale than vertical excavation and is as close to total excavation as archaeology can get. An area dig implies covering wide areas to recover building plans or the layout of entire settlements, even historic gardens. The only sites that almost invariably are totally excavated are very small hunting camps, isolated huts, and burial mounds.

FIGURE 7.5 A classic example of vertical excavation dating from the 1930s: A trench through the earthworks at Maiden Castle, England, excavated by Sir Mortimer Wheeler. *(Courtesy of the Society of Antiquaries of London, London.)*

A good example of horizontal excavation comes from St. Augustine, Florida. St. Augustine was founded on the east coast of Florida by the Spanish conquistador Pedro Menéndez de Avilés in 1565. Sixteenth-century St. Augustine was plagued with floods, fire, and hurricanes and was plundered by Sir Francis Drake in 1586. He destroyed the town, which was a military presidio and mission designed to protect Spanish treasure fleets passing through the Florida Straits. In 1702, St. Augustine was attacked by the British. The inhabitants took refuge in the Castillo de San Marcos (which still stands). The siege lasted six weeks before the attackers retreated, after burning the wooden buildings of the town to the ground. This time the colonists replaced them with masonry buildings as the town expanded in the first half of the eighteenth century.

Kathleen Deagan and a team of archaeologists have investigated eighteenth-century and earlier St. Augustine on a systematic basis since 1977, combining historic preservation with archaeological excavation. Excavating the eighteenth-century town is a difficult process on many accounts, partly because the entire archaeological deposit for three centuries is only about 3 feet (0.9 m) deep at the most, and it has been much disturbed. The excavators have cleared and recorded dozens of barrel-lined wells. They have also used horizontal excavations to uncover the foundations of eighteenth-century houses built of tabby, a cementlike substance of oyster shells, lime, and sand (Figure 7.6). The foundations of oyster shell or tabby were laid in

FIGURE 7.6 Horizontal excavation at St. Augustine, Florida, showing oyster-shell house footings from an early eighteenth-century building. *(Courtesy of Professor Kathleen Deagan, University of Florida, Gainesville, Florida.)*

footing trenches in the shape of the intended house. Then the walls were added. The tabby floor soon wore out, so another layer of earth was added and a new floor poured on top. Since the deposits outside such houses had been disturbed, the artifacts from the foundations and floors were of great importance. And selective, horizontal excavation was the best way to uncover them.

The problems with horizontal digs are exactly the same as those with any excavation: stratigraphic control and accurate measurement. Area excavations imply exposure of large, open areas of ground. A complex network of walls or postholes may lie within the area to be investigated. Each feature relates to other structures, a relationship that must be carefully recorded so that the site can be interpreted correctly, especially if several periods of occupation are involved. If the entire area is uncovered, it is obviously difficult to measure the position of the structures in the middle of the trench, far from the walls at the excavation's edge. To achieve better control of measurement and recording, it is better to use a system that gives a network of vertical stratigraphic sections across the area to be excavated. This work is often done by laying out a grid of square or rectangular excavation units, with walls several yards thick between each square. Such areas may average 12 feet (3.6 m) square or larger. This system allows stratigraphic control of large areas. Large-scale excavation with grids is extremely expensive and time-consuming. It is also difficult to use where the ground is irregular, but it has been employed with great success at many excavations, being used to uncover structures, town plans, and fortifications. Many area digs are "open excavations," in which large tracts of a site are exposed layer by layer without a grid (Figure 7.7).

Stripping off overlying areas with no archaeological significance to expose buried subsurface features is another type of large-scale excavation, normally achieved with earthmoving machinery. Stripping is especially useful when a site is buried only a short distance below the surface and the structures are preserved in the form of postholes and other discolorations in the soil. The method is widely used on sites that are about to be destroyed by construction or other activity, allowing excavators to study large areas of structures, and it has been widely used on Iroquois and Huron houses in Canada, where housing developments have threatened dozens of ancient villages (Figure 7.8).

Horizontal excavation depends, of course, on precise stratigraphic control. It is often combined with vertical trenches, which provide the information necessary for accurately peeling off successive horizontal layers.

HOW DO YOU DIG?

Archaeological excavation is an extremely precise, usually slow-moving process which is far more than mere digging. The actual mechanics of archaeological excavation are best learned in the field. There is an art in the skillful use of the trowel, brush, and other implements to clear archaeological

FIGURE 7.7 A horizontal, open-plan excavation on the Iron Age hillfort at Danebury in southern England. The Danebury research was carried out over many years, with its research designs constantly modified. *(Courtesy of Professor Barry Cunliffe, Department of Archaeology, Oxford University, England.)*

FIGURE 7.8 Horizontal excavation of an Iroquois longhouse at Howlet Hill, Onondaga, New York. The small stakes mark the house's wall plans: Hearths and roof supports are found inside the house. *(Courtesy of Professor James Tuck, Memorial University, St. Johns, Newfoundland, Canada.)*

deposits. Stripping off layers exposed in a trench requires a sensitive eye for changing soil colors and textures, especially when excavating postholes and other features, and a few hours of practical experience are worth thousands of words of instructional text.

The excavator's aim should be to explain the origin of every layer and feature encountered in the site, whether natural or humanly made. It is not enough just to excavate and describe the site; one must also explain how the site was formed. This process is achieved by removing the superimposed layers of the site one by one. In so doing, the archaeologist records the full details of each layer and its contents as they are excavated. Everything depends on a flexible research design, which provides the blueprint for the excavation and helps determine the methods used to expose the site. Such methods vary from site to site and are usually a combination of vertical and horizontal digging. Much depends on the size of the site, the kinds of finds that are made, and, above all, on the stratigraphic layers within it. Obviously, the excavation of a single-level Iroquois village site with longhouse foundations buried under a layer of topsoil can only be excavated horizontally, so one can expose as much of the large house foundations as possible. The same is true of many other archaeological sites.

When digging any site, the fundamental approach usually involves one of two basic methods, but both can be used on the same site:

- *Excavation by visible layers.*   This method involves removing every visible layer in the site separately. This slow-moving approach is commonly used in cave sites, which often have complex stratigraphy, and also on open sites such as bison kills on the North American Plains, where bone layers and other levels can be distinguished relatively easily in preliminary stratigraphic test pits.
- *Excavation by arbitrary levels.*   Here the soil is removed in standard-sized arbitrary levels, which vary in size depending on the nature of the site (between 3 and 12 inches, 5 to 20 cm, is normal). This approach is used when there is little discernable stratigraphy or variation in the occupation layers, each level being screened carefully to recover artifacts, animal bones, seeds, and other small finds.

Ideally, of course, one would like to excavate every site according to natural stratigraphic layers, but there are many instances, such as California coastal shell middens and some large occupation mounds, where one simply cannot see the natural layers, if there ever were any. The deposits are often too fine or ashy to form discrete layers, especially when riffled by wind or trampled by later occupants or cattle. I have excavated a series of African farming villages up to 12 feet (3.6 m) deep, which were most logically excavated in arbitrary levels, for the few visible occupation layers were marked by obvious concentrations of wall fragments from collapsed houses (Figure 7.9). Most levels merely yielded counts of potsherds, occasional other artifacts, and numerous fragmentary animal bones.

FIGURE 7.9 A vertical excavation through the deposits of a 1,000-year-old African village shows two clearly stratified collapsed huts in the upper levels.

In practice, most archaeologists combine both approaches when possible, making sure that, whatever method is used, features are carefully recorded in the site notebooks and in the final publication.

Tools of the Trade

Indiana Jones went into the field with gangs of laborers armed with shovels, and, of course, he had his favorite bullwhip. Today's archaeologist uses more refined tools of the trade! You can even buy prepackaged excavator's tool kits which contain everything from a backpack to work vest with convenient pockets and a leather holder for your trowel—but this is carrying things a little too far. Here are some thoughts on both personal tool kits and other equipment.

Larger tools and more expensive items are usually provided by the organization supporting the excavation, be it an academic institution or a CRM firm. Some examples include the following:

- *Earthmoving equipment* is an essential part of CRM excavations and large digs. Once shunned by purists, such equipment is now widely used, especially when sites are threatened with destruction and time is short. An expert operator can work wonders with a backhoe or front-end loader, even removing a few centimeters of soil with a delicate touch. One English archaeologist of my acquaintance describes himself as an expert on archaeology, sheep farming, and earthmoving equipment. To watch him operate such a piece of equipment is to witness serious excavation, where the equipment operator knows exactly when to stop work and the significance of what he is uncovering.

- *Shovels* are the literary trademark of the archaeologist, but, in fact, the trowel is a more appropriate symbol! Most common is the familiar long-handled, round-bladed No. 2 shovel. The square-point shovel is invaluable for moving large amounts of loose earth or sand, also for scraping. I have used this to move sterile overburden for hours with minimal fatigue (all of us were very fit at the time: We had been digging for months!).
- *Screens* are vital for recovering small finds of all kinds and come in several sizes, with meshes of 1/4 inch (60mm) or less being most common.
- *Mattocks, picks, forks, and such* are useful for loosening soil. The mattock and the pick may be considered together because they are variants on the same type of tool; when used with care, they are a delicate gauge of soil texture, an indication used often in larger sites. The old-style Mesopotamian and Egyptian excavations, such as Woolley's dig at Ur, once used teams of pickmen, shovelers, and basket carriers to remove the soil and dump it off the site.
- *Surveying equipment* includes compasses, levels, electronic recording devices, laser recorders, and mapping devices.
- *Laptop computers* are ubiquitous on modern-day excavations for data recording of all kinds. Some people keep their excavation notes on a laptop. I prefer to have both a notebook and a computer.

Personal equipment is a matter of preference, beyond some essentials. (See Doing Archaeology box on p. 202 for more information on this.)

STRATIGRAPHIC OBSERVATION

The basis of all archaeological excavation is the properly recorded and interpreted stratigraphic profile. A section through a site gives a picture of the accumulated sediments and occupation levels that constitute the ancient and modern history of the locality. Obviously, anyone recording stratigraphy needs to know as much about the history of the natural processes that the site has undergone since abandonment as about the formation of the ancient site itself. The sediments that cover the archaeological finds have undergone transformations that radically affect the ways in which artifacts are preserved or moved around in the soil. Burrowing animals, subsequent human activity, erosion, wind action, grazing cattle—all can modify superimposed layers in drastic ways.

Archaeological stratigraphy is usually much more complicated than geological layering, for the phenomena observed are much more localized and the effects of human behavior tend to be intensive and often involve constant reuse of the same location (Figure 7.10). Subsequent activity can radically alter the context of artifacts, structures, and other finds. A village site can be leveled and then reoccupied by a new community which digs the

DOING ARCHAEOLOGY

A Personal Excavation Kit

I always like to take my own small tools on an excavation or survey, simply so that I always have familiar equipment on hand. Here are the contents of my tool kit, which live in a small backpack:

- *Diamond-shaped pointing trowel,* the true archaeologist's trademark. The Marshalltown brand is widely used in the United States, with a one-piece blade and stem. Refuse all cheap substitutes! The pointing trowel is a highly versatile tool for uncovering small items or clearing soil near small features such as hearths. It is also a superb scraping tool in expert hands, ideal for tracing the dark outlines of postholes or complex stratigraphic layers in a trench wall. A holster for your trowel is convenient.
- *A small whisk broom* for cleaning up.
- *An ice pick or small set of dental picks* for delicate excavation work, such as cleaning bones in the soil. Some exca-

vators prefer handmade bamboo picks, said to be more delicate on bone.

- *Three or four paintbrushes of 2-inch (50-mm) width or less* are essential for fine cleaning.
- *A 25-foot steel measuring tape (or metric equivalent).* I always carry my own as the excavation tapes are always in use. Most digs are now metric, so you should come equipped accordingly.
- *Pencils, erasers, permanent ink pens* for note taking and marking artifacts.
- *A personal notebook.*
- *Resealable plastic bags* of various sizes. Never be without them!

Don't forget a broad-brimmed hat, sunscreen, sunglasses, and good, sturdy boots, as well as gloves and knee pads if you feel a need for them. If hardhats are required, the excavation will provide them.

A light notebook computer is an increasingly commonplace, if relatively expensive, convenience.

foundations of its structures into the lower levels and sometimes even reuses the building materials of earlier generations. Postholes and storage pits, as well as burials, are sunk deep into older strata; their presence can be detected only by changes in soil color or the artifact content. Herds of cattle can trample small artifacts lying on the ground into underlying levels.

Here are some factors to be taken into account when interpreting stratigraphy:

- Human activities at the times in the past when the site was occupied and the effects, if any, on earlier occupations.
- Human activities, such as plowing and industrial activity, subsequent to final abandonment of the site.
- Natural processes of deposition and erosion at the time of occupation. For instance, Stone Age cave sites were often abandoned at times when the walls were shattered by frost and fragments of the rock face were showering down on the interior.
- Natural phenomena that have modified the stratigraphy after abandonment of the site (floods, tree uprooting, animal burrowing).

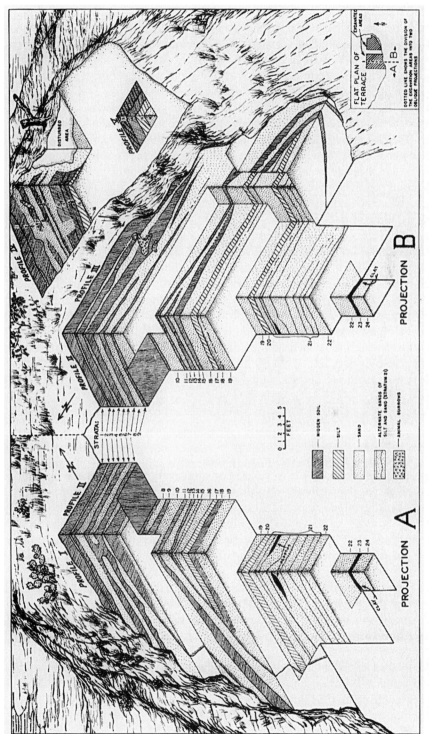

FIGURE 7.10 An exemplary stratigraphic diagram of the Devil's Mouth site, Amistad Reservoir, Texas. The diagram shows three-dimensional stratigraphy and correlates layers in different trenches one with another. (*Courtesy of the Department of Anthropology, University of Texas at Austin.*)

Interpreting archaeological stratigraphy involves reconstructing the depositional history of the site and then interpreting the significance of the natural and occupation levels observed. This analysis means distinguishing between types of human activity; between deposits that result from rubbish accumulation, architectural remains, and storage pits; and between activity areas and other artifact patterns.

Philip Barker, an English archaeologist and expert excavator, advocates a combined horizontal and vertical excavation for recording archaeological stratigraphy. He points out that a vertical profile gives a view of stratigraphy in the vertical plane only. Many important features appear in the section as a fine line and are decipherable only in the horizontal plane. The principal purpose of a stratigraphic profile is to record the information for posterity so that later observers have an accurate impression of how it was formed. Because stratigraphy demonstrates relationships—among sites and structures, artifacts, and natural layers—Barker advocates cumulative recording of stratigraphy as excavation is under way, which enables the archaeologist to record layers in section and in plan at the same time. Such recording requires extremely skillful excavation. Various modifications of this technique are used in both Europe and North America.

All archaeological stratigraphy is three-dimensional; that is to say, it involves observations in both the vertical and horizontal planes. The ultimate objective of archaeological excavation is to record the three-dimensional relationships throughout a site, for these are the relationships that provide the context of each find.

A superb example of an accurate section drawing appears in Figure 7.10.

ARCHAEOLOGICAL RECORDING

Records, records, records: Realize at once that any excavation is as much the creation of an archive as it is a dig. Your excavation destroys the site and the contexts of the artifacts found therein, so the record of your investigation is an archive as important as the undisturbed portions of the location. As the excavator, you have a responsibility both to publish the excavation in full and to deposit as complete a record of the site as possible in an appropriate, permanent repository. This responsibility means that the excavator spends much of his or her time writing in notebooks, entering records into a computer, or engaged in careful stratigraphic observation, mapping, and surveying. (See Doing Archaeology box on p. 205.)

A steady flow of artifacts, food remains, and other finds comes from every excavation. Here a computer-based recording system is invaluable, using bar codes or other methods to enter the data into the laboratory computer at the end of each day, or even during the dig. Each bag of finds or individual artifact, if important, has its own provenance number, which identifies its context in time and space. This provenance data, together with preliminary classifications of the artifacts, forms the basis of the find register in the computer.

DOING ARCHAEOLOGY

Site Records

I keep all kinds of notebooks on an excavation, of which the following are all-important:

- A *day-to-day journal* of the excavation, which begins the day we reach camp and ends when we pull out at the end of the dig. This is a general diary, in which I write about the progress of the excavation, record general thoughts and impressions, and write spontaneously about the work I am engaged in. This is also a personal account, in which I will write about conversations, discussions, and other people-related matters, such as theoretical disagreements between members of the research team. (For a sample page, see Figure 7.11*a*.) This

journal is absolutely invaluable when you are in the laboratory or writing up the excavation for publication, for it contains many forgotten details, first impressions, and passing thoughts that would otherwise not have been set down. I use a journal for all my research, even when visiting sites. When visiting the Maya center at Xunantunich in Belize, my journal reminded me about details of the excavations that had escaped my memory.

- *The site notebook* is the formal record of the excavations, which contains technical details of the dig, information on excavation and sampling methods, stratigraphic data, records of unusual finds, and major features, among other things. This is a much more organized

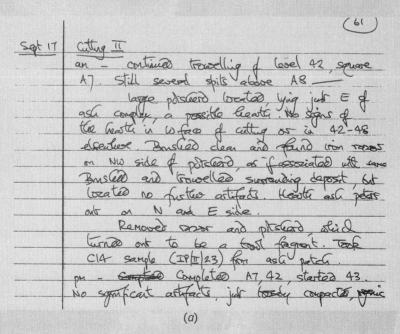

(a)

FIGURE 7.11 Site records: (a) Sample page of one of my site notebooks; (b) a sample page of one of my small-find notebooks.

(Continued)

DOING ARCHAEOLOGY

Site Records *(Continued)*

document, really a logbook of the day-to-day operation of the dig. The site notebook is also the entry point into all site records and is cross-referenced accordingly (Figure 7.11*b*). I usually use loose-leafed notebooks, so that I can insert single-page forms used for recording features and other important discoveries at the correct place in the book. Your site notebook should be compiled on archival paper, as it is the permanent record of the excavation.

As soon as possible, I photocopy all the site notebooks at once and put the originals in a safe to guard against loss.

Many excavators now use laptops and send their notes and data back to base by modem. I prefer pencil and paper. Have you ever had a computer crash because of dust at a critical moment when you have not backed up your data for a while? Once you have had this happen once, you either never do it again or you revert to pencil and paper!

Find number | Site, trench square, level | Artifact description * = action item

(b)

Maps, site plans, and photographs are an integral part of the recording process. Site plans may vary from a simple contour plan for a burial mound or small village to a complex plan of an entire prehistoric town or of a complicated series of structures. Accurate plans are important, for they provide a record not only of the site's features but also of the measurement recording grid set up prior to excavation to provide a framework for the trenching. The advent of computer-aided design (CAD) programs and computers has made the production of accurate plans much easier in expert hands. For example,

Douglas Gann has produced a three-dimensional AutoCad map of Homol'ovi Pueblo near Winslow, Arizona, which is a far more vivid reconstruction of the 150-room pueblo than any two-dimensional map. Combined with animations made with visualization software, this enables someone unfamiliar with the site to envisage what it must have been like when in use.

Classical archaeologists working at Corinth have used a laser theodolite to map the ancient city. The survey has provided the first accurate spatial record of human occupation on the site from Stone Age to Byzantine times. Corinth was laid to waste by the Roman general Mummius in 146 B.C., and was refounded as a Roman colony by Julius Caesar in 44 B.C. The laser survey has enabled the archaeologists to reconstruct the division of the site into plots for military veterans ordered by the Romans after the destruction of the city at the end of the second century B.C.

Three-dimensional recording is the recording of artifacts and structures in time and space. The provenance of archaeological finds is recorded with reference to the site grid (Figure 7.12). Traditionally, three-dimensional

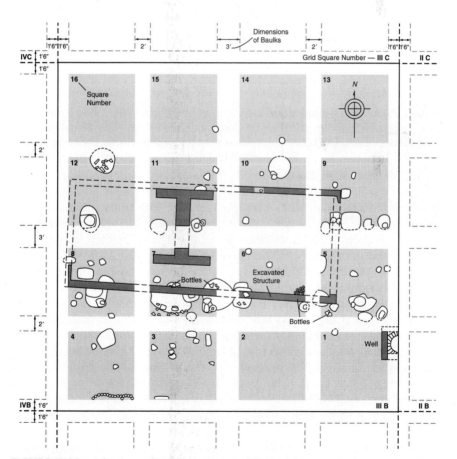

FIGURE 7.12 A horizontal grid excavation showing the layout of squares relative to an excavated structure at Colonial Williamsburg, Virginia.

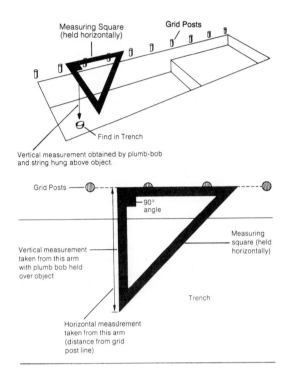

FIGURE 7.13 Three-dimensional recording the traditional way: using a measuring square *(top)*; a close view of the square from above *(bottom)*. A horizontal measurement is taken along the edge, perpendicular to the grid post line; the vertical measurement, from that arm with a plumb bob. Electronic instruments now carry out three-dimensional recording in a fraction of the time.

recording is carried out with a surveyor's level or with tapes and plumb bobs (Figure 7.13). It assumes particular importance on sites where artifacts are recorded in their original positions or on those where different periods in the construction of a building are being sorted out.

High technology is adding new accuracy to three-dimensional recording. By using theodolites equipped with laser beams, an excavation team can cut recording times dramatically. Harold Dibble has used the laser-surveying device with great success at the 50,000-year-old La Quina rock shelter in southwestern France. He estimates that the device cuts recording time by 50 percent and increases accuracy by 300 to 500 percent. A small microprocessor wired to the surveyor's tool records the measurement data, eliminating handwriting. Later, back in camp, the site laptop downloads its data into a personal computer that processes the measurements and produces a color-coded diagram of the day's work. The resulting map can be analyzed in a few minutes.

Grids, units, forms, and labels are the backbone of all recording efforts. Site grids are normally laid out with painted pegs and strings stretched over

FIGURE 7.14   Meticulous recording of an excavation at Boomplaas Cave in South Africa, where the researchers were recovering dozens of transitory Stone Age occupation horizons and fragile environmental data. The excavation removed tiny layers of deposit, recording the positions of individual artifacts with the aid of a grid suspended from the cave roof. *(Courtesy of Professor Hilary Deacon, Stellenbosch University, Stellenbosch, Cape, South Africa.)*

the trenches when recording is necessary. Small-scale recording of complex features may involve using an even smaller grid that covers but one square of the entire site grid.

At Boomplaas Cave in South Africa, Hilary Deacon used a precise grid laid out using the cave roof to record the position of minute artifacts, features, and environmental data (Figure 7.14). Similar grids have been erected over underwater wrecks in the Mediterranean, although laser recording is gradually replacing this technique. The various squares in the grid and the levels of the site are designated by grid numbers, which provide the means for identifying the location of finds as well as a basis for recording them. The labels attached to each bag or marked on the find bear the grid square numbers, which are then recorded in the site database.

ANALYSIS, INTERPRETATION, AND PUBLICATION

The process of archaeological excavation itself ends with filling in the trenches and transporting the finds and site records to the laboratory. The archaeologist retires from the field with a complete record of the excavations and with the data needed to test the hypotheses that were formulated before going into the field. But with this step, the job is far from finished; in fact, the work has hardly begun. The next stage in the research process is analyzing the finds, a topic covered in Chapters 8 and 9. Once the analysis is completed, interpretation of the site can begin.

In these days of high printing costs, it is impossible to publish the finds from any but the smallest sites in complete detail. Fortunately, many data retrieval systems enable us to store data on CD-ROM and microfilm so that they will be available to the specialists who need them. Already, one can access databases from some unpublished sites on the World Wide Web. The issues of permanent preservation of such digital records are the subject of much concern and debate.

Beyond publication, the archaeologist has two final obligations. The first is to place the finds and site records in a convenient repository where they will be safe and readily accessible to later generations. The second is to make the results available to a general audience as well as fellow professionals.

EXAMPLES OF ARCHAEOLOGICAL EXCAVATION

There is only one way to learn excavation and that is to go out in the field and work on an actual dig. You can do this in many ways—through university field schools, by going on an excavation overseas which accepts volunteers (see Chapter 13 for further information), or as a volunteer on an academic excavation. Many people gain experience digging on CRM projects, working as laborers or unskilled helpers, then graduating to more advanced work on the excavation. All I can do here is to give a general flavor of what different excavations are like and of some of the problems they encounter.

The text which follows should be read in conjunction with the accompanying photographs, taken during the course of the excavations.

Small Forager Site: Koobi Fora, Northern Kenya

The earliest archaeological sites in the world, in the East Turkana area of northern Kenya, date to about 2.5 million years ago. Such locations are little more than tiny scatters of fractured stones and broken animal bones representing a single visit, usually located in dry stream beds or other places that were sheltered from strong winds and hot sun. The excavators lay out a grid square over the site, dig test pits to establish the stratigraphy and geology of the area, then painstakingly expose and lift the entire artifact and bone scatter, recording the exact position of every find, however small. The result is an extremely accurate plan of the entire site, enabling the researchers to study the distribution of stone tools, waste flakes, and food remains in its entirely. In practice, the finds are plotted and lifted square by square, to prevent damage to fragile objects. One Koobi Fora location, site FxJj50, lay in an ancient water course close to an abundant supply of toolmaking stone (Figure 7.15). More than 2,100 fractured animal bones from 17 different mammals lay among

FIGURE 7.15   Site FxJj50. Koobi Fora, Kenya. *(Courtesy of Professor Harry Bunn, Department of Anthropology, University of Wisconsin, Madison.)*

the stone choppers and flakes used to break them up. Some sites lay in such sheltered locations that even tiny stone chips and leaf impressions were preserved in the sandy deposits.

This form of specialized area excavation is widely used on many small forager sites, among them the 1.75-million-year-old locations at Olduvai Gorge in Tanzania and on much later camps in Europe, Asia, and the Americas.

Complex Open Sites, Caves, and Rock Shelters: Gatecliff Rock Shelter, Nevada

Complex, much-stratified open sites, caves, and rock shelters are among the most challenging of all archaeological sites because they contain many, often highly compressed natural and occupation layers within very small areas (see Figure 7.10). This makes it hard to decipher both cultural sequences and individual occupations.

When David Hurst Thomas excavated Gatecliff Rockshelter in the uplands of the Great Basin in central Nevada in the 1970s and 1980s, he was confronted with more than 32 feet (10 m) of well-stratified deposits. He began with vertical excavation, with test pits and trenches that followed natural layers and established a stratigraphic sequence of 56 geological strata and 16 cultural levels. Radiocarbon dates showed that the site was occupied from about 2500 B.C. Thomas used changing stone projectile point forms and other artifacts to anchor the site to the cultural sequence for the Great Basin region, then shifted to horizontal excavation to explore short-term occupation levels in the upper deposits. As the excavation proceeded, he removed large blocks from ancient roof falls, then opened a large, deep trench with terraced walls for safety into the lowermost horizons. After years of excavation, he was able to establish that most visitors were single-sex groups engaged in specific tasks such as plant gathering some distance from their main base camp. He identified a distinctive "hearth line" 13 feet (4 m) from the back wall, situated to allow a smokefree and well-warmed work area in the shelter.

Few rock shelter excavations are on the scale of the Gatecliff project, but it offers a fine example of cave digging at its best.

Large Occupation Mounds: Çatalhöyük, Turkey

Many ancient societies occupied the same location for centuries on end, even for millennia. The early farming village at Abu Hureyra, Syria, accumulated a small *tell* between 9000 and 6000 B.C. Early cities such as Ur, Iraq, excavated by Sir Leonard Woolley in the 1920s and 1930s, cover many acres and boast not only of thousands of years of occupation debris, but temple mounds, royal cemeteries, and entire stratified city precincts. Early excavators such as Woolley uncovered enormous areas with the aid of workforces in the hundreds. Traditionally, mound excavation combines vertical and area excavation, as was the case at Ur. Karl Lamberg-Karlovsky excavated a huge stepped trench into the depths of the Tepe Yahya site on the Iranian Plateau (Figure 7.16), an approach that revealed stratigraphic evidence for increasingly important and more widespread trade in soapstone vessels.

Çatalhöyük in central Turkey was an important farming and trading community of closely huddled mudbrick houses in 6000 B.C., with as many as

FIGURE 7.16 Stepped mound excavation at Tepe Yahya, Iran. *(Courtesy of the Peabody Museum, Harvard University.)*

1,000 to 2,000 inhabitants; it was one of the largest human settlements in the world at the time. British archaeologist James Mellaart originally excavated Çatalhöyük's *tell* in the 1960s using area excavation which exposed an elaborate complex of houses and shrines, complete with vivid wall paintings and cult figures (Figure 7.17). Another British scholar, Ian Hodder, has now embarked on a long-term research project with an international research team to excavate the village anew, with all the technological and theoretical sophistication of late-twentieth-century archaeology. The excavations involve both vertical and area trenching, but especially the meticulous dissecting of individual houses and minute occupation levels within them. In one shrine, the diggers have used trowels, brushes, and dental picks to expose no less than 28 individual horizons and have recorded every item within them. This kind of "micro-excavation" is exceedingly expensive and very slow-moving, but is essential if we are to gain a closer understanding of the religious beliefs and day-to-day lives of Çatalhöyük's inhabitants.

Forts, Earthworks, and Burial Mounds: Maiden Castle, England, and Other Sites

The great British excavator Sir Mortimer Wheeler investigated the spectacular Iron Age hill fort at Maiden Castle in southern England in the 1930s and established a standard for earthwork and area excavation that has been a yardstick ever since (Figure 7.5). The Maiden Castle excavations combined vertical excavation of the serried and still steep-sided earthworks with area excavation of the entrances and interior of the fort. Wheeler adopted the classic approach of establishing the building sequence by dissecting the earthworks,

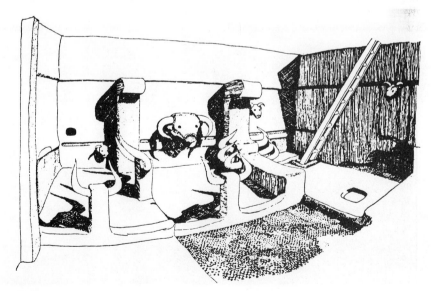

FIGURE 7.17   Shrine at Çatalhöyük, Turkey, with benches and ox heads. Such shrines were entered through the roof.

then excavating the houses and other features in the interior. He also reconstructed the Roman attack on the fort in A.D. 43 (see Chapter 2). His results were refined by further investigations in the 1980s.

The Wheeler approach influenced the way in which another British excavator, Barry Cunliffe, explored the Danebury Iron Age hill fort further north. Cunliffe devoted many seasons to large-scale area excavations in the interior of Danebury, which revealed many details of the settlement once protected by formidable earthworks. But the entire excavation (Figure 7.7) was anchored to the stratigraphy established by digging the earthworks.

Few earthwork excavations approach the scale of the Maiden Castle and Danebury digs, which were expensive, long-term academic projects. Most investigations involve a combination of test excavation, remote sensing, and careful area survey: The excavations seek to answer highly specific questions. A case in point is the Monk's Mound at *Cahokia, Illinois*, which was the focal point of a densely populated floodplain near the modern city of East St. Louis after A.D. 1050, when the Mississippian culture flourished in the region (Figure 7.18). Our knowledge of Cahokia comes from years of very large- and small-scale excavation both at the site itself and in the surrounding areas, much of it carried out as part of CRM excavations or as operations to stabilize and preserve major earthworks. For instance, a recent slump on the second of Monk's Mound's four terraces allowed archaeologists to test-pit the slump areas as part of the stabilization process. They found that the terrace was built in about A.D. 1000 to 1100.

Burial mounds are a specialized form of excavation, which involve not only investigating graves and funeral rites, but establishing the environment of the area when the mound was built and the mode of construction. Sometimes the mound is excavated totally to the original ground level, using

FIGURE 7.18 Reconstruction of the central precincts of Cahokia, Illinois, with Monk's Mound in the foreground. *(Courtesy of the Cahokia Mounds State Park, Cahokia, Illinois.)*

a quadrant method, like the slices of a cake, or some other area method, but selective investigation involving cross sections or even test pits is more common today, when conservation is as important as excavation.

Middens, Shell or Otherwise

In archaeology, **middens** are piles of discarded occupation debris, sometimes they are huge accumulations of shells (as along the California coast, in South Africa, or New Zealand) or city trash heaps, such as those at Maya cities, for instance Copán, Honduras. Midden excavation usually involves random sampling to ensure the collection of statistically valid quantitative data of pottery and other discarded artifacts, or on such topics as changes in shellfish-eating habits and climatic shifts reflected in the frequencies of different species. Test pits and vertical excavation are normally used, combined with careful screening procedures designed to recover objects as small as fish or bird bones.

Midden excavation is not the most exciting of fieldwork. Indeed, screening sea- or freshwater shells day after day is positively mind-numbing. However, the data that can be obtained from such excavations is invaluable. One of the finest shell midden excavations ever conducted was at Galatea Bay near Auckland, New Zealand, in the early 1960s, where archaeologist Wilfred Shawcross investigated a shallow Maori fishing midden using a grid form of horizontal excavation instead of the usual vertical trenches or test pits (Figure 7.19). He obtained such fine-grained data that he was able to establish the weights and seasons of many fish species in the site.

Underwater Archaeology: Uluburun, Turkey

Underwater archaeology has all the romantic aura of treasure hunting, thanks to years of *National Geographic* magazine stories that depict scuba divers raising amphora jars, copper ingots, and other spectacular finds from the seabed. In fact, underwater archaeology has exactly the same objectives as excavation on land—the meticulous recording of a sealed time capsule (a shipwreck) for information about ancient times.

Archaeologists George Bass and Cemal Pulak of Texas A&M University's Institute for Nautical Archaeology excavated a Bronze Age shipwreck off Uluburun on the southern Turkish coast, using the latest underwater techniques. They established a measurement grid over the site, just as they would on land, then plotted every ship's timber and every item of the cargo in its exact position on the seabed before lifting them (Figure 7.20). The wreck lay in 90 to 150 feet (27 to 46 m) of water on a steep slope. As the ship landed on the bottom, the cargo shifted. Bass and Pulak's meticulous area excavation recovered a wealth of information about the cargo ship and its construction and about the cargo, which included enough copper and tin to make bronze armor and weapons for an entire regiment. They were able to date the wreck with tree rings to about 1310 B.C.; they established that the ship was traveling from east to west and that she contained cargo from at least nine different regions of the eastern Mediterranean and Aegean Seas.

FIGURE 7.19 Exemplary midden excavation at Galatea Bay, New Zealand. *(Courtesy of Professor Wilfred Shawcross, Australian National University, Canberra, Australia.)*

FIGURE 7.20 Excavations on the Uluburun shipwreck. *(Courtesy of the Institute for Nautical Archaeology, Texas A&M University, College Station, Texas.)*

FRAGILE OBJECTS

Narratives of nineteenth-century excavation abound with accounts of spectacular and delicate discoveries that crumbled to dust upon exposure to the air. Regrettably, similar discoveries are still made today, but many spectacular recoveries of fragile artifacts have been made. In almost every find, the archaeologist responsible has had to use great ingenuity, often with limited preservation materials on hand. Sir Leonard Woolley faced very difficult recovery problems when he excavated the Royal Cemetery at Ur-of-the-Chaldees in the 1920s. In one place, he recovered an offering stand of wood, gold, and silver, portraying a he-goat with his front legs on the branches of a thicket, by pouring paraffin wax over the scattered remains (see Figure 1.2). Later, he rebuilt the stand in the laboratory and restored it to a close approximation of the original.

Conservation of archaeological finds has become a highly specialized field of endeavor, which covers every form of find, from textiles to leather, human skin, and basketry. Many conservation efforts, such as those used to preserve the Danish bog corpses, or the famous Roskilde Viking ships near Copenhagen, Denmark, can take years to complete (see Figure 2.11). The Bronze Age site at Flag Fen in eastern England has yielded tens of thousands of wood fragments, including house planks, oak posts, and parts of trackways. Excavators Francis and Maisie Pryor keep the wood wet during excavation with spray systems. Once the wood is lifted, the most important specimens go into freshwater tanks or are freeze-dried for permanent preservation.

BURIALS AND HUMAN REMAINS

To many people, *excavation* means human skeletons—lots of them. In fact, burial excavation is a difficult and routine task that must be performed with care because of the delicacy and often bad state of the bones. The record of the bones' position and the placement of the grave goods and body ornaments is as important as the association of the burial, for the archaeological objective is to reconstruct burial customs as much as establish chronology. Although the Maya lords of Mesoamerica were sometimes buried under great pyramids, as at Palenque, where the Lord Pacal lay under the Temple of the Inscriptions, most burials are normally located by means of a simple surface feature, such as a gravestone or a pile of stones, or through an accidental discovery during excavation. Once the grave outline has been found, the skeleton is carefully exposed from above. The first part of the skeleton to be identified will probably be the skull or one of the limb bones. The main outline of the burial is then traced before the delicate backbone, feet, and finger bones are uncovered. The greatest care is taken not to displace the bones or any of the ornaments or grave goods that surround them. Normally, the undersurfaces of the bones are left in the soil so that the skeleton may be recorded photographically before removal (Figure 7.21). Either the burial is removed bone by bone, or it is removed as a single unit to the laboratory, where it is cleaned at leisure.

FIGURE 7.21 Maya burials from Gualan in Guatemala's Motagua Valley. Note the clean excavation, the carefully brushed skeleton with bones still in position, and the stone lining of the tomb. *(Courtesy of Professor Norman Hammond, Department of Archaeology, Boston University.)*

Some burials are deposited in funerary chambers so elaborate that the contents of the tomb may reveal information not only on the funeral rites but also, as in the Sumerian royal burials at Ur, on the social order of the royal court (Chapter 1).

Excavation of Native American burials has generated furious political controversy in recent years, with native groups arguing that it is unethical to dig up even the prehistoric dead. Reburial and repatriation legislation now restricts the excavation of ancient burials (see discussion in Chapter 2).

Human skeletons are a valuable source of information on prehistoric populations. The bones can be used to identify the sex and age of the buried person as well as to study ancient diseases. A whole series of new techniques are revolutionizing studies of prehistoric diet and even DNA.

STRUCTURES AND PITS

Area excavations are normally used to uncover structures of considerable size. Grids allow stratigraphic control over the building site, especially over the study of successive occupation stages. Many such structures may have been built of such perishable materials as wood or matting. Wooden houses are normally recognized by the postholes of the wall timbers and, sometimes, foundation trenches. Clay walls collapse into a pile when a hut is burned or falls down; thus, the wall clay may bear impressions of matting, sticks, or thatch. Stone and mudbrick structures are often better preserved, especially if mortar was used, although sometimes the stone has been removed by later builders and only foundation trenches remain. Stratigraphic cross sections across walls give an insight into the structure's history. The dating of most stone structures is complicated, especially when successive rebuilding or occupation of the building is involved (Figure 7.22).

The pueblos of the American Southwest offer another type of problem in excavation. The many rooms of the pueblos contain complicated deposits

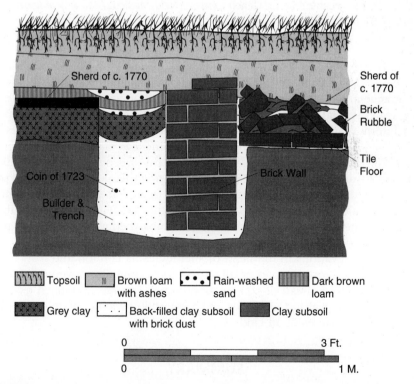

FIGURE 7.22 Dating construction of a building by its associated artifacts. The brick wall was built in a foundation trench that was filled with brick dust and clay. Someone dropped a coin dating to 1723 into the clay as the trench was being filled. Obviously, then, the building of which the wall forms a part dates to no earlier than 1723. *(Courtesy of Ivor Nöel Hume.)*

FIGURE 7.23 Pueblo Bonito, Chaco Canyon, New Mexico. *(Courtesy of Robert Harding, Photo Researchers.)*

full of occupation debris and many artifacts (Figure 7.23). Such assemblages can be used to identify the activities carried out in different spaces.

Storage and rubbish pits are commonly found on archaeological sites and may reach several feet in depth (Figure 7.24*a*). Their contents furnish important information on dietary habits with data gleaned from food residues or caches of seeds. Trash pits are even more informative. Garbage pits and privies at Colonial Williamsburg have yielded a host of esoteric finds, including wax seals from documents that were used as toilet tissue. Some historic pits can be dated from military buttons and other finds. Pits of all kinds are normally identified by circular discolorations in the soil. The contents are then cross-sectioned, and the associated finds are analyzed as an associated unit (Figure 7.24*b*).

Urban excavations in the heart of such cities as London and New York are among the most complex of all excavations, sometimes even conducted underground and ahead of construction crews (Figure 7.25). Such excavations require specialized techiques and a sound knowledge of ancient architecture and structures of all kinds.

SUMMARY

Excavation is a primary way in which archaeologists acquire subsurface data about the past. Modern archaeologists tend to carry out as little excavation as possible, however, because digging archaeological sites destroys a finite

FIGURE 7.24   Storage pit excavation: *(a)* a double storage pit at Maiden Castle, England, that was cut into white chalk sub-soil; *(b)* a cross section across an excavated storage pit. *(Courtesy of the Society of Antiquaries, London.)*

(a)

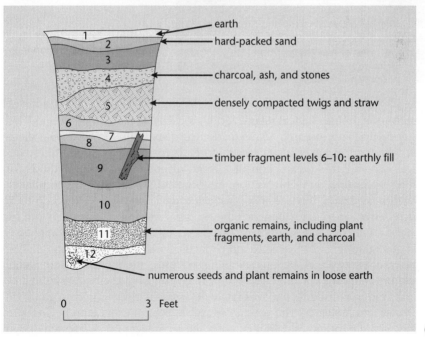

earth

hard-packed sand

charcoal, ash, and stones

densely compacted twigs and straw

timber fragment levels 6–10: earthly fill

organic remains, including plant fragments, earth, and charcoal

numerous seeds and plant remains in loose earth

0   3 Feet

(b)

FIGURE 7.25 A subterranean urban excavation in London. *(Courtesy of the Museum of London.)*

resource—the archaeological record. Today's excavations are often conducted by multidisciplinary research teams made up of specialists from several disciplines, who work together on a carefully formulated research design. All archaeological excavation is destruction of a finite resource. Accurate methods for planning, recording, and observation are essential. The Koster site in Illinois, where the excavators devised a sophisticated data flow system to keep their research design up-to-date, illustrates the essential research design. Sites can be excavated totally or, as is more common, selectively. Vertical excavation is used to test stratigraphy and to make deep probes of archaeological deposits. Test pits, often combined with various sampling methods, are dug to give an overall impression of an unexcavated site before major digging begins. Horizontal or area excavation is used to uncover far wider areas and especially to excavate site layouts and buildings. The process of archaeological excavation begins with a precise site survey and establishment of a site-recording grid. A research design is formulated, and hypotheses are developed for testing. Placement of trenches is determined by locating likely areas or by sampling methods. Excavation involves not only digging but also recording stratigraphy and the provenances of finds, as well as observations of the processes that led to the site's formation. Careful stratigraphic observation in three dimensions is the basis of all good excavation and is used to demonstrate relationships among layers and between layers and artifacts. Excavation is followed by analysis and interpretation and, finally, publication of the finds to provide a permanent record of the work carried out. Chapter 7 also describes excavations at several different site types.

KEY TERMS

Area excavation

Horizontal excavation

Midden

Physical anthropologist

Selective excavation

Site-formation processes

Test pit

Three-dimensional recording

Total excavation

Vertical excavation

GUIDE TO FURTHER READING

Manuals on excavation and field methods are surprisingly rare, but here is a selection. Look out for forthcoming series of short paperbacks on specific aspects of excavation, which several publishers are about to put on the market.

Barker, Philip. 1986. *Understanding Archaeological Excavation*. London: Batsford.

An expert guide to excavation. Strong British orientation.

Bray, Tamara L., and Thomas, W. Killion. eds. 1994. *Reckoning with the Dead: The Larsen Bay Repatriation and the Smithsonian Institution*. Washington DC: Smithsonian Institution Press.

An absolutely superb discussion of a controversial case study in repatriation, which includes valuable information on the Native American perspective.

Frankel, David. 1991. *Remains to Be Seen*. Melbourne, Australia: Longman Cheshire.

A simple manual of Australian archaeology that is crammed with helpful insights about archaeological methods in general; for the beginning reader. Excellent illustrations.

Hester, Thomas R., Harry J. Shafer, and Kenneth L. Feder 1997. *Field Methods in Archaeology*. 7th ed. Mountain View, CA: Mayfield.

An updated version of a classic field manual aimed at American archaeologists. Probably the most useful source for general information.

Joukowsky, Martha. 1986. *Complete Manual of Field Archaeology*. Englewood Cliffs, NJ: Prentice Hall.

A survey of excavation methods in both New World and Old World contexts. Recommended for general reading.

Wheeler, R. E. M. 1954. *Archaeology from the Earth*. Oxford: Clarendon Press.

An archaeological classic that describes excavation on a grand scale with verve and elegance. A must for every archaeologist's bookshelf, if only for its common-sense information.

PART IV

❂

RECONSTRUCTING PAST LIVES

*A man who has once looked with the
archaeological eye will never see again quite
normally. He will be wounded by what other
men call trifles. It is possible to refine the
sense of time until an old show in the bunch
grass or a pile of nineteenth century beer
bottles in an abandoned mining town tolls
in one's head like a hall clock. This is the
price one pays for learning to read time from
surfaces other than an illuminated dial. It is
the melancholy secret of the artifact, the
humanly touched thing.*

LOREN EISELEY, *THE NIGHT COUNTRY.*

The golden mask of Egyptian pharaoh Tutankhamun, c. 1323 B.C. (Source: Douglas Miller/ Hulton Getty/Liaison Agency, Inc.)

Artifact Analysis
Discovery: Celebrating Finds at Carchemish, Syria
   Classification
   Typology
   Types
Doing Archaeology: Archaeological Types
   Quantitative Methods
Ancient Technology
   Stone
Doing Archaeology: Lithic Analysis
   Clay (Ceramics)
Doing Archaeology: Ceramic Analysis
   Metals and Metallurgy
Site: Ancient Wine at Abydos, Egypt
   Bone, Wood, Basketry, and Textiles

Technology: We are obsessed with it. Our society can land someone on the moon, aim cruise missiles at small targets hundreds of miles away and hit them, transplant human hearts, and send pilotless aircraft powered by the sun high above the earth. Technology has changed history. The harnessing of fire just after 2 million years ago enabled our remote forebears to settle in bitterly cold climates. About 25,000 years before present, the fashioning of small ivory needles with perforated eyes led to the development of layered clothing which allowed people to survive comfortably in subzero winters. Approximately 3,000 years ago, the development of the outrigger canoe enabled people living in the southwestern Pacific to colonize offshore islands hundreds of miles beyond the horizon. Since the earliest times, our cultures and technological inventiveness have allowed us to adapt to a great range of natural environments and develop ingenious ways of intensifying the food quest, of fishing and sea-mammal hunting, and of farming the land in a world of growing population densities. All modern humanity's myriad technologies are ultimately descended from the first simple tools made by human beings over 2.5 million years ago. With over 6 billion people on earth, our technological prowess has the enormous challenge of feeding a rapidly growing global population while preserving the environmental quality of the world.

We know more about ancient technologies than any other aspect of the societies of the past because we study the material remains of long-forgotten behavior. Thus, it is hardly surprising that the analysis of artifacts is a major part of archaeological research and the follow-on from site surveys or excavations, whatever the size of the project. Chapter 8 discusses artifact analysis and the major technologies used in ancient times.

ARTIFACT ANALYSIS

Artifact analysis is labor-intensive and time-consuming, taking far longer than excavation or survey. A month's excavation can yield enough laboratory work for six months or more, and that before the final report is even drafted. This is the unspectacular part of archaeology, as opposed to excavation, but among the most important. (See Discovery box below.)

The elaborate process of analysis and classification starts in the field alongside excavation—processing and organizing the finds so that they can be analyzed. These first stages in processing newly excavated archaeological finds are entirely routine (Figure 8.1). Most excavations maintain some form of field laboratory. It is here that the major site records are maintained, stratigraphic profile drawings are kept up to date, and radiocarbon samples and other special finds are packed for examination by specialists. A small team staffs the field laboratory. Its members ensure that all finds are cleaned, processed promptly, packed carefully, and labeled and recorded precisely. A successful laboratory operation allows the director of the excavation to evaluate the available data daily, even hourly. It is here, too, that basic conser-

 DISCOVERY

Celebrating Finds at Carchemish, Syria

Early archaeologists in Egypt and parts of southwestern Asia worked with enormous teams of workers by modern standards. The workforce on Flinders Petrie's Egyptian digs in the 1890s numbered in the hundreds, as did those at Ur in Iraq in the 1920s and 1930s. Leonard Woolley of Ur fame excavated the Hittite city at Carchemish on the Euphrates River in Syria just before World War I. He and his colleague T. E. Lawrence not only excavated the great city, they also spied on German engineers building a nearby railroad to Baghdad as a sideline. Woolley was a born leader of Arab workers. He worked closely with his foreman Hamoudi, famous among archaeologists of the day for his swearing. The Carchemish excavations were always light-hearted. Woolley and Hamoudi celebrated each important discovery with a rifle volley, the number of cartridges denoting the significance of the find. The

volleys became a form of competition that were a badge of honor for the workers and a celebration of discovery. The workers labored in teams, with the job of pick-man being especially prized, for the chance of receiving a volley was much higher. But Woolley made sure that basket carriers who found something of significance were given an extra large volley, to ensure that eyes were always open.

Woolley himself admitted that the system appeared childish, but he encouraged it as a way of making the excavation proceed smoothly and be something more than what he called "a mere business." He hated dull excavations and enjoyed the company of workers who were fiercely loyal to him. The process of discovery was a game pursued with deadly seriousness and on a scale and with methods that would never be tolerated today.

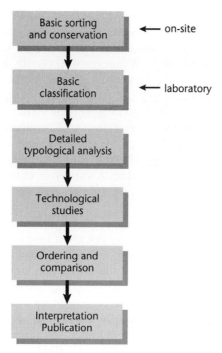

FIGURE 8.1 The process of artifact analysis.

vation work is carried out, reassembling fragmented pots, hardening bones with chemicals, or stabilizing fragile objects. Computers play an important role in the field laboratory, for they are used to code vast quantities of information for later use.

The analysis continues back in the home laboratory, whether a small ceramic study for a CRM project or an enormous, years-long activity that results from a large-scale survey or excavation. You need large, empty tables, specimen cabinets, good lighting, and good cleaning facilities in the artifact laboratory—this before you start talking about any form of microscope or high-technology device for studying such esoteric details as the composition of pottery clays or the trace elements in flaked obsidian used for stone tool manufacture. You also need a good eye for detail, an orderly mind, and, above all, infinite patience. It takes weeks to sort and classify even a relatively small artifact collection. I have colleagues who have spent years analyzing a single medium-sized excavation.

Successful artifact analysis revolves around classification and typology, two fundamental archaeological skills.

Classification

Our attitude toward life and our surroundings involves constant classification and sorting of massive quantities of data. Driving along the freeway this morning, I found myself unconsciously classifying the tide of automobiles on the road: luxury sedans, sport utility vehicles, pickups, vans. Then there were Chevrolets, Fords, Chryslers, Mercedes, and so on, all of them in different colors and model configurations. We never stop classifying artifacts, people, our surroundings. We classify types of eating utensils: knives, forks, and spoons—each type has a different use and is kept in a separate compartment in the drawer. We group roads according to their surface, finish, and size. In addition to classifying artifacts, lifestyles, and cultures, we make choices among them. If we are eating soup, we choose to use a spoon. Some people eat rice with a fork, some use chopsticks or their fingers, and others have decided that a spoon is more suitable. A variety of choices is available, but the final decision is often dictated by cultural custom rather than by functional pragmatism.

All people classify, because doing so is a requirement for abstract thought and language. But everyday classes are not often best for archaeological purposes. **Classification,** in archaeology, is the process of dividing artifacts and other data into discrete types. Like the computer, however, classification should be a servant rather than a master. Sometimes our classifications of good and bad—those based on color of skin or on our definitions of what is moral or immoral—are made and then adhered to as binding principles of life without ever being questioned or modified, no matter how much our circumstances may change. The dogmatism and rigidity that result from these attitudes are as dangerous in archaeology as they are in daily life.

In archaeology, classification is a research tool, a means for creating data. All classifications used by archaeologists follow directly from the problems they are studying. Let us say that our excavator is studying changes in pottery designs over a 500-year period in the Southwest. The classification he or she uses will follow not only from what other people have done but also from the problems being studied. How and even what you classify stems directly from the research questions asked of the data.

Taxonomy is the name given to the system of classifying concepts, materials, objects, and phenomena used in many sciences, including archaeology. Biologists classify human beings within a hierarchy developed by Carolus Linnaeus in the eighteenth century. It begins with the kingdom Animalia, the phylum Chordata (animals with notochords and gill slits), the subphylum Vertebrata (animals with backbones), the class Mammalia, the subclass Eutheria, the order Primates, the suborder Hominoidea (apes and hominidae), the family Hominidae, the genus *Homo,* the species *sapiens,* and, finally, the subspecies *sapiens.* This hierarchy is gradually refined until only *Homo sapiens sapiens* remains in its own taxonomic niche. It consists of a hierarchy of units. Each element in the hierarchy is defined and related to the others. Archaeology has built its own taxonomy of specialist terminologies and concepts quite haphazardly, but with four major objectives:

- *Organizing data into manageable units.* This step is part of the preliminary data-processing operation, and it commonly involves separating finds on the basis of raw material (stone, bone, and so on) or artifacts from food remains. This preliminary ordering allows much more detailed classification later on.

- *Describing types.*   By identifying the individual features **(attributes)** of hundreds of artifacts, or clusters of artifacts, the archaeologist can group them, by common attributes, into relatively few types. These types represent patterns of separate associations of attributes. Such types are economical ways of describing large numbers of artifacts. Which attributes are chosen depends on the purpose of the typology.

- *Identifying relationships between types.*   Describing types orders the relationships among artifacts. These stem, in part, from the use of a variety of raw materials, manufacturing techniques, and functions.

These three objectives are much used in culture-historical research. Processual archaeologists may use classification for a fourth:

- Studying assemblage variability in the archaeological record. These studies are often combined with ethnographic analogy or formal experiments with replicated technologies.

Archaeological classifications are artificial formulations based on criteria set up by archaeologists. These classificatory systems, however, do not necessarily coincide with those developed by the people who made the original artifacts.

Typology

Typology is a system of classification based on the construction of **artifact types.** It is a search for patterns among either objects or the variables that define these objects, a search that has taken on added meaning and complexity as archaeologists have begun to use computer technology and sophisticated statistical methods. This kind of typology is totally different from arbitrarily dividing up the objects and variables. I remember sitting in a Cambridge archaeological laboratory many years ago and learning the basics of stone tool classification. Our instructor laid out a series of Acheulian hand axes in front of us, magnificent specimens from the gravels of the Thames River (Figure 8.10*b*). He divided them into different categories. "These are pointed axes, these ovates [oval-shaped], these ovates with twisted edges, these linguate, with tongue-shaped ends," he declared. One of us pointed out that some of the axes in the "pointed" category were far from ideal examples of the form; in fact, one or two were distinctly oval. "They are pointed hand axes," pronounced our instructor firmly, brooking no disagreement. The arbitrariness of his classifications was just like that used by a stamp collector classifying postage stamps. It was as if prehistoric hand axes were all standardized productions turned out by an impersonal stone-flaking machine. Lost was the opportunity to examine the underlying patterns of human design and behavior, which is what interests archaeologists more than mere classification.

Typology enables archaeologists to construct arbitrarily defined units of analysis that apply to two or more samples of artifacts, so that these samples can be compared objectively. These samples can come from different sites, or from separate levels of the same site. Typology is classification to permit comparison, an opportunity to examine underlying patterns of human design and behavior. The value of typology is that it enables you to compare what has been found at two sites or in different levels of the same site. Typology, as James Deetz (1967) puts it, has one main aim: "classification which permits comparison. . . . Such a comparison allows the archaeologist to align his assemblage with others in time and space." Let us look over a group of archaeologists' shoulders as they sort through a large pile of potsherds, from one occupation level, on the laboratory table.

First, the sherds are separated by decoration or lack of it, paste, temper, firing methods, and vessel shape (Figure 8.2). Once the undecorated or shapeless potsherds have been counted and weighed, they are put to one side, unless they have some special significance. Then the remaining sherds are examined individually and divided into types, according to the features they display. Some potsherds stand out because they enable one to distinguish different vessel functions—globular pots, shallow bowls, and so on, which provides one basis for type classification by function. Many sherds tell one little about vessel form or function, but they bear different painted designs,

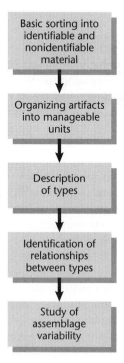

FIGURE 8.2 Classifying a collection of potsherds. The basic stages of simple classification.

a basis for distinguishing different styles. The classifier piles them on the table by style of decoration: one consists of sherds painted with black designs; a second, red-painted fragments; a third, a group of plain sherds. Once the preliminary sort is completed, the archaeologists look over each pile in turn. They have already identified three broad types in the pottery collection. But when they examine the first pile more closely, they find that the black-painted sherds can be divided into several smaller groupings: one with square, black panels; another with diamond designs; and a third with black-dotted decoration. In the end, the researchers may identify three functional types and perhaps eight or nine stylistic types on the basis of decoration and other stylistic features, each, perhaps, with several subtypes. The archaeologists study the collection in minute detail, identifying dozens—if not hundreds—of attributes, distinctive features of an artifact, for example, the thickness of a pot wall or a type of base-thinning on a stone projectile point, conspicuous and inconspicuous, stylistic or dimensional, even some based on chemical analyses. This is the process of typology, classifying artifacts so that one type can be compared with another. Obviously, the types from this one site can be compared with other arbitrary types found during laboratory sorting of collections from nearby sites.

For accurate and meaningful comparisons to be made, rigorous definitions of analytical types are needed, to define not only the "norm" of the artifact type but also its approximate range of variation, at either end of which one type merges into one or two others. Conventional analytical definitions are usually couched in terms of one or more attributes that indicate how the artifact was made, the shape, the decoration, or some other distinctive feature. These definitions are set up following carefully defined technological differences, often bolstered by measurements or statistical clusterings of attributes. Most often, the average artifact, rather than the variation between individual examples, is the ultimate objective of the definition.

Types

We all have strong opinions about how we classify artifacts, just like the people who originally made them, for each has or had a distinctive role in society. We assign different roles in eating to a knife, a fork, and a spoon. Knives cut meat; steak knives are used for eating steaks. The stone arrowhead is employed in the chase; one type of missile head is used to hunt deer, another to shoot birds, and so on. The use of an artifact may be determined not only by convenience and practical considerations but also by custom or regulation. The light-barbed spearheads used by some Australian hunting bands to catch fish are too fragile for dispatching a kangaroo; the special barbs permit the impaled fish to be lifted out of the water. Pots are made by women in most African and Native American societies, which have division of labor by sex; each has formed complicated customs, regulations, or taboos, which, functional considerations apart, categorize clay pots into different types with varying uses and rules in the culture (Figure 8.3).

FIGURE 8.3 The difficulties of artifact classification are well demonstrated by this classic example of a basketry tray for parching acorns. This finely made basket was produced by the Chumash Indians of southern California by weaving plant fibers. The design was formed in the maker's mind by several factors, most important of which was the tremendous reservoir of learned cultural experience that the Chumash have acquired, generation by generation, through the several thousand years they lived in southern California. The designs of their baskets are learned and relate to the feeling that such and such a form and color are "correct" and traditionally acceptable. But there are more pragmatic and complex reasons, too, including the flat, circular shape that enables the user to roast seeds by tossing them with red embers. Each attribute of the basket has a good reason for its presence—whether traditional, innovative, functional, or imposed by the technology used to make it. The band of decoration around the rim is a feature of the Chumash decorative tradition and occurs on most of their baskets. It has a rich red-brown color from the species of reed used to make it. The steplike decoration was dictated by the sewing and weaving techniques, but the diamond pattern is unique and the innovative stamp of one weaver, which might or might not be adopted by other craftspeople in later generations. The problem for the archaeologist is to measure the variations in human artifacts, to establish the causes behind the directions of change, and to find what these variations can be used to measure. This fine parching tray serves as a warning that variations in human artifacts are both complex and subtle.

The Chumash hunter-gatherers occupied the Santa Barbara Channel region of southern California. At the time of European contact in the fifteenth century, they dwelt in permanent villages, some housing as many as 1,000 people. They were ruled by chiefs and enjoyed a complex ritual and social life.

Furthermore, each society has its own conception of what a particular artifact should look like. Americans have generally preferred larger cars, Europeans small ones. These preferences reflect not only pragmatic considerations of road width and longer distances to travel in the New World but also differing attitudes toward traveling and, for many Americans, a preoccupation with prestige manifested in gold-leaf lettering and custom colors, hubcaps, and style. The steering wheel is on the left, and the car is equipped with turn signals and seatbelts by law. In other words, we know what we want and expect an automobile to look like, even though minor design details change—as do the length of women's skirts and the width of men's ties.

Archaeologists have to devise archaeological types that are appropriate to the research problems they are tackling, an extremely difficult task. This grouping may or may not coincide with the actual tool types designated by the original makers. Such groupings are based on criteria set up by archaeologists as a convenient way of studying ancient tool kits, style, and technology. They are useful scientific devices that provide a manageable way of classifying small and large collections of prehistoric tools and the by-products from manufacturing them. A good example comes from the world-famous Olduvai Gorge site in East Africa, where Louis and Mary Leakey excavated a series of cache sites used by very early humans, *__Homo habilis.__* Mary Leakey studied the stone tools and grouped them in the "Oldowan tradition," a tradition characterized by jagged-edged chopping tools and flakes (Figure 8.4).

(a)

(b)

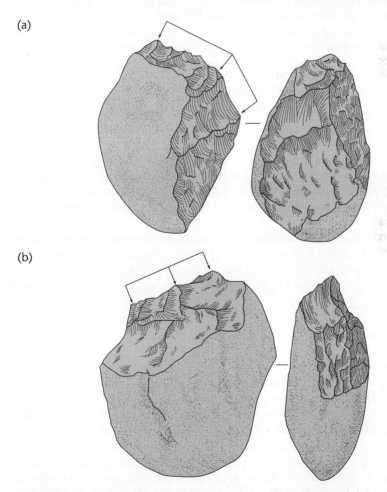

FIGURE 8.4 Oldowan "chopping tool": A simplified picture of the process of making a jagged edge by flaking a cobble from both sides *(top).* A large disc-shaped Oldowan artifact in plan and side view *(bottom).*

She based her classifications on close examination of the artifacts, and an assumption that the first human tool kit was based on crude stone choppers soon became archaeological dogma.

Recently, Nicholas Toth of Indiana University has taken a radically different approach to classifying Oldowan artifacts. He has spent many hours not only studying and classifying the original artifacts, but also learning Oldowan technology for himself, replicating hundreds of artifacts made by *Homo habilis* 2 million years ago. His controlled experiments have shown that *Homo habilis* was not using chopping tools at all. The primeval stone workers were more interested in the sharp-edged flakes they knocked off lumps of lava, for cutting and butchering the game meat they scavenged from predator kills. The "chopping tools" were, in fact, just cores or the end product of knocking flakes off convenient lumps of lava.

Controlled experiments like Toth's provide useful insights into how prehistoric peoples manufactured the tools they needed. Toth and other experts are now trying to study the telltale patterns of edge wear on the cutting edges of Oldowan flakes, for the polish, striations, and microflake scars left by working, for example, fresh bone as opposed to hide or wood are highly distinctive. With controlled experimentation and careful examination of edge wear, they hope to achieve a closer marriage between the ways in which the first humans used stone tools and the classifications devised by the archaeologist hundreds of thousands of years later.

Archaeological types are based on clusters of similar attributes or on clusters of objects. The archaeologist constructs typologies based on the reoccurrence of formal patterns of physical features of artifacts. Many of these formal types have restricted distributions in space and time, which suggest they represent distinctive "styles" of construction and/or tasks that were carried out in the culture to which they belong. For example, the so-called *Chavín* art style was widespread over much of coastal and highland Peru after 900 B.C. The jaguar, snake, and human forms of this art are highly characteristic and mark the spread of a distinctive iconography over a large area of the Andean region. Chavín art, and the characteristic styles associated with it, had a specific role in Peruvian society of the time (Figure 8.5). (See Doing Archaeology box on p. 238.)

Attribute Analysis   As archaeologists work out their typologies, they find themselves examining hundreds of individual fragments of stone tools, potsherds, and other artifacts, each of which bears several distinctive attributes.

Every commonplace artifact we use can be examined by its attributes. The familiar glass beer mug has a curved handle which extends from near the lip to the base, often fluted sides, a straight, rounded rim, and dimensions that are set by the amount of beer it is intended to contain. It is manufactured of clear, relatively thick glass (the thickness can be defined by precise measurement). You can find numerous attributes on any human artifact, be it a diamond ring or a prehistoric pot. For example, a collection of 50 potsherds lying on a laboratory table may bear black-painted designs,

FIGURE 8.5 A Chavín carving on a pillar in the temple interior at Chavín de Huantar, Peru. This reconstruction makes the temple walls seem more regular and the background more open than they actually were. The distinctive motifs exhibit the style of Chavín art spread throughout highland and coastal Peru, marking an interval termed the Chavín "Horizon" that cuts across many local sequences. *(Courtesy of Professor Gordon Willey, Harvard University.)*

while 8 have red panels on the neck, 10 are shallow bowls, and so on. An individual potsherd may come from a vessel made of bright red clay mixed with powdered seashells so that the clay fires better. It may come from a pot with a thick rim made by applying a rolled circle of clay before firing and a crisscross design cut into the wet clay with a sharp knife during manufacture. Each of the many individual features is an attribute, most of which are obvious enough. Only a critically selected few of these attributes, however, will be used in classifying the artifacts (Figure 8.8). (If all were used, then no classification would be possible: Each artifact would be an individual object identified by an infinite number of attributes.) Attribute analysis emphasizes combinations of distinctive attributes that distinguish and isolate one artifact type from another. Thus, the archaeologist works with only those attributes considered most appropriate for the classificatory task at hand. A group of potsherds can be divided into different decorative styles

DOING ARCHAEOLOGY

Archaeological Types

Archaeologists tend to use four "types of types," described briefly here. **Descriptive types** are based solely on the form of the artifact—physical or external properties. The descriptive type is employed when the use or cultural significance of the object or practice is unknown. Descriptive types are commonly used for artifacts from early prehistory, when functional interpretations are much harder to reach.

Chronological types are defined by decoration or form, but are time markers. They are types with chronological significance. Chronological types are defined in terms of attributes that show change over time. For example, on the Great Plains of North America, Clovis and Folsom points were used for short periods of prehistoric time, the former for about five centuries from about 11,300 to 10,950 B.C. (Figure 8.6). Projectile points have long been used as chronological markers in North American archaeology.

Functional types are based on cultural use or role in their user's culture rather than on outward form or chronological position, for example "weapons," "clothing," "food preparation," and so on. Although in some cases, obvious functional roles, such as that of an arrowhead for hunting or warfare or of a pot for carrying water, can be correctly established in the laboratory, functional classifications are necessarily restricted and limited (Figure 8.7).

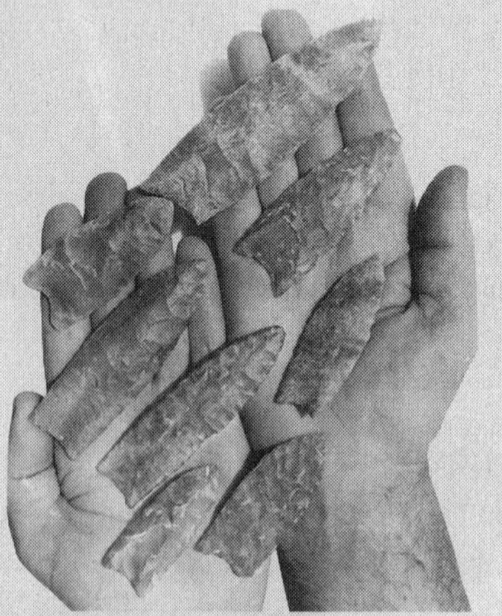

FIGURE 8.7 An example of a functional classification. This form of Scandinavian flint dagger of about 4000 B.C. is a beautifully made, pressure-flaked tool, a copy of the bronze daggers so fashionable at the time in central Europe. This tool has been classified by generations of archaeologists as a *dagger*, by implication, a weapon of war and defense, worn by Scandinavian farmers who still had no metal and made a slavish imitation of a more-advanced metal tool. This instinctive designation may seem obvious, but we really do not know whether our functional classification is correct. Does use wear on the blade show that a dagger was actually used in warfare and for personal defense? Was it a weapon, or was it purely an object of prestige for the owner, perhaps with some religious function?

FIGURE 8.6 Clovis points from the North American Great Plains. *(Courtesy of the Arizona State Museum, University of Arizona, Tucson.)*

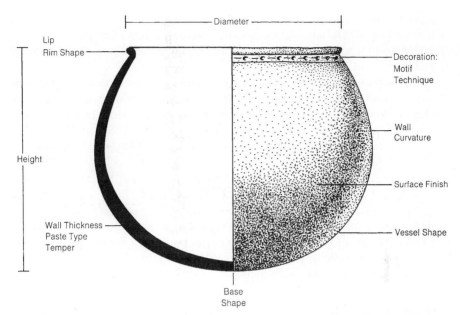

FIGURE 8.8 Some common attributes of a clay vessel. Specific attributes that could be listed for this pot are the concave shoulder, dot-and-drag decoration, the mica used to consolidate the clay, round base, and thickness of the wall at the base.

based on motifs, paints and other surface treatments, and colors. The selected attributes are then hand-recorded, and a series of artifact types is erected from them. The definition of the type here can depend on the order in which the attributes are examined and on the researcher's decision as to which are important.

Quantitative Methods

Until the late 1950s, almost all archaeological classification was qualitative, based to a great extent on instinct and experience rather than on numerical methods or empirical testing. Since the 1960s, a new generation of quantitative methods has revolutionized the finer details of typology.

The concept of quantitative methods refers not only to the standard techniques of statistical analysis and inference that readily come to mind but also to various techniques of numerical analysis and numerical manipulation, as well as graphical techniques for displaying data so that the patterns in the data are more readily apparent. Modern archaeology relies heavily on all manner of quantitative methods. They provide us with very powerful tools for answering such fundamental questions as "How old is it?" "Where does it come from?" and "What was it used for?"

An understanding of the process of applying quantitative methods to archaeological problems and a basic level of computer literacy are fundamental skills for all modern archaeologists. Quantitative methods are no longer the sole province of the specialist but rather are fundamental tools employed by all archaeologists at some level. (Readers interested in exploring this complex subject in more detail should consult one of the sources listed at the end of this chapter.)

Certainly as far as stone tools are concerned, it is likely that classifications based on function and technology will become more widespread as a result of highly precise research into such phenomena as edge wear on modern artifacts. This provides a basis for testing hypotheses about tool use in the past and a firm foundation for classifications based on actual human behavior.

ANCIENT TECHNOLOGY

Our forebears made use of an enormous range of natural materials to make artifacts and developed highly elaborate technologies for the purpose. We cannot possibly hope to describe them all here, so this discussion is confined to the more commonplace materials.

Stone

Watching an expert stoneworker (or "lithic technologist" as they prefer to be called, from the Greek *lithos*: "stone") is a true pleasure. With seemingly effortless skill, a rough lump of fine-grained stone changes shape into an elegant projectile point or a replica of a delicate, straight-edged hand ax fashioned by a Stone Age forager over 250,000 years ago. Some archaeologists have become experts at ancient stone technology. They have learned to feel and "read" the subtle textures and contours of toolmaking stone to the point where they can make a hand-ax in less than two minutes or replicate the finest products of ancient Egyptian or Maya stone artisans. These skills enable them to decipher the technology of long-vanished societies and provide such fascinating detail, such as information on left-handed stoneworkers.

The prehistory of humankind is literally wrought in stone, for this most durable of all toolmaking materials provides the framework for thousands of years of gradually evolving human technology, since the first hominid put stone cobble to stone cobble before 2.5 million years ago. The evolution of stoneworking over the millions of years during which it has been practiced has been infinitely slow. Nonetheless, people eventually exploited almost every possibility afforded by suitable rocks for making implements.

The manufacture of stone tools is what is called a **reductive** (or subtractive) **technology,** for stone is acquired, then shaped by removing flakes until the desired form is achieved. Obviously, the more complex the artifact, the more reduction is required. Basically, the process of tool manufacture is linear. The stoneworker acquires the raw material, prepares a **core** of stone (the lump of stone from which flakes or blades are removed), then carries out the initial reduction by removing a series of flakes. These flakes are then trimmed and shaped further depending on the artifact required. Core tools are those made from the core, flake tools are those made from flakes removed from a core. Later, after use, a tool may be resharpened or modified for further use.

Principles of Manufacture The making of stone tools depends on **conchoidal fracturing** (Figure 8.9). The simplest way of producing a stone that will cut or chop—surely the basic tool of prehistoric people—was simply produced by breaking off a piece and using the resulting sharp edge. But to make a tool that has a more specialized use or that can be employed for several purposes requires a slightly more sophisticated flaking technique. First, an angular fragment or smooth pebble of suitable rock can be brought to the desired shape by systematically flaking it with another stone. The flakes removed from this core, or lump, are then primarily waste products, whereas the core becomes the implement that is the intentional end product of the toolmaker. Furthermore, the flakes struck from the core can themselves be used as sharp-edged knives, or they can be further modified to make other artifacts.

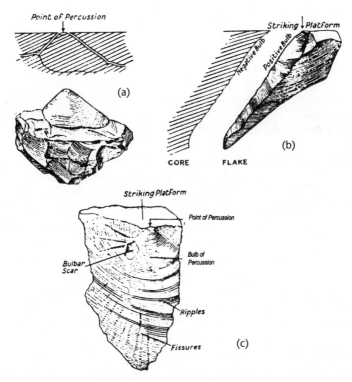

FIGURE 8.9 The conchoidal fracture, which forms when a blow is struck on homogeneous types of rock: *(a)* when a blow is struck, a core of percussion is formed by the shock waves rippling through the stone; *(b)* a flake is formed when the block (or core) is hit at the edge and the stone fractures along the edge of the ripple; *(c)* features of a struck flake.

Generally, Stone Age people and other makers of stone tools chose flint, obsidian, and other hard, homogeneous rocks from which to fashion their artifacts. All these rocks break in a systematic or predictable way, like glass. The effect is similar to that of a hole in a window produced by a BB gun. A sharp blow by percussion or pressure directed vertically at a point on the surface of a suitable stone dislodges a flake, with its apex at the point where the hammer hit the stone. This results in a conchoidal fracture (Figure 8.9). When a blow is directed at a stone slab obliquely from the edge, however, and the break occurs conchoidally, a flake is detached. The fractured face of the flake has a characteristic shape, with a bulge extending from the surface of the piece outward down the side. This is known as the bulb of percussion (or force); there is a corresponding hollow or flake scar on the core from which the flake has been detached. The bulb of percussion is readily recognized, as Figure 8.9 shows, not only by the bulge itself but also from the concentric rings that radiate from the center of the impact point, widening gradually away from it.

Methods Figure 8.10 shows some of the major stone-flaking methods prehistoric peoples used. The simplest and earliest was direct fracturing of the stone with a hammerstone (Figure 8.10*a*). After thousands of years, people began to make tools flaked on both surfaces, such as Acheulian hand axes (Figure 8.10*b*). As time went on, the stoneworkers began to use bone, "soft" antler, or wood hammers to trim the edges of their tools. The hand ax of 150,000 years ago had a symmetrical shape; sharp, tough working edges; and a beautiful finish.

As people became more skillful and specialized, such as the hunter-gatherers of about 100,000 years ago, they developed stone technologies producing artifacts for highly specific purposes. They shaped special cores that were carefully prepared to provide one flake or two of a standard size and shape (Figure 8.10*c*). About 35,000 years ago, some stoneworkers developed a new technology based on preparing cylindrical cores from which long, parallel-sided **blades** were removed by indirect percussion with a punch and hammerstone (Figure 8.10*d*). These regular blanks were then trimmed into knives, scraping tools, and other specialized artifacts.

Blade technology was so successful that it spread all over the world. It was highly efficient. Controlled experiments resulted in 6 percent of the raw material being left on one exhausted blade core; 91 percent of it formed 83 usable blades. The entire process is strongly reminiscent of the Leatherman or Swiss Army knife, in which a chassis with strong springs supports a variety of specialized tools such as knife blades, corkscrews, or spikes. In the same way, a blade core produced blades, which in turn produced more specialized artifacts, some of which were then used to cut antler and other raw materials (Figure 8.11).

Pressure flaking became so refined that it became the most common technique of later prehistory, especially in the Americas (Figure 8.7). The stoneworker used a small billet of wood or antler pressed against the

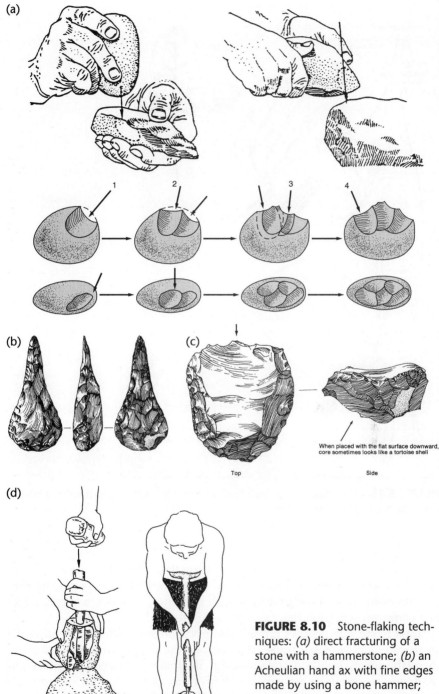

FIGURE 8.10 Stone-flaking techniques: *(a)* direct fracturing of a stone with a hammerstone; *(b)* an Acheulian hand ax with fine edges made by using a bone hammer; *(c)* a carefully prepared core designed to produce standard-sized flakes; *(d)* blade technology, using a punch.

When placed with the flat surface downward, core sometimes looks like a tortoise shell

Top   Side

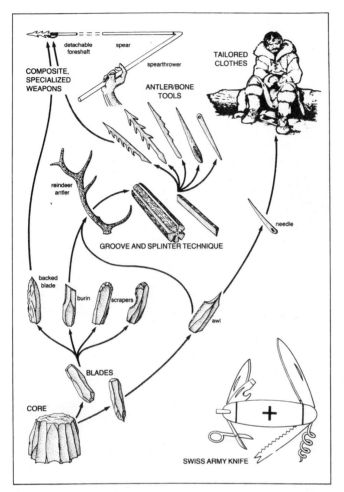

FIGURE 8.11 The "Swiss Army knife" effect. How a blade core produced a wide range of more specialized artifacts.

working edge to exert pressure in a limited direction and remove a fine, thin, parallel-sided flake. This formed one of many flake scars that eventually covered most of the implement's surfaces. Pressure flaking facilitates the production of many standardized tools with extremely effective working edges in a comparatively short time.

Later Stone Age peoples ground and polished stone when they needed a sharp and highly durable blade. They shaped the edges by rough flaking and then laboriously polished and ground them against a coarser rock, such as sandstone, to produce a sharp, tough working edge. Modern experiments have demonstrated the greater effectiveness of polished stone axes in felling forest trees, the toughened working edge taking longer to blunt than that of a flaked axe. Polished stone axes became important in many early farming societies, especially in Europe, Asia, Mesoamerica, and parts of temperate North America. They were used in New Guinea as early as 28,000 years ago and in Melanesia and Polynesia for the manufacture of canoes, which were essential for fishing and trade.

Expert stoneworkers still fashion artifacts to this day, especially gunflints for use in flintlock muskets. Gunflint manufacture was a flourishing industry in Britain and France into the twentieth century and is still practiced in Angola, Africa, where flintlock muskets are still in use for hunting.

Lithic Analysis **Lithic analysis,** the study of stone tool technology, involves far more than merely classifying different stone artifact types, as was the practice a half-century ago. Today, astoundingly minute details of long-forgotten human behavior come from combining several powerful analytical approaches. (See Doing Archaeology box on p. 246.)

It is all too easy to think of stone artifacts as merely lifeless objects, when, in fact, they once had a life of their own. Belgian archaeologist Daniel Cahen's reconstruction of stoneworking at the 9,000-year-old *Meer* site in northern Belgium is a classic example of the "new" lithic analysis. He and colleague Lawrence Keeley combined edge-wear analysis with refitting to reconstruct a fascinating scenario. They used the evidence from three borers that had been turned counterclockwise to show that a right-handed artisan walked away from the settlement, sat on a boulder, and made some tools, using some prepared blanks and cores he or she had brought there. Later a left-handed artisan came and sat nearby, bringing a previously prepared core, from which he or she proceeded to strike some blanks that this stoneworker turned into tools.

Some of the most productive analyses of artifact manufacturing processes have come from meticulous combinations of debitage analysis with experimental replications of early technology. Nicholas Toth of Indiana University spent months replicating very early hominid technology as used at Olduvai Gorge more than 1.75 million years ago. He compared his own cores and debitage with the originals and was not only able to show that the flakes removed from the cores were more important than the cores themselves, often called chopping tools, but that some of the world's very early stone toolmakers were left-handed as well.

Marvin Kay of the University of Arkansas is using three-dimensional Nomarski optics, which enable him to examine artifact surfaces with different colors of polarized light, to focus on polishes and on microscopic striations that result not only from hafting projectile points, but from the impact on the head when it strikes an animal. Kay compares the use wear on prehistoric artifacts to different use patterns resulting from modern experiments with artifact replicas against elephants and other animals. He has found, for example, that 13,000-year-old Clovis points from North America display minute scratches near the base that result from the head absorbing the shock of impact during the hunt. There are clear signs that many of them were

DOING ARCHAEOLOGY

Lithic Analysis

Modern lithic analysis is as much concerned with processes of manufacture and tool use as it is with complete artifacts. A combination of sophisticated methods reveals valuable information about human behavior.

Debitage analysis involves reconstructing the "reduction sequence" the original toolmaker used to create a finished artifact. Most steps in stone tool manufacture can be recognized by studying finished artifacts, cores, and the debris, often called debitage (French: "discarded waste") left behind by the stoneworker. By close examination of debitage, an expert lithic technologist can separate primary flakes, flakes resulting from the rough blocking out of the core, from the finer flakes that were removed as the artisan prepared the striking platform on the top or sides of the core. Then there are the flakes that all this preparatory work was aimed at— the artifact blanks struck from the core. Finally, there are the fine retouching flakes that turn the blank into the finished projectile point, scraper, or whatever other implement was needed.

Refitting (sometimes called **retrofitting**) is the reconstruction of ancient stone tool manufacture by retrofitting flakes to the core. Watch someone making stone tools and you will find that they are sitting in the middle of a pile of ever accumulating debris—chips, flakes, abandoned cores, and discarded hammerstones. Prehistoric stoneworkers produced the same sort of debris—hundreds, if not thousands, of small waste fragments, by-products of toolmaking that are buried on archaeological sites of all ages. Vital information on prehistoric lithic technology comes from careful excavation of all the debitage from a place where a prehistoric artisan worked, then trying to fit the pieces together one by one to reconstruct the procedures used.

Refitting requires great patience, but can provide valuable information about stone tool manufacture by individuals. You can sometimes trace the movement of individual fragments or cores horizontally across a site, a process that requires even more patience than simple refitting. This procedure is of great value in reconstructing the functions of different locations in, say, a rock shelter site, where a stoneworker might make tools in one place, then carry a core to a nearby hearth and fashion another blade for a quite different purpose.

Experimentation. Archaeologists have experimented with the making of stone tools since the mid-nineteenth century. Today many archaeological laboratories ring to the sound of people trying to make stone tools and replicate ancient technology—and cutting their fingers in the process.

Modern experimenters have drawn on both experimentation and ethnographic observation to work out ancient techniques. Recent research has focused on reconstructing reduction sequences and also on quarry sites as part of efforts to reconstruct prehistoric trade in obsidian and other rocks, which can be traced back to their source, and to achieve closer understanding of the relationships between human behavior and lithic technology.

Use-wear analysis involves both microscopic examination of artifact working edges and actual experiments using stone tools, in an effort to interpret tell-

(Continued)

DOING ARCHAEOLOGY

Lithic Analysis *(Continued)*

tale scratches and edge luster resulting from their use. Many researchers have experimented with both low- and high-power magnification and are now able to distinguish with considerable confidence between the wear polishes associated with different materials such as wood, bone, and hide. The approach is now reliable enough to allow one to state whether a tool was used to slice wood, cut up vegetables, or strip meat from bones, but relatively few archaeologists are trained in using the microscopes and photographic techniques required for analyzing wear. Another approach studies organic residues, the trace elements of debris from use adhering to tool edges.

Petrological analyses have been applied with great success to the rocks from which stone tools are made, especially ground stone axes in Europe. Petrology is the study of rocks (Greek *petros:* "stone"). A thin section of the ax is prepared and examined under a microscope. The minerals in the rock can then be identified and compared with samples from ancient quarry sites. British archaeologists have had remarkable success with this approach and have identified more than 20 sources of ax-blade stone in Britain alone. Spectrographic analysis of distinctive trace elements in obsidian has yielded remarkable results in southwestern Asia and Mesoamerica, where this distinctive volcanic rock was traded widely from several quarry centers (Chapter 11).

used, then reshaped and used again, often serving as knives after their usefulness as points was over. Kay's methodology is so sophisticated that he can even detect planing effects on tough stone such as quartzite, the planing resulting from use of the artifact for butchery. This kind of research will one day allow archaeologists to develop histories of individual artifacts as part of a larger-scale analysis of activities on archaeological sites.

The important thing about lithic analysis is not just the study of the implements themselves; it is the understanding of what the implements mean in terms of human behavior. And the new, multifaceted approaches to lithic analysis offer a real chance that methods such as edge-wear analysis will provide definitive ways of classifying stone tools in terms of their original functions.

Lithic technology has a modern application as well. Obsidian flake and blade edges are so sharp that they are widely used by modern eye surgeons, on the grounds that such cutting tools are superior to modern steel!

Clay (Ceramics)

Fired-clay objects are among the most imperishable of all archaeological finds, but pottery is a relatively recent innovation, dating to some 10,000 years ago in Japan and somewhat later in southwestern Asia. From the very earliest times, people used animal skins, bark trays, ostrich eggshells, and wild gourds for carrying loads beyond the immediate surroundings of their settlements.

Such informal vessels were ideal for hunter-gatherers, who were constantly on the move. The invention of pottery seems to have coincided with the beginnings of more lasting settlement. Fired-clay receptacles have the advantage of being both durable and long-lived. We can assume that the first clay vessels were used for domestic purposes: for cooking, carrying water, and storing food. They soon assumed more specialized roles in salt making, in ceremonial activities, and as oil lamps and burial urns.

Broken ceramic vessels are among the most common archaeological finds. **Ceramic analysis,** analysis of their shape, style, and form, has provided the foundations for thousands of archaeological analyses.

Pottery Manufacture Modern industrial potters turn out dinnerware pieces by the millions, using mass-production methods and automated technology. Prehistoric artisans created each of their pieces individually, using the simplest of technology but attaining astonishing skill in shaping and adorning their vessels.

The clay used in pot making was invariably selected with the utmost care; often it was even traded over considerable distances. The consistency of the clay is critical; it is pounded meticulously and mixed with water to make it entirely even in texture. By careful kneading, the potter removes the air bubbles and makes the clay as plastic as possible, allowing it to be molded into shape as the pot is built up. When the clay is fired, it loses its water content and can crack, so the potter adds a **temper** to the clay, a substance that helps reduce shrinkage and cracking and also ensures even firing and cooling. Although some pot clays contain a suitable temper in their natural state, pot makers commonly added many other materials such as fine sand, powdered shell, or even mica as artificial temper.

Pot making **(ceramics)** is a highly skilled art, with three major methods:

1. *Coil.* The vessel is built up from a clay lump or with long coils or wedges of clay that are shaped and joined together with a mixture of clay and water (Figure 8.12). Such hand methods were common wherever pot making was a part-time activity satisfying local needs.
2. *Mold.* The vessel is made from a lump of clay that is either pressed into a concave mold or placed over the top of a convex shape. Molding techniques were used to make large numbers of vessels of the same size and shape, as well as figurines, fishing net weights, and spindle whorls. Sometimes several molds were used to make the different parts of a vessel.
3. *Potter's wheel.* Wheel-made pots came into wide use after the invention of the potter's wheel in Mesopotamia about 5,000 years ago. The vessel is formed from a lump of clay rotating on a platform turned by the potter's hands or feet. The wheel method has the advantage of speed and standardization and was used to mass-produce thousands of similar vessels, such as the bright red Samian ware found throughout the Roman empire.

FIGURE 8.12 A Pueblo woman making pottery using the coil method. *(Courtesy of the University of New Mexico Museum.)*

Surface finishes provided a pleasing appearance and also improved the durability of the vessel in day-to-day use. Exterior burnishing and glazing with a tough surface coating made vessels watertight or nearly so. Often a wet clay solution, known as a slip, was applied to the smooth surface. Brightly colored slips were often used and formed painted decorations on the vessel (Figure 8.13). When a slip was not applied, the vessel was allowed to dry slowly until the external surface was almost leatherlike. Many utilitarian vessels were decorated with incised

FIGURE 8.13 Mimbres bowl. *(Courtesy of Steven A. LeBlanc.)*

or stamped decorations, using shells, combs, stamps, and other tools. Some ceremonial pots were even modeled into human effigies or given decorations imitating the cords used to suspend the pot from the roof (Figure 8.14).

Most early pottery was fired over open hearths. The vessels were covered with fast-burning wood, whose ash would fall around the vessels and bake them evenly over a few hours. Far higher temperatures were attained in spe-

FIGURE 8.14 Moche portrait head from Peru. *(Courtesy of the Art Institute of Chicago.)*

cial ovens, known as kilns, which would not only bake the clay and remove its plasticity but also dissolve carbons and iron compounds. Once fired, the pots were allowed to cool slowly, and small cracks were repaired before they were ready for use.

Ceramic Analysis   An enormous expenditure of archaeological energy has gone into ceramic analysis. As with stone technology, the emphasis has shifted in recent years from pure classification to broader-based research into the behavior of pot makers and the role of their products in society. (See Doing Archaeology box below.)

DOING ARCHAEOLOGY

Ceramic Analysis

- *Analogy and experiment.* Controlled experiments to replicate prehistoric ceramic technology provide data on firing temperatures, properties of tempers, and glazing techniques. Ethnographic analogy has been a fruitful source of basic information on potters and their techniques.

- *Form and function analysis.* Two features of prehistoric pottery are immediately obvious when we examine a collection of vessels: **form** (shape) and decoration. Functional analysis depends on the common assumption that the shape of a vessel directly reflects its **function**—bowls were used for cooking and eating, portrait head pots were ceremonial vessels, large pots were used for water storage, and so on. Such functional classifications bristle with obvious difficulties when one is separated from the pot makers by many centuries, even millennia, so form analysis is a more viable option. Form analysis is based on careful classification of clusters of different vessel shapes. These shapes can be derived from complete vessels or from potsherds that preserve the rim and shoulder profiles of the vessel. It is possible to reconstruct the pot form from these pieces by projecting measurements of diameter

and vessel height. Such analyses produce broad categories of vessel form that are capable of considerable refinement.

- *Stylistic analysis.* This form of analysis is much more commonly used, for it concentrates not on the form and function of the vessel but on the decorative styles used by the potters. These are assumed to be at least somewhat independent of functional considerations. In such areas as the American Southwest, pottery styles have been used to trace cultural variations over thousands of years. Most stylistic analyses use small numbers of distinctive attributes, which appear in associated sets of features that provide the basis for erecting types and varieties of pottery styles. These are assumed to represent the social system behind the pots studied. For instance, Attic and Corinthian pottery from Greece reflect standardized styles which can be dated accurately. Although a variety may represent the activities of only one family of potters, a type can represent the work of several villages or an entire community. Thus, goes the argument, standardized pottery types reflect a fairly rigid social system that prescribes what pottery styles are used, but less-formal designs are characteristic of a

(Continued)

DOING ARCHAEOLOGY

Ceramic Analysis *(Continued)*

less-restrictive society. However, can one really assume that pottery styles reflect social behavior? We do not yet know.

• *Technological analysis.* The more elaborate, computer-generated classifications of today reveal that many of the archaeologist's classificatory cornerstones, such as pottery temper, are in fact subject to complex behavioral and environmental factors rather than being the simple barometers of human behavior they were once thought to be. Technological analyses of pottery focus on the fabric and paste in potting clays, and relate ceramic vessels to locally available resources. These also provide useful, statistically based yardsticks for interpreting variation between different pottery

forms. Throughout later prehistory, clay vessels were major trade commodities, not only for their own qualities but also because they were convenient receptacles for such products as olive oil, wine, or salt. Numerous other procedures yield valuable information on ancient ceramics, including X-ray diffraction studies and ceramic petrology. These approaches can be used in combination to study what can be called "ceramic ecology," the interaction of resources, local knowledge, and style that ultimately lead to a finished clay vessel. Even the sediment found inside ancient pots can be examined spectrographically, and sometimes identified, as was the case with a wine storage jar from Iran dating to 4000 B.C.

The potsherd is hardly a glamorous artifact, but, in expert hands, one that is capable of providing astounding quantities of information about ancient human behavior, especially when technology and conventional analysis are combined. (See Site box on p. 253.) For instance, *Mississippian* pottery, manufactured in the southeastern United States between A.D. 1000 and 1500, was fired to a temperature between 800°C and 900°C. The Mississippians used crushed shell to temper their pots, so their vessels should not vitrify at these temperatures. But the pots did. Mississippian settlement was concentrated in valley bottoms, where the potters used clays heavy in montmorillonite and added crushed shell to them so that the unfired vessels would dry more evenly.

Metals and Metallurgy

"Hough!" "Hough!" The goatskin bellows emit a steady puffing noise as the African smith raises and lowers the bags with his hands, singing along the way. Every 20 minutes, another member of the team takes over as the master smith keeps a close eye on the clay furnace loaded with iron ore and charcoal. He adds charcoal, then more ore, then charcoal again. The smelt continues for seven hours until the master is satisfied. Then he rakes out the white-hot charcoal and recovers a lump of slag and smelted iron from the fire. All the preparation time and seven hours of arduous bellows work pro-

SITE

Ancient Wine at Abydos, Egypt

Some of the most remarkable ceramic research involves not the vessels themselves, but their contents. In 1988, German Egyptologist Günter Dreyer excavated the tomb of one of Egypt's first leaders at *Abydos* on the Middle Nile. Scorpion I lived in about 3150 B.C. His elaborate tomb contained four rooms stocked with at least 700 jars, which held a total of about 1,200 gallons (4,550 liters) of wine. Forty-seven of the jars contained wine pips, together with remains of sliced figs that were once suspended on strings in the wine, probably to sweeten it. The crusty residues adhering to the insides of the pots were analyzed with an infrared spectrometer and liquid chromatography which revealed the remains of tartaric acids (found naturally in grapes), also of terebinth resin, which ancient vintners used to prevent wine from turning into vinegar. Neutron activation analysis of the jar clay yielded trace element clusters that were compared to a large database of samples from Egypt and the eastern Mediterranean. The database pointed to the southern hill country of Israel and Transjordan as the source of the vessels, an area where vine growing was well established in 3100 B.C. The wine probably traveled the Nile across an ancient trade route, "the Way of Horus," that linked southern Israel with Egypt via the Sinai Desert. By 3000 B.C., wine growing was well established in the Nile Deltas in northern Egypt, the source of the pharaoh Tutankhamun's wines 1,500 years later.

duced just enough iron to make one small hoe. In these days of mass-produced steel and all kinds of exotic metals, we forget just how much labor went into producing even a single iron tool. The development of metallurgy is one of humanity's great innovations, but it was certainly not a labor-saving invention.

Metals first became familiar to people in the form of rocks in their environment. Properties of metal-bearing rocks—color, luster, and weight—made them attractive for use in the natural state. Eventually, people realized that heat made such stone as flint and chert easier to work. When this knowledge was applied to metallic rocks, stoneworkers discovered that native copper and other metals could be formed into tools by a sequence of hammering and heating. Of the 70 or so metallic elements on earth, only eight—iron, copper, arsenic, tin, silver, gold, lead, and mercury—were worked before the eighteenth century A.D. Properties of these metals that were important to ancient metalworkers were, among others, color, luster, reflecting abilities (for mirrors), acoustic quality, ease of casting and welding, and degrees of hardness, strength, and malleability. Metal that was easily recycled had obvious advantages.

Copper The earliest metal tools were made by cold-hammering copper into simple artifacts. Such objects were fairly common in Near Eastern villages by 6000 B.C. Eventually, some people began to melt the copper. They may have achieved sufficiently high temperatures with established methods used to fire pottery in clay kilns. The copper was usually melted or smelted into shapes and ingots within the furnace hearth itself. Copper metallurgy was widespread in the eastern Mediterranean by about 4000 B.C. European smiths were working copper in the Balkans as early as 3500 B.C. In the Americas, copper working achieved a high degree of refinement in coastal Peru among the Moche (see Figure 1.9) and Chimu, also in western Mesoamerica. The Archaic peoples of Lake Superior exploited the native deposits of copper ore on the southern shores of the lake, and the metal was widely traded across eastern North America and cold-hammered into artifacts from Archaic to Woodland times.

Bronze The real explosion in copper metallurgy took place midway through the fourth millennium B.C., when southwest Asian smiths discovered that they could improve the properties of copper by alloying it with a second metal such as arsenic, lead, or tin. Perhaps the first alloys came about when smiths tried to produce different colors and textures in ornaments. But they soon realized the advantages of tin, zinc, and other alloys that led to stronger, harder, and more easily worked artifacts. Most early bronzes contain about 5 to 10 percent alloy material (10 percent is the optimum for hardness). An extraordinary development in metallurgical technology occurred during the third millennium B.C., perhaps in part resulting from the evolution of writing. By 2500 B.C., practically every type of metallurgical phenomenon except hardening of steel was known and used regularly. The use of tin alloying may have stimulated much trading activity, for the metal is relatively rare, especially in the eastern Mediterranean region. Bronze working was developed to a high pitch in northern China after 2000 B.C.

Gold Gold played a vital part in prestige and ornament in many ancient societies. The pharaoh Tutankhamun is sometimes called the "Golden Pharaoh": His grave was rich in spectacular gold objects (see Figure 1.7). The burials of Moche lords around A.D. 400 at Sipán, on the northern coast of Peru, revealed the remarkable wealth of this desert civilization. One shroud-wrapped warrior-priest wore a pair of gold eyes, a gold nose, and a gold chin-and-neck visor; his head was lying on a gold, saucerlike headrest (see Figure 1.9). Hundreds of minute gold and turquoise beads adorned the Lord of Sipán, who wore 16 gold disks as large as silver dollars on his chest. There were gold-and-feather headdresses and intricate ear ornaments, one of a warrior with a movable club. The Aztecs and the Inca also were talented goldsmiths whose magnificent products were shipped off to Europe and melted down for royal treasuries in the sixteenth century. Spanish conquistadors marveled at the Coricancha, the temple of the Sun god Inti in the Inca capital at Cuzco high in the Andes. The outside of the beautifully built stone temple was gilded with gold and silver, while inside lay a garden with golden clods of earth, golden maize, and golden herdsmen guarding golden llamas (Figure 8.15).

Gold is a metal that rarely forms compounds in its natural state. It was collected in this form, or in grains gathered by crushing quartz and concentrating

FIGURE 8.15 A silver llama fashioned by an Inca smith. *(Courtesy of the American Museum of Natural History, New York.)*

the fine gold by washing. The melting point of gold is about the same as that of copper, so no elaborate technology was needed. Gold is easily hammered into thin sheets without annealing—heating and cooling of metal to make it less brittle. Prehistoric smiths frequently used such sheets to sheath wooden objects such as statuettes. They also cast gold and used appliqué techniques, as well as alloying it with silver and other ores. Gold was worked in the Near East almost as early as copper, and it was soon associated with royal prestige. The metal was widely traded in dust, ornament, and bead form in many parts of the world.

Iron Bronze Age smiths certainly knew about iron. It was a curiosity, of little apparent use. They knew where to find the ore and how to fashion iron objects by hammering and heating. But the crucial process in iron production is carburization, in which iron is converted into steel. The result is a much harder object, far tougher than bronze tools. To carburize an iron object, it is heated in close contact with charcoal for a considerable period of time. The solubility of carbon in iron is very low at room temperature but increases dramatically at temperatures above 910°C, which could easily be achieved with charcoal and a good Bronze Age bellows. It was this technological development that led to the widespread adoption of iron technologies in the eastern Mediterranean area at least by 1000 B.C.

Iron tools are found occasionally in some sites as early as 3000 B.C., but such artifacts were rare until around 1200 B.C., when the first iron weapons in eastern Mediterranean tombs appeared. The new metal was slow to catch on, partly because of the difficulty of smelting it. Its widespread adoption may coincide with a period of disruption in eastern Mediterranean trade routes as a result of the collapse of several major kingdoms, among them that of the Hittites, after 1200 B.C. Deprived of tin, the smiths turned to a much more readily available substitute—iron. It was soon in use even for utilitarian tools and was first established on a large scale in continental Europe in the seventh century B.C. by the Hallstatt peoples.

Iron ore is much more abundant in the natural state than copper ore. It is readily obtainable from surface outcrops and bog deposits. Once its potential was realized, it became much more widely used, and stone and bronze were relegated to subsidiary, often ornamental, uses. The influence of iron was immense, for it made available abundant supplies of tough cutting edges for agriculture. With iron tools, clearing forests became easier, and people achieved even greater mastery over their environment. Ironworking profoundly influenced the development of literate civilizations. Some people, such as the Australian Aborigines and the pre-Columbian Americans, never developed iron metallurgy.

Metal Technologies   Copper technology began with the cold-hammering of the ore into simple artifacts. Copper smelting may have originated by the accidental melting of some copper ore in a domestic hearth or oven. In smelting, the ore is melted at a high temperature in a small kiln and the molten metal is allowed to trickle down through the charcoal fuel into a vessel at the base of the furnace. The copper is further reduced at a high temperature, then cooled slowly and hammered into shape. This annealing adds strength to the metal. Molten copper was poured into molds and cast into widely varied shapes.

Copper ores were obtained from weathered surface outcrops, but the best material came from subsurface ores, which were mined by expert diggers. Many early copper workings have been found in southern Africa, where the miners followed surface lodes under the ground (see Figure 8.16).

Some of the most sophisticated bronze working was created by Chinese smiths, who cast elaborate legged cauldrons and smaller vessels with distinctive shapes and decoration in clay molds.

Ironworking is a much more elaborate technology that requires a melting temperature of at least 1537°C. Prehistoric smiths normally used an elaborate furnace filled with alternating layers of charcoal and iron ore, which was maintained at a high temperature for many hours with a bellows. A single firing often yielded only a spongy lump of iron, called a bloom, which then had to be forged and hammered into artifacts. It took some time for the metallurgists to learn that they could strengthen working edges by quenching the tool in cold water. This process gave greater strength, but it also made the tool brittle. The **tempering** process, reheating the blade to a temperature below

FIGURE 8.16 Excavation in an ancient copper mine at Kansanshi, Zambia, Central Africa. The miners followed copper ore outcrops deep into the ground with narrow shafts, the earth filling of which have yielded both radiocarbon samples and artifacts abandoned by the miners. *(Courtesy of Professor Michael Bisson, Department of Anthropology, McGill University, Montreal, Canada.)*

727°C, restored the strength. Iron technology was so slow in developing that it remained basically unchanged from about 600 B.C. until medieval times.

Analysis of Metal Artifacts   Again, the focus is on human behavior rather than objects alone, so researchers combine typological and technological analyses. *Typological analyses* study the stylistic changes in European bronze brooches, swords, axes, and iron artifacts which were very sensitive to fashion and to changing trading patterns. From such changes, the evolution of bronze pins or iron slashing swords, for example, can be traced across Europe, with small design changes providing both relative dating and occasional insights into the lifeways of the people using them. In many ways, such studies are similar in intent to those carried out with stone implements or potsherds.

Technological analyses are often more important than the study of finished artifacts. Such studies start with ethnographic analogies and actual reconstructions of prehistoric metallurgical processes. Chemists study iron and copper slag and residues from excavated furnaces.

We know much about ancient metallurgy because prehistoric artifacts preserve traces of their thermal and mechanical history in their metallic microstructure. This structure can be studied under an optical microscope. Each grain of the metal is a crystal that forms as the metal solidifies. The shape and size of the grains can reveal whether alloys were used and indicate the cooling conditions and the type of mold used. At first, prehistoric metallurgists used "pure" metals, which could be worked easily but produced only soft tools. Then they discovered how to alloy each of these metals with a second one to produce stronger, harder objects with lower melting points. The basic data for studying prehistoric alloys come from phase diagrams, which relate temperature and alloy composition, showing the relative solubility of metals when combined with other metals. Phase diagrams were developed under controlled conditions in a laboratory and tend to reflect ideal conditions. By examining the object under an optical microscope, researchers can often spot differences in chemical composition, such as the cored, treelike structure that is characteristic of cast copper-tin alloys. Metals contain insoluble particles that can give clues to the smelting procedures and types of ores used. An energy-dispersive X-ray spectrometer and a scanning electron microscope are used to identify the particles. This impressive battery of analytical techniques has enabled archaeologists to study how 6,000 years of experimentation took humanity from simple manipulation of rocks to the production of steel in about 1000 B.C. The record of these millennia is read in the lenses of the microscope and reveals the triumphs and frustrations of the ancient smith.

Africa is the only region where a handful of village smiths still use ancient methods to smelt iron, or, more often, to recycle modern metals. Peter Schmidt of the University of Florida has spent many years studying traditional iron smelting in the Great Lakes area of East Africa, where he has found that such activities unfold within a rich fabric of history, myth, and ritual. Over many centuries, the East African ironworkers have innovated continually in response to ever changing circumstances, such as changing ritual identities and new economic opportunities among neighboring groups. Ironworking was sometimes organized around competitive family or clan groups, who produced high-phosphorus iron, steel, and cast iron, using such innovations as larger ore fragments, closely packed furnace pits, and reflecting bellows pipes to create higher temperatures inside the fire. Any research into ancient metallurgy requires a multidisciplinary approach that focuses not only on technology, but on society itself.

Bone, Wood, Basketry, and Textiles

This chapter focuses on the most durable technologies, on the grounds that these are the ones most commonly encountered by archaeologists everywhere. But good preservation conditions sometimes yield rich information on more perishable technologies, which we summarize briefly here.

Bone and Antler   These materials were probably used from the beginnings of human history. The earliest artifacts apparently consisted of little more than fragments of fractured animal bone used for purposes that could not be fulfilled by wood or stone implements. The earliest standardized bone tools date from after about 100,000 years ago, but they assumed much greater levels of sophistication during the late Ice Age, when *Homo sapiens sapiens* used sharp-edged stone chisels to cut long splinters from antlers and turn them into spear points, harpoons, and fishing spears, as well as creating many specialized tools for foraging, fishing, and ceremonial purposes from them. They also used antler and bone as palettes for fine carvings and engravings of animals and geometric designs. The humble bone or ivory needle appeared about 25,000 years ago, a revolutionary artifact, because it enabled humans to manufacture layered, tailored clothing, essential for colonizing the bitterly cold open plains of Europe and Eurasia with their nine-month winters.

Bone and ivory technology achieved great sophistication in the Bering Strait area of the far north, where a highly specialized sea mammal hunting tool kit came into use over 2,000 years ago. Elaborate typological studies have been made of the stylistic and functional changes in such diverse items as harpoons and the winged ivory objects fastened to the butts of harpoons. Other artifacts include picks made of walrus tusk and snow shovels and wedges of ivory and bone, as well as drills and domestic utensils.

Wood   Like bone, wood was used for human artifacts from the earliest times. Only occasionally do such artifacts survive, the earliest being a series of 400,000-year-old long wooden throwing spears from Schoningen, Germany, which would have been lethal against large game. The bogs and marshes of northern Europe have preserved entire wooden tool kits made by foraging families as early as 7000 B.C., including dugout canoes, fishing spears, traps, and spear points, and also wooden trackways across waterlogged ground. The dry conditions of western North America have yielded rich finds of such artifacts as throwing sticks, and even duck decoys used to pursue waterfowl. Delicately made furniture survives in pharaoh Tutankhamun's tomb. (See also the Ozette cedar wood whale fin, illustrated in Figure 2.12.)

The manufacture of wood tools involves such well-understood mechanical processes as cutting, whittling, scraping, planing, carving, and polishing. Fire was often used to harden sharpened spear points. Oil and paint imparted a fine sheen and appearance to all kinds of wood artifacts. Even more revealing are wood fragments from abandoned buildings, fortifications, and even track walkways. Microscopic analysis of wood fragments and charcoal can provide information on the wood types used to build houses, canoes, and other such objects. On very rare occasions, stone projectile heads and axes have been recovered in both waterlogged and dry conditions in which their wood handles and shafts have survived together with the thongs used to bind stone to wood. The Ozette excavations yielded complete house planks and even some wood boxes that had been assembled by the skillful grooving and bending of planks.

Wood was probably the most important raw material available to our ancestors. The thousands upon thousands of ground stone axes in the archaeological record all once had wooden handles. Wood was used for house building, fortifications, fuel, canoes, and containers. Most skilled woodworking societies used the simplest technology to produce both utilitarian and ceremonial objects. They used fire and the ringing of bark to fell trees, stone wedges to split logs, and shells and stones to scrape spear shafts.

Basketry and Textiles   Basket production is one of the oldest crafts. Basketry includes such items as containers, matting, bags, and a wide range of fiber objects. Textiles are found in many later, dry sites, and they are well preserved along the Peruvian coast. Some scholars believe that basketry and textiles are among the most sensitive artifacts for the archaeologist to work with, culturally speaking, on the grounds that people lived in much more intimate association with baskets and textiles than with clay vessels, stone tools, or houses. Furthermore, even small fragments of basketry and textiles display remarkable idiosyncrasies of individual manufacture. When preserved, baskets are amenable to the same kinds of functional and stylistic analyses as other artifacts.

Patricia Anawalt is a textile expert who has spent many years studying pre-Columbian garments depicted on Mexican Indian codices. This research has enabled her to work out some of the complicated sumptuary rules that governed military uniforms and other clothing. For example, the lengths, material, and decoration of Aztec men's cloaks were regulated precisely by the state. Even the type of knot was specified.

The dry climate of the central Peruvian coast has preserved the wardrobes of *Paracas* nobles buried between 600 and 150 B.C. Paracas rulers wore mantles, tunics, ponchos, skirts, loincloths, and headpieces. These garments were embroidered with rows of brightly colored anthropomorphic, zoomorphic, and composite figures (Figure 8.17). Interpreting the iconographic patterns

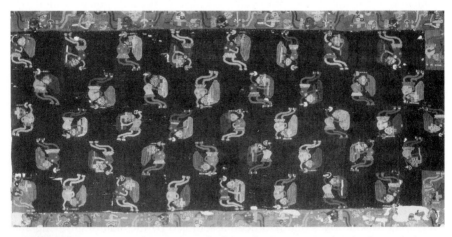

FIGURE 8.17   A cotton funerary textile from the Paracas Peninsula, Peru, dating to c. 300 B.C.

that appear on these ancient garments tells us something of Paracas religious and social customs. Many of the rulers' garments were adorned with shaman figures, showing that the wearer had a special relationship with the super-natural. From this we might conclude that one of the important functions of a Paracas ruler was to mediate between people and the supernatural forces that influenced and determined life's events.

People have accused archaeologists of being obsessed with the minute details of artifacts and technology to the exclusion of almost anything else. Doubtless there are such obsessives among us, but most researchers know that priceless information about people and human behavior lies behind even simple artifacts. We have only begun to tap the potential of multidisciplinary research into ancient technologies.

SUMMARY

This chapter describes the principal technologies used by ancient human soci-eties and some of the ways archaeologists study them.

Classifying artifacts in archaeology is somewhat different from our day-to-day classification of the objects around us. The objectives of archaeological classification are to organize data into manageable units, to describe types, and to identify relationships among types. Archaeological types are group-ings of artifacts created for comparisons with other groups. These groupings may or may not coincide with the actual tool types designed by the manu-facturers. Archaeological classification begins with identifying artifact attrib-utes, the characteristics that distinguish one artifact from another. Attributes can be selected by closely examining a collection of artifacts, or they can be derived statistically. Culture history in archaeology is based on classification of artifacts and assemblages, defined as associations of artifacts that are thought to be contemporary. This view of culture history has been replaced by perspectives in which environment and culture play important roles.

One of the main inorganic materials used by prehistoric people was stone, especially hard, homogeneous rock, which fractures according to the con-choidal principle. We described the basic techniques for manufacturing stone tools, which start with the stone-on-stone technique, then the cylinder-hammer method, and the prepared cores used to produce blanks for more standardized artifacts. Blade technology came into use about 45,000 years ago. Lithic experimentation and ethnoarchaeology have leading roles in the study of stone technologies; edge-wear and sourcing studies throw light on the trade in raw materials and the uses to which tools were put.

Ceramics (clay objects) are a major preoccupation of archaeologists and such artifacts date to the last 10,000 years. This chapter described the process of pottery manufacture, the various methods used, and the surface finishes employed. Ceramic analysis proceeds by analogy and experiment, research in which controlled experiments with firing and the properties of clay have had leading parts. The vessels themselves are studied through form and functional analyses. Many archaeologists prefer to use stylistic analyses. Clusters of attributes are used now, also, in attempts to standardize stylistic classifications.

Prehistoric metallurgy is a phenomenon of the past 6,000 years. We described the basic properties of copper, bronze, gold, and iron and some of the cultural contexts in which metallurgy developed. Typological and technological analyses are used to study prehistoric metallurgy. We also briefly described the importance of bone, wood, basketry, and textiles to ancient technology.

KEY TERMS

Artifact types
Attributes
Blades
Ceramic analysis
Ceramics
Chronological types
Classification
Conchoidal fracture
Core
Debitage analysis
Descriptive types
Experimentation
Form

Function
Functional types
Homo habilis
Lithic analysis
Petrological analysis
Reductive technology
Retrofitting (or refitting)
Taxonomy
Temper
Tempering
Typology
Use-wear analysis

GUIDE TO FURTHER READING

The literature on archaeological classification is both complex and enormous. I strongly advise you to obtain expert advice before delving into even key references. Here, however, are some useful starting points.

Cowgill, George L. 1982. "Clusters of Objects and Associations between Variables: Two Approaches to Archaeological Classification," in Robert A. Whallon and James A. Brown, eds., *Essays in Archaeological Typology,* pp. 30–55. Evanston, IL: Center for American Archaeology.

An excellent comparison of attribute-based and object cluster-based classifications in archaeology.

Drennan, Robert D. 1997. *Statistics for Archaeologists: A Commonsense Approach.* New York: Plenum.

An admirable introduction to quantitative archaeology, complete with practice problems.

———1986. "Methodological Issues in Americanist Artifact Classification," *Advances in Archaeological Method and Theory* 9:149–208.

A specialist essay on artifact classification that summarizes the major controversies surrounding the subject.

Dunnell, R. C. 1971. *Systematics in Prehistory*. New York: Free Press.

A highly technical introduction to systematic classification in archaeology.

Shennan, Stephen. 1996. *Quantifying Archaeology*. 2nd ed. Orlando, FL: Academic Press.

Another introduction to quantitative archaeology for the advanced student. Includes simple exercises.

Literature on ancient technologies includes the following:

Arnold, Dean E. 1985. *Ceramic Theory and Cultural Process*. Cambridge: Cambridge University Press.

A well-written and closely argued discourse on ceramic ecology.

Crabtree, Don E. 1972. *An Introduction to Flintworking*. Pocatello: Idaho State Museum.

The best simple account of basic lithic technology ever written, by an expert with a lifetime of experience. Valuable glossary and clear illustrations.

Knecht, Heidi, ed. 1997. *Projectile Technology*. New York: Plenum Press.

Essays on projectile points and their technology, a vital issue in American archaeology.

Muhly, James D., and Theodore Wertime, eds. 1980. *The Coming of the Age of Iron*. New Haven, CT: Yale University Press.

Essays on early metallurgy, ranging more widely than just ironworking.

Odell, George H., ed. 1996. *Stone Tools: Theoretical Insights into Human Prehistory*. New York: Plenum Press.

Essays on the connections between lithics and human behavior.

Rice, Prudence M. 1997. *Pottery Analysis: A Sourcebook*. Chicago, IL: University of Chicago Press.

An excellent reference book for anyone interested in ceramics.

Schmidt, Peter, ed. 1996. *The Culture and Technology of African Iron Production*. Gainesville: University of Florida Press.

No one studying ancient metallurgy should miss the essays on the relationship between ironworking and society in this book.

Sutton, Mark Q., and Brooke S. Arkush, eds. 1997. *Archaeological Laboratory Methods*. Dubuque, IA: Kendall Hunt.

A useful manual of laboratory methods of all kinds, as applied to artifacts, raw materials, and food remains.

Whittaker, John. 1994. *Flintknapping*. Austin: University of Texas Press.

An introduction to lithic technology for beginners.

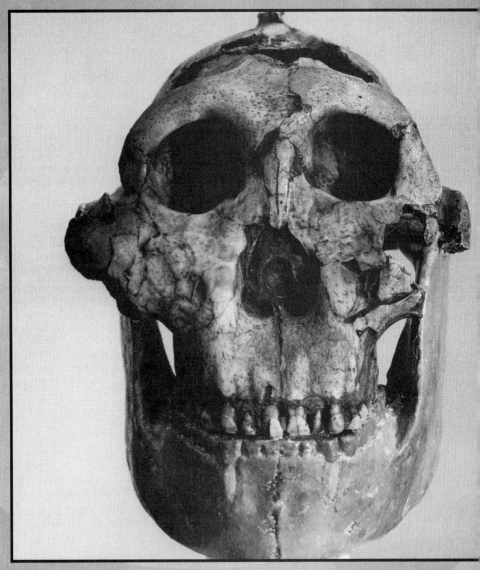

Reconstructed skull and jaw of Australopithecus boisei, a robust Australopithecine found by Mary Leakey, from Olduvai Gorge, Tanzania, East Africa. (Source: R.I.M. Campbell.)

Studying Subsistence
Animal Bones (Zooarchaeology)
    Taphonomy
    Studying Animal Bones
    Comparing Bone Assemblages
Doing Archaeology: Identifying Animal Bones
    Species Abundance and Cultural Change
    Game Animals
    Seasonal Occupation
    Domestic Animals
    Slaughtering and Butchery
Plant Remains
Site: Olsen-Chubbuck Bison Kill Site, Colorado
    Flotation
    Plant Phytolith Analysis
Doing Archaeology: Flotation of Plant Remains
    Interpreting Plant Evidence (Paleoethnobotany)
Birds, Fish, and Mollusks
    Birds
    Fish
    Mollusks
Subsistence Data from Rock Art
Discovery: Recording the Behistun Inscription, Iraq
Ancient Diet

Take the forelimb of a deer, a handful of wild grass seeds, a maize cob, and a few grinding implements, study them closely in a laboratory, and come up with a reconstruction of the diet of the people who lived at the site where you found these few food remains. This is basically what archaeologists attempt to do when they study the subsistence practices of ancient societies.

We can boast of some remarkable progress in the study of ancient lifeways. We know, for example, that the earliest hominids scavenged meat from predator kills under the noses of lions and other formidable cats. Late–Ice Age Cro-Magnon people of 20,000 years ago followed spring and fall reindeer migrations and butchered animals in their prime. In a remarkable piece of detective work, botanist Gordon Hillman was able to reconstruct the plant foods eaten by a group of foragers who lived at *Wadi Kabbaniyah* on the banks of Egypt's Nile River in 16,000 B.C. from the feces of infants recovered from small hearths. They relied on at least 13 edible plants, most commonly wild nut grass, which is still a staple for Egyptian villagers to this day. Similarly, we know that some of Thomas Jefferson's slaves at Monticello, Virginia, dined off better cuts of meat than some of the lesser servants. Food remains open unusual and often fascinating windows into the past, which tell us a great deal about contemporary social conditions and adaptations to changing environments. Chapter 9 describes some of the methods archaeologists use for studying ancient subsistence and diet.

STUDYING SUBSISTENCE

Archaeologists reconstruct ancient lifeways from the surviving material remains of subsistence activities, which come in many forms. Like every other form of archaeological research, the perspective is multidisciplinary, for we rely on the expertise of scientists from many other fields, among them botanists, ecologists, and zoologists.

- *Environmental data.* Background data on the natural environment is essential for studying subsistence. Such data can include information on such phenomena as animal distributions, ancient and modern flora, and soils—the range of potential resources to be exploited.
- *Animal bones (faunal remains).* These are a major source of information on hunting practices and domestic animals.
- *Plant remains.* Plant remains can include both wild and domestic species, obtained using flotation methods and from actual seeds found in dry sites or carbonized by fire.
- *Human bones.* Stable carbon isotopes of skeletal collagen from human bones provide vital information on ancient diets. Bones also give evidence of anatomical anomalies, ancient diseases, and dietary stress.
- *Feces (coprolites).* These yield vital evidence for reconstructing prehistoric diet in both animals and, in our context, humans.
- *Artifacts.* The picture of human subsistence yielded by artifacts can be limited because of poor preservation, but implements such as plow blades can be useful sources of evidence.
- *Rock art.* Occasionally, rock art depicts scenes of the chase, fishing, and food gathering and can provide useful information on subsistence activities.

Most reconstructions of ancient lifeways rely on evidence from several different sources. For instance, the excavators of the Wadi Kabbaniyah site found Nile catfish bones, the bones of gazelle (a desert antelope) and wild oxen, plant remains preserved in infant feces, and the bones of winter-migrating waterfowl. They painted a composite portrait of foragers who moved along the Nile in search of different seasonal foods 11,000 years before the pharaohs founded ancient Egyptian civilization.

ANIMAL BONES (ZOOARCHAEOLOGY)

The Old Testament prophet Ezekiel unwittingly defined the task of the zooarchaeologist: "And I prophesied as I was commanded; and as I prophesied, there was a noise, and behold, a rattling; and the bones came together, bone to its bone. And as I looked, there were sinews on them, and flesh had come upon them, and skin had covered them" (Ezekiel 37:10). Zooarchaeologists literally put the flesh on long-dead animals, reconstructing the environment and behavior of ancient peoples to the extent that animal remains allow. **Zooarchaeology** is a specialized expertise which requires a background in paleontology or zoology.

Taphonomy

Paleontologists studying dinosaurs and ancient mammals have it relatively easy compared with zooarchaeologists. They deal much of the time with relatively complete bones, whereas the archaeologist studies collections of food-related bones that have literally been smashed to bits as part of the butchery process. This means that zooarchaeologists rely heavily on modern animal skeletons as a basis for identifying ancient food bones. They also pay close attention to *taphonomy* (Greek, *taphnos:* "tomb"; *nomos:* "law"), the study of the processes that operate on organic remains after the organism dies and leaves the **biosphere.**

Anyone carrying out **faunal analysis** (the study of ancient fauna through the analysis of bones) must solve two problems: the statistical problem of estimating the characteristics of a fossil assemblage from a sample, and the taphonomic problem of inferring which animal bones were abandoned on-site as opposed to those preserved in the archaeological context (Figure 9.1).

Many questions about the processes that transform living organisms into "archaeological" bones remain unanswered, despite some research into such topics as the ways in which bones can be transported and disarticulated by both carnivores and natural agents such as water. For example, experiments with captive hyenas have shown that they choose to eat backbones and hip bones first which they usually destroy completely. Then limb bone ends are often chewed off, but shafts are often left intact. Esoteric research, perhaps, until you realize that the patterns of bone fractures tell us that the 1.75-million-year-old hominid bone caches at Olduvai Gorge, Tanzania, were picked over by hyenas after the site's human owners had departed. Humans butchered and disarticulated animals with tools long before the carcasses were dispersed by natural phenomena or by carnivores, so the study of such systematic activities are at least a baseline for examining patterns of damage on archaeological bones.

Interpretation of prehistoric camps and kill sites has to be undertaken with great care, for the apparent patterns of bones and artifacts on such prehistoric land surfaces represent not only human activity but complex and little-understood natural processes as well. The classic example of how misleading animal bone concentrations can be comes from South Africa. In the 1950s, the bones of Australopithecines and other early hominids came from enormous assemblages of fractured mammal bones in ancient sinkholes and caverns. At first, Raymond Dart, the discoverer of *Australopithecus,* claimed the hominids had killed and butchered the other mammals with a simple but brutal tool kit of bone, ivory, and sharp teeth. Dart was a vivid lecturer, who would seize fossil jaw bones and demonstrate to enthralled audiences how *Australopithecus* had run down and slaughtered fleet-footed

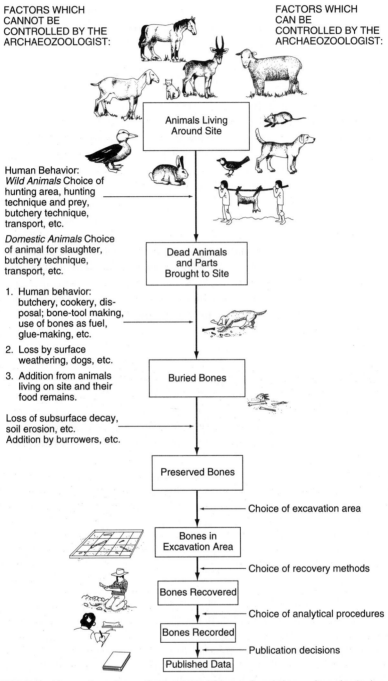

FIGURE 9.1 Zooarchaeology: the analysis of bone from the archaeological record. This figure shows some of the factors that affect faunal data. Factors that the archaeologist cannot control are on the left; those that he or she can control are on the right.

antelope. Unfortunately for this compelling scenario, zoologist C. K. Brain undertook a minute study of the broken animal bones in the 1970s and proved they had been dumped in caves and sinkholes by hyenas, whose distinctive teeth marks could be seen on the bones.

Studying Animal Bones

Faunal remains are usually fragmentary, coming from dismembered carcasses butchered either on-site or out in open country. To some degree, how much of the carcass is carried back to camp depends on the animal's size. Small deer may be taken back whole, slung over the shoulder. Hunter-gatherers sometimes camped at the site of a kill of a large animal, where they ate parts of the carcass and dried parts for later use. This is what the organizers of the Olsen-Chubbuck mass bison drive did when they drove over 150 bison into a narrow gully. Many of the bones were so complete that excavator Joe Ben Wheat was able to reconstruct the entire butchery process. Almost invariably, however, the bones found in occupation sites have been broken to splinters. Every piece of usable meat was stripped from the bones; sinews were made into thongs; and the skin was formed into clothing, containers, or sometimes housing materials. Even the entrails were eaten. Limb bones were split for their delicious marrow; some bones were made into such tools as harpoon heads, arrow tips, or mattocks (Figure 9.2).

FIGURE 9.2 The Olsen-Chubbuck bison kill site, showing exposed bones. *(Courtesy of University of Colorado Museum, Boulder.)*

You cannot assume that the fragmentary bones found in an archaeological deposit will give you either an accurate count of the number of animals killed by the inhabitants or accurate insights into the environment at the time of occupation. Taphonomic processes often result in major changes in buried bone, perhaps even destroying the bones of smaller animals though not of larger ones. Then there are human factors: People may carry in some game from far away, yet kill all of their goats at the village. Also, we have no means of knowing what spiritual role some animals possessed in ancient societies or of studying taboos and other prohibitions that may have caused certain animals to be hunted and others to be ignored. Nor do we know precisely what the relative frequencies of different animal species were in the ancient environment. The "archaeological animal" consists of a scatter of broken bones that have been shattered by a butcher, then subjected to hundreds or thousands of years of gradual deterioration in the soil, something very different from a once-living animal that was butchered, its abandoned bones scattered on the ground.

Most bone identification is done by direct comparison with bones of known species. It is fairly simple and easily learned by anyone with sharp eyes. (See Doing Archaeology box on p. 271.)

The identification stage of a bone analysis is the most important, for several fundamental questions need answering: Are domestic and wild species present? If so, what are the proportions of each group? What types of domestic stock did the inhabitants keep? Did they have any hunting preferences that are reflected in the proportions of game animals found in the occupation levels? Are any wild species characteristic of, say, cooler or warmer climatic conditions in the region?

Comparing Bone Assemblages

Zooarchaeologists Richard Klein and Kathryn Cruz-Uribe use two measures of taxonomic abundance for assessing whether differences between assemblages are real or the result of biased collecting or other factors. They also use the same measures to make estimates of the relative abundance of different species. *The number of identified specimens present* (NISP) is a count of the number of bones or bone fragments from each species in a bone sample. This measure has obvious disadvantages, especially since it can overemphasize the importance of one species that has more bones than another or has carcasses that were butchered more thoroughly than those of other species. Both human activities such as butchering and natural processes such as weathering can affect the NISP as well. The NISP does have a certain value, though, especially when used in conjunction with an estimate of the minimum number of individuals from which the identified bones have come.

The *minimum number of individuals* (MNI) is a count of the number of individuals necessary to account for all the identifiable bones. This count is smaller than the NISP and is often based on careful inventories of such individual body parts as heel bones. The MNI overcomes many limitations of the NISP because it is a more accurate estimate of the actual number of animals

Identifying Animal Bones

I learned bone identification on a huge collection of Stone Age animals from a cave in Libya, North Africa. After a few weeks of examining bag after bag of broken bones, I became an expert on a wild sheep *(Ammotragus.)* My particular specialty was toe bones, which are remarkably diagnostic in *Ammotragus.* Later, I graduated to tropical African animals, which are far more complex, as there are many species of antelope, but the same simple comparisons apply.

The drawing of a dog in Figure 9.3 illustrates a typical mammalian skeleton. Small skull fragments, vertebrae, ribs, scapulae, and pelvic bones are normally of little use in differentiating a domestic animal from a wild one or one species of antelope from another. Upper and lower jaws and their dentition, individual teeth, the bony cores of horns, and sometimes the articular surfaces of long bones are easy to identify. Teeth are identified by comparing the cusp patterns on their surfaces with those on comparative collections carefully taken from the site area (Figure 9.4). In some parts of the world, the articular ends of long bones can be used as well, especially in such regions as southwestern Asia or parts of North America, where the indigenous mammalian fauna is somewhat restricted. It is even possible to distinguish the fragmentary long bones of domestic stock from those of wild animals of the same size in southwestern Asia, provided that the collections are large enough and the comparative material is sufficiently complete and representative of all ages of individuals and of variations in size from male to female. But in other areas, such as sub-Saharan Africa, the indigenous fauna is so rich and varied, with such small variations in skeletal anatomy, that only horn cores or teeth can help distinguish between species of antelope and separate domestic stock from game animals. Even teeth are confusing, for the cusp patterns of buffalo and domestic cattle are remarkably similar, often distinguishable only by the smaller size of the latter.

Experts disagree as to what constitutes identifiability of bone, so it is best to think in terms of levels of identifiability rather than simply to reject many fragments out of hand. For example, you can sometimes identify a fragment as coming from a medium-sized carnivore even if you have no way of telling that it is from a wolf as opposed to a dog.

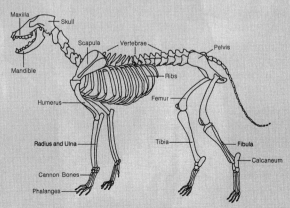

FIGURE 9.3 Identifying animal bones. The skeleton of a dog showing the most important body parts from the zooarchaeological standpoint.

(Continued)

Identifying Animal Bones   *(Continued)*

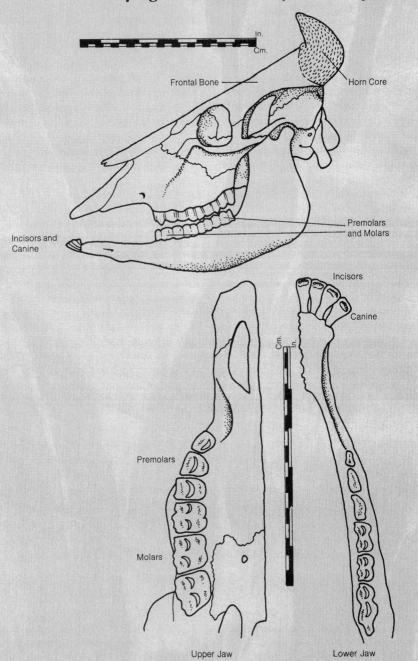

In.
Cm.

Frontal Bone ——————

Horn Core

Incisors and
Canine

Premolars
and Molars

Incisors

Canine

Cm.
In.

Premolars

Molars

Upper Jaw

Lower Jaw

FIGURE 9.4 Identifying animal bones. The skull and mandible (jaw) of a domestic ox showing the important osteological features (one-fourth actual size).

present. However, everything depends on the experts using the same method of calculating the MNI—which they often do not.

One of the best ways of obtaining an accurate MNI is on game drive sites, such as those on the North American Plains. The famous *Head-Smashed-In* kill site in southern Alberta, Canada, was used occasionally for more than 5,000 years and intensively after A.D. 300. A natural amphitheater above a precipitous cliff allowed the hunters to guide, then drive, bison herds to their death (Figure 9.5). Bone fragments from stratified deposits at the foot of the cliffs testify to staggering numbers of bison slaughtered and butchered over the past 1,800 years. Unfortunately, the bones from different kills are so jumbled that accurate MNI counts are impossible. The Olsen-Chubbock site in Colorado preserves a single kill, dating to about 8,000 years ago, when a group of hunters stampeded no less than 190 bison into a narrow gully. Of those, 110 were females, 80 males. Excavator Joe Ben Wheat was able to

FIGURE 9.5 Reconstruction of a bison drive at Head-Smashed-In, Alberta, Canada. *(Courtesy of the Head-Smashed-In Interpretative Center, Alberta, Canada.)*

obtain relatively accurate counts both from complete skeletons of animals jammed into the lowermost levels of the arroyo and from partial skeletons and other body parts butchered systematically after the hunt. He could even establish that 57 percent of the bison were adults.

The NISP and MNI together permit us to estimate the number of animals present in a bone sample, but they are highly imperfect ways of measuring abundance of animals in an archaeological sample, let alone of providing a means for relating the bone materials to a living animal population in the past. Sophisticated computer programs are now used to overcome some of the limitations of NISP and MNI, programs that lay out the basic information that is vital for intersample comparisons.

Species Abundance and Cultural Change

Climatic rather than cultural change was probably responsible for most long-term shifts in animal species abundance in the Ice Age. Some shifts must reflect human activity, changes in the way in which people exploited other animals. These changes are, however, very difficult to distinguish from environmental changes.

One of the few places where it has been possible to document such changes is in South Africa. Richard Klein has studied large faunal samples from two coastal caves in the Cape Province. The *Klasies River* cave was occupied by Stone Age hunter-gatherers between about 130,000 and 95,000 years ago, during a period of warmer climate, and thereafter until about 70,000 years ago, when the weather had become much cooler. The seashore was close to the cave during the earlier, warmer millennia. Numerous mollusks, seal bones, and penguin remains tell us much about Stone Age diet in the cave. Seabirds and fish are rare. Eland, a large antelope, is the most common large mammal, more than twice as common as the Cape buffalo. The rest of the land mammals are species common in the area during modern historic times.

In contrast, the nearby *Nelson's Bay* cave contains evidence of later Stone Age occupation dating to after 20,000 years ago, much of it during a time when the sea was some miles from the cave during the coldest part of the last Ice Age glaciation with its low sea levels. Bones of flying seabirds and fish are abundant in this cave, whereas eland are only a third as common as buffalo.

Klein points out that the tool kits are quite different in the two caves. The Klasies River cavepeople used large flake tools and spears. In contrast, the later Nelson's Bay hunters had bows and arrows and a rich tool kit of small stone tools and bone artifacts, many of them for specialized purposes such as fowling and fishing. These innovations allowed them to kill dangerous or more elusive species with greater frequency. Thus, the reason that the Klasies River people took more eland was not that eland were more abundant in earlier times but that more elusive creatures were captured less frequently. There is every indication that the Klasies people were less sophisticated behaviorally.

Klein combines some other faunal evidence with his mammalian and climatic data. The Klasies River site contains larger tortoise and limpet remains, as if these creatures were permitted to grow to a larger size than in later times. This implies less pressure on the tortoise and shellfish populations from a smaller human population before technologically more advanced people arrived.

Game Animals

Though the listing of game animals and their habits gives an insight into hunting practices, in many cases the content of the faunal list gains particular significance when we seek to explain why the hunters concentrated on certain species and apparently ignored others. Dominance by one game species can result from economic necessity, convenience, or it can simply be a matter of cultural preference. Many societies restrict hunting of particular animals or consumption of certain game meat to one or the other sex. The !Kung foragers of southern Africa's Kalahari Desert have complicated personal and age- and sex-specific taboos on eating mammals. No one can eat all 29 game animals regularly taken by the !Kung; indeed, no two individuals will have the same set of taboos. Some mammals can be eaten by everyone, but with restrictions on which parts certain individuals may eat. Such complicated taboos occur with innumerable variations in other hunter-gatherer and agricultural societies and have undoubtedly affected the proportions of game animals found in archaeological sites.

Examples of specialized hunting are common, even if the reasons for the attention given to one or more species are rarely explained. The specialized buffalo-hunting economies of the Plains Indians are well known. Another factor is overhunting, or the gradual extinction of a favorite species. One well-known example is *Bos primigenius* (Figure 9.6), the European aurochs or wild ox, which was a major quarry of late Ice–Age hunters in western Europe and was still hunted in Holocene times and after agriculture began. The last aurochs died in a Polish park in 1627. We know from illustrations and contemporary descriptions what these massive animals looked like. The bulls were large, up to $6\frac{1}{2}$ feet (2 m) at the shoulder and often had very long horns. The male coat was black with a white stripe along the back and white curly hair between the horns. Through careful, long-term breeding and selecting for the physical features of the aurochs, German and Polish biologists have "reconstituted" these beasts successfully. Reconstituted aurochs are fierce, temperamental, and extremely agile if allowed to run wild. The biological experiments have provided a far more convincing reconstruction of a most formidable Pleistocene mammal than could any number of skeletal reconstructions or artists' impressions.

Seasonal Occupation

Many prehistoric hunter-gatherers and farmers, like their modern counterparts, lived their lives in regular, seasonal cycles in which subsistence

FIGURE 9.6 *Bos primigenius,* the aurochs, now extinct. A drawing by S. Von Heberstain in 1549.

activities changed according to the seasons of the year. The Pacific Northwest Indians congregated near salmon rivers when the summer runs upstream took place. They would catch thousands of salmon and dry them for consumption during the winter months. The early dry season in Central Africa brings into season an abundance of wild fruit, which formed an important part of early farmers' diets 1,500 years ago. How do archaeologists study seasonal activities and reconstruct the "economic seasons" of the year? Every aspect of prehistoric life was affected by seasonal movements. The Northwest Indians enjoyed a complex ceremonial life during the sedentary winter months. The settlement pattern of the Khoi Khoi pastoralists of the Cape of Good Hope changed radically between dry and wet seasons. During the dry months they would congregate at the few permanent water holes and near perennial rivers. When the rains came, the cattle herders spread out over the neighboring arid lands, watering their herds in the standing waters left by rainstorms.

A variety of approaches have been used to document seasonality. The simplest method uses bones or plant remains. To illustrate this technique in one case, bird bones were used to establish that a San Francisco Bay shell midden site was visited around June 28, when cormorants were young. The presence of cod bones in early Norwegian fishing sites indicates that they were occupied during the winter and early spring. This type of analysis is fine, provided that the habits of the animals or of the plants being examined are well known or have not changed through time. Some plants are available for much of the year but are edible only during a few short weeks.

Knowledge about the ecology of both animals and plants is essential, for the "scheduling" of resource exploitation, though perhaps not explicit, was certainly a major factor in the evolution of cultural systems.

Then there are physiological events in an animal's life that an archaeologist can use to establish seasonal occupation. During the fifteenth century A.D., a group of Plains hunters regularly took bison near a water hole at *Garnsey, New Mexico.* John Speth analyzed the body parts at the kill site and discovered that the hunters had a strong preference for male beasts during the spring, the season in which the hunts took place. The butchers had abandoned body parts with low meat yields such as skulls and upper-neck bones. In contrast, bones that yielded a great deal of meat, marrow, or grease were underrepresented at Garnsey. Many more high-utility bones like these were taken from males than females. Speth believes that the hunters concentrated on males because their meat had a higher fat content and they were in better condition after the winter months than the females.

Growth patterns in animal bones can sometimes yield clues about seasonal occupation. The **epiphyses** at the ends of limb bones are slowly joined to the main bones by ossification as an animal ages. This approach can certainly give some clues as to the general age of an animal population in, say, a hunting camp, but such variables as nutrition or even castration in domesticated animals can affect the rate of fusion. Some species, such as ducks, mature much faster than others, such as deer. Clearly, knowledge of the different ages at which epiphyses fuse is essential to this approach.

Everyone knows that teeth erupt from upper and lower jaws as one grows into adulthood, often causing wisdom teeth problems in people. Teeth are such durable animal remains that many archaeologists have tried to use them to age game and domestic animal populations. It is easy enough to study tooth eruption from complete or even fragmentary upper and lower jaws, and it has been done with domesticated sheep, goats, and wild deer.

In some cases, too, archaeologists have used deer antlers to study seasonal occupations. The males of the deer family shed their antlers after the fall breeding season. By studying and X-raying the antlers in the site and knowing the migration habits of red deer, scientists believe that an 11,000-year-old hunting camp at Star Carr in northeast England was occupied from late spring through early summer

Interpretation of seasonal occupation depends heavily on ethnographic analogies. One classic example is wild wheat. Botanist Gordon Hillman has studied the gathering of wild wheat in southwestern Asia and has shown that the collectors must schedule their collecting activities very precisely if they are to gather the harvest before the ears fall off the stems or the grain is consumed by birds and other animals. It is reasonable to assume that the same precise scheduling was essential during prehistoric times, an analogy that has enabled archaeologists to interpret seasonal occupations on sites in Syria and elsewhere.

Seasonality is still a surprisingly neglected subject in the archaeological literature, but it has great potential. By studying not only large mammals and obvious plant remains but also tiny mollusks and even fish bones and fish scales, it may be possible to narrow the window of seasonal occupation at many sites to surprisingly tight limits.

Domestic Animals

Nearly all domestic animals originated from a wild species with an inclination to be sociable, facilitating an association with humans. Domestic animals did not all originate in the same part of the world; they were domesticated in their natural area of distribution in the wild. Domestication everywhere seems to begin when a growing population needs a more regular food supply to feed larger groups of people; domestication is dependent on such conditions and is a prerequisite for further population growth.

Wild animals lack many characteristics that are valuable in their domestic counterparts. Thus, wild sheep have thick coats, but their wool is not the type produced by domestic sheep, which is suitable for spinning; aurochs, ancestors of the domestic ox, and wild goats produce sufficient milk for their young, but not in the quantities so important to humans. Considerable changes have taken place during domestication, as people develop characteristics in their animals that often render the animals unfit for survival in the wild.

The history of domestic species is based on fragmentary animal bones found in the deposits of innumerable caves, rock shelters, and open sites. A number of sites have produced evidence of gradual osteological change toward domesticated animals. If the bones of the wild species of some prehistoric domesticated animals are compared with those of the domestic animals throughout time, the range of size variations first increases, and eventually selection in favor of smaller animals and less variation in size appears. This transition is fluid, however, and it is difficult to identify wild or domestic individuals from single bones or small collections.

The bones of domestic animals demonstrate that a high degree of adaptability is inherent in wild animals. People have found it necessary to change the size and qualities of animals according to their own needs, with corresponding effects on the animals' skeletal remains. Different breeds of cattle, sheep, and other domestic animals have been developed since the beginning of domestication.

Slaughtering and Butchery

Some insights into peoples' exploitation of wild and domestic animals can be obtained by studying not only animal bones themselves but also their frequency and distribution in the ground. The problem is not to record distributions and frequencies alone but to establish what they mean in terms of human behavior. Ethnoarchaeological studies of such peoples as the Nunamiut Eskimo of Alaska have provided a wealth of information on modern-day butchery practices.

Sex, Age, and Slaughter Patterns   Clearly, determining the sex of an animal and the age at which it was killed may provide a way of studying the hunting or stock-raising habits of the people who did the slaughtering. In many mammal species, males and females vary considerably in size and build. For example, male horses have canine teeth, but females usually lack them.

In humans, the female pelvis is very different from that of the male in order to accommodate the birth canal. We can estimate the proportions of males and females in such sites as the Garnsey bison kill by comparing the ratio of male to female body parts; in this case the differences between male and female beasts are known. Such analyses are much harder when less is known of size differences or when bones are very fragmentary. Zooarchaeologists use a variety of bone measurements to distinguish sex, but such approaches are fraught with statistical and practical difficulties; they work best on complete bones. Even then, it may only be possible to identify different measurement distributions that may or may not reflect differences between the sexes.

How old were these cattle when they were slaughtered? Did the inhabitants concentrate on immature wild goats rather than on fully grown ones? These are the kinds of questions that are important at many sites. To answer them, researchers must establish the age at death of the animals in the faunal sample. The skeletal parts most commonly used to determine the age of an animal at death are teeth and the epiphyses at the ends of limb bones. In almost all mammals, bones where the epiphyses are unfused come from younger animals. This enables us to construct two age classes: immature and fully grown. If we know the ages at which epiphyses fuse, as is sometimes the case in species such as domestic cattle, we can add additional classes. Unfortunately, epiphyseal fusing is too coarse a method to provide the kind of data that archaeologists need.

Fortunately, teeth and upper or lower jaws provide a more accurate way of establishing animal age. Teeth provide an almost continuous guide to the age of an individual from birth to old age. Complete upper and lower jaws allow us to study immature and mature teeth as they erupt, so we can identify not only the proportion of young animals but very old animals as well.

Individual teeth can also be a mine of information on animal age. Some biologists are using growth rings on teeth, but this method is still highly experimental. A far more promising approach measures the height of tooth crowns. Richard Klein, an expert on African bones, has measured crown heights on Stone Age mammal teeth found at the Klasies River and Nelson's Bay caves in the Cape Province of South Africa. Taken as two groups, the teeth measurements probably give interesting general impressions of the hunting habits of middle– and late–Stone Age peoples in this area. Klein compared the mortality distributions from the Cape buffalo and other large and medium-sized species to mortality curves from modern mammal populations. He identified two basic distributions:

> The **catastrophic age profile** is stable in size and structure and has progressively fewer older individuals. This is the normal distribution for living ungulate populations (Figure 9.7, *left*) and is that normally found in mass game kills achieved by driving herds into swamps or over cliffs.
>
> The **attritional age profile** (Figure 9.7, *right*) shows an underrepresentation of prime-age animals relative to their abundance in living populations, but young and old are overrpresented. This profile is thought to result from scavenging or simple spear hunting.

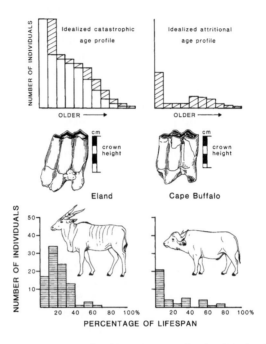

FIGURE 9.7 Two common South African game animals, the eland and the Cape buffalo, provide mortality data based on the molar crowns: idealized catastrophic age profile *(left);* idealized attritional age profile *(right).*

Klein found that the Cape buffalo age distributions from both sites were close to those observed for modern buffalo killed by lions, where both young and old males are vulnerable to attack because they are isolated from the large herds of formidable prime animals. Thus, he argued, the Stone Age hunters at both caves enjoyed a lasting, stable relationship with their prey populations of buffalo. The distributions for eland and bastard hartebeest (smaller, gregarious antelopes) were much more similar to the catastrophic profile. Klein speculates that they were similar because these species were hunted in large game drives, like the bison on the Great Plains. Thus, entire populations would be killed at one time.

Age distributions can reflect all kinds of other activities as well. The Star Carr site in northeastern England contains no young red deer. Most of the animals were three to four years old, inexperienced juveniles killed as they were leaving their mothers.

Hunting and slaughter patterns are subject to all manner of subtle variables. While studying hunting practices among the Nunamiut Eskimo of Alaska, Lewis Binford found that the hunters butchered animals as part of a much broader subsistence strategy. The Nunamiut rely heavily on stored meat for most of the year and thus orient their hunting practices toward storage objectives, as well as many other considerations. In the fall, they may hunt caribou calves to obtain skins for winter clothing, and the heads and tongues of these animals provide the meat for the people who process the skins. Binford stresses that it is difficult to interpret slaughter patterns without closely understanding the cultural systems of which hunting was a part.

Domestic animals are a controllable meat supply and subject to quite different selection criteria. In more advanced agricultural societies, cattle or horses might be kept until old age for draught purposes, surplus males being castrated and females being retained until they stopped lactating or were of no further use for breeding or plowing. Even if riding or work animals were not kept, the problem of surplus males persists. This surplus is an abundant source of prime meat, and these animals were often slaughtered in early adulthood. Cattle stood for wealth in many traditional societies, as they do in some today; and they were slaughtered on such special occasions as funerals or weddings. The herd surplus was consumed in this manner, and the owner's social obligations were satisfied.

Butchery The fragmentary bones in an occupation level are the end product of the killing, cutting up, and consumption of domestic or wild animals. To understand the butchery process, the articulation of animal bones must be examined in the levels where they are found, or a close study must be made of fragmentary body parts. The Olsen-Chubbuck kill site in Colorado yielded evidence of a slaughtered bison herd, reconstructed in astonishing detail. (See Site box on p. 282.)

Interpreting butchery techniques is a complicated matter, for many variables affected the way in which carcasses were dismembered. The Nunamiut relied heavily on stored meat, and the way they dismembered a caribou varied according to storage needs, meat yield of different body parts, and proximity to the base camp. The animals' size may also have affected the number of bones found at a base site: goats, chickens, or small deer could have been carried to the village as complete carcasses, but, of larger beasts, often only small portions were brought in. Sometimes animals with high meat yield were consumed where they were killed and every scrap of flesh and entrails utilized.

Once again, the problem is to establish the meaning of archaeological distributions in terms of human behavior. Just how complicated this is in the context of butchery can be appreciated from Binford's observation that the Nunamiut criteria for selecting meat for consumption are the amount of usable meat, the time required to process it, and the quality of the flesh. So, anyone interpreting butchery, or any other hunting or herding activities for that matter, must take into account everything known about the culture as a whole.

PLANT REMAINS

Wild vegetable foods were a staple of the prehistoric world from the earliest times up to the moment when people first began to cultivate the soil some 10,000 years ago and are still important in many farmers' diets. Unfortunately, seeds, fruits, grasses, leaves, and roots are among the most fragile of organic materials and do not survive long unless they are carbonized or preserved under very wet or arid conditions. Grain impressions in the walls of clay

SITE

Olsen-Chubbuck Bison Kill Site, Colorado

Joe Ben Wheat's excavation of the Olsen-Chubbuck site, 16 miles (25.7 km) southeast of Kit Carson, Colorado, is a remarkable story of a successful bison drive in about 6500 B.C. Using the remains of over 150 bison trapped in a narrow dry gully, Wheat reconstructed a hunt which began when some hunters approached an unsuspecting herd from downwind (see Figure 9.2).

On the day of the hunt, the wind was blowing from the south. (We know this because the bison faced south in the gully.) The hunters stampeded a large herd into a narrow defile. The leading animals stumbled and were swept on by the beasts galloping immediately behind them. They fell into the gully and were trampled to death as the hunters speared the other helpless animals as they floundered in confusion. The stampede over, the band turned to butchery. With quiet efficiency, they maneuvered carcasses into a position where they could be cut up at the edge of the arroyo. The butchers worked in teams as they rolled the animals on their bellies, slit the hides down the back, and pulled them down the flanks to form carpets for the meat. Then they removed the prime flesh from the back, also the forelimbs, shoulder blades, and other favored parts, eating the soft intestines as they worked and piling the bones to one side.

Wheat was able to reconstruct the butchery process from the jumble of bison bones at the site. He estimated the hunters butchered 75 percent of the animals they killed, acquiring about 54,640 pounds (24,752 kg) of meat in the process, much of which they probably dried. He estimated they acquired enough meat to last 100 people for a month or more.

vessels or adobe brick, made by seeds pressing into the wet clay, are sometimes useful sources of information. Numerous grain impressions have been found in European handmade pottery from the end of the Stone Age. Fortunately, refined **flotation** methods and AMS radiocarbon-dating techniques (Chapter 3) are yielding a wealth of new information.

Carbonized and unburned seeds are normally found in cooking pots, in midden deposits, or among the ashes of hearths, where they were dropped by accident. The extremely dry conditions of the western North American desert and of the Peruvian coast have preserved thousands of seeds, as well as human coprolites which contain a wealth of vegetal material. *Hogup Cave* in Utah was occupied as early as 7000 B.C. From about 6400 to 1200 B.C., the inhabitants relied so heavily on pickleweed seeds in their diet that the early deposits are literally golden with the chaff threshed from them. After 1200 B.C., deposits of pickleweed and the milling stones used to process them decline rapidly. An abrupt rise in the nearby Great Salt Lake may have drowned the marsh where the seed was collected, so the cave was only visited by hunting parties thereafter.

Richard MacNeish has excavated more than a dozen sites in Mexico's dry Tehuacán Valley, five of which contained the remains of ancient maize; 80,000 wild-plant remains and 25,000 specimens of corn came from the sites. He was able to document an increasing reliance on maize and bean agriculture before 2700 B.C., although foraging remained important.

The wild ancestor of maize was an indigenous grass, teosinte *(Zea mays parviglumis)*, which still grows in Central America. Botanists now believe that both maize and beans were domesticated from wild ancestors in the Guadalajara region, some 155 miles (250 km) west of Tehuacán, where both teosinte and a population cluster of wild beans still flourish. Early maize cobs, dried ears no more than three-quarters of an inch (20 mm) long, came from the lowest occupation level in San Marcos Cave. This was fully domesticated maize, incapable of dispersing its kernels naturally, as wild plants do to regenerate. The mature plants would have stood about 4 feet (1.2 m) high with one to five ear-bearing lateral branches, each plant producing 10 to 15 small corn ears (Figure 9.8).

(c)

(d)

(a) (b) (e)

FIGURE 9.8   The evolution of maize from the wild grass teosinte. The earliest teosinte form is *(a)*, which evolves to the stabilized maize phenotype *(e)*. The harvesting process increased the condensation of teosinte branches and led to the husks becoming the enclosures for corn ears. *(Courtesy of the Museum of Anthropology, University of Michigan. After Walter Galinat.)*

Flotation

Until a generation ago, the early history of crops was written from tiny samples of seeds preserved mainly in dry caves. Only a handful of plant remains came from even the best-preserved sites until the development of flotation methods in the Midwest during the 1960s revolutionized our knowledge of early plant utilization. (See Doing Archaeology box on p. 285.)

Flotation is rewriting the early history of farming in all parts of the world, partly because it yields much larger samples of domestic and wild seeds to work with. Andrew Moore used flotation with great efficiency on the Stone Age farming village at Abu Hureyra on the Euphrates River in Syria. He acquired 712 seed samples from soil deposits that comprised a bulk of more than 132 U.S. gallons (500 liters). Each sample contained as many as 500 seeds from over 150 plant taxa, with many of them edible. By dissecting these large samples, Botanist Gordon Hillman was able to document the retreat of oak forests in the region and the changes in plant gathering which accompanied environmental change. He showed how Abu Hureyra was in the grip of a prolonged drought in about 8800 B.C. At first, the people turned to drought-resistant small-seeded grasses, then they deliberately cultivated them to expand their food supplies. As more favorable conditions returned in about 7700 B.C., a farming settlement appeared at Abu Hureyra, based on the cultivation of emmer, einkorn, and barley, staple cereal crops that were rotated with pulses such as lentils, vetches, and chick peas. But they still supplemented their diet by collecting significant quantities of wild vegetable foods. The Abu Hureyra people lived in the same place for a long period of time because they rotated their crops and used a simple fallow system that allowed exhausted fields to recover before being replanted.

Plant Phytolith Analysis

Opal **phytoliths,** minute particles of silica from plant cells, are created from hydrated silica dissolved in groundwater that is absorbed through a plant's roots and carried through its vascular system. Silica production is continuous throughout the growth of a plant. Phytolith samples are collected in much the same way as pollen samples, then studied by identifying individual species such as cultivable grasses.

Anna Roosevelt used phytolith analysis on sites in the Orinoco River valley of Venezuela. She found that the percentages of grass phytoliths increased dramatically at the very moment when maize was introduced to the area, as indicated by carbon 13 and carbon 12 analysis of skeletal material and actual seeds.

Phytolith analysis has many potential applications in archaeology in the study of diet, through the use of coprolites and even phytoliths embedded in jawbones, but research is still in its infancy. It is likely to become as important as palynology in the years to come.

Flotation of Plant Remains

Early excavators recovered seeds from hearths and dry storage pits and obtained but a tiny fraction of what lay in the deposits. Flotation uses water or chemicals to free the seeds, which are often of microscopic size, from the fine earth or occupation residue that masks them; the vegetal remains usually float and the residue sinks. Although this technique enables us to recover seeds from many sites where it was impossible before, by no means can it be applied universally because its effectiveness depends on soil conditions. The methods used are being refined as more experience is gained with them under varied field conditions. At first, researchers simply used converted oil drums and processed samples laboriously through a series of screens, but the pace of sample processing was too slow. A number of ingenious machines have been developed to carry out large-scale flotation (Figure 9.9). The sample of earth is poured into the screened container and agitated by the water pouring into the screen. The light plant remains and other fine materials float on the water and are

carried out of the container by a sluiceway that leads to fine mesh screens, where the finds are caught, wrapped in fine cloth, and preserved for the botanists to study. The heavy sludge, in the meantime, sinks to the bottom of the container inside the oil drum.

The advantage of flotation is obvious. It provides much larger samples of plant remains that can reflect not only human consumption and exploitation of edible plants, but also the surrounding natural vegetation. In eastern North America, for example, regular use of flotation has yielded thousands of tiny seeds and a slowly emerging story of a gradual shift from foraging of wild plant foods to subsistence patterns that relied heavily on the deliberate cultivation of native plants, long before maize and beans arrived in the region. Flotation comes into its own when studying the contents of storage pits, where seed crops and other foods were kept for many months. It has also been used to study the contents of historic privies and the fills of individual rooms in Southwestern pueblos.

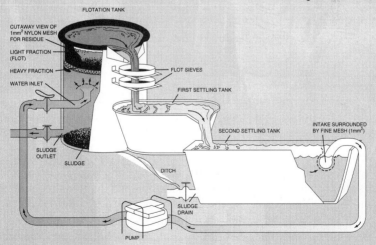

FIGURE 9.9 A water flotation device used for recovering plant remains using recycled water, developed by botanist Gordon Hillman. The lightest remains float to the surface and are caught in the float sieves. The heavier material sinks and is caught in light nylon mesh.

Interpreting Plant Evidence (Paleoethnobotany)

Like zooarchaeology, **paleoethnobotany** is a specialized field of archaeology involving the study of the uses of plant remains in the past. Paleoethnobotany requires skilled detective work which combines archaeology with botany and ethnographic studies of uses of plant remains by living peoples.

No matter how effective the recovery techniques used for vegetal remains, the picture of either food gathering or agriculture is bound to be incomplete. A look at modern hunter-gatherers reveals the problem. The !Kung of the Kalahari Desert in southern Africa appear in every book on ethnography. Many early writers on hunter-gatherers assumed that the !Kung relied on game alone and lived in perennial starvation that was relieved periodically by meat-eating orgies. In fact, nothing could be further from the truth. Much subsistence activity of the !Kung and other hunter-gatherers is conducted by the women, who gather wild vegetable foods which comprise a substantial part of the !Kung diet. Today, vegetable foods have a leading part in the !Kung diet and have presumably increased in importance as the large game herds have diminished. The !Kung know of at least 85 species of edible fruit, seeds, and plants; of this enormous subsistence base, they eat regularly only some nine species, especially the bauhinia. In a famine year or when prime vegetable food sources are exhausted, they turn to other species, having an excellent cushion of edible food to fall back on when their conventional diet staple is scarce. Theoretically, therefore, the !Kung can never starve, even if food is scarce at times—but even then, they have social mechanisms to share food. Their territory, of course, is delineated in part by available sources of vegetable foods as well as by water supplies; its frontiers, in many cases, represent a day's walking distance to the gathering grounds and back to the base camp. The data acquired by researchers into !Kung foraging is of enormous value to archaeologists studying Stone Age peoples in many parts of the world.

BIRDS, FISH, AND MOLLUSKS

Birds

Bird bones have been sadly neglected in archaeology, although some early investigators did realize their significance. As long ago as 1926, zoologist Hildegarde Howard studied a large collection of bird remains from a large shell midden at Emeryville on the eastern shores of San Francisco Bay. She found that waterbirds were the predominant species, especially ducks, geese, and cormorants, and that land birds distinctive of hill country were absent. All the geese were winter visitors, mostly found in the bay area between January and April of each year. The cormorant bones were nearly all immature, suggesting that the Native Americans had been robbing cormorant rookeries; most of the cormorant bones equaled adult birds' in size, but ossification was less complete, equivalent to that in modern birds about five to six weeks old. Howard examined rookery records and estimated that a date of June 28 each year would be the approximate time when the rookeries could be raided. She concluded that the Emeryville mound was occupied during both the winter and the early summer and probably all year.

Bird hunting has often been a sideline in the struggle for subsistence. In many societies, boys have hunted winged prey with bows and arrows while training for hunting larger game. A specialized bird-hunting kit is found in several cultures, among them the postglacial hunter-gatherer cultures of northern Europe. Though bows and spears were used in the chase, snaring was obviously practiced regularly. The birds found in some African hunting and farming sites are almost invariably species such as guinea fowl, which fly rarely and are easily snared. Surprisingly little has been written on prehistoric fowling, perhaps because bird bones are fragile and present tricky identification problems. British scientists are even experimenting with scanning electron microscopes and computer neural network techniques to identify bird species from fragmentary eggshells found in archaeological sites. In one case, from a farming site at Skara Brae in the Orkney Islands, they identified 17 different species.

Fish

Fishing, like fowling, became increasingly important as people began to specialize in different and distinctive economies, and as their environmental adaptations became more sophisticated and their technological abilities improved. Evidence for this activity comes from both artifacts and fish bones and even fish scales preserved in dry or waterlogged sites (Figure 9.10). Fish bone analysis is a highly specialized field, but one which can yield valuable information on such topics as the age and forms of salmon taken by different households, as was the case at the Keatley Creek site in British Columbia (see Chapter 10).

Freshwater and ocean fish can be caught in various ways. Nets, basket traps, and dams were methods in wide use from 10,000 years ago on, but their remains rarely survive in the archaeological record except in dry sites or waterlogged deposits. Fishhooks, harpoons, and barbed spearheads are frequent finds in lakeside or riverside encampments.

Artifacts alone tell us little about the role of fish in the prehistoric economy or about the fishing techniques of prehistoric peoples. Did they fish all year or only when salmon were running? Did they concentrate on bottom fish? Such questions can be answered only by examining the fish bones themselves—or actual fish scales.

The Chumash Indians of southern California were remarkably skillful fishers, venturing far offshore in frameless plank canoes and fishing with hook and line, basket, net, and harpoon. Their piscatory skill is reflected in the archaeological sites of Century Ranch, Los Angeles, where the bones of such deep-sea fish as the albacore and oceanic skipjack were found,

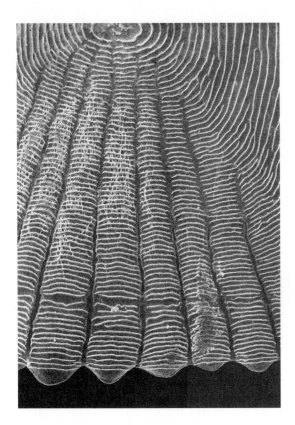

FIGURE 9.10 A fish scale found in a human coprolite from an archaeological site in Texas. *(Courtesy of Dr. Vaughn Bryant, Department of Anthropology, Texas A&M University, College Station.)*

together with the remains of large deep-water rockfish that live near the sea bottom in water too deep to be fished from the shore. Five other species normally occurring offshore, including the barracuda, were found in the same midden. The bones of shallow-water fish, among them the leopard shark and the California halibut, were discovered in the same sites, indicating that both surf fishing and canoe fishing in estuaries with hook and line, basket, or net were also practiced. The degree to which a community depends on fishing can be impressive. Lakeside or seaside fishing encampments tend to be occupied longer than hunting camps, for the food supply, especially when combined with collection of shellfish, is both reliable and nourishing. For example, lakeside groups in the western United States tended to exploit younger small fish such as the tui chub, a staple for many centuries.

Mollusks

Shellfish from seashores, lakes, or rivers formed an important part of the prehistoric diet for many thousands of years. The identification of the mollusks in shell middens is a matter for expert conchologists, who possess a mine of information on the edibility and seasons of shellfish.

Freshwater mollusks were important to many archaic bands living in North America, but because each mollusk in itself has limited food value, the amount of mollusks needed to feed even a small band of about 25 people must have been enormous. It has been calculated that such a band would need between 1,900 and 2,250 mussels, and a colossal accumulation of between 57,000 and 67,000 each month. A group of 100 persons would need at least 3 tons of mussels each month. Confronted with such figures, no one can believe that mollusks were the staple diet of any prehistoric peoples. Rather, they were a valuable supplemental food at times of scarcity during the year or a source of variety in a staple diet of fish, game, or vegetable foods.

When freshwater or seawater mollusks were collected, the collectors soon accumulated huge piles of shells at strategic places on the coast or on the shores of lakes, near rocky outcrops or tidal pools where mollusks were commonly found. Modern midden analysis involves systematic sampling of the deposits and counting and weighing of the various constituents of the soil. The proportions of different shells are readily calculated, and their sizes, which sometimes change through time, are easily measured.

California shell middens have long been the subject of intensive research, with the changes in frequency of mollusks projected against ecological changes in the site areas. The La Jolla culture middens of La Batiquitos Lagoon near San Diego are a notable example of such analysis. Claude N. Warren took column samples from one shell mound and found that the remains of five species of shellfish were the dominant elements in the molluscan diet of the inhabitants. The changes in the major species of shellfish were then calculated for each excavated level. They found that *Mytilus,* the bay mussel, was the most common in the lower levels and was gradually replaced by *Chione,* the Venus shell, and *Pecten,* the scallop, both of which assumed greater importance in the later phases of the site's occupation, which has been radiocarbon-dated from the fifth to the second millennia B.C. Warren found that *Ostrea,* the oyster, a species characteristic of a rocky coast, was also most common in the lower levels, indicating that the San Diego shore was rocky beach at that time, with extensive colonies of shellfish. By about 6,300 years ago La Batiquitos Lagoon was silted to the extent that it was ecologically more suitable for *Pecten* than the rock-loving *Mytilus.* Soon afterward, however, the lagoons became so silted that even *Pecten* and *Chione* could no longer support a large human population dependent on shellfish. The inhabitants then had to move elsewhere.

Many peoples collected mollusks seasonally, but it is difficult to identify such practices from the archaeological record. Growth bands in mollusk shells have been used to measure seasonality, but the most promising approach is to measure the oxygen-isotopic ratio of shell carbonate, which is a function of the water temperature. Using a mass spectrometer, researchers can measure the oxygen 18 composition at the edge of a shell, obtaining the temperature of the water at the time of the mollusk's death. It is difficult to obtain actual temperature readings, but you can gain an idea of seasonal fluctuations, thereby establishing whether a mollusk was taken in winter or summer.

Both freshwater and seawater shells had ornamental roles as well. Favored species were traded over great distances in North America. Millions of *Mercenaria* and *Busycon* shells were turned into wampum belts in New England in early Colonial times. *Spondylus gaederopus,* a mussel native to the Black Sea, the Sea of Marmara, and the Aegean, was widely distributed as far north and west as Poland and the Rhineland by European farmers in the fifth millennium B.C. The *Conus* shell, common on the East African coast, was widely traded, finding its way into the African interior and becoming a traditional perquisite of chieftainly prestige. The nineteenth-century missionary and explorer David Livingstone records that, on his visit to Chief Shinte in western Zambia in 1855, the going price for two *Conus* shells at that time was a slave; for five, a tusk of elephant ivory. Such shells are occasionally found in ancient village sites far from the coast dating to the past 2,000 years.

SUBSISTENCE DATA FROM ROCK ART

Rock art is a major source of information on economic activities. Upper Palaeolithic cave art in southwestern France depicts dozens of mammal species, perhaps meant to represent large, meaty animals that were economically (and symbolically) valuable. Some of the paintings of bison and reindeer are so accurate that researchers believe they can identify the season of the year that the animals were painted from the coloring of their coats!

The Stone Age rock paintings of southern Africa are of great importance for the information on ancient ritual beliefs encoded in them (see Chapter 12 and Discovery box on p. 291), but are also valuable for their precise depictions of ancient weapons, hunts and camp scenes, even of people raiding bees' nests with the angry bees swarming around their heads. There are depictions of hunters pursuing eland (a large antelope), of men and women walking with stone-weighted digging sticks (the weights look just like those found in archaeological sites), even of a man wearing an ostrich skin and carrying a bow stalking in the midst of a herd of unsuspecting ostrich. These many paintings provide a great deal of informative data on ancient hunting methods which does not survive in the archaeological record. For instance, the rock paintings in eastern South Africa provide fascinating information on fishing practices and the boats associated with them. Patricia Vinnecombe recorded a fishing scene in the Tsoelike River rock shelter in Lesotho, southern Africa (Figure 9.11). The fishermen, armed with long spears, are massed in boats, apparently cornering a shoal of fish that are swimming around in confusion. Some boats have lines under their hulls which may represent anchors; the fish cannot be identified with certainty, but they may be freshwater catfish or yellowfish.

DISCOVERY

Recording the Behistun Inscription, Iraq

Persian King Darius (548–486 B.C.) was a bombastic conqueror who liked to boast of his conquests. Fortunately for archaeology, Darius commemorated his victory over five rebel chiefs with a trilingual inscription set high on the great Rock of Behistun in the Iranian highlands. The inscription, in Old Persian, Elamite, and Babylonian cuneiform, was the Rosetta Stone of Mesopotamia, for it provided clues for the decipherment of the wedge-like script, the major diplomatic writing of its day. Unfortunately, Darius placed his inscription on a virtually inaccessible cliff face. English cavalry officer Henry Rawlinson was both an adventurer and an expert on Asian languages. He was posted to Kurdistan, near the Great Rock in 1833 and spent 10 years gradually recording the inscriptions, climbing high above the ground without scaffolding. He copied the more accessible script by hanging by one hand from a ladder while holding a notebook. But the cuneiform inscription was said by the local hillspeople to be unreachable. Rawlinson could copy the script with a powerful telescope, but wanted to make paper casts of the individual impressions. Eventually he persuaded a "wild Kurdish boy" to scale the slope. The boy swung himself across with wooden pegs and seemingly insecure foot holds until he could pass a rope across the cliff. Then he formed a swinging seat like a window cleaner's cradle and made paper casts under Rawlinson's supervision. This was a simple process, involving the hammering of wet sheets of paper into the crevices with a stout brush. When dry, they provided an accurate cast of the inscription.

The Behistun inscription helped unlock the secrets of cuneiform. As for the casts, once finished with, they moldered in the British Museum and were eaten by mice.

FIGURE 9.11 A rock painting showing a fishing scene, from Lesotho, southern Africa.

ANCIENT DIET

The ultimate objective of economic archaeology is not only to establish how people obtained their food but also to reconstruct their actual diet. Dietary reconstruction is difficult, mainly because of incomplete economic information. Yet the problems involved are fundamental. What proportion of the diet was meat? How diverse were dietary sources? Did the principal sources of diet change from season to season? To what extent did the people rely on food from neighboring areas? Was food stored? What limitations or restrictions did technology or society place on diet? All these questions lie behind any inquiry into ancient subsistence.

Diet (what is eaten) and nutrition (the ability of a diet to maintain the body in its environment) must be studied in close conjunction, for they are quite distinct from subsistence, the actual process of obtaining resources. Despite such recovery methods as flotation, it is still impossible to assess the intake of vitamins, minerals, and milk products in prehistoric diets. Nor do we have adequate data on the waste of food during preparation and storage or on the effects of different cooking techniques. Archaeological data can only indicate some of the foods eaten by prehistoric communities and show, at least qualitatively, how important some of them were generally. We are far from being able to ascribe precise food value to animal and plant remains, as would be demanded for precise studies of diet and nutrition.

Human skeletal remains can sometimes provide evidence of ancient malnutrition and other dietary conditions. Physical anthropologist Jane Buikstra has studied diet and health among the prehistoric populations of the lower Illinois valley. As early as 5500 B.C., the inhabitants of this area began harvesting hickory and other nuts on an ever larger scale. Nuts provided a high-quality food resource, but to support large numbers of people, they had to be harvested over large areas. As time went on, the growing population of the valley turned more and more to wild seeds, especially oily ones such as marsh elder, which were high in protein and were a concentrated source of food energy. In time, they actually cultivated marsh elder as well as sunflowers, whose seeds had equivalent food value. They supplemented the oily species with starchy seeds such as erect knotweed, which were highly dependable and easily stored. In the last half of the first millennium A.D., the starchy seeds gave way to cultivated maize. By this time there was considerable competition for game and other wild-animal foods, and Illinois valley populations may have ranged in the thousands of people. As much more complex social organization and regional trade evolved, Buikstra observes that dental diseases became much more common and tuberculosis spread among the village populations. The introduction of maize appears to have coincided with a deterioration in child health, too. However, the effects of intensification of food production on prehistoric diet and health are still little understood.

One useful technique involves identifying types of plant foods from the **carbon isotope analysis** of prehistoric bone and hair. By using the ratio between two stable carbon isotopes—carbon 12 and carbon 13 in animal tissue—researchers can establish how much corn was consumed or how much marine food was eaten as opposed to terrestrial resources. Research on controlled animal populations has shown that as carbon is passed along the food chain, the carbon composition of animals continues to reflect the relative isotopic composition of their diet. Carbon is metabolized in plants through three major pathways: C3, C4, and Crussulacean acid metabolism. The plants that make up the diet of animals have distinct carbon 13 values. Maize, for example, is a C4 plant. In contrast, most indigenous temperate flora in North America is composed of C3 varieties. Thus, a population that shifts its diet from wild vegetable foods to maize will also experience a shift in dietary isotopic values. Because carbon 13 and carbon 12 values are stable and do not change after death, you can study archaeological carbon from food remains, soil humus, and skeletal remains to gain insight into ancient diet.

This approach is of great importance to archaeologists studying dietary patterns, especially when combined with information from other sources. For example, excellent organic preservation at the Windover burial grounds in eastern Florida allowed a team of researchers to combine an archaeobotanical analysis with bone-collagen stable isotope and nitrogen-isotopic studies of human skeletal remains. They were interested in the degree of reliance on marine as opposed to terrestrial food resources among the people buried at Windover between about 6000 and 5000 B.C. A comparison of nitrogen-isotopic values of human bone collagen from Windover and coastal sites shows that the inhabitants of the former made little use of marine resources. Many C3 plants were part of the Windover diet, along with duck and catfish, with intermediate C3/C4 values also significant. The plant remains from the site, such as elderberry, included virtually all C3 plants, confirming the isotopic data and data from well-preserved stomach contents. The research team believes it has evidence for seasonal foraging based on wild plant foods and freshwater and estuarine resources over a long period of time.

A detailed bone chemistry analysis of adult burials from *Grasshopper Pueblo* in east-central Arizona shows the great potential of this approach. Archaeologist Joseph Ezzo was able to show that between A.D. 1275 and 1325 males had greater access to meat and cultivated plants, while females had greater access to wild plants. Between 1325 and 1400, both men and women ate virtually the same diet, one in which meat and wild plant foods were less important. This may have resulted from a combination of social and environmental factors: increased population, drought cycles, or use of marginal farming land, which compelled the Grasshopper people to live on agricultural products. The people responded to food stress by increasing storage capacity, reducing household size, and eventually by moving away.

The stable-carbon-isotope method is not restricted to use with agriculture; it has been applied with success to measure the reliance on marine species of prehistoric Northwest Coast populations in British Columbia. Forty-eight samples from prehistoric human skeletons from 15 sites along the coast revealed a dietary reliance of about 90 percent on marine sources, a figure much higher than crude ethnographic estimates. The same data suggest that there has been little dietary change along the British Columbia coast for the past 5,000 years, which is hardly surprising, given the rich maritime resources of the shoreline.

Concentrations of strontium, a stable mineral component of bone as opposed to calcium, can be used to measure the contribution of plants to diet. For instance, Stone Age people in the eastern Mediterranean ate much the same proportions of meat and plant foods from 100,000 years ago up to the end of the Ice Age. Then, there was a significant shift toward the consumption of plant foods. At Chalcatzingo, an Olmec site in Mexico, strontium analysis has shown that the elite, buried with valuable jade ornaments, had a lower strontium level, for they ate more meat compared to commoners who consumed very little.

Stomach contents and **feces** provide unrivaled momentary insights into meals eaten by individual members of a prehistoric society at specific moments in the year. Dietary reconstructions based on these sources, however, suffer from the disadvantage that they are rare and represent but one person's food intake. Furthermore, some foods are more rapidly digested than others. But even these insights are better than no data at all. The stomach of Tollund Man, who was executed around the time of Christ, contained the remains of a finely ground meal made from barley, linseed, and several wild grasses; no meat was found in the stomach contents.

Many American scholars have studied coprolites (human droppings) from dry caves in the United States and Mexico (Figure 9.10). Such researches include analyses of microscopic food remains found in the feces, and also of pollen, phytoliths, and parasites. Over the past 20 years, researchers in southwest Texas have obtained coprolite evidence for a basically stable hunter-gatherer diet over 9,000 years of hunting and gathering in this arid region.

Recent coprolite studies in North America have analyzed pollen grains found in human feces. Vaughn Bryant analyzed coprolite pollen from a site near the mouth of the Pecos River in southwestern Texas. He found that the inhabitants of the site between 800 B.C. and A.D. 500 spent the spring and summer months at this locality. During their stay, they ate many vegetable foods, including several flowers. One danger of using pollen grains is that of contamination from the background pollen "rain" that is always with us. But Bryant was able to show that all but two of the species represented in the pollen were local plants. In all these instances, too, valuable insights were obtained into minor details of prehistoric diet, as well as into intestinal parasites that were commonplace among peoples living on a diet of game meat that was often slightly rotten.

Because the ultimate objective is explaining how people lived in the past, new theoretical frameworks, systematic use of ethnographic analogy, and quantitative methods will, it is hoped, intensify research on the dietary requirements of ancient peoples.

The study of ancient subsistence has made remarkable strides in recent years, as archaeologists draw increasingly on the methods of high-tech science and multidisciplinary approaches.

SUMMARY

Archaeologists rely on many sources to reconstruct prehistoric subsistence. These include environmental data, animal bones, vegetal remains, human feces, artifacts, and prehistoric art. Zooarchaeology involves the study of animal bones. Bone identification is carried out by direct comparison between modern and ancient bones. Game animal remains can give insights into prehistoric hunting practices. The proportions of animals present can be affected by cultural taboos, the relative meat yields of different species, and hunting preferences. Early domesticated animals are very difficult to distinguish from their wild ancestors. Domestication alters both the characteristics of an animal and its bone structure. Slaughtering and butchery practices can be derived from the frequency and distribution of animal bones in the ground. Hunting and slaughter patterns are subject to all manner of subtle variables, including convenience and season of the year.

Carbonized and unburned vegetable remains are recovered from hearths and pits, often using a flotation method to separate seeds from the matrix around them. Dry sites, such as the rock shelters and camps in the Tehuacán Valley of Mexico, provide evidence for early crop domestication. Bird bones provide valuable information on seasonal occupation; fish remains reflect specialized coastal adaptations that became common in later prehistoric times. Freshwater and saltwater mollusks were both consumed as food and traded over enormous distances as prestigious luxuries or ornaments.

Prehistoric diet and nutrition must be studied together, for they are distinct from subsistence, which is the actual process of obtaining food. Human skeletal remains, stomach contents, and feces are the few direct sources available to us for information on prehistoric diet. Carbon isotope analysis offers promise as a way of studying dietary changes through time and between social classes.

KEY TERMS

Attritional age profile
Biosphere
Catastrophic age profile
Carbon isotope analysis
Epiphyses
Faunal analysis

Feces
Flotation
Paleoethnobotany
Phytoliths
Taphonomy
Zooarchaeology

GUIDE TO FURTHER READING

Binford, Lewis R. 1981. *Bones: Ancient Men and Modern Myths.* Orlando, FL: Academic Press.
    A provocative essay on animal bones, concentrating both on ethnographic analogy and faunal analysis.

Davis, Simon J. M. 1987. *The Archaeology of Animals*. London: Batsford.

    A superbly illustrated, definitive book on zooarchaeology for beginners. Strongly recommended; comprehensive.

Klein, Richard G., and Kathryn Cruz-Uribe. 1984. *The Analysis of Animal Bones from Archaeological Sites*. Chicago: University of Chicago Press.

    The authors describe statistical approaches to faunal analysis. A book for more advanced readers.

Pearsall, Deborah. 1989. *Paleoethnobotany: A Handbook of Procedures*. Orlando, FL: Academic Press.

    A useful introduction to this complex subject.

Smith, Bruce D. 1994. *The Emergence of Agriculture*. New York: Scientific American Library.

    A superb introduction to early agriculture for the general reader, with special emphasis on AMS radiocarbon dating of seeds.

CHAPTER 10
Settlement and Landscape

Chinese Terracotta soldiers. Tomb of Emperor Zhihuangdi, China. c. 221 B.C. (Source: Hulton Getty/Liaison Agency. Inc.)

Settlement Archaeology
Discovery: Catherwood and Stephens at Copán, Honduras, 1839
Households
    Earthquake at Kourion, Cyprus
    Excavating a Household
    Cerén, El Salvador
Communities
Doing Archaeology: Winter Houses at Keatley Creek, British Columbia
    Larger Communities
Site: The Creation of the Aztec World at Teotihuacán
Distribution of Communities
    The Savannah River Valley, Southeastern United States
    The Basin of Mexico Survey
    Geographic Information Systems at Roman Wroxeter, England
Population
    Collapse at Copán, Honduras
Doing Archaeology: Studying the Maya Collapse at Copán, Honduras

"I am my own aborigine," Irish archaeologist Seamus Caulfield once told me. We were standing on the forbidding limestone cliffs of County Mayo in northwest Ireland, gazing at the rolling bogland of Céide Fields. Caulfield grew up in nearby Belderigg, a hamlet of small houses surrounded by ancient field walls built and rebuilt over thousands of years. As a small boy, he went barefoot for six months of the year, feeling underfoot the texture of narrow pathways, marshlands, and small fields. Years later, Seamus Caulfield still has a tactile relationship with his home community and with the farmland that once sustained it, the kind of close relationship with environment and landscape once enjoyed by preindustrial societies all over the globe. He calls these familiar farmlands his "landscape of memory." Thanks to archaeology, Caulfield has traced his ancestry back on this land to a long-forgotten Stone Age field system built before 3000 B.C.

Caulfield inherited a passion for archaeology from his schoolteacher father, who had discovered stone walls deep under the peat which mantles the local landscape. In 1983, Caulfield began to map the buried stone walls at nearby Céide Fields. First, he tried using aerial photographs to identify the field systems, but the peat covered everything. Then he turned to the low-tech tools of his youth, a 6-foot-long (2-m-long) iron T-bar and a special spade used for cutting peat sods. Caulfield and his students laid out lines across the hills and ran transects of probes at one-foot intervals across the bogland. The peat was much shallower where the buried stone walls lay. Soon, hundreds of bamboo poles marked walls and fields.

Season after season, Caulfield returned to Céide Fields until he had mapped more than four square miles (103 sq. km) of intact farming landscape, undisturbed since 2400 B.C. (Figure 10.1). With the help of geologists and palynologists, Caulfield showed how the warmer and wetter climate after

FIGURE 10.1 Céide Fields Stone Age field system, County Mayo, Ireland. The building in the center background is the visitor center. *(Source: Consulate General of Ireland.)*

the Ice Age brought pine forests to the area. Tree rings tell us the forest suddenly vanished in 2800 B.C., opening up grassland ideal for cattle grazing. For nearly 500 years, small groups of farmers separated their pastures with low stone walls, dividing the land into a patchwork of lines, rectangles, and squares. Each family lived in a small thatched round house set within a stone enclosure amidst a mosaic of constantly changing fields modified over successive generations.

Like Seamus Caulfield thousands of years later, the Stone Age farmers knew every boulder, every tree, and every stream. They knew the qualities of grazing grass and how the subtle movements of clouds forecast rain and wind. Judging from their communal tombs set among their fields, they valued their close relationship to the land in more than material terms. Generations of the dead lay in the cramped side chambers of the sepulchers. The living made offerings to their ancestors in the small outside court by the entrance to the tomb, their gifts ensuring the continuity of human existence and the orderly passage of the seasons that governed their lives.

After five centuries, the damp climate defeated the farmers. Wet bog, with its mosses, heathers, and moor grass, spread inexorably across the hills. The grasslands vanished, the cattle herders retreated inland, and the boundary walls disappeared under peat. County Mayo was a peaceful part of Ireland. No Roman armies or social catastrophes disrupted life at Céide Fields, ensuring a high level of cultural continuity in this corner of Ireland. Seamus Caulfield's family has lived at Belderigg for generations. Thanks to his research, he feels he can safely claim himself as an "aborigine," a distant descendant of the local farmers of some 200 generations ago.

The Céide Fields project is a classic example of **settlement archaeology,** the topic of this chapter—the ways in which archaeologists study households, communities, and ancient cultural landscapes.

SETTLEMENT ARCHAEOLOGY

The archaeology of landscape and settlement is what archaeologists call settlement archaeology. Such research requires a combination of common sense, careful mapping and survey combined with fine-grained excavation, and, often, high-technology science. (See Discovery box below.)

Settlement patterns are the result of relationships between people, who decided for economic, social, and political reasons to place their houses, settlements, and religious structures where they did. Archaeologists can study settlement patterns at several levels—the internal layout of a single dwelling, its relationship to others in the community, and the relationship of this settlement to its neighbors and more distant ones across an ever changing landscape. At one level, settlement archaeology allows us to examine not only relationships between different communities, but trading networks, ways in which people exploited their environment, and social organization as well.

For instance, the Chumash Indians of southern California lived on the islands and shores of the Santa Barbara Channel, where ocean upwellings

DISCOVERY

Catherwood and Stephens at Copán, Honduras, 1839

In 1839, New York traveler-turned-lawyer John Lloyd Stephens and Scottish artist Frederick Catherwood journeyed deep into the Central American rainforest, following rumors of vanished civilizations and great ruins masked by primordial jungle. They came first to the tiny village of Copán, in what is now Honduras, where "around them lay the dark outlines of ruins shrouded by the brooding forest. . . . The only sound that disturbed the quiet of this buried city was the noise of monkeys moving around among the tops of the trees" (Stephens, 1841, 48). I vividly remember visiting an unexcavated Maya center at Naranjo, Guatemala, where you walk among eroding pyramids that vanish into the forest canopy high overhead. You can still imagine the powerful effect Copán had on Catherwood and Stephens over 150 years ago.

While Catherwood drew the intricate hieroglyphs he had found on stone columns still standing among the ruins, Stephens tried to buy the ancient city of Copán for $50, so he could transport it block by block to New York. The deal fell through when he found he could not float any antiquities down the nearby Copán River.

Stephens and Catherwood subsequently visited many other famous Maya cities, among them Palenque, Uxmal, and Chichén Itzá. They were the first travelers to recognize the Maya as the builders of these great sites. Stephens wrote: "These cities . . . are not the works of peoples who have passed away . . . but of the same great race . . . which still clings around their ruins" (1841, 222). All subsequent research into the Maya civilization is based on the work of these two tough pioneers.

nourished one of the richest inshore fisheries on earth. Seven hundred years ago, this rich, if unpredictable, bounty of marine resources allowed some Chumash to live in densely populated, permanent settlements with as many as 1,000 inhabitants. The most important of these villages were clustered at sheltered spots on the coast with good canoe landings, kelp fisheries close offshore, and sea mammal rookeries within easy reach. If you find a series of coastal Chumash settlements in sheltered positions that protect them from the southeastern storms of winter, you can reasonably assume that there were sound, practical reasons behind the site distribution. Within the village itself, we know that a complex variety of social, economic, and even personal factors dictated the layout of houses in relation to one another.

At another level, an entire village or city may reflect a society's view of their world and the cosmos. The ancient Mesoamericans placed great emphasis on lavish public ceremonies set in the heart of large ceremonial centers. Fifteen hundred years ago, great lowland Maya cities such as Copán and Tikal were replicas in stone and stucco of the layered Mesoamerican spiritual world of the heavens, the living world, and the underworld (Figure 10.2). Their pyramids were sacred mountains, the doorways of the temples atop them the sacred openings by which the ruler, as intermediary to the spiritual world, traveled to the Otherworld up and down the *Wacah Chan,* the symbolic World Tree that connected the layers of the Maya universe. A thousand years later, the vast plaza of the Aztec capital Tenochtitlán stood at the center of the ancient Mexican world. When Spaniard Hernán Cortés and his conquistadors climbed to the summit of the great temple of the sun god Huitzilopochtli and the rain god Tlaloc in 1519, they stood at the axis of the Aztec universe. The four quarters of the Aztec world radiated from a temple so sacred that pyramid after pyramid rose at the same location.

FIGURE 10.2 Temple I at the Maya city of Tikal, which dates to about A.D. 700, is a replica of a sacred mountain and was once a sacred pathway to the Maya Otherworld. *(Source: Robert Frerck/Odyssey Productions.)*

The relationship between an individual and the landscape can be as complex as that of an entire society. A Central African farmer once showed me his land, a patchwork of small gardens, some intensely cultivated, others lying fallow as the soil regenerated after years of use. I saw just land until he pointed out the subtle signs of regenerating soil, different kinds of grasses to be eaten by his cattle in the weeks ahead, the flowering nut trees that would be harvested at the end of the wet season. The landscape came alive, a quilt of gardens, plants, and animals protected by his ancestors, who were now the spiritual guardians of the land. My friend's relationship to his surroundings was like Seamus Caulfield's "landscape of memory" at Céide Fields.

Settlement archaeology is about these many layers of dynamic relationships, some of which are nearly impossible to discern without the careful use of analogy with living societies (see Chapter 2).

For working purposes, many archaeologists divide these layers of relationship into a loose hierarchy of three general levels—households, communities, and distribution of communities (Figure 10.3).

HOUSEHOLDS

I once worked in the low-lying Middle Zambezi valley in Central Africa excavating a 500-year-old trading settlement lying among modern farming villages. The local Tonga people farmed an environment where the midday temperature often exceeded 100°F (37°C) and the nights were hot for most of the year. Their pole-and-mud huts had thatched roofs that projected far from the walls to form large and shady verandas. As we started work at dawn, we would see each household coming awake in the cool of morning, the women setting out for the fields with their baskets and hoes, boys driving goats and sheep to pasture. Each day, the rhythm of the household would repeat itself—the morning walk to the fields, the return at midday, the monotonous pounding of wooden pestles and mortars that signaled the preparation of the evening meal. Come twilight, the people would eat, settling down to smoke and gossip as the sun set and darkness fell. There was a timeless rhythm to the passing days, which varied little, as the same artifacts were used day after day, and lain down after use in the same place each night.

We found traces of collapsed, 500-year-old mud huts in our excavations. I made a point of examining ruined houses in modern-day villages, photographing the disintegrating walls and roofs, plotting the distribution of hearths, stone grinders, and other artifacts abandoned when the owners left. We tried to reconstruct the activities of individual households from the patterns of artifacts we found near hearths and on hut floors. In this particular instance, we were unsuccessful, for the people had swept their houses clean before abandoning them. However, the same approach, using artifact patternings, has provided insights into ancient households in many parts of the world.

We should never forget that **households** are chronicles of human interactions and communities even more so. A household unit is defined by the artifact patterns that reflect activities which take place around a house; they

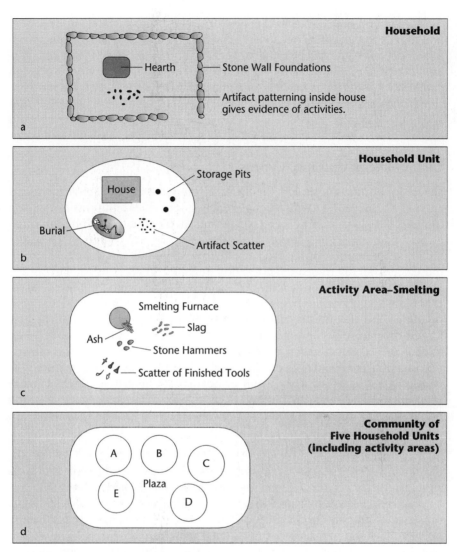

FIGURE 10.3   Spatial units used by archaeologists to study human settlement: *(a)* household; *(b)* household unit; *(c)* activity area; *(d)* community.

are assumed to belong to one household. Archaeological sites, whether small hunting camps, humble farming villages, or vast cities, are archives of human interaction. People lived and died in these places. They grew up, got married, had children, quarreled with neighbors. These daily interactions, between men and women, rich and poor, traders and their customers, slaves and masters, come down to us in the form of distinctive artifact patternings and community settlement patterns. The anonymous testimony of artifacts from individual houses, neighborhoods, palaces, and temples reveals the full, and often unsuspected, diversity of ancient human communities.

Careful and meticulous excavation can reveal the activities of individual households, provided the house has remained isolated from surrounding occupation debris. Fortunately for the archaeologist, many societies used more-or-less standardized hut designs, so researchers can use the variations in design and artifact patterings between individual houses as evidence for different subsistence activities, social status, wealth, and manufacturing activities. Like a shipwreck on the seabed, a well-excavated ancient house can be a sealed capsule of a moment in the past, which can be read by an expert like a book.

Earthquake at Kourion, Cyprus

Seventeen hundred years ago, the Romans controlled the Mediterranean world and its lucrative trade routes through a network of cities and ports from Spain to Egypt. On July 21, A.D. 365, an early morning earthquake ripped through a small Roman port at *Kourion* in southwestern Cyprus. Three shock waves flattened the town. The quake caused huge tsunamis that rolled ashore in the eastern Mediterranean. Thousands perished in Alexandria, Egypt, 250 miles (402 km) away. Archaeologist David Soren recovered a treasure trove of information about the households in Kourion by excavating the individual buildings and plotting the time capsules of daily life preserved in the collapsed dwellings. A computer database of the patterned finds allows Soren to analyze individual rooms from different angles. He recovered the skeletal remains of a family still abed. The husband died vainly trying to shield his young wife and infant from a rain of beams and limestone blocks (Figure 10.4). In a nearby courtyard, Soren's excavators found a stable where a young girl died trying to calm a restless mule, whose skeleton lay by a stone trough.

Excavating a Household

Kourion is a dramatic find—individual households preserved by the very cataclysm that destroyed them. More often, the archaeologist finds more subtle patternings of household activities—stone toolmaking, cooking, or domestic crafts preserved within the boundaries of long-vanished dwellings. By excavating every artifact and other debris and leaving them in place, archaeologists can plot the exact positions of individual artifacts and food remains where they lie.

Every time I have dug a house with its contents intact, I have tried to define a larger "household unit." The unit comprises not only the dwelling itself but any surrounding storage pits and graves, also areas for food preparation and other tasks associated with them. To begin, the researchers lay out a lettered and numbered grid of squares over the household unit, connected to the larger recording grid that covers the entire site. (Alternatively, they may rely on electronic plotting.)

Households require slow-moving area excavation, so that the exact position of every artifact, features such as hearths or pits, and the tiniest of food remains such as seeds and broken animal bones can be recorded electronically and photographically before anything is lifted from the dwelling. Sometimes, I have managed to identify the activities of different individuals while still excavating the house floor—stoneworking activity surviving as a

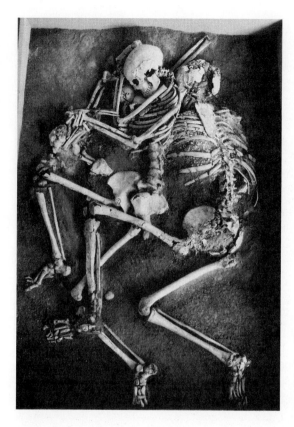

FIGURE 10.4 Kourion, Cyprus. A 28-year-old man tries to shield his 19-year-old wife and their one-and-a-half-year-old baby from falling roof timbers. *(Source: Martha Cooper/NGS Image Collection.)*

scatter of stone tools and the waste flakes and cores used to make them, butchering of a rabbit by a cluster of broken bones (Figure 10.5). More often, however, the database in the laboratory computer is the best source of information, allowing researchers, for example, to call up the position of every potsherd of a certain style or all ox forelimb bones. It is then that they can discern unexpected associations, subtle signposts to long-forgotten domestic activities, or even of children playing. Short of a burial or a house belonging to a known historical individual, this is about as close as one can get in archaeology to individuals as opposed to households. This type of excavation is invaluable when studying male and female roles or the cultural diversity of a household revealed by distinctive artifacts (see Chapter 11).

Household archaeology is a classic application of the law of association described in Chapter 2. The distinctive patterning of artifacts in houses, storage pits, and other areas forms **activity sets,** groups of artifacts associated with specific activities, such as wire-making tools and copper rods: These are evidence that someone was making fine copper wire ornaments.

Cerén, El Salvador

Activity sets sometimes provide startlingly complete stories of the past, especially at sites where preservation conditions are exceptional. One August

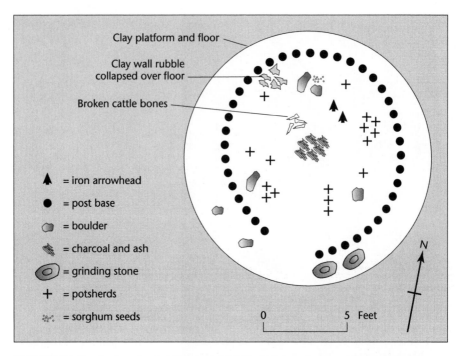

FIGURE 10.5 A plot of a 1,000-year-old African farmer's house from Kalomo, Zambia.

evening in the sixth century A.D., a sudden rumble shook a quiet Maya village at Cerén in El Salvador (see also Chapter 2). An underground fissure less than a mile away erupted without warning. A fast-moving cloud of ash darkened the twilight sky. The villagers fled for their lives, leaving everything behind. Minutes later, their houses lay under a thick layer of volcanic debris. Fifteen hundred years later, archaeologist Payson Sheets used subsurface radar to locate several buried houses deep under the ash (see Chapter 6). He then excavated the dwellings. Plotting every artifact, even individual wall fragments, seeds, and pieces of thatch, he discovered households where the people fled cascading ash at the end of the evening meal.

One household lived in a complex of four buildings: a kitchen, a workshop, a storehouse, and a residence, where the residents socialized, ate, and slept. The residence had a front porch open on three sides. The main room covered 43 square feet (4 sq. m), with storage pots against the back wall (Figure 10.6). One pot contained a spindle whorl for making cotton thread. A large adobe bench on the east side of the room served as a sleeping place. During the day, people rolled up their mats and stored them among the rafters. Even the sharp-edged obsidian knife blades, stored high in the roof for safety, still lay among the thatch.

A walkway linked the dwelling to a nearby storehouse, passing by a food-grinding area where a metate (grinding stone) still stood on forked

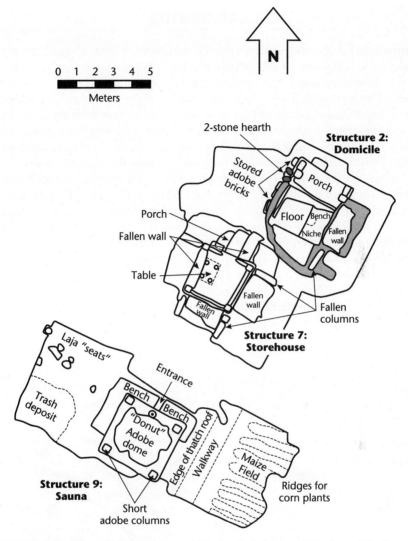

0 1 2 3 4 5
Meters

N

2-stone hearth

Structure 2: Domicile

Stored adobe bricks

Porch

Porch

Floor Bench

Fallen wall

Niche Fallen wall

Table

Fallen wall

Fallen wall

Fallen columns

Structure 7: Storehouse

Laja "seats"

Entrance

Trash deposit

Bench Bench

"Donut" Adobe dome

Edge of thatch roof

Walkway

Maize Field

Structure 9: Sauna

Short adobe columns

Ridges for corn plants

FIGURE 10.6 Plan of a Maya house at Cerén, El Salvador. *(Courtesy of Professor Payson Sheets, University of Colorado, Boulder.)*

sticks about 20 inches (50 cm) above the ground. The household owned a well-tended garden along the side of the storehouse with carefully spaced rows of three species of medicinal herbs standing about 3 feet (1 m) apart, each plant standing in a small mound of soil. Just to the south an ash-covered field contained ridges of young maize plants about 8 to 15 inches (20 to 38 cm) high, typical corn growth for August in this environment.

The study of individual households gives us an intimate look at daily life. By expanding the inquiry to the community level, researchers gain a broader impression of how people interacted with one another.

COMMUNITIES

Communities are the arrangement of structures within a single group. A community is a group of individuals and households who normally reside in face-to-face association. The archaeology of communities covers a vast spectrum of human settlements, from tiny hunter-gatherer camps to enormous cities. Expanded versions of the same survey and excavation methods used to investigate households operate at the community level, but a researcher's concerns range far wider than the character and layout of the settlement itself. Both environmental conditions and subsistence limit the size and permanence of human settlements. Most hunter-gatherer societies such as the !Kung of southern Africa's Kalahari Desert or the Hadza of Tanzania, East Africa, are constantly on the move, so their camps are short-lived, sometimes occupied for little more than a few days. In contrast, the farmers of Çatalhöyük, a Turkish farming settlement of 6000 B.C., lived in the same crowded village of mud houses separated by narrow alleys for many centuries, because they were anchored to their nearby fields (Figure 10.7).

In such small communities, family and kin ties were of overwhelming importance, affecting the layout of houses, household compounds, and

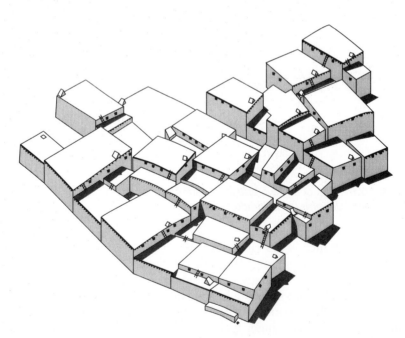

FIGURE 10.7 A schematic reconstruction of houses at Çatalhöyük, Turkey. The inhabitants entered their houses from the roof, and the outside walls formed a simple town wall. *(Courtesy of Thames and Hudson, London.)*

groups of dwellings. By mapping and analyzing artifact patterns and house inventories, excavators can sometimes find traces of different residential clusters within a single community. Kent Flannery and a University of Michigan research team used such data plots to find at least four residential wards (barrios) within the rapidly growing village of San José Mogote, which flourished in Mexico's Valley of Oaxaca after 1350 B.C. A trash-filled erosion gully separated each cluster of square thatched houses from its neighbors.

Small communities, like cities, are never static entities. Peoples' children grow up, marry, and start new households nearby. Houses burn down or collapse, so new dwellings are built in their place. As often happened with Iroquois villages in the American northeast, a settlement would outgrow its fortifications, then erect an extended palisade to protect new houses (Figure 10.8). The study of an ancient community is a study of constant interactions between individuals, households, and members of the settlement discerned through the careful study of **activity areas** and artifact patternings. (See Doing Archaeology box on p. 310.)

The Keatley Creek excavations revealed possible evidence for social organization, but other lines of evidence were needed to confirm the hypothesis.

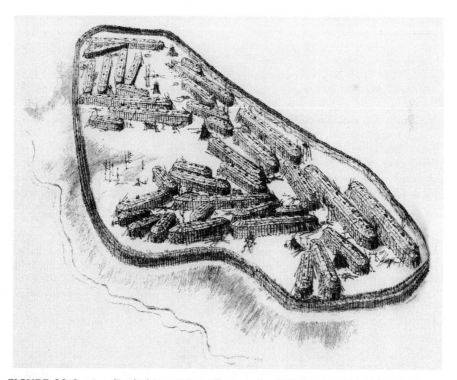

FIGURE 10.8 A palisaded Iroquoian village at the Draper site, Ontario, Canada, dating to c. A.D. 1500. This settlement was expanded several times. *(Courtesy of the Museum of the American Indian, London, Ontario, Canada.)*

DOING ARCHAEOLOGY

Winter Houses at Keatley Creek, British Columbia

When archaeologist Brian Hayden excavated a series of large winter houses at *Keatley Creek* near the Fraser River in British Columbia, he unearthed over 115 house depressions, excavated partially into the ground, some over 66 feet (20 m) across. The dwellings were dug up to 6 feet (2 m) into the subsoil, then roofed with timber, bark, grass, or mats. Access was usually by ladder through the smoke hole. The site lies on a dry terrace above the Fraser River in a semiarid environment. Mountains rise behind the site. There are a number of important salmon harvesting sites nearby, which were among the most productive in the region in early historic times. Many surrounding groups came to the area to trade for dried salmon, which probably gave Keatley Creek unusual importance as a settlement.

Most of the house pits excavated by Hayden and his colleagues date to between 3500 B.C. and A.D. 950. The excavators excavated each housepit carefully, recording not only basic dimensions, but the sizes of hearths and storage pits, also the depth of fire-reddening beneath each hearth. Using fine screens, they acquired as much accurate information on the positions of individual artifacts and food remains as possible. In addition, they sampled house-floor deposits for their soil chemistry and used flotation to recover small plant remains, tiny artifacts, and bone fragments. They combined this data with sourcing studies of toolmaking materials (see Chapter 11)

and studied ways of distinguishing floor surfaces from the remains of collapsed thatched roofs.

The analysis of all these data revealed some interesting social differences. One large pithouse had a series of hearths forming a circle about 6 feet (2 m) wide inside the pit wall, as if a series of domestic groups resided in the same dwelling. Each hearth had its own fire-cracked rocks and stone tools used for domestic activities. The distributions of stone artifact fragments and waste byproducts reveal that the messier tasks such as animal butchery and spear making took place in the center of the dwelling, where there was more space and headroom, while such activities as projectile point manufacture and sewing occurred in the domestic areas, which were more comfortable.

The layout of hearths in the same house revealed another interesting pattern. The deeper, more fire-reddened hearths were in the western area of the dwelling, while the smaller and more superficially reddened ones were to the east. By the same token, the larger storage pits were also to the west. Hayden believes these patterns reflect not separate activity areas, but socioeconomic variations between wealthier, more powerful people living by the larger hearths and pits, and poorer families located elsewhere. Pine bedding fragments and domestic refuse come from all hearth areas, also a hint that some social factors were at work.

In fact, other excavations on Northwest Coast houses and ethnographic accounts from living groups support Hayden's theory, for they reveal large dwellings where the richer and more powerful families occupied one-half of the house.

Ethnographic accounts speak of the most important fishing sites in the region being owned by members of individual households, perhaps passed down from one generation to the next. Analysis of the salmon bones from Keatley Creek by Ken Berry reveals that poorer families consumed mostly "pink salmon," readily identified by the two-year growth rings in their back- bones. Pink salmon are the easiest to catch, but are the smallest and have the lowest fat content. In contrast, the inhabitants of the larger dwellings ate not only pink salmon, but also chinook and sockeye, both larger forms that can only be caught in quantity from rocks projecting far into the water or from specially constructed platforms. The fact that such salmon bones only occur in larger houses strongly confirms ethnographic accounts which state that such sites were owned by only a few families or kin groups. Salmon provided over 70 percent of the protein in the local diet. Dried fish was traded widely in historic times, and presumably earlier; it was a trade controlled by elite families, who retained others, both commoners and slaves, to do the monotonous fishing and processing work.

Finally, archaeologist Ed Bakewell studied the sources of the toolmak- ing chert found in the large housepits. Each such dwelling had its own distinctive source, or a constellation of sources which it drew on, as if they formed separate economic entities, each exploiting their own stone sources and hunting grounds in the mountains. Furthermore, analysis of the stone tools in the middens along the rims of the house pits revealed remarkably little change over the long duration of the site, as if the same corporate groups had exercised control over local fishing rights and their own territories for more than 1,000 years. Hayden claims this is the longest-lived example of such economic and social stability known any- where.

The Keatley Creek excavations are a remarkable example of the ability of fine-grained excavation to reveal long-term social and economic rela- tionships.

Larger Communities

The behaviors and interactions of people living in much larger communi- ties like cities are also reflected in artifact patternings and in the settlement pattern of the city as a whole. While economic and environmental realities often affect the siting of a smaller community, more complex factors such as religious authority come into play with ancient cities. For example, the city of *Eridu* in southern Iraq was the largest human settlement on earth in 4000 B.C. Eridu lay close to the Euphrates River, with easy access to the wider world of the Persian Gulf. Approximately 5,000 people clustered in the crowded precincts of the city, perhaps, at first, little more than an agglomeration of villages of close kin or specialist artisans living close to one another for mutual protection and economic interest. They lived in the shadow of the great mudbrick *ziggurat* temple-mound of the god Enlil, a veritable artificial mountain that reached toward the wide heavens above

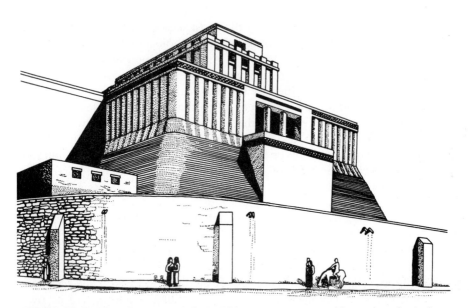

FIGURE 10.9 The *ziggurat* temple at Eridu, as reconstructed by archaeological excavations. The drawing shows successive shrines built at the same location between 5000 and 3000 B.C. *(After Nicholas Postgate, 1992.* Early Mesopotamia. *London: Routledge, figure 23.)*

(Figure 10.9). Eridu's temple was the highest point in the flat countryside for many miles around, a symbol of an intensely sacred place favored by the gods. Compelling political and religious factors helped determine the site of Eridu, the chosen city of Enlil. Like many other ancient cities, this oldest of human cities was a symbolic center of the universe, the holiest place on earth.

We tend to think of ancient cities in terms of their signature public structures—palaces, pyramids, and magnificent temples. But archaeology allows us to look far beyond the lavish facade and huge plazas into a humbler world. The city of Teotihuacán at the edge of the Basin of Mexico was a cluster of villages in 250 B.C. Over the next two centuries, the villages became a city of an estimated 40,000 people. Five hundred years later, between 100,000 to 200,000 nobles, artisans, and common folk dwelt within its precincts, which covered seven square miles (Figure 10.10). Teotihuacán had become rich on obsidian trade, and it was a place of sacred pilgrimage ruled by powerful lords. In its heyday, the city dwarfed medieval London with its few tens of thousands of citizens and was one of the largest human settlements in the world. Then, in about A.D. 750, Teotihuacán abruptly collapsed, for reasons that are still not understood. The Aztecs still revered its sacred pyramids eight centuries later. They believed Teotihuacán was the place where their world began. (See Site box on p. 314.)

FIGURE 10.10   A general view of Teotihuacán, Mexico. *(Courtesy of Lesley Newhart.)*

Archaeologists René Millon, Bruce Drewitt, and George Cowgill undertook the ambitious task of mapping the entire city of Teotihuacán in the 1960s (Chapter 6). They showed how, unlike most ancient cities, Teotihuacán did not grow haphazardly. The mapping project showed how the city's architects worked to a layout devised early in the city's existence and adhered to for centuries. This brilliant conception was a symbolic landscape of artificial mountains (pyramids) and foothills separated by open spaces. The famous Street of the Dead bisects the city on a north-south axis, bordered on its east side by the 200-foot (61-m)-high Pyramid of the Sun, built in five stages over a natural cavern discovered during excavations in 1971. This cave was the most sacred place in the city, a gateway to the Otherworld. The pyramid itself marked the passage of the sun from east to west and the rising of the Pleiades constellation on the day of the equinox. An east-west avenue crosses the Street of the Dead near its southern end, dividing the city into segments coinciding with the four quadrants of the Mesoamerican spiritual world. For its entire existence, Teotihuacán was a model in clay, stone, and stucco of an all-pervasive spiritual world.

Thanks to the Mapping Project data, we know that teeming neighborhoods of single-story, flat-roofed, rectangular apartment compounds complete with courtyards and passageways lay beyond the ceremonial precincts. Narrow alleyways and streets about 12 feet (3.6 m) wide separated each compound from its neighbors. Each housed between 20 and 100 people, perhaps

SITE

The Creation of the Aztec World at Teotihuacán

A remarkable Franciscan friar, Fray Bernardino de Sahagun (c. 1499–1590), arrived in New Spain (Mexico) less than 10 years after the Spanish Conquest of the Aztec empire. He devoted his life to recording Aztec history and culture before it died out with the deaths of his elderly informants. All of them had learned their history in schools where the students learned by oral recitation. Sahagun learned how the Aztecs believed they lived in a finite world. Theirs was the fifth of five successive worlds, which was destined to perish as a result of catastrophic earthquakes. His informants recited the story of the creation of the Aztec world, known as the Fifth Sun, high on the pyramids of Teotihuacán. They told how the gods assembled atop the Pyramid of the Sun when all was darkness after the destruction of the Fourth Sun. They "took counsel among themselves there in Teotihuacán. . . . Who will carry the burden? Who will take it upon himself to be the sun, to bring the dawn?" (Anderson and Dibble 1955, 4).

Two gods presented themselves as volunteers. They fasted for four days and nights, just as Aztec rulers did in later centuries when they visited Teotihuacán. Then they dressed in the correct ceremonial regalia and cast themselves into a great fire as the other gods watched. The god Nanautzin jumped eagerly into the flames. His partner Tecuziztecatl hesitated. So, Nanautzin leapt out of the fire as the Sun and smote him in the face with a rabbit. Tecuziztecatl became the moon, with the imprint of the rabbit causing the dark shadows on its surface. Then, the wind god Ehecatl "arose and exerted himself fiercely and violently as he blew. At once he could move him [the Sun] who thereupon went his way. . . . When the Sun came to enter the place where he set, then once more the Moon moved" (Anderson and Dibble 1955, 5).

Thus was born the world of the Fifth Sun, kept in motion, the Aztecs believed, by the constant offerings of blood from human hearts sacrificed on the altar of the Sun God.

members of the same kin group. Judging from artifact patternings, some sheltered skilled artisans, families of obsidian and shell ornament makers, weavers, and potters.

What was life like inside Teotihuacán's anonymous apartment compounds (barrios)? Mexican archaeologist Linda Manzanilla has investigated one such complex close to the northwest edge of Teotihuacán, searching for traces of different activities within the complex. The stucco floors in the apartments and courtyards had been swept clean, so Manzanilla and her colleagues used chemical analyses of the floor deposits to search for human activities. She developed a mosaic of different chemical readings, such as high phosphate readings where garbage had rotted and dense concentrations of carbonate from lime (used in the preparation of both tortillas and stucco) which indicated cooking or building activity. Manzanilla's chemical plans of the compound are accurate enough to pinpoint the locations of cooking fires and eating places where the inhabitants consumed such animals as deer, rabbits, and turkeys. She was able to identify three nuclear families of about 30 people who lived in three separate apartments within this community inside a much larger community. Each apartment had specific areas for sleeping, eating, religious activities, and funeral rites.

Teotihuacán's barrios have revealed intense interactions between people who knew one another well and between these tight-knit communities and the wider universe of the city itself. Walking along one of the cleared streets, you can imagine passing down the same defile 1,500 years earlier, each side bounded by a bare, stuccoed compound wall. Occasionally, a door opens onto the street, offering a view of a shady courtyard, of pots and textiles drying in the sun. The street would have been a cacophony of smells and sounds—wood smoke, dogs barking, the monotonous scratch of maize grinders, the soft voices of women weaving, the passing scent of incense.

Teotihuacán was a vast urban community made up of hundreds of smaller communities, with a market that sold commodities and exotic luxuries from all over the Mesoamerican highlands and lowlands. The Teotihuacános valued their foreign trade so highly that they allowed foreigners to settle among them in special barrios occupied over many centuries. Immigrants from the Veracruz region of the lowlands lived in a neighborhood on the city's eastern side, identified from the remains of distinctive circular adobe houses with thatched roofs identical to those of the inhabitants' Gulf Coast homeland (Figure 10.11). These people, easily identified by their orange-, brown-, and cream-painted pots, probably traded in exotic tropical luxuries such as brightly colored bird feathers. Another neighborhood on the western side housed Zapotec traders from the Valley of Oaxaca, 250 miles (402 km) south of Teotihuacán. Potsherds from their segregated compounds allow us to identify their presence in the crowded city.

Today, Teotihuacán is an archaeological skeleton. However, thanks to the Mapping Project and later researches, we can easily imagine the city in its heyday 1,500 years ago, the brightly painted ceremonial precincts lapped by thousands of flat apartment roofs and the city surrounded by a green patchwork of irrigation canals and cornfields.

The major objective of the ongoing Teotihuacán project is to understand the diverse internal workings of this remarkable city as a going organization throughout its long history. This understanding can only come from years of surface survey and excavation that rely on the study of artifact patternings, house contents, and entire neighborhoods through the ancient city.

DISTRIBUTION OF COMMUNITIES

"I am my own aborigine." Seamus Caulfield's remark epitomizes the problem that archaeologists face when studying ancient landscapes. Caulfield was lucky enough to discover an intact Stone Age farming landscape with such rich environmental data that he was able to reconstruct the complex history of farming at Céide Fields over many centuries. Few archaeologists are so

FIGURE 10.11 Reconstruction drawing of the Veracruz enclave at Teotihuacán. *(Source: Chuck Carter/NGS Image Collection.)*

lucky, so they rely on cultural ecology and other theoretical models to help them interpret archaeological surveys (for cultural ecology, see Chapter 4).

The Savannah River Valley, Southeastern United States

Cultural ecology is at the heart of all settlement archaeology because the **distribution of communities** (the density and distribution of communities across the landscape, as determined by economic, environmental, social and religious, subsistence, and technological constraints) across ancient landscapes depended on many factors. Some were environmental, such as the availability of game, wild plant foods, or good grazing grass. For instance, a research team headed by archaeologist David Anderson used tree rings from bald cypress trees to record the severity of drought cycles on the coastal plain of the Savannah River in the southeastern United States. Bald cypresses are highly sensitive to temperature and rainfall changes, to the point that the researchers could compile statistics on drought severity, hours of sunshine, and amount of rainfall per growing season from about A.D. 1005 to 1600. They combined these figures with estimates of agricultural reserves available to the local farmers derived from historical records, oral traditions, and archaeological observations of ancient storage pits. During these six centuries, Mississippian farmers lived in the Savannah River valley. Anderson and his colleagues were able to show that the farmers were able to maintain a year's reserve grain supply for three-quarters of these 600 years. When drought occurred, there were large enough food surpluses to allow time for people to switch to other food sources such as fish and wild plant foods.

In the Savannah River valley, as elsewhere, compelling political developments also affected settlement patterns. During the sixteenth century, for instance, the local chiefdoms were caught between two powerful, competing neighbors. The Savannah chiefdoms were too small and lacked the political clout to acquire large food surpluses to feed dense populations. Within a few years, these small chiefdoms collapsed as the people dispersed into smaller communities or moved elsewhere.

The Basin of Mexico Survey

For years, the study of community distributions depended on large-scale archaeological surveys that combined aerial photographs with months of systematic foot survey on the ground. William Sanders and a large research team from Pennsylvania State University surveyed the entire Valley of Mexico, center of the Aztec civilization, in the 1970s. They compiled distribution maps of every known archaeological site and plotted them against comprehensive environmental data, with dramatic results. Sanders showed how the population of the basin ebbed and flowed over many centuries, with the rise and fall of the great city of Teotihuacán in the first millennium A.D.

The most dramatic changes came some centuries later when the growing Aztec capital Tenochtitlán achieved overwhelming dominance. By the end of the fifteenth century A.D., the imperial capital housed at least 200,000 people, living in dense residential areas now buried under the concrete jungle of Mexico City. The concentration of sites nearby was such that Sanders estimated at least 400,000 city and country dwellers occupied a 230-square-mile (370-sq.-km) zone of foothills, plains, and lake-bed areas near the capital. He calculated that about 1 million people lived within the confines of the Basin of Mexico at the time. Tenochtitlán was a magnet to outlying populations. Its very presence skewed the entire settlement pattern of the basin. So many people lived there that the Aztecs now farmed every local environment in the region to ensure there was enough food to go around.

Tenochtitlán stood at the center of an organized landscape, created by ambitious rulers who thought nothing of building nearly 25,000 acres (10,000 hectares) of highly productive swamp gardens in the southern part of the basin alone. Over less than two centuries, the local settlement pattern changed from a patchwork of small states and major centers to a highly centralized agricultural landscape capable of meeting the basic food needs of at least half a million people.

Few settlement patterns show such dramatic changes as those in the Basin of Mexico. Sanders was a pioneer in combining environmental and archaeological data in settlement archaeology, but his project was unsophisticated by the standards of some of today's projects, which rely on high technology to integrate field surveys with a wide variety of spatial data.

Geographic Information Systems at Roman Wroxeter, England

Virconium Cornoviorum, the Roman town at present-day Wroxeter near Shrewsbury in west-central England, was the fourth-largest urban center in Roman Britain. Wroxeter started as a legionary camp in A.D. 60, then became a town 30 years later, flourishing until the fifth or sixth century. Most Roman towns lay under modern cities such as London or York. Fortunately for archaeologists, much of Wroxeter is in open country. For more than a century, generations of excavators investigated the major public buildings and commercial zone of the town. They used aerial photographs and surface collections of potsherds and other artifacts to plot the general outlines of the settlement and to develop a detailed chronology of its buildings.

But these simple approaches could not answer fundamental questions about the history of a once-strategic military gateway into neighboring and unconquered Wales. Many Roman forts and camps lay close to the town. What impact did these army encampments have on the rural population? What were the consequences of the Roman conquest on local Iron Age farmers? Vince Gaffney and an international team of researchers have combined the powerful technology of Geographic Information Systems (GIS) with aerial photographs and ground survey to provide some answers.

The Wroxeter archaeologists could draw on a massive archive of aerial photographs of the surrounding countryside, taken under every kind of weather condition imaginable over more than half a century. They located over 40 farming enclosures and the remains of a once-extensive field system. The researchers "warped" digital images of the aerial photographs onto Britain's national map grid, turning the images into GIS maps so accurate a fieldworker can measure and interpret such features as the Roman street grid at Wroxeter itself with margins of error as small as 3 feet (1 m) (Figure 10.12).

The Wroxeter project is unusual in that the archaeologists working on the ground have the ability to manipulate all available archaeological data on the screen before they go into the field. The fieldworkers rely heavily on volunteers, who are recording the Roman town's topography by taking measurements every 33 feet (10 meters). A magnetometer survey combined with ground-penetrating radar has revealed hitherto unknown buildings on the edge of the town. For generations, experts on Roman Britain had called Wroxeter a carefully planned "garden city" with parks and open spaces. GIS and remote sensing have revealed a less well organized community with uncontrolled expansion at its margins as it drew people from the surrounding countryside.

At Céide Fields, I walked an ancient landscape discovered with the simplest of field surveys. At Wroxeter, I explored a dynamic, ever changing settlement pattern on the World Wide Web. Within a few years, Wroxeter's

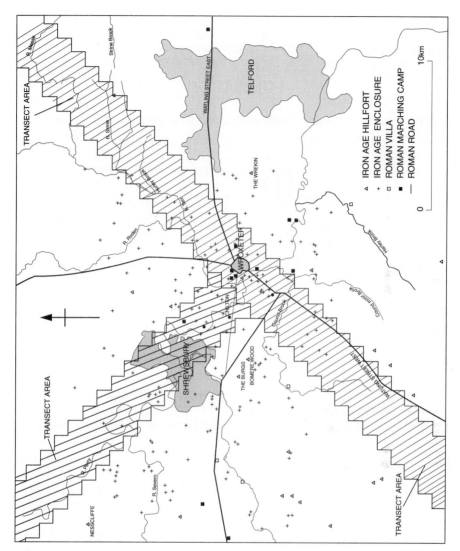

FIGURE 10.12 GIS research in the Wroxeter region. GIS data derived from many sources, including generations of aerial photographs, provided the background data for the survey of Roman Wroxeter's hinterland. The map shows the Roman city and outlying sites, also the three transects walked by archaeologists on the ground. Wroxeter is unique among Roman towns in Britain in not being buried under a modern city, which makes it unusually important for settlement studies. *(Courtesy of Dr. Vincent Gaffney, Birmingham University.)*

archaeologists will be able to answer questions about changing patterns of supply and demand. By assuming the town was the economic hub of the surrounding area, they will be able to show how mass-produced pottery from remote sites flowed through the region along an existing infrastructure of roads, tracks, and rivers accessible through the GIS data base. But a final word of caution: The archaeological data in GIS databases is selected by the researcher and is subject to subjective judgment. GIS has important limitations as a means of even partially reconstructing ancient landscapes.

POPULATION

Settlement patterns across a landscape evolve in response to three broad variables: environmental change, interactions between people, and shifts in population density. Of these three, population is the hardest to study.

Global population growth was not a major factor in human history until after the Ice Age, which ended about 10,000 years ago. Growing population densities were probably a factor in the development of agriculture in southwestern Asia in about 9000 B.C. and in the appearance of the first cities and civilizations about 6,000 years later. In the case of farming, much drier conditions, diminished supplies of wild plant foods, and many more mouths to feed turned many hunter-gatherer groups in the Jordan valley and modern-day Syria into sedentary farmers within a few centuries. Unfortunately, estimating population densities is often little more than guesswork. Despite attempts to develop censuses from house counts and refuse accumulation, most population estimates are little more than guesses. For instance, one estimate places the population of Britain in 11,000 B.C. at about 10,000 people, another estimates the average population of early states in southern Iraq was about 17,000.

Nevertheless, changing population distributions are of great importance, for there is a clear cause-and-effect relationship between population and the potential **carrying capacity** (the number of people per square mile that a specified area of land can support, given a particular subsistence level, for example, hunting and gathering) and productivity of agricultural land. As populations grow, goes one popular argument, so people try to collect or produce more food, perhaps by developing highly efficient ways of fishing or hunting or by turning to agriculture. Like the ancient Egyptians, farmers may have faced the challenge by developing large-scale irrigation systems capable of producing several crops a year and feeding many more people.

Population, then, is a critical variable in settlement archaeology, as William Sanders and his colleagues showed with the rapid growth of the Aztec capital in the Basin of Mexico. While Sanders's population estimates were little more than highly informed guesses, he was able to show a dramatic rise over several centuries. Such general trends are of great interest, for they enable one to monitor large-scale processes such as the rise or fall of an entire civilization. An excellent example of such a study comes from the Maya civilization.

Collapse at Copán, Honduras

The collapse of Classic Maya civilization in the southern lowlands of Mesoamerica during the ninth century A.D. is one of the great controversies of archaeology. For generations, scholars have argued ferociously over this sudden collapse. Was the sudden decline caused by social unrest, warfare, or ecological collapse? Or did the Maya nobility place too many demands on their farmer subjects? The debate continues, marked by a lack of reliable scientific data from the field, except from a remarkable study of changing settlement patterns and population distributions at the city of Copán in Honduras.

Copán was one of the greatest Maya cities, founded in a fertile valley before the fifth century A.D. On December 11, A.D. 435, a Maya lord named Kinich Yax Kuk Mo ("Sun-eyed Green Quetzal Macaw") founded a dynasty that ruled for four centuries. Copán soon became a major kingdom of the Maya world with a spectacular urban core that covered 36 acres (14.6 ha) (Figure 10.13; see also Chapter 7). Between 550 and 700, the Copán state expanded dramatically, with most of the population concentrated in the urban core and immediately around it. By 800, between 20,000 and 25,000 people lived in the general Copán valley area. Then, in 822, the royal dynasty ended and the kingdom collapsed. (See Doing Archaeology box on p. 322.)

The dry evidence from years of settlement survey give us a bare-bones outline of changing settlements, communities, and landscapes in the past. Behind these changing distributions and activities lie the people of the past, the main players on the ancient stage. In Chapter 11, we learn how archaeologists study the all-important interactions between individuals, small groups, communities, and societies that shaped the human past.

FIGURE 10.13   The central precincts at Copán, as reconstructed by artist Tatiana Proskouriakoff. *(Courtesy of the Peabody Museum, Harvard University.)*

DOING ARCHAEOLOGY

Studying the Maya Collapse at Copán, Honduras

How and why did Copán collapse? Archaeologists David Webster and William Sanders and many colleagues working on a long-term investigation of the city decided to investigate the collapse by studying changing settlement patterns and shifting population densities around the abandoned city. They developed a large-scale settlement survey modeled after the famous Basin of Mexico survey of some years earlier to examine more than 52 square miles (135 sq. km) around the urban core. Using aerial photographs and systematic field surveys, the research team recorded more than 1,425 archaeological sites containing more than 4,500 structures. Team members mapped and surface-collected each location. Two hundred fifty-two sites were test-pitted to obtain artifact and dating samples so they could be placed within the general chronological framework for the valley.

As the data flowed into the laboratory, the researchers developed a classification of site types using size and other criteria, classifying them in a hierarchy from simple to complex as a way of developing a portrait of shifting landscape use over many centuries. At the same time, they obtained 2,300 dates, using volcanic glass fragments that could be dated using the obsidian hydration method (see Chapter 3). The survey yielded a bird's-eye view of dramatic population changes as human settlement expanded and contracted over the valley landscape.

The earlier sites found in the survey documented rapid population growth, especially in the city itself and nearby. There was only a small, scattered rural population. Between 700 and 850, the Copán valley reached its greatest sociopolitical complexity, with a rapid population increase to between 20,000 and 25,000

people. These figures, calculated from site size, suggest the local population was doubling every 80 to 100 years, with about 80 percent of the people living within the urban core and immediate periphery. Rural settlement expanded outward along the valley floor, but was still relatively scattered. Now people were farming foothill areas, as the population density of the urban core reached over 8,000 people per 0.3 sq. mile (1 sq. km), with the periphery housing about 500 people per 0.3 sq. mile (1 sq. km). Some 82 percent of the population lived in relatively humble dwellings, an indication of the pyramid-like nature of Copán society.

After A.D. 850, the survey showed dramatic shifts. The urban core and periphery zones lost about half their population, while the rural population increased by almost 20 percent. Small regional settlements replaced the scattered villages of earlier times, a response to cumulative deforestation, overexploitation of even marginal agricultural land, and uncontrolled soil erosion near the capital. By 1150, the Copán valley population had fallen to between 2,000 and 5,000 people.

The Copán research does not explain why the city collapsed, but it chronicles the dramatic impact of rapidly growing populations on ecologically fragile landscapes. The evidence hints that environmental degradation was a major factor in the Maya collapse. Maya writings tell us that Maya lords considered themselves the intermediaries between the living and supernatural worlds. However, when the inexorable forces of environmental decline took hold, their authority evaporated and a centuries-old spiritual relationship between farmers and an elaborate cosmic world vanished into near oblivion.

SUMMARY

Settlement archaeology studies the changing distributions of human settlements over the changing prehistoric landscape. These settlement patterns result from relationships between people and from a complex set of environmental, economic, and population-related variables. Archaeologists commonly distinguish between the study of settlements, households, communities, and the distribution of communities across the landscape as convenient ways of thinking about settlement archaeology. Investigating households involves horizontal excavation and careful mapping to recover household clusters and activity sets, assemblages of artifacts that reflect different human activities. The same approaches allow us to investigate small settlements such as camps and villages and enormous cities such as Mexico's Teotihuacán. Large-scale settlement surveys such as those conducted in the Basin of Mexico provide valuable information about changing settlement patterns and relationships between communities. In recent years, archaeologists have made increasing use of Geographic Information Systems (GIS) to study interactions between people, settlements, and the environment. Changing population densities and distributions were the subject of an important settlement survey around the Maya city of Copán, which chronicled drastic changes in population as the state collapsed in the ninth century A.D.

KEY TERMS

Activity areas
Activity sets
Carrying capacity
Communities

Distribution of communities
Households
Settlement archaeology
Settlement patterns

GUIDE TO FURTHER READING

Butzer, Karl W. 1982. *Archaeology as Human Ecology.* Cambridge: Cambridge University Press.
    An authoritative account of basic environmental and spatial concepts in archaeology.
Flannery, Kent V., ed. 1976. *The Early Mesoamerican Village.* Orlando, FL: Academic Press.
    Flannery's University of Michigan research team carried out exemplary settlement archaeology in the Valley of Oaxaca. The dialogues about the nature of archaeology in its pages are well worth the price of admission.
Millon, René. 1973. *The Teotihuacán Map: Urbanization of Teotihuacán, Mexico.* Austin: University of Texas Press.
    The preliminary monograph on the mapping of this great city.

Sanders, William T., Jeffrey R. Parsons, and Robert S. Santley. 1979. *The Basin of Mexico: Ecological Processes in the Evolution of a Civilization.* 2 vols. Orlando, FL: Academic Press.

The technical monograph on the Basin of Mexico survey, which is a classic example of this kind of archaeology. Not for beginners!

Sheets, Payson. 1992. *The Cerén Site.* New York: Harcourt, Brace, Jovanovich.

A straightforward account of the Cerén excavations that describes many details of Maya household life.

Soren, David, and Jamie James. 1988. *Kourion: The Search for a Lost Roman City.* Garden City, NY: Anchor/Doubleday.

Soren tells the dramatic story of the Kourion excavations and of the tragic earthquake which flattened the settlement.

Visit the Wroxeter Project! The Wroxeter surveys and excavations feature prominently on the World Wide Web. You should begin your visit at http://www.english-heritage.org.uk/wroxet.html.

Here you will find links to other Wroxeter pages. The Hinterland project is at http://www.birmingham.ac.uk/BUFAU/ Projects/WH/ Docs/bm95/htm.

PART V

⟲

INTERACTIONS

Imagine a dinner table of a thousand guests, in which each man is sitting between his own father and his own son. (We might just as well imagine a ladies' banquet ...) At one end of the table there might be a French Nobel laureate in a white tie and tails and with the Legion of Honor on his breast, and at the other end a Cro-Magnon man dressed in animal skins and with a necklace of cave-bear teeth. Yet each one would be able to converse with his neighbors to his left and right, who would either be his father or his son. So the distance from then to now is not really very great.

ATTRIBUTED TO AXEL KLINCKOWSTRÖM AND QUOTED BY BJORN KÜRTEN, *HOW TO DEEP-FREEZE A MAMMOTH*, 1986, 61.

People of the Past

Harappan priest-king, Mohenjo-daro, Pakistan. c. 1900 B.C. (Source: Embassy of Pakistan.)

Egyptian pharaoh, Maya lord, Pueblo farmer, or Ice Age forager—all are equal in the face of death and modern archaeological and medical science. Human skeletons, frozen corpses, and mummies are the medical records of the past, one of the few ways we can study actual individuals from ancient societies. Some famous individuals from the past are known to us by name. The Egyptian king Rameses II's mummy reveals his height (5 feet 8 inches, or 1.4 m) and that he suffered from arthritis, dental abscesses, and poor circulation (Figure 11.1). Maya Lord Pacal lay in a magnificent stone sarcophagus adorned with his genealogy under the Temple of the Inscriptions at Palenque, Mexico. The glyphs on the sarcophagus lid revealed the dates of his reign (A.D. 615 to 683). Most individuals from the past, though, survive as nameless corpses or skeletons, members of long-forgotten communities far from royal courts and magnificent temples. For all their anonymity, their bodies yield priceless information about their lives.

Chapter 11 turns from settlements and landscapes to the actual people of the past and their interactions—as men and women, as small groups within diverse societies, as communities trading with one another.

AN INDIVIDUAL: ÖTZI THE ICE MAN

Only rarely do archaeologists have the chance to study a well-preserved individual from the remote past. When they do, the full array of modern medical sciences comes into play.

In September 1991, German mountaineers Helmut and Erika Simon made their way around a narrow gully at 10,530 feet (3,210 m) near Hauslabjoch in the Italian Alps. Erika suddenly spotted a brown object projecting from the ice and glacial meltwater in the bottom of the gully. At first she thought it was merely a doll, but soon identified the skull, back, and shoulders of a

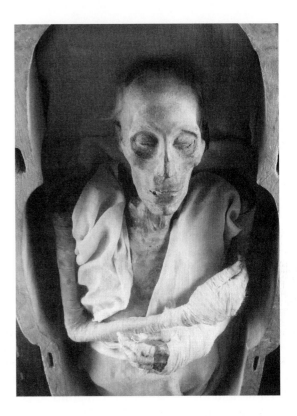

FIGURE 11.1 The mummy of Egyptian pharaoh Rameses II (1279–1212 B.C.). *(Source: O. Louis Mazzatenta/NGS Image Collection.)*

man with his face lying in water. She had stumbled across a casualty of a 5,000-year-old mountain accident.

The first police on the scene also assumed the man was a climbing victim. A unique archaeological find became corpse number 91/619 on the local coroner's dissection table. Within days, the authorities realized the body was very old and called in archaeologist Konrad Spindler of the University of Innsbruck, Austria. Local archaeologists organized a dig at the site, which was already under 2 feet (0.6 m) of snow. They used a steam blower and a hair dryer to recover parts of a grass cloak, leaves, tufts of grass, and wood fragments. By the end of the excavation, they had established that the man, now nicknamed "Ötzi the Ice man," had deposited his ax, bow, and backpack on a sheltered ledge. He had lain down on his left side, his head on a boulder, perhaps taking shelter from rapidly deteriorating weather in the small gully. Judging from his relaxed limbs, the exhausted man had gone to sleep and frozen to death a few hours later. For 5,000 years, Ötzi's body lay in the gully, which protected his corpse as a glacier flowed overhead.

The Innsbruck University research team called on the latest archaeological and medical science to conserve and study the 47-year-old man. Within a few weeks, five AMS radiocarbon tests dated Ötzi's body to between 3350 and 3150 B.C. Biological anthropologists estimated his height as about 5 feet 2 inches (1.6 m) and took DNA samples, which showed his genetic makeup was similar to late Europeans. (See Doing Archaeology box on p. 330.) Ötzi's stomach was empty, so he was probably weak and hungry at the time of his death. He also suffered from parasites. Smoke inhaled while living in small dwellings with open hearths had blackened his lungs as much as those of a modern-day smoker. Ötzi had endured prolonged malnutrition in his ninth, fifteenth, and sixteenth years. His hands and fingernails were scarred from constant manual labor. He had groups of tattoos—mostly parallel vertical lines—on his lower back, left calf, and right ankle.

On his last day alive, Ötzi wore a leather belt that held up a loin cloth. Suspenders led from the belt to a pair of fur leggings. He wore an outer coat of alternating stripes of black and brown animal skin, also an outer cape of twisted grass, just like those worn in the Alps a century ago. Ötzi's bearskin cap fastened below his chin with a snap. On his feet he wore bearskin and deerskin shoes filled with grass held in place by a string "sock" (Figure 11.2).

Ötzi was a self-sufficient man on the move. He carried a leather back-pack on a wooden frame, a flint dagger, a copper-bladed ax with wooden handle, and a yew longbow and skin quiver filled with 14 arrows. His equipment included dry fungus and iron pyrite, for fire lighting, and spare arrowheads.

Today, Ötzi lives in a special freezer, which replicates glacial conditions. Scientists are still puzzling over the reason why he was so high in the mountains. A few wheat seeds lodged in his fur garments tell us he had recently been in a farming village. Some wild seeds come from a valley south of the Alps, as if he climbed from the Italian side. Was he a shepherd caught out at high altitude? Had he fled to the mountains to escape a family feud, or was he simply hunting wild goats? Nearly 150 scientists have collaborated on the Ötzi project, but the circumstances of his death remain a complete mystery.

Ötzi the Ice man is the earliest European to survive as an identifiable individual, one of the few people of the past to come down to us so well preserved that we know almost more about him than he knew himself—his injuries, his diseases, his parasites. This remarkable discovery comes as somewhat of a jolt, because we come face to face with a once-living person, who laughed and cried, worked, played, loved, hated, and interacted with others.

SOCIAL RANKING

Social inequality has been a feature of human life since the first appearance of farming some 10,000 years ago, and it was institutionalized in civilization since before 3000 B.C.

Social ranking (social distinctions between individuals, communities, and other units of society) exists in several forms: as social distinctions between individuals (often reflected in graves), including relationships between individuals, communities, and the wider society (discerned from the study of architecture, settlement patterns, and distributions of luxury goods such as

DOING ARCHAEOLOGY

DNA and Archaeology

Ever since the identification of the ABO blood system in the early twentieth century, genetics has had a profound effect on the study of human evolutionary history. Modern molecular biological techniques have made it much easier to detect and analyze new polymorphic genes (genes present in slightly different forms in different people) that might have medical or anthropological interest. All humans carry in their genes the record of their past history. In recent years, studies of mitochondrial DNA (mtDNA) present outside the cell nuclei in small structures called mitochondria have attracted particular attention. mtDNA is inherited through the female line and is passed from mothers to offspring virtually unaltered except for rare changes caused by mutation. Large-scale studies of human mtDNA in present-day populations from all parts of the world have shown that there is relatively little mtDNA variation throughout the globe, suggesting that there was a relatively recent branching-out of human populations. The African mtDNAs were the most variable, having had more time to accumulate genetic changes, consistent with the theory that the African human lineages were the oldest ones. Molecular biologists Rebecca Cann, Mark Stoneking, and Alan Wilson proposed that all modern humanity is descended from a single anatomically modern human, who lived in tropical Africa about 200,000 years ago. This hypothesis has been widely criticized and refined, but it seems increasingly likely that *Homo sapiens sapiens* (ourselves) evolved in Africa, then spread into other parts of the Old World and eventually to the Americas. mtDNA research on Native American populations links them to Siberian ancestors, as one might expect.

The first ancient DNA sequences were reported by Swedish scientist Svaante Pääbo, who, in 1985, extracted and characterized DNA from the skin of a Predynastic Egyptian of about 4000 B.C. Since then, DNA has been extracted from bones, teeth, and plant remains using a new technique called polymerase chain reaction (PCR). Pääbo used this technique on a human brain of 3000 B.C. from a hunter-gatherer site at Windover, Florida, and identified an mtDNA strain not previously observed in North America. In recent years, scientists have succeeded in extracting DNA from a Neanderthal bone over 50,000 years old and have shown that these archaic Europeans were genetically distinct from the modern humans who succeeded them. mtDNA analysis of ancient human skeletons from Easter Island in the Pacific has also shown that the ultimate origins of the Easter Islanders lies in Polynesia, for this remote land mass was colonized from the Society Islands (the Tahiti region) by A.D. 500.

Molecular biology is playing an increasingly important role in the study of ancient human populations and population movements.

gold ornaments, see Chapter 10), and in social diversity (ethnicity), which is social inequality reflected in the relationships between groups within society.

Ancient Egyptian pharaohs ruled over a long-lived, socially stratified civilization along the Nile River—their civilization was broken down into distinct social classes; **social stratification** is a term commonly used in

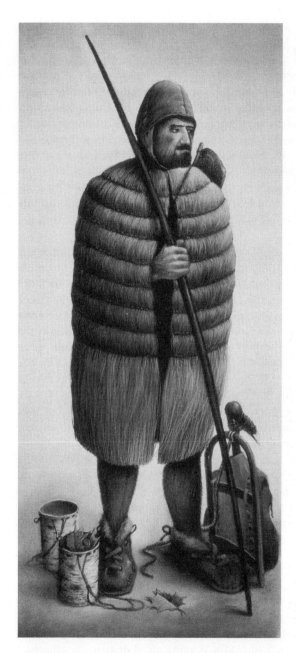

FIGURE 11.2
Reconstruction of the Ice
Man in his grass cloak.
(Courtesy of Stern/Black Star.)

archaeology to refer to the social organization of state-organized societies,
where groups (classes) have unequal access to the means of production.
The pharaohs and their high officials commanded the loyalty of several million commoners, who supported the state with their labor and products.
All early civilizations flourished for the benefit of a tiny minority at the

pinnacle of society. A vast social chasm separated ruler and nobles from commoners at the bottom of the social pyramid. Such highly centralized societies as those of the Egyptians or the Aztecs controlled every aspect of life, with all wealth and secular or religious power concentrated in a few hands. Powerful religious beliefs unified these increasingly complex societies. Usually, their rulers reigned as living gods. For generations, archaeologists have speculated about the origins of the early civilizations, in which social ranking was pronounced and supreme power expressed by enormous public works such as the Pyramids of Giza or the Pyramid of the Sun at Teotihuacán. Elaborate paintings, sculptured reliefs, and public inscriptions reinforced divine messages, the social inequality sanctioned by gods and goddesses. These large-scale manifestations of social ranking, though, reveal less than burials, which were part of the ritual of passage from the living to the afterworld.

The expectation that life would continue uninterrupted after death is still a powerful force in human society and has been for thousands of years. As early as the late Ice Age, more than 15,000 years ago, some human societies blurred the distinction between the living and spiritual worlds, from which the ancestors watched over the interests of their descendants. The Egyptians believed that the souls of well-behaved people enjoyed immortality in the afterlife. Maya lords interceded with the ancestors, those who had gone before. In many ancient societies, the dead set out on their journey to the next world adorned in all their finery and accompanied by their finest possessions. These artifacts might be little more than a necklace of shell beads, or the enormous wealth of a Moche warrior-priest (see Figure 1.9), but they are a barometer of social ranking, of the power and prestige that set one individual, or class of individuals, off from another.

A remarkable example of social ranking came from the *Khok Phanom Di* mound, near Bangkok, Thailand. The 23-foot (7-m) mound lies on a river floodplain; it was occupied between about 2000 and 1400 B.C. Khok Phanom Di was both village and burial ground, with clusters of graves separated by occupation debris and perhaps wooden barricades. Archaeologists Charles Higham and Rachanie Thoserat unearthed a raised platform containing the burial of a woman interred with several elaborately decorated pots, thousands of shell beads, and a clay anvil she once used to fashion pots (Figure 11.3). She wore shell disks on each shoulder and an exotic shell bangle on her left wrist. Alongside her lay the skeleton of a child whose head rested on a shell disk, presumably her daughter.

The Khok Phanom Di burials were a mirror of a community that produced fine pottery for export, with potting skills conferring high status on the best practitioners, such as the woman buried on the special platform. Higham and Thoserat believe prestige and status came from personal achievement in a community dominated by women potters, who held most of the wealth. So many clusters of burials came from the mound that they could trace the rising and declining fortunes of generations of different families by the richness of the artifacts deposited with successive women.

FIGURE 11.3 The woman of Khok Phanom Di, Thailand. *(Courtesy of Professor Charles Higham, University of Otago, New Zealand.)*

This important excavation reveals the great complexities behind the study of social ranking in wealthy societies. In instances of affluent societies, the differences between, say, rulers, merchants, and commoners are easy to discern from grave furniture. But what about humbler, more egalitarian societies where differences in rank and status are more muted? Many variables such as age, sex, personal ability, personality, and even circumstances of death can affect the way in which people were buried. Even the position of the grave may have depended on kin relationships or social status. As a general rule, the greater and more secure a ruler's authority, the more effort and wealth is expended on his or her burial. Thoroughly and carefully studied, an ancient cemetery can provide invaluable information on social ranking.

A thousand years ago, a series of powerful **chiefdoms** ruled over major river valleys in the North American southeast. Their rulers enjoyed exceptional supernatural powers and special relationships with the supernatural world. Only a small number of people governed these *Mississippian* societies, which were like social pyramids known to us from contemporary cemeteries. The Mississippian center at *Moundville,* Alabama, was in its heyday in the thirteenth and fourteenth centuries A.D., about two centuries before European contact. More than 20 mounds topped by earthworks and the

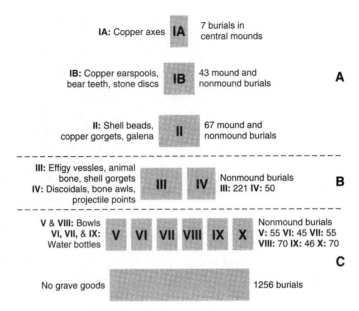

FIGURE 11.4 Moundville, Alabama. Peebles' pyramidlike social hierarchy of Moundville burials based on the analysis of more than 2,000 graves. Artifacts listed against individual skeletons are grave goods found with them.

residences of nobility lay inside a wooden palisade covering 370 acres (150 ha) on the banks of the Black Warrior River. The highest-ranking people with the richest graves were buried in or near the earthen mounds at the hub of the site (Figure 11.4). A second group had fewer grave goods and were not buried in mounds, while the lowest-ranking people lay in almost undecorated graves at the edge of the site.

The moundville study and other such cemetery researches are often more concerned with general patterns of social organization than with the complex interactions between people as individuals and groups as they vie for authority and prestige. Such "horizontal" interactions between men and women, between factions within a nobility, or among religious and ethnic groups have been largely ignored until recent years. (See Discovery box on p. 335.)

GENDER: MEN AND WOMEN

Archaeologists have long studied people and households, but only recently have turned their attention to the complex issues of gender and gender relations, a promising avenue of new research.

Gender is not the same as *sex,* which refers to the biological male or female. Gender is socially and culturally constructed. Gender roles and relations acquire meaning in culturally and historically meaningful ways. This

DISCOVERY

The Sepulcher of the Maya Lord Pacal, Palenque, Mexico

Palenque is a Maya city, famous both for its architecture and for a long dynasty of talented lords, starting with Chan-Bahlum (Snake-Jaguar), who ascended to the throne on March 11, A.D. 431. The dynasty flourished for just under four hundred years, achieving the height of its power under the rule of Pacal (Shield) and his son in the seventh century. Pacal ruled for 63 years and turned Palenque into a major political force in the Maya lowlands. When he died, he was buried in an underground sepulcher beneath a pyramid and the celebrated Temple of the Inscriptions, built over a period of 15 years.

In 1949, Mexican archaeologist Alberto Ruz, convinced that a royal tomb lay beneath the pyramid, lifted a flagstone in the floor of the temple and cleared a rubble-filled stairway leading into the heart of the artificial mountain. Five months of backbreaking work over two seasons cleared a stairway with 45 steps, then a sharp U-turn, which led to another short 21-step stair and a corridor at the same level as the foot of the pyramid. After removing a stone and lime obstruction, Ruz came to a triangular doorway slab, guarded by six young sacrificial victims. He moved the stone enough to slip into an enormous rock-cut crypt with a procession of priests in stucco around the walls. A huge stone slab bearing intricate hieroglyphs filled the floor of the chamber. To lift the five-ton stone, Ruz's workers felled a hardwood tree, lowered four sections of the trunk down the stairway, then levered up the sarcophagus lid with car jacks and the timbers. Inside the sepulcher lay a tall man wearing jade and mother-of-pearl ornaments. He wore a jade mosaic mask with eyes of shell, each iris of obsidian. At the time of the excavation, no one could read Maya glyphs, so the identity of the ruler remained unknown. We now know it was Pacal. His carved sarcophagus lid commemorates his divine ancestry.

means that gender is a vital part of human social relations and a central issue in the study of ancient human societies.

The expression of gender varies and has always varied from society to society and through time. Some archaeologists, such as Margaret Conkey and Joan Gero, write of "engendering archaeology," an attempt to reclaim men and women in nonsexist ways in the past. This goes much further than merely demonstrating that pots were made by women and stone projectile points by men or trying to identify womens' activities in the archaeological record. The archaeology of gender deals with the ideology of gender, with roles and gender relations—the ways in which gender intersects with all aspects of human social life. How are roles and social relationships constructed? What contributions did men and women make to ancient societies? An **engendered archaeology** uses a wide diversity of archaeological methods and approaches to find how out gender "works" in ancient societies, to unravel its cultural meanings.

Grinding Grain at Abu Hureyra, Syria

Farmers' bones reveal telling secrets about male/female roles. The Abu Hureyra farming village in Syria, described in Chapter 9, is the earliest known agricultural settlement in the world. In about 8800 B.C., the inhabitants switched from hunting and foraging to growing cereal crops. A thousand years later, they founded a close-knit community of rectangular, one-story mudbrick houses, separated by narrow alleyways and courtyards set in the midst of their fields. For hours on end, the Abu Hureyra women would labor on their knees, grinding grain for the evening meal, as the monotonous scraping sound of grinding corn echoed through the settlement. Thanks to some exciting detective work by biological anthropologist Theya Molleson, we can be certain that women rather than men ground grain.

Molleson is an expert on human anatomy and pathological conditions in bones caused by stress and disease. She studied the many skeletons found under the Abu Hureyra houses and soon found out the people were remarkably healthy, except for bone deformities caused by arduous and repetitive tasks. Then she noticed some adolescents had enlarged portions on their neck vertebrae, the result of carrying heavy loads. She also identified many knee bones with bone extensions on their articular surfaces, the result of repeated kneeling for long periods of time. many people also had stressed lower-back vertebrae, enlarged toe joints, and gross arthritic conditions of the big toe (Figure 11.5).

Molleson was puzzled by these deformities, until one of her colleagues visited Egypt and noticed that kneeling supplicants on the walls of ancient

FIGURE 11.5 A woman's deformed toe bone from Abu Hureyra, Syria. *(Courtesy of Dr. Theya Molleson.)*

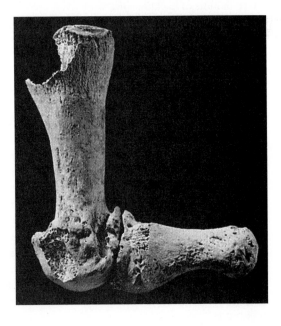

temples always had their toes curled forward. The only activity at Abu Hureyra that could produce the same effect was kneeling in front of the stone grinding querns found set into the house floors. Intrigued, Molleson now reconstructed the grinding process. The grinder put grain on the quern and gripped the grinding stone with both hands. He or she then knelt with the toes bent, pushing the stone forward, arms turning inward as the stone reached the end of the quern. At the end of the stroke, the upper body was almost parallel to the floor. Repeated every day, such back-and-fro movement would cause backbone damage identical to those on the skeletons, would also place bending stress on the knee and hip joints, and would eventually cause arthritic conditions in the toes—all conditions found in the Abu Hureyra bones.

Next, Molleson asked who had done the grinding. She measured the first metatarsal bone of the foot. The larger male bones showed little wear, whereas the shorter womens' metatarsals displayed signs of heavy wear. Theya Molleson is virtually certain that women and girls suffered repetitive-stress injuries because they shouldered the laborious task of preparing food.

This extraordinary and meticulous research is one of the few instances in which we have clear archaeological evidence for the division of labor between men and women in the past.

The Engendered Past

To engender the past means to focus not only on major material achievements such as metallurgy or pot making, or on ancient environments, but also on interpersonal relations and the social dynamics of everyday activity. These are the activities that take up most of peoples' daily lives—hunting, gardening, preparing meals, building houses, and so on. But gender also impacts on trade, craft specialization, state formation, religion, and ritual—to mention only a few major human activities.

Gender research in archaeology is concerned not just with women, but with people as individuals and their contributions to society. Archaeologist Elizabeth Brumfiel has studied Aztec women, who were expert weavers; indeed, weaving was a fundamental skill for an Aztec noblewoman (Figure 11.6). However, she points out that to characterize them merely as weavers ignores the vital links between weaving, child rearing, and cooking (to mention only a few womens' tasks), and the wider society in which the women lived. For instance, the population of the Valley of Mexico rose tenfold during the four centuries before the conquest, a striking testimony to the success of the Aztec household economy. Women wove textiles and the capes that were the badges of social status in Aztec society. Their woven products were vital to the enormous tribute system on which Aztec civilization depended. Cotton mantles even served as a form of currency. Cloth was a primary way of organizing the ebb and flow of goods and services that sustained the state.

FIGURE 11.6 An Aztec woman teaches her daughter how to weave and prepare food. *(Courtesy of the Bodeleian Library, Oxford University.)*

Brumfiel shows that the Aztec household and the roles of women were much more varied than those attributed to them by early Spanish observers. Furthermore, the skills of cooking and weaving were important political tools, ways of maintaining social and political control. Thus, she argues, the idealization of these skills in both Aztec folklore and schooling developed because women were makers of both valuable goods and of people. It was they who assured the continuity of Aztec kin groups.

More simplistic views of Aztec life mask the dynamic and highly adaptive role that women played in this remarkable civilization.

What, then, is an "engendered past?" Scientific reporting tends to obliterate the actors and actresses, whose deeds created the past. An engendered archaeology ventures into new territory, using innovative approaches to present the multiple voices of the past in order to report both data and stories of the past. Such research requires exceptionally complete data and meticulously excavated sites.

ETHNICITY AND INEQUALITY

Archaeology of inequality is the archaeology of how people have exercised control over one another. Feminist archaeology concerns itself with male/female roles and social inequality, which is also becoming a major topic of concern in archaeology.

For the most part, archaeologists have focused their attention on two broad topics. Culture historians have described long-lasting cultural traditions in many parts of the world, while cultural ecologists and advocates of processual archaeology have studied the ever changing relationships between human societies and their natural environments. In recent years, however, an increasing number of scholars have used archaeology's unique perspective to study ethnic diversity and what is sometimes called the archaeology of inequality: the ways in which people have exercised economic and social power over others. This is a reaction against approaches that minimize the importance of social power and assume that ancient societies enjoyed a high degree of cultural uniformity. In fact, many archaeological studies have shown that cultural change can occur very rapidly, at times at a speed that is well within the limits of human memory, as it does in our society. Nor should one minimize the importance of social power in the appearance of early states, such as those of the Maya or Aztecs. Despite a few studies that are now focusing on the importance of social ranking and the political power of kings and nobles, almost no archaeologists have studied the phenomenon of resistance to overwhelming social and political power and the archaeology of ethnic minorities.

Ideologies of Domination

Elites have used many tactics to exercise power over others, everything from gentle persuasion to divine kingship, precedent, economic monopolies, and naked force. Perhaps most important of all are the **ideologies of domination.** The ancient Maya lords built great ceremonial centers with towering pyramids and vast plazas that were symbolic models of the sacred landscape, of the Maya universe. Their pyramids were sacred mountains, the sites of sacred openings that were the threshold to the spiritual world of the ancestors. It was here that the ruler went into a shamanistic trance, communicating with the gods and ancestors in lavish public ceremonies. Everything validated the complex relationship between the living and the dead and between the ruler and the commoner, displayed in lavish, pointed metaphors that confirmed the divine power of the supreme lords (see also Chapter 12).

Archaeologist Mark Leone has even used eighteenth-century landscaping in Annapolis, Maryland, to show how a crisis of confidence in an existing social order resulted in an ambitious example of public display. William Paca, a wealthy landowner, lawyer, and governor of Maryland, was a fervent believer in individual liberty. He signed the Declaration of Independence,

FIGURE 11.7 William Paca's garden in Annapolis, Maryland.

with its strong emphasis on individual liberty, while living in a slave-owning Colonial society. Paca lived a life of contradictions, which he expressed in the powerful, symbolic layout of his garden (Figure 11.7) with its paths, terraces, and plantings, all carefully calculated to bolster their owner's civil and social authority, which he also expressed in the law. Some scholars have criticized Leone's interpretation on the grounds that Paca used well-established traditions of landscape construction in his garden. These were not necessarily a reflection of ideology, but they may have played a role in Paca's long-term social aspirations.

Artifacts, Social Inequality, and Resistance

Political and social power are extremely heterogeneous phenomena that are exercised in many forms. From the archaeologist's point of view, it is fascinating that one can use material objects such as pottery to study how people negotiated their social positions and resisted the submergence of their own culture. Artifacts offer a unique way of examining the history of the many communities that kept no written records, but expressed their diverse feelings and cultures through the specific artifacts and commodities that they purchased and used.

Promising studies of such resistance are coming from the American South, where the earliest Africans to reach North America brought their own notions of religion, ritual, and supernatural power to their new homes. They even maintained small shrines in their living quarters. Historical records rarely refer to such shrines, but archaeologists have found blue beads and other charms at many slave sites in the North American Southeast. At the Garrison and Kingsmill plantations in Maryland and Virginia, engraved pewter spoons bear motifs remarkably similar to those executed by African Americans living in Suriname in South America. Bakongo-style marks like those made in Central Africa have come from bowls found in other Southern sites. Everything points to people who arrived in North America with cultural values and a world-view radically different from those of their masters.

Slave plantations were part of very complex, much wider networks that linked planters to other planters, planters to slaves, and slaves to slaves on other plantations. It is significant that slaves within these harsh, oppressive, and racist environments were able to maintain important elements of their own culture. Despite such conditions, African Americans maintained their own beliefs and culture, which they melded over the generations with new ideas and material innovations from their new environment. They believed that their culture, their way of living—everything from cuisine to belief systems—was the best way. African spiritual beliefs in all their variety were highly flexible and were often responses to outside influences, whether political, religious, or economic. Thus, existing spiritual beliefs adapted readily to the new American environment, with the people adopting new artifacts or modifying existing ones over the generations. For example, archaeologists working at Thomas Jefferson's Monticello estate have recovered crystals, pierced coins, and other ritual artifacts from Mulberry Row, where his slaves resided.

Traditional practitioners were operating in a hostile environment, so they were careful to disguise their activities. At the Levi Jordan cotton and sugar plantation in south Texas, archaeologists Kenneth Brown and Doreen Cooper have excavated a cabin occupied by an African-American healer-magician. The cabin yielded animal bones, iron spikes, and other artifacts that were part of the paraphernalia of a traditional West African healer. But the same simple artifacts had other uses, too, so much so that an outside observer would not suspect that their owner was engaged in traditional medicine. To the African-American workers on the plantation, the same objects had an entirely different symbolic meaning that was not revealed to outsiders. For this reason, none of the healer's tools-in-trade bore any telltale symbolic decoration that might reveal their true purposes.

African archaeologists and historians have pointed out that the sheer diversity of West African cultures makes it foolhardy to make direct comparisons between African-American and African artifacts. But the survival of African beliefs and culture in African-American society is well documented as a general phenomenon and has persisted into recent times. All these finds suggest that African Americans maintained their own distinctive culture in the face of repressive slavery. They were disenfranchised from white people in their own villages and slave quarters, to the point that their masters and mistresses may well have been more like parts of their environment than key players in their social lives. In South Carolina and Georgia, slaves even spoke a distinctive African-American language. Children growing up in this culture used material objects such as earthen bowls that were made by members of this culture and heard stories of magic and religious chants that were important ways of establishing African-American identity, maintaining ideological power, and molding values. While many slaves may not have resisted their inferior, white-bestowed social status on a day-to-day basis, they ignored European-American culture in favor of their own and rejected an ideology that rationalized their enslavement.

Historical archaeologist Leland Ferguson has documented this resistance in South Carolina, where, in 1740, blacks outnumbered whites by almost 2 to 1, and one-half of that majority was African-born. Here, as elsewhere along the south Atlantic coast, African women arrived with a knowledge of pot making that they used to fashion domestic wares in their new homes. Their distinctive unglazed earthenware products occur in slave quarters, on plantations, and in cities (Figure 11.8). Once considered Native American

FIGURE 11.8 Colono Ware. *(Courtesy of the South Carolina Institute of Archaeology and Anthropology, University of South Carolina.)*

pots that had been traded to slaves, these wares were the product of complex demographic and cultural forces that resulted from interactions between blacks and whites, and between both of those groups and Native Americans. Ferguson undertook a study of this "Colono Ware" from the Southeast, focusing on complete vessels recovered from all manner of locations, including slave quarters, free Native American villages, plantations, and missions. He found that what he calls the "container environment" of South Carolina consisted of wood, basketry, and earthenware manufactures broadly similar to those of the slaves' African homeland. Not only that, but the bowls and other vessels mirrored basic eating habits in Africa, for they were used for preparing and serving carbohydrate porridges with a vegetable or meat relish on the side.

Ferguson believes that African-American eating habits were quite similar to those of the peoples of West Africa and radically different from those of the European Americans around them. Colono Ware is remarkably similar over a large area, made by people living in an ethnic environment where reciprocal relationships with one another were of vital importance and where there were strong ties to ancestral African culture. It was, Ferguson says, an unconscious resistance to slavery and the plantation system. The development of Southern culture, he concludes, was a long process of quasipolitical negotiation. It is exciting that one can use archaeology to look at the early stages of this complex process of negotiation from both sides.

Another fascinating chronicle of ethnic resistance comes from an archaeological investigation of the route taken by a small group of Northern Cheyenne when they broke out of Fort Robinson, Nebraska, on January 9, 1879. They fought a running battle with the garrison, across the White River, up some bluffs, and into open country, where it took the military 11 days to capture them. This much is beyond controversy, but the route that the Cheyenne took out of the river valley is disputed. According to military accounts, the escaping party moved up an exposed sandstone ridge to reach the bluffs. This exposed route was illogical, indeed foolhardy, for there was a full moon. Cheyenne oral traditions insist on another route to the bluffs through a well-protected drainage that would have offered excellent cover from pursuing riflemen.

Archaeologists from the University of South Dakota Archaeology Laboratory investigated the escape routes with the collaboration of local Cheyenne representatives. They used random shovel testing and metal detectors to search for spent bullets in three areas—two drainages and the exposed ridge mentioned in military accounts. The survey recovered no bullets from the exposed ridge, but did find them in the drainages, thereby confirming the oral account of the Cheyenne Outbreak. This may seem like a footnote to modern history, but it is important to remember that the Outbreak has become a classic story of the American West from the white perspective immortalized by John Ford's movie "Cheyenne Autumn." This film tells the story from the victors' perspective and is a form of moral tall tale of the Old West. Now oral tradition and archaeology have shattered part of the myth, telling the story from the Native American perspective in circumstances where science has helped fashion a mosaic of the recent past that is the historical truth rather than myth.

The most compelling studies of ethnic minorities' resistance to social domination, at present, come from the United States, from historical sites where written records amplify the archaeological record in important ways. As so often happens, methods developed on historical sites will ultimately be applied to prehistoric situations. What, for example, was the social position of Oaxacan merchants living in Teotihuacán, Mexico, in A.D. 600? Were they treated differently from citizens of the city? Does their material culture reflect carefully orchestrated responses to the dominant culture around them? What was the lifeway of slaves and workers in Egypt? How did their relationships with their noble masters change through, say, the New Kingdom?

Artifacts tell powerful stories about the lowly and the anonymous, the men and women who labored in the shadow of great states and mighty rulers. The lives of ordinary folk are as compelling in the tales they tell as those recorded on papyri, in government archives, or on clay tablets. (See Site box below.)

SITE

War Casualties at Thebes, Egypt

Few tales of ordinary people are as vivid as a remarkable discovery made at Thebes in 1911 by Egyptologist Herbert Winlock in a sepulcher close to the tomb of the Middle Kingdom pharaoh Mentuhotep (2061–2010 B.C.). Sixty soldiers killed in battle were stacked in the tomb dressed in linen shrouds. All the soldiers were young men in the prime of life, each with a thick mop of hair bobbed off square at the nape of the neck. Their dried-out bodies were so well preserved that they began to decay when removed from the tomb. Winlock used biological and archaeological data to reconstruct their last battle: All had perished in an attack on a fort, for their wounds came from arrows shot from above or from the crushing blows of stones thrown down from a fortification. Contemporary pictures show the attackers sheltering themselves under thin shields as they attempted to breach the defenses under a rain of missiles. In this case, the fire was too fierce, so the men had run out of range. Some of them, however, were overtaken by a shower of arrows. At least one was hit in the back with an arrow that came out on the other side of his chest. He pitched forward and the slender reed shaft broke off as he fell and bled to death. The defenders of the fort then sallied forth and mercilessly clubbed at least a dozen of the wounded attackers to death with heavy blows. Then, waiting vultures and ravens descended on the corpses and worried away the flesh with their beaks. A second attack was successful, and the torn bodies were recovered and buried with honor in a special tomb next to their pharaoh. We do not know where the battle took place, but it was somewhere in Egypt, for the arrows that killed the attackers were of Egyptian design. Few discoveries make such a powerful statement about the lives of the anonymous players of the past as this one.

Archaeology, with its rich potential for studying the mundane and the trivial, the minutest details of daily life, is an unrivaled tool for the dispassionate study of social inequality and ethnicity. It also studies broader interactions between people and groups through artifacts passed along exchange and trade routes.

TRADE AND EXCHANGE

Many Americans drive Japanese cars. French teenagers like the taste of hamburgers. Pacific Islanders crave Mexican-made television sets. We live in an international world, where economic ties link nations many thousands of miles apart. Over the past 2,000 years, and especially during the European Age of Discovery after A.D. 1500, human societies throughout the world have become part of a vast web of economic interconnectedness. But the ultimate roots of our modern-day global economic system date back more than 5,000 years, to the dramatic growth of long-distance trade which preceded the appearance of the world's first civilizations in Egypt and Mesopotamia.

Exchange systems were part of human life long before the Sumerians and ancient Egyptians. Black Sea shells appear in late–Ice Age hunting encampments deep in the Ukraine from at least 18,000 years ago. The Paleo-Indians of the Great Plains exchanged fine-grained toolmaking stone over long distances as early as 9000 B.C. Few human societies are completely self-sufficient, for they depend on others for resources outside their own territories. And, as the need for raw materials or for prestigious ornaments increased, so did the tentacles of exchange and trade between neighbors near and far. This trade often had powerful political or symbolic overtones, conducted under the guise of formal gift giving or as part of complex exchange rituals.

People make trade connections and set up the exchange systems that handle trade goods when they need to acquire goods and services that are not available to them within their own site-catchment area. The movement of goods need not be over any great distance, and it can operate internally, within a society, or externally, across cultural boundaries—within interaction spheres. Both exchange and trade always involve two elements: the goods and commodities being exchanged and the people doing the exchanging. Thus any form of trading activity implies both procurement and handling of tools and raw materials and some form of social system that provides the people-to-people relationships within which the trade flourishes. Not only raw materials and finished objects but also ideas and information passed along trade routes.

Conventionally, exchange and trade are recognized in the archaeological record by the discovery of objects exotic to the material culture or economy of the host society. For instance, glass was never manufactured in sub-Saharan Africa, yet imported glass beads are widespread there in archaeological sites of the first millennium A.D. Until recently, such objects were recognized almost entirely on the basis of style and design—the appearance of distinctive pottery forms far from their known points of origin, and so on. Sometimes exotics such as gold, amber, turquoise, or marine shells, commodities whose general area of origin was known, provided evidence of long-distance exchanges. Between 5,000 and 2,000 years ago, Late Archaic and Woodland peoples in the North American Southeast used native copper from outcrops near Lake Superior and conch shells from the Gulf Coast, both commodities of known origin.

In the early days of archaeology, such exotica were deemed sufficient to identify trade, even what were loosely called "influences" or even "invasions." The assumptions made about the nature of human interactions were very limited and never precise. Today, however, studies of prehistoric exchange are far more sophisticated, owing to two major developments. The first is a new focus throughout archaeology on cultural process and on regional studies. The second is the development of a wide range of scientific techniques that are capable of describing the composition of certain types of raw material and even of identifying their sources with great precision.

Types of Exchange and Trade

Exchange can be internal, within a society, or external, with other groups. Internal distribution of artifacts and commodities is commonplace even in the least-complex societies.

Gift Exchange   Much internal exchange is gift giving. Perhaps the most famous example is that of the *kula* ring of Melanesia in the southwestern Pacific. An elaborate network of **gift exchanges** passes shell necklaces in one direction, arm shells in the other. They are passed as ceremonial gifts from one individual to another, in gift partnerships that endure for decades. These gift exchanges enjoy great prestige, yet serve as a framework for the regular exchange of foodstuffs and other more day-to-day commodities. With all gift exchange, much depends on the types of commodities being exchanged. In the case of the *kula* ring, precious seashell ornaments pass between individuals of higher status; foodstuffs are a more common form of transaction involving many individuals and families. And, of course, not only objects but also information can be exchanged, which may lead to technological innovation or social change.

Gift giving is a common medium of exchange and trade in societies that are relatively self-supporting. The exchange of gifts is designed primarily to reinforce a social relationship between both individuals and groups. The gifts serve as gestures that place obligations on both parties. This form of exchange is common in New Guinea and the Pacific and was widespread in Africa during the past 2,000 years, as well as in the ancient Americas. Gift giving and bartering formed a basic trading mechanism for millennia, a simple means of exchanging basic commodities. But this sporadic interaction between individuals and communities reduced peoples' self-sufficiency and eventually made them part of a larger society whose members were no longer so self-sufficient and who depended on one another for basic commodities and also for social purposes.

Reciprocity   **Reciprocity** is the mutual exchange of goods between two individuals or groups; it is at the heart of much gift giving and barter trade. It can happen year after year at the same place, which can be as humble as someone's house. Such central places become the focus of gift giving and trade. When a village becomes involved in both the production of trade goods and their exchange with other communities, it will probably become an even more important center, a place to which people will travel to trade.

Redistribution   **Redistribution,** the distribution of goods or commodities received by an individual through a community or group, of trade goods throughout a culture requires some form of organization to ensure that it is equitable. A redistributive mechanism may be controlled by a chief, a religious leader, or some form of management organization. Such an organization might control production of copper ornaments, or it might simply handle distribution and delivery of trade objects. Considerable social organization is needed for the collection, storage, and redistribution of grain and other commodities. The chief, whose position is perhaps reinforced by religious power, has a serious responsibility to his community that can extend over several villages, as his lines of redistribution stretch out through people of lesser rank to the individual villager. A chief will negotiate exchanges with other chiefs, substituting the regulatory elements of reciprocal trading for a redistributive economy in which less trading in exotic materials is carried out by individual households.

Prehistoric exchange was an important variable that developed in conjunction with sociopolitical organization. In many areas, external trade proceeded from simple reciprocal exchange to the more complex redistribution of goods under a redistributor. In other words, trading is closely tied to growing social and political complexity, although it does not necessarily imply the special production of exotic artifacts specifically for exchange.

Markets   The term market covers both places and particular styles of trading. The administration and organization encourages people to set aside one place for trading and to establish relatively stable prices for staple commodities. This stability does not mean regulated prices, but some regulation is needed in a network of markets in which commodities from an area of abundant supplies are sold to one with strong demand for the same materials. The mechanisms of the exchange relationship, particularly, require some regulation.

Markets are normally associated with more-complex societies. No literate civilization ever developed without strong central places, where trading activities were regulated and monopolies developed over both sources of materials and trade routes themselves. Successful market trading required predictable supplies of basic commodities and adequate policing of trade routes. For example, most early Mesopotamian and Egyptian trade was riverine, where policing was easier. When the great caravan routes opened, the political and military issues—tribute, control of trade routes, and tolls—became paramount. The caravan, predating the great empires, was a form of organized trading that kept to carefully defined routes set up and maintained by state authorities. The travelers moved along these set routes, looking neither left nor right, bent only on delivering and exchanging imports and exports. These caravans were a far cry from the huge economic complex that accompanied Alexander the Great's army across Asia or the Grand Mogul's annual summer progress from the heat in Delhi to the mountains, which moved a half-million people, including the entire Delhi bazaar.

Sourcing

Studying long-distance trade involves far more sophisticated inquiry than merely plotting the distributions of distinctive artifacts hundreds of miles away from their place of manufacture. Fortunately, modern scientific technology allows us to trace the sources of many important trade materials.

By far the most significant of these materials is obsidian, volcanic glass that is ideal for fabricating stone tools, ornaments, and, in Mesoamerica, highly polished mirrors (Figure 11.9). The first studies focused on the Mediterranean and southwestern Asia, where obsidian was a major trade community for many thousands of years. (See Doing Archaeology box on pp. 349–350.)

In Mesoamerica, many scholars have attempted to trace the trade routes over which obsidian traveled from highlands to lowlands. The use of source data enables researchers to conceive of exchange on a regional basis, an approach used with success at Copán combined with obsidian hydration dating to trace changes in obsidian trade networks over many centuries. Nowadays, the ultimate research goal is to identify the exchange mechanisms that distributed the obsidian within each exchange zone. Thus the data requirements have changed. No longer is it sufficient to know the approximate source of a raw material or an artifact. Sources must be pinpointed accurately, and distributions of traded goods or commodities must be quantified precisely. Such data provide the groundwork for studies of trade. However, it remains to translate these distributions and the source data into characterizations of human behavior.

Most obsidian studies have concentrated on the use of the rock and the amount of it traded from settlement to settlement. Future studies will have to monitor exchange by taking analogies from ethnohistorical and historical studies of quarrying and trade, and by developing new ways of inferring behavior from the archaeological record. Chipped stone is useful in this regard, for one can reconstruct the reduction strategies used to produce traded raw material and finished artifacts and thereby gain insights into efficiency of production and other such facets of human behavior. This approach has worked well with Paleo-Indian sites in North America, for such groups exchanged fine toolmaking stone over enormous areas or traveled long distances to obtain supplies. Ancient quar-

ᛃᛃᛃᛃ DOING ARCHAEOLOGY

Obsidian Sourcing

Scientists studied the sources of toolmaking stone long before the advent of spectrographic analysis, relying both on petrology and on distinctive rocks, such as the butter-colored and easily recognized Grand Pressigny flint, widely used in France by Stone Age farmers. Hi-tech analytical methods have revolutionized sourcing since the 1960s, when British archaeologist Colin Renfrew and others used spectrographic analysis to identify no fewer than 12 early farming villages that had obtained obsidian from the Ciftlik area of central Turkey (Figure 11.9). This

FIGURE 11.9 Obsidian mirror from Mesoamerica. *(Courtesy of the Department of Library Services, American Museum of Natural History, New York.)*

(Continued)

DOING ARCHAEOLOGY

Obsidian Sourcing *(Continued)*

pioneer study showed that 80 percent of the chipped stone in villages within 186 miles (300 km) of Ciftlik was obsidian. Outside this "supply zone," the percentages of obsidian dropped away sharply with distance, to 5 percent in a Syrian village and 0.1 percent in the Jordan valley. If these calculations were correct, each village was passing about half its imported obsidian further down the line (Figure 11.10). Renfrew and his colleagues identified no fewer than nine obsidian "interaction zones" between Sardinia and Mesopotamia, each of them linked to well-defined sources of supply, each yielding obsidian with its own distinctive trace elements identifiable spectrographically.

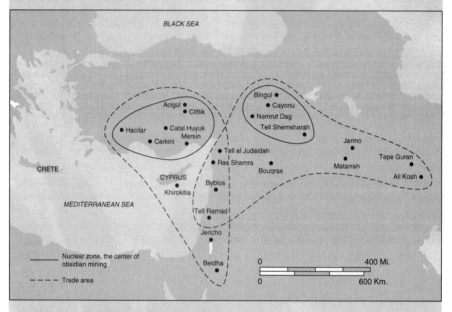

FIGURE 11.10 Obsidian trade in the eastern Mediterranean region. Sourcing studies reveal that early farming communities in Cyprus, Anatolia, and the Levant obtained their obsidian from two sources in central Anatolia. Meanwhile, villages such as Jarmo in the Zagros Mountains and Ali Kosh far to the southeast relied on sources in Armenia. Settlements such as Çatalhöyük in Anatolia were so close to obsidian sources that they probably collected their own supplies. More than 80 percent of their stone artifacts are made of the material, while obsidian tools are much rarer down the line, the further one travels from the source.

ries, such as those in Greece, Mesoamerica, and Australia, are potentially valuable sources of information on the exchange of exotic materials.

Archaeologist Robin Torrence studied Aegean obsidian trade, finding that the exchange was noncommercial and noncompetitive: The prehistoric stoneworkers visited quarries and prepared material for exchange with minimal concern for economical use of the raw material. On the island of melos, for example, the visitors simply quarried what they wanted and left. There is no evidence of specialized production. During early farming times, obsidian mining may have been a seasonal occupation, but during the Bronze Age it became a specialized occupation requiring special voyages to melos and other quarries. The reason for the shift is unknown. Perhaps it was connected to a rising demand that outstripped the yield from seasonal visits.

Sourcing studies are sometimes called **characterization studies,** as they involve petrology and other approaches for identifying the characteristic properties of the distinctive raw materials used to fashion, say, stone axes. One should stress the word *distinctive,* for the essence of these methods is that one be able to identify the specific source with great accuracy. For example, obsidian from Lipari Island off Sicily, traded over a wide area of the central Mediterranean, has highly specific characteristics which show it came from Lipari and nowhere else.

Isotopic chemistry has been highly effective in studying metal sources. For example, the isotopic composition of lead depends on the geological age of the ore source. Lead mines were few and far between in antiquity. Provided their location is known, it is possible to study lead sources in bronze artifacts, and also those of silver, for the latter is extracted from lead ores. This technique has been used to distinguish between classical Greek silver coins made from mainland ore and those manufactured with metal from the Aegean island of Siphnos and other locations.

A Unique Portrait of Ancient Trade: The Uluburun Ship

Merely studying the distribution of artifacts gives one a grossly inadequate picture of ancient trade, for such factors as the logistics of transportation, as well as local political and economic conditions affected every aspect of trade and exchange.

Few archaeological finds rival the extraordinary cargo found aboard a Bronze Age ship wrecked off the rugged Uluburun cliffs in southern Turkey. Shipwrecks like this offer unique opportunities to study ancient trade, for each ship on the seabed is a sealed capsule, its holds a mirror of trading conditions at the time. George Bass and Cemal Pulak's excavation of the Uluburun ship has yielded a mine of information on the commercial world of the eastern Mediterranean in the fourteenth century B.C. The heavily laden ship was sailing westward from the eastern Mediterranean when it was shattered on the jagged rocks of Uluburun in about 1316 B.C. (a date from tree rings in firewood found in the wreck). It sank in 151 feet (48 m) of water. Bass and Pulak have plotted the exact position of every timber and every item of the ship's equipment and cargo as they lift artifacts from the seabed. They have recovered a unique portrait of eastern Mediterranean trade from more than 3,000 years ago.

The Uluburun ship was laden with six tons of copper ingots, probably mined in Cyprus, and with tin ingots and artifacts (see Figure 7.21). The tin may have come from southern Turkey. Canaanite jars from Palestine or Syria held olives, glass beads, and resin from the terebinth tree, used in religious rituals. The ship's hold contained Baltic amber that probably reached the Mediterranean overland, ebony-like wood from Africa, elephant and hippopotamus ivory, and ostrich eggshells from North Africa or Syria. Egyptian, Levantine, and Mycenaean daggers, swords, spearheads, and woodworking tools were aboard, and also sets of weights, some fashioned in animal forms. There were costly glass ingots, Mesopotamian cylinder seals, a Mycenaean seal stone, even a gold cup and parts of a tortoiseshell lute. The ship carried Egyptian scarabs, dozens of fishing weights, fishhooks, and 23 stone anchors, vital when anchoring in windy coves. Even the thorny burnet shrub used to pack the cargo was preserved. One unique find: a diptych, a wooden cover for a wax tablet used to record commercial transactions (Figure 11.11).

By using find distributions from land sites and a variety of sourcing techniques, Bass and Pulak have reconstructed the anonymous skipper's last journey. They believe he started his voyage on the Levant coast, sailed north up the coast, crossed to Cyprus, then coasted along the southern Turkish shore. The ship called at ports large and small on its way west, along a well-traveled route that took advantage of changing seasonal winds, to Crete, some Aegean Islands, and perhaps to the Greek mainland. The skipper had traversed this route many times, but on this occasion his luck ran out and he lost his ship, the cargo, and perhaps his life on Uluburun's pitiless rocks. From the archaeological perspective, the Uluburun shipwreck is a godsend,

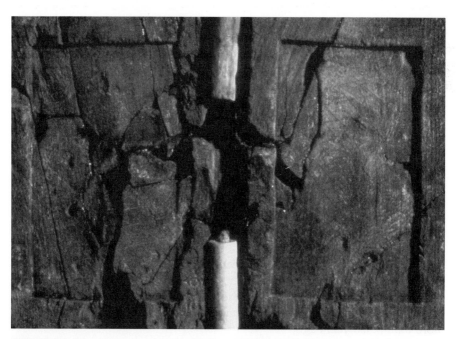

FIGURE 11.11 Diptych from the Uluburun shipwreck. *(Courtesy of the Institute for Nautical Archaeology, Texas A&M University, College Station, Texas.)*

for it allows researchers to fill in many details of an elaborate trade network that linked the eastern Mediterranean with Egypt, the Aegean, and Greece more than 3,300 years ago. Bass and Pulak suspect that the Uluburun ship may have been carrying an unusually valuable cargo, but the owners remain a mystery.

The study of prehistoric trade is a vital source of information on social organization and the ways in which societies became more complex. Trade itself developed a great complexity, in both goods traded and in the interactions of people involved. Colin Renfrew identified no fewer than 10 types of interaction between people that can result from exchange and trading, ranging from simple contact between individuals to trading by professional traders, such as the pochteca of the Aztec, who sometimes acted as spies.

SUMMARY

A new generation of archaeological research is turning away from impersonal cultural processes toward the study of people and small groups. Such research marries modern archaeological data recovery methods with new interpretative approaches that consider the archaeologist as an "active mediator" of the archaeological record of the past. Discoveries of actual individuals from the past allow us to make detailed studies of the health, diet, and activities of individual people, like the Ice Man discovery in the European Alps.

Social ranking is difficult to study from archaeological evidence. It can be studied in the archaeological record by using burials and associated grave furniture, as at Ur in Mesopotamia, and by using structures or artifact patterns.

The archaeology of gender is assuming increasing importance as a means of identifying changing male-female roles in the past and of studying individuals in prehistory. These researches involve detailed studies of grave furniture, studies of female pathology, which reflects such activities as constant grain grinding, and extrapolations of material data into hypothetical scenarios of changing gender relations.

Ethnicity and social inequality have been studied by archaeologists working with African-American and other sites in North America. Such researches involve identifying distinctive artifacts that reflect African religious beliefs and material signs of silent resistance to the dominant culture.

Trade and exchange were important means of human interaction from the earliest times. Much early trade probably took the form of gift exchanges and the bartering of food and other commodities between neighboring settlements. Trade is normally recognized in the archaeological record by the discovery of exotic objects far from their places of origin. Prehistoric trade networks are studied by examining the distributions of such objects and the sources of raw materials used to make artifacts. One example is the Uluburun shipwreck off southern Turkey, which revealed the complexity of eastern Mediterranean trading in the fourteenth century B.C.

KEY TERMS

Archaeology of inequality
Characterization studies
Chiefdoms
Engendered archaeology
Exchange systems
Gift exchanges

Ideologies of domination
Market
Reciprocity
Redistribution
Social ranking
Social stratification

GUIDE TO FURTHER READING

Earle, Timothy K., and Jonathan E. Ericson, eds. 1977. *Exchange Systems in Prehistory.* Orlando, FL: Academic Press.

   Articles dealing with method and theory in the study of prehistoric trade. For the more-advanced reader.

Ferguson, Leland. 1992. *Uncommon Ground.* Washington, DC: Smithsonian Institution Press.

   An exemplary study of African-American culture in the archaeological record.

Gero, J. M., and M. W. Conkey. 1991. *Engendering Archaeology.* Oxford: Blackwell.

   An influential series of essays on gender in archaeology.

Nelson, Sarah M. 1997. *Gender in Archaeology.* Walnut Creek, CA: AltaMira Press.

   A critical analysis of gender research for the beginner and advanced readers alike. Strongly recommended.

Orser, Charles E., and Brian M. Fagan. 1995. *Historical Archaeology.* New York: HarperCollins.

   A basic text on historical archaeology with numerous examples of studies of social conditions and social inequality with archaeological data.

Sabloff, Jeremy A., and C. C. Lamberg-Karlovsky, eds. 1975. *Early Civilization and Trade.* Albuquerque: University of New Mexico Press.

   Conference papers that cover a wide range of problems in the study of prehistoric trade. Strong on theory and actual case studies.

CHAPTER 12

The Archaeology of the Intangible

A painting of the Aztec sun god Tonatiuh. He wears an elaborate feathered headdress while dancing and waving a snake scepter. (Source: Neg./Transparency no. 332105, courtesy the Library, American Museum of Natural History.)

Whenever I visit the great city of Teotihuacán, I am haunted by the past. I look down from the summit of the Pyramid of Sun at the tiny human figures dwarfed by the massive artificial mountain and wonder at the scale of a city built by thousands of people working in the service of divine lords and powerful gods. I stand in the plaza at the foot of the pyramid and sense the overwhelming weight of power and supernatural might that the builders wished to convey. Teotihuacán is a powerful statement, but so much is lost. The pyramid was once the setting for dazzling spectacles, a stage where masked lords appeared in trance, where brilliantly colored dancers performed, where chants and incense rose into the evening sky. The colors have long faded. No banners fly over temples, the stories told by narrators and priests have vanished on the wind. Teotihuacán is now an empty stage, devoid of the transparent things through which the cosmos once came to life. All that is left are the material remains of the spiritual and the sacred— mirrors of the intangible. (See Figure 12.1 and Discovery box on p. 358.) Chapter 12 describes how archaeologists wrestle with the toughest problem of all: reconstructing the intangible religious beliefs, ideologies, and social relationships of the past.

A FRAMEWORK OF COMMON BELIEF

We are *Homo sapiens sapiens,* capable of subtlety, of passing on knowledge and ideas through the medium of language. We have consciousness, self-awareness, and are capable of foresight. We can express ourselves and show emotions. Mitochondrial DNA researches trace the roots of modern humans back to tropical Africa between 100,000 and 200,000 years ago. Archaeology tells us *Homo sapiens sapiens* settled in western Asia by 90,000 years ago, and in western Europe, replacing earlier Neanderthal populations, by 35,000 years before present. Sometime during this ancient diaspora, we anatomically modern people developed a unique capacity for symbolic and spiritual thought, for defining the boundaries of existence, and the relationship between the individual, the group, and the cosmos. We do not know when

FIGURE 12.1 A Minoan priestess from Crete in ceremonial regalia, clasping two snakes. *(Source: Hirmer Fotoarchiv.)*

these capabilities first developed, but late–Ice Age cave art tells us humans melded the living and spiritual worlds at least 30,000 years ago.

By 10,000 years ago, when the first farming societies appeared in western Asia, human cosmology probably began to share several common elements, which are often reflected in archaeological evidence.

First, the world of living humans formed part of a multilayered cosmos, sometimes comprising primordial waters, with the heavens and an underworld. Gods, goddesses, spirit beings, and ancestors inhabited the supernatural layers of the cosmos. This universe often began as a dark sea of primordial waters, or, as *Genesis* puts it, a world "without form."

Second, a vertical axis, often a symbolic tree, or support for the bowl of heaven, linked the various cosmic layers. Mircea Eliade, one of the greatest religious historians of the twentieth century, stresses the importance of this *axis mundi* (axis of the world), which joined the living and spiritual worlds at a mythic center, a sacred place, either a natural feature such as a cave or mountain or a humanly made structure such as a pyramid.

Such sacred places, and the mythic landscapes associated with them, played vital roles in all societies. Eliade calls them "instruments of orthogenetic transformation," settings for the rituals that ensured the continuity of cultural

DISCOVERY

Hiram Bingham at Machu Picchu, Peru

The "Lost City of the Incas" was one of the great archaeological mysteries of the late nineteenth century, a legend of a last Inca stronghold where their rulers found refuge from rapacious Spanish conquistadors after Francisco Pizarro overthrew their empire in 1534. A young Yale University graduate named Hiram Bingham fell under the spell of the mystery and penetrated to the remote Vilcabamba site high in the Andes and realized this was not the settlement. He persuaded his wealthy Yale classmates to finance a second expedition to the Andes.

Tough and intensely curious, the young Bingham was a competent mountaineer and had a sound historical background. He left Cuzco in 1911 with a well-equipped mule train and traveled along the Urubamba River, admiring the extraordinary palimpsest of snowy peaks, mountain streams, mist, and tropical vegetation. A chance encounter with a local farmer named Melchor Arteaga brought a report of some ruins on a hillside across the river. On July 24, 1911, Bingham and the farmer, accompanied by a Peruvian sergeant, crossed the Urubamba by a log bridge. There was lit-

tle margin for error. Bingham got down on his hands and knees and crawled across six inches at a time. Then he climbed 2,000 feet (600 meters) up a narrow path through the forest on the other side of the river. After pausing for lunch in an Indian homestead high above the valley, Bingham set out reluctantly to climb further. Just round a spur, he sighted a flight of a hundred recently cleared stone terraces climbing about 1,000 feet (300 meters) up the hillside. Above the terraces, which the Indians had cleared, he plunged into thick forest and found himself wandering among building after building, including a three-sided temple with masonry as fine as that at Cuzco or Ollantaytambo. He found himself confronted with the walls of ruined houses built of the highest quality of Inca stonework. He plunged through the undergrowth and entered a semicircular building whose outer wall, gently sloping and slightly curved, bore a striking resemblance to the famous Temple of the Sun in Cuzco. Bingham had stumbled on the most famous of all Inca ruins, Machu Picchu.

traditions, a place where the word of the gods rang out in familiar chants passed from one generation to the next. Sacred mountains such as the Hindu Mount Meru, the Greeks' Olympus, or the Lakota Indians' Black Hills often served as the cosmic axis. The Egyptian pharaohs erected pyramids as sacred mountains linking the domain of the sun to the realm of earth. Maya lords built great ceremonial centers as symbolic representations of their world of sacred mountains, caves, trees, and lakes. To demolish a sacred place was to destroy the essence of human existence itself. In 1521, Spanish conquistador Hernan Cortés razed the Aztec capital Tenochtitlán in the Valley of Mexico, knowing its temples and plazas replicated a cherished and all-encompassing supernatural world.

Third, the material and spiritual worlds formed a continuum, with no boundary between them. An "external" landscape on earth was also an "internal" landscape of the mind, or "landscape of memory," where colors, jagged peaks, streams, groves of trees, cardinal directions, and other phenomena had spiritual associations and their places in local mythology. Usually, ancestors, those who had gone before, were the intermediaries between the living and the supernatural worlds. They looked after the welfare of the living and were guardians of the land.

Fourth, individuals with unusual supernatural powers, either shamans or spirit mediums, had the ability to pass effortlessly into altered states of consciousness between the material and spiritual realms, to fly free in the supernatural world through ritual and performance. Such men and women "of power" had direct and personal links to the supernatural world. Shamans moved easily into the spiritual world. There they "dreamt," going through visionary experiences where they saw dots, lines, spirit animals, even gods, and also ancestors. From their dream journeys, they acquired the wisdom to keep their worlds in balance with the sacred, and the power to influence events in the natural world. They were healers, they brought rain, they became sorcerers who could bring disease, cause factional strife, or even war. The shaman was a spiritual actor who functioned as an intermediary to the ancestors and the spiritual world.

Last, human life was governed by the cycles of the seasons, by seasons of planting, growth, and harvest, identified by movements of the heavenly bodies. Notions of fertility, procreation, life, and death lay at the core of such a cyclical human existence. Myth and ritual played an important part in defining this world order. They allowed the material and spiritual worlds to pass one into the other as a single constellation of belief. Through poetry, music, dance, and evocative surroundings, a deep sense of sacred order emerged.

The intangible assumed many forms, but these commonalities, observed by anthropologists and religious historians in many human societies throughout the world, provide a viable framework for scientific investigation of ancient sacred places, the settings for mythic performance. The stone circles at Avebury and Stonehenge in Britain, the courts of the Palace of Knossos on Crete, and Maya pyramids—all tell us much of long-vanished religious beliefs.

A generation ago, many archaeologists threw their hands up in despair when confronted with ancient religion. One anonymous, and cynical, archaeologist described religion as "the last resort of cynical excavators." About a generation ago, a small group of archaeologists challenged their colleagues to move beyond artifacts and food remains. They asked: Why should we interpret the past in terms of purely ecological, technological, and other material factors? Some of the best minds in archaeology are grappling with a scientific methodology for studying human consciousness, especially religion and belief. As we discussed in Chapter 4, they are straddling a fine line between rigorous science and fantasy. This emerging "archaeology of mind" is a marriage of cultural systems theory, settlement archaeology, environmental reconstruction, ethnographic analogy, and the decipherment of written records. We approach this complex subject with specific examples.

ETHNOGRAPHIC ANALOGY AND ROCK ART

The late–Ice Age rock paintings of southwestern France and northern Spain are justly famous for their brilliant depictions of long-extinct game animals, painted between 15,000 and 30,000 years ago. For generations, scholars have grappled with the meaning of the paintings, for they realized long ago that they were far more than merely art for art's sake. In an era when AMS radiocarbon dating allows researchers to date individual paintings, and chemical analyses are deciphering the composition of the ancient paints, we can reasonably hope that we can achieve a greater understanding of the meaning of the art in the future. This greater comprehension will result, in part, from some remarkable research in southern Africa. (See Doing Archaeology box on p. 361.)

The rock paintings painted by Stone Age artists in southern Africa are also justly famous, but very different from those of late–Ice Age Europe. Whereas most European paintings and engravings depict animals, human hands, and numerous signs, the southern African art commemorates not only animals, but scenes of the hunt, women gathering, people in camp, and elaborate ceremonies (see Figure 9.10). Until recently, we had no idea of the meaning of these paintings, until archaeologist David Lewis-Williams came across the long-forgotten research notebooks of a German linguist named Wilhelm Bleek. Bleek made a lifetime's study of African languages. In 1870, he discovered there were 28 San convicts working on the breakwaters of Cape Town harbor, arranged for them to be released into his supervision, and used them as informants. Bleek and his sister-in-law Lucy Lloyd recorded an enormous body of San mythology and folklore over a period of nearly 20 years, which lay neglected in the University of Cape Town Library until Lewis-Williams discovered them in the 1970s.

The Bleek archive contained numerous accounts of rainmaking and other rituals recounted by men who had practiced them themselves. Bleek himself was familiar with a few rock paintings and his informants were able to explain scenes of men charming a mythic rainmaking animal with sweet-smelling grasses. Lewis-Williams realized the paintings were the result of thought patterns that reflected shared beliefs and behavior over large areas where the paintings were to be found. He talked to living !Kung in the Kalahari Desert and showed them pictures of paintings. His informants were able to identify antelope of different sexes and groupings of them painted at different times of year. Lewis-Williams became particularly interested in the eland, a large, fat antelope that is so slow on its feet that a hunter can run it down on foot. A single eland can feed a small band for days, which meant such animals assumed great importance in environments where food supplies could be irregular. Bleek's informants had recited myths that associated the scent of recently killed eland with honey. Lewis-Williams has examined hundreds of eland paintings in the Drakensburg Mountains and elsewhere, including scenes of

DOING ARCHAEOLOGY

Copying South African Rock Paintings

All research into the meaning of rock art starts with accurate copies. Scientists have striven for a high degree of accuracy ever since the early twentieth century, when color photography was unknown. The French priest and archaeologist Abbé Henri Breuil was a gifted artist, whose copies of late-Ice Age paintings at such sites as Altamira in northern Spain are justly famous. He spent weeks on end lying on his back tracing paintings onto translucent rice paper by the light of a flickering acetylene lantern. He taped the paper to the rock or had an assistant, who was roundly cursed if he fidgeted, hold it there. Many times, he made a sketch, then finished it later. Breuil had inadequate lighting and materials, but achieved miracles of improvisation. Today's rock art copyist has an arsenal of superior materials and photographic methods at his or her disposal. Artists set up sheets in front of a wall to avoid direct contact with the painting, then trace, checking their drawings with photographs and measurements. Color photography allows accurate recording without impacting the images, but today's researchers use both color and black-and-white film, diverse light sources, and a wide array of filters to enhance different colors. Infrared film or light makes red ochers transparent, so the observer can see other pigments under red figures. Ultraviolet light sources cause calcite and living organisms on cave walls to fluoresce, which allows assessment of damage caused by wall growths. The sophisticated recording processes of today go hand in hand with AMS radiocarbon dating using tiny flecks of charcoal and other paints.

As in Europe, scholars in southern Africa have experimented with various rock art copying methods. In the 1890s, Abbé Breuil was the first archaeologist to make color reproductions of South African rock art, using butcher's paper. Another early scholar, Walter Battiss, painted in watercolors. The beginnings of a revolution in San culture rock art studies came with the development of affordable color photography in the 1950s. A South African rock art expert, Alex Willcox, photographed thousands of paintings, especially in the Drakensberg Mountains, where some of the finest cave paintings in Africa are to be found. Willcox was somewhat of a romantic. Captivated by the beauty and variety of the paintings, he waxed lyrical about the leisurely, prosperous life of the ancient San. He wrote of expert artists who took great joy in their depictions of animals and people. This, he said, was "art for art's sake." In reality, the paintings were an invaluable source of information about ancient San life and hunting practices. Patricia Vinnecombe also worked in the Drakensberg region and compiled a remarkable statistical record with drawings and color photography. A 1970s scholar, Harold Pager, photographed the paintings in black and white, measured the drawings, and then returned to the site to color in the photographs. Another photographer, Neil Lee, used color film, shooting the art from an overall perspective, then moving closer and closer to take detailed close-up photographs. This approach allowed him to study the painter's technique, the draughtsmanship, the types of brushes used, and the different paint types.

Today's sophisticated theories about San rock art are based on a growing database of carefully recorded paintings. To accumulate such a database is an urgent priority, for many paintings are vanishing rapidly through natural causes, excess tourism, or vandalism.

eland staggering in their death throes as dancers cavort around the animal. White dots depict the sweat dripping from a dancer who is "dying" in trance. Lewis-Williams believes that these dancers were acquiring the potency released by the death of the eland, a process shown by the antelope heads, feet, and hair on the dancers. He realized that painting after painting linked society with the supernatural, the medium responsible for this linking being a shaman, who induced trance by intense concentration, prolonged rhythmic dancing, and hyperventilation. Today, the !Kung still dance next to the carcass of a freshly killed eland as a shaman enters trance.

By combining careful observations from ethnographic data with archaeological observations, Lewis-Williams believes he can "read" some of the rock paintings as meaningful scenes. Dance, miming, and sounds made the dead eland "appear" real before the participants. As the shaman danced, he hallucinated and "saw" the eland standing in the darkness beyond the glow of the fire. As the dance continued, the dancers became as one with the eland spirit and the transfiguration was complete. Afterward, the shaman-artists remembered their trance experiences and painted what they had hallucinated on the walls of rock shelters. The visions of the unconscious were painted, then transferred to the world of the conscious. Lewis-Williams points out that many of the hallucinogenic experiences of Stone Age artists were very similar to those induced in modern times by LSD, peyote, or other hallucinogens.

The Lewis-Williams research shows that paintings were far more than art; they were objects of significance in and of themselves—images with potent ingredients of ocher and eland blood. In many paintings, a figure or an animal enters or leaves a crack in the wall, climbs an uneven rock surface, or emerges from the shelter wall. These paintings may reflect a belief that an underground world takes a shaman to the spiritual world. An informant showed Lewis-Williams how San once danced in the painted rock shelter to which she took him. They raised their hands during the dance and turned to the paintings to identify their potency. Thus, the paintings began to affect the flow of mental images that entered the dancers' minds as they moved, clapped, and sang. The people may have visited the same locations again and again, which would account for the jumble of paintings at some presumably potent locations.

The symbolic meaning of at least some southern African art is well documented, but we certainly cannot use the San experience and ethnography to interpret late–Ice Age paintings in Europe. But there are some general similarities: the placement of animal images in dark caves, the presence of occasional human-animal figures, and a combination of naturalistic and geometric images that carry an undertone of altered consciousness. And one scene in the Grotte de Chauvet in southeastern France depicts a man in a bison skin as part of an animal frieze; he's facing the entrance of the chamber as if awaiting his audience. Native American rock art, such as that of the Chumash of southern California, has strong and well-documented shamanistic overtones.

THE ARCHAEOLOGY OF DEATH

The Maya lord Pacal ruled over the city of Palenque and its surrounding domains from A.D. 615 for no less than 67 years. He turned Palenque into a major political force in the Maya lowlands by political marriages, diplomatic offensives, trade, and conquest. Pacal erected the Temple of the Inscriptions as his burial place, one of the masterpieces of Maya architecture. The builders dug a large burial chamber with an immense sarcophagus below ground, then erected the temple pyramid atop it. A secret internal stairway led to the sanctuary of the temple on the summit of the sacred mountain. Pacal remained undisturbed until 1949, when Mexican archaeologist Alberto Ruz probed under the temple floor, cleared the stairway of rubble, and entered the burial chamber. Pacal lay under a richly carved sarcophagus lid that depicted his sacred genealogy. The great ruler wore a magnificent jade mask, his hair adorned with jade tubes, elaborate ornaments masking his body, and all the grave furniture reflecting his status as a powerful personage with supernatural powers.

The symbolism of death and burial is an important source of information on ancient religious beliefs as well as social ranking, most notably in the regalia and artifacts deposited with the deceased. For Egyptian pharaohs, the actual disposal of the corpse was really a minimal part of the sequence of mortuary practice in that society. Funerary rites are a ritual of passage and are usually reflected not only in the position of the body in the grave but also in the ornaments and grave furniture that accompany it. For instance, the Egyptian pharaoh Khufu expended vast resources on building his pyramid and mortuary temple at Giza in 2550 B.C. (see Figure 2.6). Thousands of laborers moved more than 2.3 million limestone blocks weighing between 1.5 and 2.5 tons to build his pyramid during his 23-year reign. The royal tomb was looted within a few centuries, but the pyramid shape endures, a powerful statement of Egyptian kingship. Egyptian pharaohs were considered to be the living embodiment of the Sun God Ra and joined him in the skies upon their deaths. The pyramids were symbolic sun rays, like the sun bursting through clouds overhead, a type of ladder to heaven for their owners.

Some Native American groups, notably the Hopewell people of eastern North America, buried magnificent ceremonial artifacts with prominent individuals. Such artifacts as soapstone pipes, copper sheet portraits, and masks reflected not only the status of the owner, but that person's clan affiliation and importance as a shaman or priest.

ARTIFACTS: THE IMPORTANCE OF CONTEXT

In 1953, British archaeologist Kathleen Kenyon unearthed a cache of plaster human heads in a pit under a house floor at Jericho in the Jordan valley. Each head was a naturalistic, individual portrait, with nose, mouth, and ears modeled with remarkable delicacy (Figure 12.2).

FIGURE 12.2 Plastered human skull from *Jericho,* Jordan, thought to be a portrait of an ancestor. *(Courtesy of the British School of Archaeology in Jerusalem.)*

Apparently, they were portraits of ancestors. The cowrie-shell eyes of the others glare unblinkingly at the beholder, giving an impression of inner wisdom. We will never know what ritual surrounded these ancestor portraits, but their context, buried under a hut floor, speaks volumes about the close relationship between living households and their ancestors. Plastered human heads are, I suppose, the ultimate artifacts, but they, like other art objects and tools of all kinds, can give us insights into ancient beliefs. Very often, their contexts within sites are as important as the objects themselves. Nowhere is this context more important than in the controversies surrounding the existence of an ancient Mother Goddess in Mediterranean lands.

The cycle of birth, death, and rebirth; fecundity, child bearing, the planting and harvesting of grain lies at the heart of ancient thinking about creation. In many farming societies, the earth is considered female, the source of life and rich harvests. When archaeologists with classical educations found clay female figurines in early farming villages throughout western Asia, the Aegean Islands, and southeast Europe, they remembered their Homer, espousing the notion of an age-old, universal Earth Mother, the primordial Mother Goddess. Worshipped from the earliest days of farming, and perhaps much earlier, the myth flourished when less-rigorous scientific interpretations allowed the archaeologist to speculate. The creator goddess became a universal Great Earth Mother long before archaeological evidence gave such a goddess validity. It made sense that farming and fertility went together. So, it seemed logical to add an Earth Mother, a Mother Goddess, to the equation.

The credibility of the Mother Goddess cult depends on archaeological context, not mere stylistic resemblances. Archaeologists have found hundreds of human figurines in western Asia over the past century: figures with no signs of divinity from Mesopotamia; anthropomorphic male and female depictions from 6,000-year-old Egyptian villages; figures of a female deity at the village of Çatalhöyük in central Turkey; and a range of figurines of both sexes and without sex from all over the rest of Turkey, the Aegean Islands, and Greece. British archaeologist Peter Ucko studied every known early female figurine from the eastern Mediterranean region in 1968 and found that few of them had precise cultural contexts. Many were thrown out of houses with the domestic garbage. Some were childrens' toys, others trade objects, mourning figures in tombs, ancestral spirit figures, or tokens to encourage pregnancy.

Despite Ucko's rigorous, critical analysis over a quarter of a century ago, archaeologists and others have persisted in writing about universal Mother Goddess cults. In a recent study of painted figurine fragments found in early Greek farming villages, Lauren Talalay showed that 18 widely scattered fragments were not goddess figurines, as they had once been labeled, but perhaps trading tokens, split into two halves by parties to an exchange transaction (Figure 12.3).

Despite the figurine controversy, the occurrence of distinctive artifacts and ritual buildings in a site or a society may be significant. In Mexico's

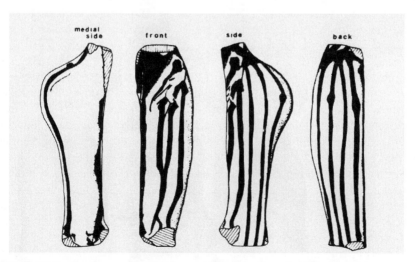

FIGURE 12.3   Fragment of a clay human leg from Franchthi Cave, southern Greece. One-half full size. *(Courtesy of Dr. Lauren Talalay, University of Michigan.)*

Valley of Oaxaca, public buildings appear between 1400 and 1150 B.C., many of them oriented 8 degrees west of north and built on adobe and earth platforms. Rare conch-shell trumpets and turtle-shell drums traded from the coastal lowlands were apparently used in public ceremonies in such buildings. Clay figurines of dancers wearing costumes and masks that make them look like fantastic creatures and animals, as well as pottery masks, are also signs of communal ritual (Figure 12.4). The personal

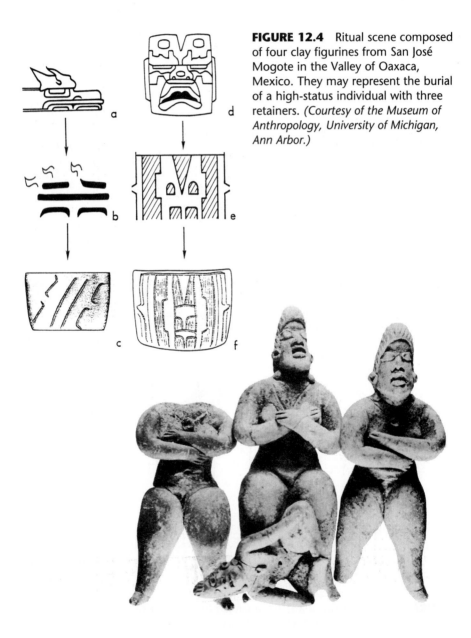

FIGURE 12.4 Ritual scene composed of four clay figurines from San José Mogote in the Valley of Oaxaca, Mexico. They may represent the burial of a high-status individual with three retainers. *(Courtesy of the Museum of Anthropology, University of Michigan, Ann Arbor.)*

ritual of self-mutilation by bloodletting was widespread in early Mesoamerica. The Spanish described how the Aztec nobles would gash themselves with knives or with fish and stingray spines in acts of mutilation that were penances before the gods, imposed by religion. A few stingray spines have come from early Oaxacan villages, probably traded far into the interior for the specific use of community leaders. Flannery suggests that bloodletting fish spines were kept and used at home, and that they were also used in public buildings. The ritual artifacts in the Oaxacan villages enabled Flannery and his colleagues to identify three levels of religious ceremony: personal bloodletting; dances run by kin groups, which cut across household lines; and public rituals in ceremonial buildings, involving a region wider than one village. (See Site box below.)

 SITE

The Shrine at Phylakopi, Greece

The small Mycenaean town of Phylakopi on the island of Melos in the Aegean Sea was home to an estimated 1,400 to 2,100 people between 1390 and 1090 B.C. The settlement was a maze of small stone houses, narrow alleyways, and courtyards, excavated by Colin Renfrew using a 33-foot (10-m) grid that allowed him to record architectural changes and stratigraphy with great precision. This excavation method, combined with meticulous studies of the Mycenaean pottery provided very precise contexts for the finds and enabled Renfrew to identify an important shrine in the town.

He first suspected a shrine when he recovered broken animal and human figurines in his trenches. Slow-moving excavation over the floors of the putative shrine rooms revealed stone platforms and exotic objects like seal stones. But the evidence for religious activity was modest at best, until the excavators uncovered a side chamber and a wall niche in the westernmost shrine room. This contained a pedestalled vase, the fragments of an oxlike figure, other figurines, and a remarkable female figurine, which stood

upright in the room. "The Lady of Phylakopi," as Renfrew named her, had a conical stem painted like a long skirt, a bulbous body with small breasts, a painted brown chin, staring eyes, and eyebrows and hair outlined in brown. Another complete female figurine stood to one side.

The figurines could have come from a store room, so Renfrew studied the design of the chambers. He found that the builders had laid them out in such a way that the symmetrically placed platforms were the focus of attention. The objects displayed on them would have caught attention at once. Furthermore, the "shrines" yielded conch-shell trumpets, identical to those blown by priestesses depicted on seals from Crete. Perforated tortoiseshell fragments were the remains of lyre bodies. The fine pottery found inside the two shrines was of much better quality than that from elsewhere on the site.

The precise contexts of these finds allowed Renfrew to conclude that he had found the town shrine, which is duplicated, at least superficially, at other sites on Crete and the Greek mainland.

ARTIFACTS AND ART STYLES

Ideology is a product of society and politics, a body of doctrine, myth, and symbolism associated with a social movement, an institution, class, or group of individuals, often with reference to some political or cultural plan, along with the strategies for putting the doctrine into operation.

Writing is power, especially in societies where only a tiny proportion of the population is literate. For most people, knowledge of all kinds—hunting expertise, farming know-how, weaving skills, and religious beliefs—is passed from one generation to the next by word of mouth, through chants, rituals, and many other means. Art and architecture are powerful ways of propagating religious beliefs and ideologies, especially in highly centralized societies where the entire fabric of society depends on social conformity.

Strong ideologies drove all preindustrial civilizations. The Egyptian pharaohs were seen as living personifications of the sun god Ra. Maya lords had divine ancestry and unique abilities to intercede with the supernatural world. The supreme Inca ruler epitomized the sun. The ideologies that reinforced these beliefs surrounded everyone and were depicted with familiar motifs on textiles and pottery, on temple walls and carvings. Artifacts and buildings were often expressions of widely held religious beliefs.

Such ideologies come down to us in highly attenuated form. We see them on the snarling faces of Olmec portrait heads, axes, and altars from lowland Mesoamerica, where lords and jaguars had close associations, and where human shamans transformed themselves in trance into fierce beasts (Figure 12.5). We see them on the fine copper portraits of rulers and animals crafted

FIGURE 12.5 Olmec figure with snarling lips. *(Courtesy of the British Museum, London.)*

by Hopewell artisans and buried with prominent individuals over 2,000 years ago. Mississippian art motifs preserved on shell ornaments, pots, and other artifacts reflect religious beliefs that have survived, in modified form, into historic times. Decoding such messages is extremely difficult, especially when there are no ethnographic or historical accounts to guide the researcher.

The Moche state on the North Coast of Peru enjoyed a flamboyant ideology and set of religious beliefs, which are known to us only from the magnificent burials of the lords of Sipán (see Figure 1.9) and from detailed studies of sculpted and painted clay vessels crafted by Moche artisans. Archaeologist Christopher Donnan has attempted to decode the iconography behind the pottery, but has only succeeded in doing so in the most general terms. For example, he has identified a complex ceremony involving human sacrifice that was performed before warrior-priests wearing regalia precisely the same as that worn by the Lords of Sipán. The Sipán regalia reflect an ancient Andean duality between sun and moon, day and night, but to go into more detail without written sources is well nigh impossible. Fortunately, some exceptional studies of native South American religions, ancient and modern, give insights into such institutions as shamanism and ancestor worship in earlier times.

Research like Donnan's requires exceptional rigor, for it is all too easy to rely on intuition and aesthetic sense rather than demanding analysis. Another scholar, Olga Linares, has studied the ideology behind high-status cemeteries in central Panama. Using sixteenth-century Spanish eyewitness accounts of local Panamanian chiefdoms engaged in constant warfare and raiding and the detailed information on local animal species, Linares studied graves and the associated flamboyant polychrome vessels found in them. They were open pots designed to be seen from above, where mourners could see the animal motifs painted upon them. Sometimes, apparently, the pots were so valuable that they were exhumed from one grave and put in another. Ethnohistorical accounts mention that the highly competitive chiefs vied constantly for leadership and prestige, painting and tattooing their bodies with badges of rank and bravery. Each group of warriors wore different symbols that associated them with their leader. They went to their graves with helmets, weapons, other military paraphernalia, and painted pottery. Linares noticed that the art styles rarely depicted plants, but rather many animal species, motifs that commemorated qualities of aggression and bravery. Crocodiles, large felines, sharks, stingrays, scorpions, and even poisonous snakes were the animals that were dangerous, and therefore symbols of bravery. They often appeared on clay vessels, and sometimes parts of the animals' bodies, such as sharks' teeth and stingray spines, were buried with the dead. In contrast, prey species and animals with soft parts like, say, monkeys, were largely ignored by the artists. Thus, the Panamanian chiefdoms used carefully selected animals to communicate the qualities most admired in chiefs and warriors.

Most of what we know about ancient religion comes from literate societies, where documents and inscriptions amplify the archaeological record in dramatic ways. We know a great deal about Mesopotamian and ancient Egyptian religion, but the most dramatic advances of recent years have come with the decipherment of Maya glyphs, already mentioned in Chapter 4. (See Doing Archaeology box on p. 371.) David Friedel and Linda Schele have studied Maya images and hieroglyphs and have used changes in them to trace changes in the meaning of symbols associated with political power. For example, they theorize that the religious symbolism of the late Preclassic era 2,000 years ago was based on the passage of Venus as morning and evening star with the rising and setting of the sun. The people of any Maya community could identify and verify their cosmos simply by observing the sky.

As time went on, Maya cosmology was expanded and elaborated. The names of late Preclassic rulers were not recorded publicly. Perhaps such permanent verification on public monuments was not yet deemed necessary. Classic rulers followed a quite different strategy. They legitimized their rule through genealogies, public ceremonies, and monuments—much Classic Maya art was erected as part of this process of legitimizing rulers, who claimed identity with gods in the Maya cosmos. Friedel and Schele believe that the metaphor of the twin ancestors—Venus and the sun—provided a potent image for lateral blood ties between lineages, communities, and everyone who believed in the same myths. Since twins are of the same womb and blood, so the Maya are all of common ancestry and blood.

Research on Maya glyphs and archaeological sites shows that archaeologists should never think of religion and ritual in isolation but rather as integral to social organization, economic life, and political systems. The ideas and beliefs, the core of all religions, are reflected in many aspects of human life, especially in art and architecture. Every society has its own model of how the world is put together, its own ultimate beliefs. These sacred propositions are interpreted for the faithful through a body of theology and rituals associated with it. The rituals are more or less standardized, religious acts often repeated at regular times of the year—harvests, plantings, and other key times. Others are performed when needed: marriages, funerals, and the like. Some societies, such as those of the ancient Egyptians and the Maya, made regular calendars to time religious events and astronomical cycles. These regular ceremonies performed important functions not only in integrating society but also in such activities as redistributing food, controlling population through infanticide, and dispersing surplus male cattle in the form of ritually accumulated wealth.

Religious experiences are predominantly emotional, often supernatural and awe-inspiring. Each aspect of religion—sacred propositions, ritual, experience—supports the others. A religion will operate through sanctified attitudes, values, and messages, an ethic that adds a sacred blessing, derived from the ultimate sacred propositions of the society, to elicit predictable responses from the people. Such predictability, sparked by directives from some central religious authority, ensures orderly operation of society. In time, as in Mesopotamia, that authority can become secular as well. The institutions and individuals associated with these messages can become sanctified, for they are associated with the sacred propositions that lie at the heart of the society's beliefs. As societies became more complex, so did the need for

♕ DOING ARCHAEOLOGY

The Ancient Maya World through Glyphs

The decipherment of Maya glyphs was a magnificent scientific triumph, which resulted from inspired teamwork between epigraphers living in many countries. The process of decipherment continues to this day, to the point that we now have a rudimentary understanding of the intricate cosmology and religious beliefs of the ancient Maya, even if many details remain controversial. The glyphs give us a new understanding of the complex, multilayered Maya world. Great cities such as Copán, Palenque, and Tikal depicted the geography of the sacred world. Maya glyphs tell us the world was alive and imbued with a sacredness that was concentrated at sacred points such as caves and mountains. The gods created these spots when they created the cosmos. Living people built cities and communities within the matrix of the sacred landscape, which merged with divinely created patterns in caves and at the summits of humanly raised pyramids. At the same time, the world of human beings was connected to the Otherworld along the axis of a World Tree, which ran through the center of existence. This axis moved constantly, but could be materialized through powerful rituals at any point in the natural and humanly made landscape.

Glyphs tell us how Maya lords went into hallucinogenic trances atop pyramid-mountains. They gashed their penises with stingray spines, a bloodletting ritual that brought the World Tree into existence through the middle of the temple atop the pyramid. The temple doorway became a sacred entrance to the Otherworld. Here, the ruler would mediate between the people and the gods and ancestors. Clouds of incense rose high above the temple as the ritual unfolded. This was the Vision Serpent, whose twisting coils symbolized the path of communication that linked the living and supernatural worlds.

Maya artists depicted the cosmos on special tripod plates designed to catch the blood that helped open the door to the Otherworld. A great bearded serpent with gaping jaws emits the pure, life-bearing waters of the earth. Below flow the dark waters of the Underworld, with the World Tree emerging from the head of the Eveningstar god as he rises from primordial black waters.

A new generation of Maya research is combining glyphs with archaeology in efforts to decipher royal genealogies, to identify the builders of temples and pyramids, and to untangle the complex political history of a flamboyant, volatile civilization.

a stable framework to administer the needs of the many increasingly specialized subgroups that made up society as a whole. And architecture and sacred places played a central role in this ideological framework.

SACRED PLACES

Notre Dame de Chartres Cathedral, France, built in a mere quarter-century in about A.D. 1195, is the sixth church built on the same site, a masterpiece where the infinite becomes a miracle in stone and glass. The cathedral is all windows, the great rose window of the western front symbolizing the Virgin Mary herself. Stained glass windows were a major element in Gothic architecture, ethereal settings among soaring beams and graceful arches. At Chartres, they became a form of new language, bringing together ancient principles of Christianity, many of them derived from even older cosmic beliefs. The rose was a powerful symbol, which evoked soul, eternity, wheel, sun, and the cosmos. The rose was sacred to the Egyptian goddess Isis, to Greek Aphrodite, and to Venus, as a symbol of human love transcending passion, which signified the Virgin Mary in Christianity. The major rose windows at Chartres depict the Virgin and Child (north), martyrs who spread the Word and the New Testament (south), and the wounded Christ at the center of the Last Judgment (west). Each uses the same vocabulary of color, form, geometry, and symbol. The gemlike transmutation of the light shining through the windows created transcendental effects that could heal and revivify worshippers crowded in the nave. The pictures in the windows communicated the message of God for the illiterate who came to pray.

Like ancient Egyptian artists, the medieval artisans followed a standard vocabulary of forms as far as the disposition of figures and backgrounds were concerned. They made use of unique geometrical compositions to structure the motifs of the windows, often with close ties to astrological and cosmological images and also zodiacal symbolism. Like the Aztec great temple at Tenochtitlán, Mexico, the Egyptian pyramids, and Maya centers, Chartres' windows were an integral part of a setting which brought heaven to earth and joined the secular and spiritual.

Chartres served the same purpose as much older sacred places. The cathedral was a magnet. The permanent population of medieval Chartres may have been no more than 1,500 people. The cathedral regularly attracted 10,000 worshippers, an offering to God as powerful as the human sacrifices of the Aztecs and the propitiating killing of children for Minoan deities. The cathedral provided a way of connecting the divine to the living world, for all things emanated from the Kingdom of God. Requiring enormous expenditures of human labor and sometimes extreme deprivation, Gothic cathedrals were expensive outpourings of love for the Lord, also metaphorical sacrifices in stone and material goods offered in the expectation of divine favors in return. Chartres was the setting for dazzling spectacles. Sung masses and mystery plays depicting the life of Jesus or episodes in the lives of saints brought on intense emotional reactions among the faithful. The great cathedral bells tolled at times of joy, at moments of mourning. They sounded warnings, rang out in exultation, and in crisis. Great preachers attracted huge crowds. Baptisms, marriages, funerals and prayers for the dead, ordinations and excommunications, victory celebrations and public meetings: The cathedral was the focus of human life.

Like Mesoamerican Indians, medieval Christians worried about the fertility of the land, the continuity of life itself. Every Easter Eve, a New Light was kindled, celebrating the Resurrection and the year's start. A thousand tapers were lit and carried from town to village, village to household, as life renewed. Autumn harvest festivals saw churches decorated with the fruits of the soil, commemorating the bounty of the soil, like the Green Corn Ceremonies of eastern North American groups.

Seven centuries ago, the medieval cathedral was the Bible of the poor, an image of the cross and of the body of Christ, a corner of God's kingdom.

Sacred places were among ancient humanity's greatest achievements, often mirrors of the spiritual world. Great Maya cities such as Copán and Tikal were vast replicas of the spiritual world wrought in stone and stucco, with sacred mountains (pyramids), carved stelae (trees), and reservoirs (lakes). They were oriented with the heavenly bodies and were settings for elaborate ceremonies when powerful lords in trance would appear before their subjects. Angkor Wat in Cambodia is one of the masterpieces of the ancient world (see Figure 6.7). Khmer King Suryavarman II erected Angkor Wat as an observatory, shrine, and mausoleum in the early twelfth century A.D. The temple honors Vishnu, ruler of the western quarter of the compass. The five multitiered towers of the temple depict Mount Meru, home of the Hindu gods and center of the universe. Celestial maidens twist and cavort in endless dances on Angkor's walls, depicting the pleasures of paradise. More than a dozen Khmer princes built their shrines near this sacred place.

The great temple or ceremonial center was the focus of human life, the sanctified terrain where scheduled rituals guaranteed the seasonal renewal of cyclic time, and where the splendor, potency, and wealth of rulers symbolized the well-being of the whole community. Such centers ensured the continuity of cultural traditions; the religious and moral models of society were laid down in sacred canons recited in temples in reassuring chants passed from generation to generation.

Such sacred places lay at the heart of much wider cultural landscapes, defined by generations of experience with supernatural qualities. They were the focus of much wider worlds, which is why settlement archaeology plays such an important role in the study of ancient religions. For instance, the celebrated stone circles at Avebury in southern Britain formed part of a much larger sacred landscape, defined not only by natural landmarks but by burial mounds, sacred avenues delineated by stone uprights, and structures where the bodies of the dead were exposed before burial in communal tombs (see Figure 6.1). In recent years, teams of archaeologists have been gradually reconstructing this long-vanished, fragmentary landscape with survey and excavation that reveals its gradual evolution over many centuries.

Cahokia, the great Mississippian center, lies in the heart of a pocket of extremely fertile bottomland on the Mississippi floodplain near modern-day St. Louis known as the American Bottom. At the height of its powers between A.D. 1050 and 1250, Cahokia covered an area of more than 5 square miles (13 sq. km), about the size of the ancient city of Teotihuacán in the Valley of Mexico. Several thousand people lived in pole-and-thatch houses covering about 2,000 acres (800 ha) of ground, which were clustered on either side of a central east-west ridge. More than 100 earthen mounds of various sizes, shapes, and functions dot the Cahokia landscape, most grouped around open plazas. The largest, Monk's Mound, dominates the site and the surrounding landscape. Monk's Mound rises in four terraces to a height of 100 feet (31 m) and covers 16 acres (6.4 ha), slightly larger an area than Egypt's Great Pyramid of 13 acres (5.3 ha, see Figure 7.19). Fortunately for science, the ancient cosmology and religious beliefs behind Cahokia can be pieced together, at least partially, from a combination of archaeology in the American Bottom and ethnohistory derived from historic southeastern Indian groups (Figure 12.6).

The layout of Cahokia reflects a traditional Southeastern cosmos with four opposed sides, reflected in the layout of their platform mounds, great mounds, and imposing plazas. By A.D. 1050, the rectangular plaza surrounded by mounds replicated the ancient quadripartite pattern of the cosmos, seen in much earlier settlements along the Mississippi. Four-sided Mississippian platform mounds may portray the cosmos as "earth-islands," just as modern-day Muskogean Indians thought of the world as flat-topped and four-sided. Archaeologist John Douglas uses ethnographic and archaeological data to

FIGURE 12.6 An artist's reconstruction of the ceremonial precincts at Cahokia, Illinois. *(Courtesy Cahokia Mounds State Park.)*

argue that the four-sided cosmos had a primary axis which ran northwest to southeast, with an opposite axis dividing the world into four diamond-shaped quarters. Cahokia is oriented along a slightly different north-south axis, but it certainly perpetuates the notion of spiritual links between opposites and a cosmos divided into quarters. Researchers believe the orientation reflects observations of the sun rather than the moon. Astroarchaeologist Anthony Aveni thinks Cahokia's rulers used the sun to schedule the annual rituals which commemorated the cycles of the agricultural year.

Southeastern cosmology revolved around dualities. In the case of Cahokia, these may have included the Upper and Lower Worlds, also a powerful and pervasive fertility cult linked to commoners and the elite. These dualities were carried through to the smallest ritual centers. Changing settlement layouts imply that, at first, local communities and kin groups controlled fertility rituals in dispersed households divided into symbolic quarters, with ceremonial structures facing a central square. Later, centers display more formal layouts, with central plazas, elaborate sacred buildings, and storage and ritual pits filled with offerings made during fertility and world-renewal ceremonies. By this time, experts believe, power was passing from local kin leaders to a powerful elite based at Cahokia, a shift reflected in increasingly elaborate ceremonial architecture, residences for local leaders at local centers and special mortuary complexes. Their carefully laid out centers brought two central ritual themes together: the spiritual realm of fertility and life, and the validation of living rulers, who were intermediaries with the supernatural realm.

Cahokia and other Mississippian centers reflect an ancient cosmology in a symbolic language intelligible to noble and commoner alike.

ASTROARCHAEOLOGY AND STONEHENGE

Astroarchaeology is the study of ancient astronomical observances. The movements of the sun and moon and other heavenly bodies played an important role in many ancient societies, among them ancient Egyptian civilization, the Maya, and many Andean cultures. Astroarchaeology, the study of ancient astronomy, is an important source of information about ancient religious beliefs and cosmologies.

Astroarchaeology is a far cry from the crazy theories of cultists, who claim Egypt's Pyramids of Giza were giant, highly sophisticated astronomical observatory complexes run with computers. (Correspondence from such "theorists" lands in a file in my office named "Pyramidiots.") Modern research into ancient astronomy uses computer software to examine the sky over the Maya homeland on specific years and makes highly accurate observations of astronomical alignments at Stonehenge, Hopewell monuments in Ohio, and other sites known to have astronomical associations.

More nonsense has been written about the stone circles at Stonehenge, England, than about almost any other archaeological site in the world (see Figure 1.5). After more than three centuries of sporadic research, scientists are still deeply divided about the significance of this extraordinary monument, the prehistoric equivalent of a Norman cathedral, used and modified from about 2950 to 1600 B.C. Was it the center of some long-forgotten religious cult, or was it an observatory, a sophisticated place of dialogue with the sun and stars?

In the 1960s, Boston astronomer Gerald Hawkins used an IBM mainframe computer to plot the positions of 165 key points: stones, stone holes, earthworks, and other fixed points. He found "total sun [and moon] correlation" with a network of 13 solar and 11 lunar alignments, all of them based on features of early, rather than later, Stonehenge, where the alignments were less precise. Hawkins called Stonehenge a "Neolithic computer" used for predicting lunar eclipses. From the archaeologists' point of view, the fatal flaw in Hawkins' reasoning was his assumption that any alignments he saw, as a twentieth-century astronomer, were also known to the original builders. Hawkins was familiar with abstruse astronomical data. How could one assume Stone Age or Bronze Age farmers had the same expertise, especially since they had to cope with the cloudy and unpredictable sighting conditions of the British heavens? Hawkins's astronomy was little more than an anecdotal way of explaining Stonehenge. A decade later, retired engineering professor Alexander Thom announced that Stonehenge's stone circles were a central "backsight" for observing heavenly bodies, used with no less than eight "foresights," mostly earthworks identified on the visible horizon. Unfortunately, Thom failed to reconcile the archaeological and astronomical evidence. Nearly all his "foresight" earthworks are of later date than the stone circles of the "backsight."

Was Stonehenge an observatory? One cannot speak of it in the same breath as sophisticated Maya observatories, or of the builders as astronomers on par with Babylonian priests. We have known since the seventeenth century that Stonehenge was aligned on the axis of the midsummer sun. But the stone circles were never an elaborate device for predicting eclipses or measuring the sky. Rather, Stonehenge reflects a distinctive *idea* of time, which revolved around the cyclical movements of sun, moon, and stars across the heavens, as indicators of the passing seasons.

The farmers who built the later Stonehenge lived in a demanding environment where the passage of the seasons governed their lives. Every year, the eternal cycles of planting, growth, and harvest, of symbolic life and death, repeated themselves in endless successions of good and bad harvests, of drought and excess rainfall, of famine or plenty. The people placed great store by death rituals, on reverence of the ancestors, the guardians of the land. They devoted enormous resources to the great stone circles in the midst of their sacred landscape, where their priests and shamans used the stone uprights and simple stone alignments to observe the passage of the seasons. At midsummer sunrise and, perhaps, on the shortest day of the year, about December 21, the priests stood at the open side of the horseshoes to observe sunrise or sunset. In winter, the setting of the winter sun at the solstice signaled the beginning of lengthening days and the certainty that the cycle of the seasons would begin anew.

We have great difficulty envisaging Stonehenge in its heyday, sitting as it does in the midst of a late-twentieth-century landscape. Our only impressions can come from our physical perceptions of what it was like to move around both outside and inside the monument. These perceptions must be fundamentally similar to those of the ancients, for the stone uprights still tower overhead and restrict the view, as they did 4,500 years ago. With the exercise of ritual power, setting is everything. Stonehenge was such a setting.

The lesson of Stonehenge lies in the continuities of farming life, rather than changes. Chieftains lived and died, achieved great power and supernatural authority, and, in time, became ancestors. As villages prospered and more people crowded the densely farmed landscape, always at the center of this busy world lay a set of ancient values and beliefs epitomized by the weathered stone circles of Stonehenge. The seasons came and went, and so did human life itself, while Stonehenge remained an idea of time, a place where relationships between the living, the dead, and the supernatural were commemorated in stone.

SOUTHWESTERN ASTRONOMY AND CHACO CANYON

Agriculture and religion intersected the lives of the ancient Pueblo Indians of the Southwest, living as they did in a region of unpredictable rainfall, where the timing of harvest and planting was everything. The Pueblo world was one of close interdependence between farming and religious observance and between isolated communities large and small. The major ceremonies of the summer and winter solstices brought people together in implicit recognition of this interdependence.

The Pueblo tied their world to the horizon and the heavens by making a calendar out of the environment around them. The Hopi oriented themselves to the points on the horizon that mark the places of sunrise and sunset at the summer and winter solstices. The Pueblo anchored time, and their ritual cycles, to these events, especially to the winter solstice, when the sun is at its southernmost point. They believed that if the sun does not turn round, then it would fall off into the underworld. Some groups observed a period of "staying still," to keep the sun in its winter house. Winter solstice ceremonies guided the sun in the correct direction. The Sun Priests set the days for these ceremonies, as well as the lesser celebrations in the annual calendar, starting their prayers and observations about 28 days before the winter solstice and 29 days before the summer. They used a chosen spot in the village for their work, tracking the sun's seasonal position with the aid of horizon markers, which showed up clearly at sunrise. Sometimes, they employed windows in buildings to manipulate light and shadow.

Sun watching required much more than observation of solstices and other events. The Sun Priest had to make anticipatory observations over three weeks before an event such as a solstice celebration to allow for preparations to be made. He also required lengthy training, so he could still predict events during times of bad weather. This is why he had to know the position of sunrise relative to horizon markers several weeks *before* the event. At the solstice, the sun stands still on the horizon for four days, making the observation of the actual solstice day impossible beforehand. So, the Sun Priest had to make his observations at a time when the sun is still moving perceptibly everyday, in human-eye terms, about 10 minutes of arc (arcmins) a day. He could have predicted the day of the solstice by making the observation and then keeping a tally of days on a notched stick. This approach solved the problem of cloud cover and bad weather. By using any clear day well ahead of time, the observer may have used his notched stick to calculate the correct day of solstice even if the sky was overcast. The predictions of the summer solstice were remarkably accurate, almost invariably to within a day and a half. Such accuracy was essential. A major disaster would transpire if the ceremonies took place and the sun had already turned or was still moving toward its turning point, as if it were about to fall off the earth. Accurate predictions reinforced priestly power and strengthened bonds within the community, as well as validated the worldview.

Ecological time served the Pueblo well. They lived a well-regulated life attuned to the solstices and to the realities of their arid environment. The yearly cycle repeated itself endlessly. As one year ended, another began, measured in the passage of moons and days.

Fortunately for science, pre-Columbian astronomers used buildings, pictographs, and other humanly manufactured objects for their observations, enabling us to trace Pueblo astronomy back to the Anasazi, "the ancient ones," whose primordial roots extend back as far as 2,500 years ago.

The best archaeological evidence for Pueblo astronomy comes from Hovenweep Pueblo in Colorado, erected by Anasazi people related to nearby Mesa Verde communities between the late twelfth and mid-thirteenth centuries. The pueblo includes round, square, or D-shaped towers. At least one, Hovenweep Castle, has special sun-sighting ports aligned with the summer and winter solstices. Nearby, Holly House contains petroglyph panels with symbols that may represent the sun and other heavenly bodies.

The first farmers of the Southwest dwelt in small communities of pit houses. By A.D. 900, Southwestern farming populations rose considerably. Many Anasazi communities moved into large, well-constructed towns, epitomized by the great pueblos of Chaco Canyon. For two and a half centuries the Chaco Canyon pueblos flourished, during a time of constant climatic change. By 1050, the Chaco Phenomenon (an archaeological term) was in full swing. The Phenomenon expanded from its canyon homeland to encompass an area of more than 65,000 square kilometers (25,000 sq. miles) of the surrounding San Juan Basin and adjacent uplands. Roads and visual communication systems linked outlying communities with the canyon. Great pueblos such as semicircular Pueblo Bonito housed hundreds of people (see Figure 7.24). The population of Chaco Canyon rose from a few hundred to at least 5,500 inhabitants, with many more people visiting for major ceremonies and trading activities.

During the 1970s and 1980s, aerial photographs and side-scan radar placed Chaco at the center of a vast ancient landscape. A web of over 400 miles (650 km) of unpaved ancient roadways link Chaco with over 30 outlying settlements. The Anasazi had no carts or draft animals, but they built shallow trackways up to 40 feet (12 m) wide, cut a few inches into the underlying soil or demarcated by low banks or stone walls. Each highway runs straight for long distances, some for as much as 60 miles (95 km), each linked to a major pueblo at the canyon itself. The people approached the canyon along straight walkways, descending to the pueblos down stonecut steps in the cliffs (Figure 12.7). The Chacoan "roads" are a mystery. Were they used for travel or transportation of vital commodities? For years, archaeologists have argued for some form of integrating Chacoan cultural system which would have unified a large area of the Southwest a thousand years ago. One authority, archaeologist James Judge, believes the San Juan Basin's harsh and unpredictable climate with its frequent droughts, caused isolated Anasazi pueblos to form loosely structured alliances for exchanging food and other vital commodities. Chaco lay at the hub of the exchange system and also served as the ritual center for major rainmaking ceremonies and festivals. The canyon's great houses were the homes of privileged families who were able to predict the movements of heavenly bodies and controlled ritual activity.

FIGURE 12.7   A stairway carved into a sandstone mesa near Casa Rinconada in Chaco Canyon, part of the canyon's road system. *(Courtesy of Mick Sharp.)*

In Judge's scenario, the roads were pilgrimage and trading walkways. However, archaeologist John Roney of the Bureau of Land Management points out that there are no signs of domestic rubbish or encampments along the roads. On the ground, he has followed many of the fuzzy lines on air photographs, verifying more than 60 road segments, many of them short and without specific destination. Roney is certain that major north and south tracks radiated from Chaco, but he is cautious about joining segments into long lines uniting distant places on the map. He is sure of a mere 155 miles (250 km) of roads and believes the Chacoans constructed the walkways as monuments, as a ritual gesture, not to be used.

Do roads have to lead to a destination, as we Westerners always believe? The answer to the Chaco road mystery may lie not in the archaeological record, but in Pueblo Indian cosmology. The so-called Great North Road is a case in point. Several roadways from Pueblo Bonito and Chetro Ketl ascend Chaco's north wall to converge on Pueblo Alto. From there, the road travels 13 degrees east of north for about 2 miles (3 km) before heading due north for nearly 30 miles (50 km) across open country to Kutz Canyon, where it vanishes. North is the primary direction in the mythology of modern-day Keresan-speaking Pueblo peoples, who may have ancestry among Chaco communities. North led to the place of origin, the place where the spirits of the dead went. Chaco's Great North Road may have been an umbilical cord to the underworld, a conduit of spiritual power. Another Pueblo concept, that of the Middle Place, was the point where the four cardinal directions converged. Pueblo Bonito, with its cardinal layout, may have been the Middle Place.

The Great Houses and trackways of Chaco Canyon may have formed a sacred landscape, a symbolic stage where the Anasazi acted out their beliefs and commemorated the passage of seasons. Fortunately, new scientific technologies such as Geographic Information Systems are combining multispectrum imagery, color infrared photographs, and 1930s half-tone images. By enhancing different light, heat, and vegetational conditions, fieldworkers can go into the field with information on hitherto invisible features, locating themselves on the ground with the satellite-driven Global Positioning System, which can fix their positions within a few feet. A new generation of survey work will establish the true extent of Chacoan roads and place them in a precise topographical context.

It is hard for us to reconstruct the intangible religious beliefs of the remote past, separated as we are from them by many centuries. Just how hard can be imagined by listening to modern-day storytellers as they recite well-known tales to an audience that has heard them over and over, but never tires of the stories and their morals. I have heard Pueblo Indian storytellers recite from memory, face to face with their audiences, often for as long as an hour at time, holding their listeners spellbound with tales that bind living people to the world of the sun and moon, of animals and plants like humans. The plots twist and turn, with heroes and terrifying hazards, tests of skill and wisdom. Almost invariably, the tales involve deeply felt religious beliefs and the spiritual world. Only a fraction of these tales survive, lovingly transcribed, edited, and translated as a permanent record of a vanishing world. Many tell of the sun, whose powers of warmth and light sustained life itself. One Hopi tale recounts how a young man was conceived by the sun and journeyed to visit his father. After many adventures, including a journey across the heavens, he returns happy: "I saw for myself how he attends to our needs every single day of our lives. Therefore we must live out our lives in a good manner, and he will never forsake us" (Swann 1994, 678).

Fortunately, a new generation of archaeological research is beginning to study the fascinating and complex world of the intangible.

SUMMARY

Archaeologists study the religious beliefs of ancient societies by using material remains and information from a variety of sources. Many ancient religions shared common features: a multilayered cosmos, a cyclical existence, important locations that were axes of the world, and a concern with ancestors and shamanism.

Ethnographic analogy plays an important role in studying ancient rock art, thanks to anthropological research among the San of southern Africa a century ago. Richly adorned burials can provide information on religious beliefs as well as social ranking, but the major source of such information comes from art and artifacts. The context of artifacts in time and space is of vital importance, as this can often reveal more information than the objects themselves. Rigorous studies of art styles, such as that of the Moche of Peru or the Maya, can yield valuable information on ancient ideologies, especially if combined with ethnographic or written records.

Sacred places such as Cahokia, Illinois, medieval cathedrals, or Maya cities were vital catalysts for religious beliefs, for they were the settings for rituals of validation and other ceremonies. Settlement archaeology plays an important role in studying such locations in the context of their wider landscape. So does astroarchaeology, the study of ancient astronomy, notably successful in the American Southwest, at Stonehenge, England, and with the Maya civilization.

KEY TERM

Astroarchaeology

GUIDE TO FURTHER READING

Aveni, Anthony. 1993. *Ancient Astronomy*. Washington D.C.: Smithsonian Books.
    An excellent summary of what we know about astronomy of the ancients, for the wider audience.

Chippindale, Christopher. 1994. *Stonehenge Complete*. 2nd ed. London: Thames and Hudson.

The best source on Stonehenge for the general reader.

Fagan, Brian. 1998. *From Black Land to Fifth Sun*. Reading, MA: Helix Books.

A survey of the archaeology of mind for the general reader which consists mainly of case studies.

Lewis-Williams, David. 1981. *Believing and Seeing: Symbolic Meanings in Southern San Rock Paintings*. New York: Academic Press.

A beautifully written and argued study of rock art and ethnographic analogy.

Linares, Olga. 1997. *Ecology and the Arts in Ancient Panama: On the Development of Social Rank and Symbolism in the Central Provinces*. Washington D.C.: Dumbarton Oaks.

The exemplary monograph on her research.

Pauketat, Thomas R., and Thomas E. Emerson, eds. 1997. *Cahokia: Domination and Ideology in the Mississippian World*. Lincoln: University of Nebraska Press.

A technical series of essays on Mississippian religious beliefs and archaeology.

Schele, Linda, and David Friedel. 1990. *A Forest of Kings*. New York: William Morrow.

A popular account of Maya civilization that is a mine of information on religion, iconography, and social ranking. Controversial, engrossing, and readable.

———. 1993. *Maya Cosmos*. New York: William Morrow.

A companion to the previous reference, which explores the Maya heavens.

Sullivan, Lawrence. 1989. *Icanchu's Drum*. New York: Free Press.

Sullivan's study of ancient and modern Latin American indigenous religions is a remarkable monograph that should be read by every archaeologist.

PART VI

RESOURCES

A mere hole in the ground, which of all sights is perhaps the least vivid and dramatic, is enough to grip their attention for hours at a time.

P. G. WODEHOUSE, *A DAMSEL IN DISTRESS*

Archaeology is the only branch of anthropology where we kill our informants in the process of studying them.

KENT V. FLANNERY, *THE GOLDEN MARSHALLTOWN*

Ear ornament worn by a Lord of Sipan, Peru. c. A.D. 400. (Source: Earspool, from Sipan, Peru. Moche culture, c. 300 ce. Gold turquoise, quartz, and shell, diameter approximately 5" (12.7 cm). Bruning Archeological Museum, Lambayeque, Peru. (Courtesy of UCLA Fowler Museum of Cultural History. Photo by Susan Einstein.).)

Archaeology as a Profession
    Deciding to Become an Archaeologist
Doing Archaeology: The Personal Qualities of an Archaeologist
    Gaining Fieldwork Experience
    Career Opportunities in Archaeology
Doing Archaeology: Fieldwork Opportunities
    Academic Qualifications: Graduate School
Thoughts on Not Becoming a Professional Archaeologist
Our Responsibilities to the Past
Doing Archaeology: A Simple Code of Archaeological Ethics for All

I became an archaeologist by sheer accident, having entered Cambridge University in England without any idea of potential careers. I was admitted on condition I studied anything except Greek or Latin, for which I had no aptitude whatsoever! So, I took a list of potential subjects and chose archaeology and anthropology on a whim with no intention of making them a career. My first lecturer was a Stone Age archaeologist named Miles Burkitt, who was famous for his classroom stories. He had studied late–Ice Age rock art under the legendary French archaeologist Henri Breuil before 1910. His enthusiastic reminiscences triggered my interest in the past. By chance, while still an undergraduate, I met another famous archaeologist, the African prehistorian Desmond Clark, and ended up working in a museum in Central Africa after I graduated. I have been an archaeologist ever since, a career choice I have never regretted.

    Chapter 13 is about archaeology as a career and a hobby, as an avocation and part of all of our lives. In short, it's about archaeology and you.

ARCHAEOLOGY AS A PROFESSION

I gave up saying I was an archaeologist at cocktail parties after learning the hard way! Say you are an archaeologist and immediately your questioner brightens up. "How exciting! What a fascinating job," your new acquaintance almost invariably says. They think you are some kind of Indiana Jones, perpetually traveling to remote lands in search of some archaeological Holy Grail. When you tell them you study stone tools and recently spent three months searching for fossil rodents (which is usually the truth), their eyes glaze over and they often do not believe you. There's another scenario, too, where questioners' eyes light up when they learn of your occupation and they ask you, confidentially: "Is it true that the Egyptian Sphinx is 12,000 years old?" or, "What about the Lost Continent of Atlantis? Isn't it in the Bahamas?" or, most common of all, "What's the latest on the Dead Sea Scrolls?" I must confess, in such situations, I am a coward and say I am a historian, which, in a sense, I am. My interlocutors soon lose interest.

    Archaeology still has an aura of romance and spectacular discovery about it, which probably accounts for why many of you took the course that assigned this book in the first place. You learn pretty fast that modern-day archaeology, while often fascinating and sometimes conducted in remote lands, is a highly technical discipline where spectacular discoveries are few and far between. True, exciting finds occasionally hit the headlines, such as the Moche Lords of Sipán or the Uluburun shipwreck, but the fact remains that most archaeologists labor far from the public eye, often on unspectacular and sometimes downright monotonous sites or obscure problems. An Indiana Jones–like personality is certainly not a qualification for archaeology; indeed it has never been. Indiana Jones himself is complete fiction, a composite built up from a group of well-known pioneer archaeologists of the early twentieth century, whose collective discoveries and adventures were indeed larger than life. Today's archaeologist is about as far from Professor Jones as you can get and probably works a long way from the halls of academe.

What, then, are the qualities that make a good archaeologist in these days of highly specialized research and wide diversity of career options? Quality of character is as important as academic qualifications, which we discuss subsequently, for you will never become rich as an archaeologist. This is a profession that has its own unique rewards. Money is not one of them. (See Doing Archaeology box on p. 387 for a description of the characteristics of good archaeologists.)

In many senses, archaeology is not a profession, but a calling to which many people devote their lives. In these days of instant gratification and ardent materialism, there is nothing wrong with that, provided you do not take yourself too seriously.

Deciding to Become an Archaeologist

I became an archaeologist almost by chance, for the occasional fieldwork experiences I had as an undergraduate were interesting and left me wanting more. This is not like becoming a priest or a nun, or signing up with the military, where a high degree of initial commitment is needed. You can ease your way into the field, up to the point when you apply to graduate school, and have a great time doing so.

Almost everyone I meet who is contemplating a career in archaeology either encountered the subject in high school or became interested as a result of taking an introductory course at college or university. Many people are lucky enough to have had a truly inspiring teacher, who fires them with enthusiasm for a career possibility they have never encountered before. What, then, should you do next once your appetite for the past is whetted?

First, take more courses in archaeology at the upper division level from as broad a cross section of instructors as possible. Begin with an advanced method and theory course (if that does not turn you off, then you know you are on to something, for such courses are not remarkable for their excitement!). Then take a selection of area courses, so you find out which general areas of specialty interest you and which do not. Remember, if you apply to

DOING ARCHAEOLOGY

The Personal Qualities of an Archaeologist

Anyone wanting to become an archaeologist needs far more than academic credentials (discussed later). Here are some essentials:

- *Enthusiasm,* indeed a passion for archaeology and the past, is the baseline for anyone who enters this field. Archaeology thrives on enthusiasm, for the best archaeologists are those with the kind of fire in their bellies that enables them to raise money, overcome major practical obstacles, and carry out their work. Personal charisma breeds good archaeological leaders, provided they have the patience for the small details as well.
- *Infinite patience* to carry out fieldwork and other research that can involve slow-moving repetitive tasks and dealing with sometimes-difficult people.
- *A mind that thrives on detail,* since a great deal of archaeology is minutiae—small attributes of stone tools and potsherds, analyzing computerized data, studying tiny details of the past for weeks on end. Both excavation and survey, to say nothing of laboratory work, require great patience and a concern for detail.
- *Adaptability,* an ability to put up with long journeys, sometimes uncomfortable fieldwork, and often primitive living conditions. You need to be fit enough to walk long distances and to thrive on improvisation under difficult conditions. Imagine, for example, fashioning Land Rover wheel bearings out of nails when you are several hundred miles from a service station and need to get home. I know archaeologists who have done that. They had to.
- *Good organizational skills,* since a great deal of archaeology is logistics and organization of field crews, site archives, even camp kitchens. A good mind for organization is a great asset.
- *Cultural sensitivity and good people skills* are essential. Many of archaeology's most successful practitioners invest enormous amounts of time in cultivating people and communicating with Native Americans and other cultural groups. Such skills require great patience and sensitivity, but the personal satisfaction and rewards are immense. This is one reason why a background in anthropology is so important to an archaeologist.
- *A commitment to ethical archaeology* is also necessary. Do not become an archaeologist unless you are prepared to adhere to the ethical standards demanded of such professionals, some of which are spelled out in Chapter 2.
- *A sense of humor* may seem self-evident, but it is vital, for many archaeologists take themselves far too seriously. Have you ever spent a week writing a paper, then had your computer implode before you have backed up your text? Moments like that beset all field research. That's why archaeologists need a sense of humor, because sometimes everything that can go wrong goes wrong—all at once.

The most important considerations are commitment and enthusiasm, which will carry you through almost anything.

graduate school, you will need some specific interest as the potential focus of your degree.

Second, give yourself as thorough and as broad an education in general biological studies and cultural anthropology as possible, both to focus your interests and to see whether living people interest you more than dead ones. If you do go on to become a professional, you will never regret this exposure.

Third, take as many courses as you can in related disciplines, so that you emerge with strongly developed multidisciplinary interests. The most important and fascinating problems in archaeology, for example, the origins of agriculture, can only be approached from a multidisciplinary perspective. Much CRM archaeology is strongly multidisciplinary, too.

Last, gain significant field and laboratory experience while still an undergraduate. Such experience looks good on graduate applications, especially if it is broadly based. Even more important, it allows you to experience the challenges, discomforts, and realities of field and laboratory work before they become your job (and you should think of graduate school as a job). Only a few months ago, I had a student come in to see me who had been all enthusiasm for archaeology. She had gone in the field in the Southwest for a month and hated every moment of it. She still likes archaeology but has decided to enjoy it from afar.

If you take the trouble to acquire a broad-based experience of archaeology in your undergraduate years, you will be well equipped for graduate education and its pathways to a professional career.

Gaining Fieldwork Experience

"How do I go on a dig?" I am asked this question dozens of times a year, especially when I teach the introductory archaeology course. The good news is that there are more opportunities to go in the field as an undergraduate then ever before, provided you are prepared to make the effort to find them. Begin by taking your department's field course, if it offers one, then look further afield, using personal contacts and departmental bulletin boards as a start. (See Doing Archaeology box on p. 389 for more details.)

Career Opportunities in Archaeology

This is not a good time to become an academic archaeologist, for jobs are rare and the competition intense. But it is certainly an excellent time to consider a career in government or the private sector, both of which effectively administer or carry out most archaeology in North America.

Academic Archaeology This field is shrinking. A generation ago, almost all archaeologists were faculty members at academic institutions or worked in museums or research institutions. Purely academic archaeology still dominates both undergraduate and graduate training, and there are many people who enter graduate school with the resolute ambition of becoming a "traditional" research scholar. But growth in academic positions is now very slow. Some programs are even shrinking.

Most archaeology in North America and many parts of Europe is now conducted as CRM projects, much of it mandated by law. This means that most

DOING ARCHAEOLOGY

Fieldwork Opportunities

Fieldwork opportunities abound, if you take the trouble to look for them. Here are some possible choices after that, or in lieu of fieldwork:

- *Volunteering on an excavation or survey sponsored by your own institution.* Ask your instructors about possible opportunities. Once they see you are serious, they may be delighted to use you in the field or laboratory.
- *Volunteering on fieldwork sponsored by some other local or national organization, such as a historical society, museum, or government agency.* Many of my students have served as interns for the National Park Service and other organizations. The World Wide Web is a useful source of information on such opportunities, as is your department bulletin board, which probably advertises fieldwork opportunities.
- *Attending field school.* Many institutions sponsor summer field schools for credit. Some programs such as the Grasshopper Pueblo Field School run by Arizona State University have been running successfully for years. The most popular and rigorous field schools are in heavy demand and are filled by competitive application, sometimes by graduate students. General field schools are worthwhile because they combine excavation, laboratory analysis, and academic instruction into one intensive experience. And the camaraderie among participants in such digs can be memorable. Very often, attendance at a field school gives you a basic qualification that will help in getting summer work with a research institute or private contract firm. The Society for American Archaeology (address is in the "Useful Addresses" section at the end of this chapter) and the World Wide Web will provide information, as will mailings sent to your department. Choose your field school with care! All are not equal and you should take advice from your instructors before committing yourself. A word to the wise: Beware of summer field schools that offer you a chance to excavate on archaeological sites in remote lands. Some of them, especially in the eastern Mediterranean, charge high fees and use students as unskilled labor, so you learn little. Check carefully before signing up and insist on getting names of former students you can contact beforehand.

- *Participating in professional excavations overseas.* The Archaeological Institute of America and the Council for British Archaeology (addresses are in the "Useful Addresses" section) maintain lists of professional excavations that rely on serious volunteers. Sometimes they provide cheap or even free accommodation if you stay for a while. I have had many students who have had excellent experiences with such digs, but again, check carefully ahead of time. (One of my students even met his wife on an excavation in Britain!)
- *Volunteering on CRM excavation.* Many of my students receive their first fieldwork experience by working as laborers on local CRM projects. Many of them begin as volunteers and are later paid for their work. It is worth checking with any private-sector CRM firms in your area, or consult your instructor, who may have contacts.

(but certainly not all) academic archaeology in American universities is carried out overseas, most commonly in Europe, Mesoamerica, or the Andes. Over the years, this means that there is intense competition for the rare vacant academic jobs in such well-trodden areas as Mesoamerica and even more applicants for academic positions in North American archaeology.

A recent study of American archaeologists found that only about 35 percent worked in academia, and the number is shrinking every year. The moral is simple: If you want to become an academic archaeologist, beware of overspecializing or of working in too-crowded fields and have other qualifications such as CRM or computer skills at your disposal.

Museum jobs are rare, especially those that are purely research positions. A career in museum work is rewarding, but hard to come by and requires specialized training in conservation, exhibits, curation, or some other aspect of collections care in addition to academic training.

Cultural Resource Management and Public Archaeology These offer almost open-ended opportunities to those who are seeking a career managing and saving the archaeological record. Time was when academic archaeologists looked down on their CRM colleagues and considered them second-rate intellectual citizens. The reverse has been true, too, for I have met CRM archaeologists who consider academics tweed-suited dilettantes! All this is nonsense, of course, for all archaeologists are concerned with careful stewardship of the human past. The greatest opportunities in archaeology during the next century lie in the public archaeology arena and the private sector, where the challenges are far more demanding than the traditional academic concerns. Adapting to this reality will lead to many changes in undergraduate and graduate curricula in coming years.

If you are interested in public archaeology or CRM, you have the choice of either working in government or for some form of organization engaged in CRM activity, which can be either a nonprofit group perhaps attached to a museum, college, or university or a for-profit company operating entirely in the private sector. The latter come in many forms and sizes, with larger companies offering the best opportunities and career potential, especially for entry-level archaeologists. Most public archaeology activity operates through government, although a few private-sector firms also specialize in this work. If you choose to work in the public sector, you can find opportunities in many federal government agencies, among them the National Park Service and the Bureau of Land Management. Many archaeologists work for state archaeological surveys and other such organizations. Historical societies, such as that in Ohio, often employ archaeologists.

Whichever career track you choose, you will need a sound background in academic archaeology and fieldwork experience as well as suitable degrees to follow a career in these areas. Although you may receive some background training in CRM or public archaeology during your undergraduate or graduate career, much of your training will come on the job or through specialized courses taken as part of your work.

Whatever your interests in professional archaeology, I strongly advise you to obtain background and experience in CRM field- and laboratory work as part of your training.

Academic Qualifications: Graduate School

An undergraduate degree in archaeology qualifies you to work as a gopher on a CRM excavation or an academic dig and little else, except for giving you a better knowledge than most people have of the human past—not something to denigrate as a source of enlightenment and enjoyment in later life. Many people work on CRM projects for a number of years and live in motels: They even have their own informal newsletters!

Any form of permanent position in archaeology requires a minimum of an M.A. (Master of Arts), which will qualify you for many government and private-sector positions. All academic positions at research universities, and, increasingly, teaching posts require a Ph.D.

Typically, an M.A. in archaeology requires two years of course work and some form of data-based paper and, at some institutions, oral examination. The M.A. may have a specialized slant, such as CRM or historic preservation, but most are general degrees, which prepare you to teach at some two- or four-year colleges and universities and open you to many CRM or government opportunities. The advantage of the M.A. degree is that it gives you a broad background in archaeology, which is essential for any professional. It is the qualification of choice for many government and CRM or public archaeology positions.

The Ph.D. is a specialized research degree, which qualifies you as a faculty member to teach at a research university and at many institutions that stress teaching and not research. This is the professional "ticket" for academic archaeologists and is certainly desirable for someone entering government or the private sector, in which complex research projects and management decisions are often needed. The typical Ph.D. program requires at least two years of comprehensive seminar, course, and field training, followed by comprehensive examinations (written and often oral), M.A. papers, then a formal research proposal and a period of intensive fieldwork that, in written form, constitutes the Ph.D. thesis. The average doctoral program takes about seven years to complete and turns you into a highly specialized professional, with some teaching and research experience. After those seven years, you then must find a job in a highly competitive marketplace. Yes, it is a daunting prospect to face seven years or more of genteel poverty, but the intellectual and personal rewards are considerable for someone with a true passion for archaeology and academic research.

Applying to graduate school is a complex process, which lies outside the scope of this book, but some important points are worth thinking about a long time before you compile an application.

Do not consider applying for a graduate program in archaeology unless you have the following:

- An academic record well above average, with in-depth coverage of archaeology and anthropology. An A-minus grade point average is a minimal requirement for good graduate schools; also you need good GRE (Graduate Record Exam) scores. A strong background in anthropology and a multidisciplinary perspective are essential.
- Some field experience on a dig or survey.
- An ability to write good, clear English and to speak fluently in public (both skills acquired by experience).
- Strong and meaningful support from at least two qualified archaeologists who are able to write letters for you, *who know you really well.* The old adage about getting to know your professors is so true. A letter written by someone who knows you both as a person and a student stands out from the crowd.
- A specific research interest, which is spelled out carefully in the statement of intent required on most graduate applications. It is very important that your emerging specialist interests coincide with those of the department of your choice and with the faculty members who work there. For example, it's no use applying to the University of California at Santa Barbara for Ph.D. study in eastern North America. We have no one who teaches it! An obvious point, one would think, but one often ignored.
- A strong passion for archaeology and for teaching as well as research, a realistic expectation as far as the tight job market is concerned, and a moral commitment not to collect artifacts for profit or for personal gain are also essential.

A final word to the wise: If you feel your passion and interest in archaeology waning as you progress through your graduate years, do not hesitate to quit. The experience may be traumatic in the short-term, but there are many people in archaeology who quietly wish they had never chosen a career with seemingly limited prospects. They may not readily admit it, but they are out there. Do not join them!

THOUGHTS ON NOT BECOMING A PROFESSIONAL ARCHAEOLOGIST

Over many years of teaching archaeology, I have introduced thousands of people to the subject. Only a handful have become professional archaeologists. Most students who pass through my courses go on to an enormous variety of careers—Army rangers, bureaucrats, international businesspeople, lawyers, politicians, real estate tycoons, teachers, and even chefs and pastry cooks. At least two of my former students are in jail! But every one of them is aware of archaeology and its role in the contemporary world, of the remarkable achievements of our ancient forebears. This is by far the most important teaching that I do, of far greater significance than any amount of professional training I may give graduate students.

My task as a beginning course teacher is not to recruit people to the field, to create an "in-group" who know all about radiocarbon dating and the archaeology of the central Ohio valley or eastern Siberia, but to help create what the National Science Foundation calls "an informed citizenry." Many of my students end up with no interest in archaeology whatsoever; they find it boring and irrelevant to their lives (this quite apart from finding me tiresome!). But you can be sure they have heard of the subject and its remarkable achievements and have decided where it fits in their lives. This is, after all, one of the objectives of an undergraduate education.

Having said this, many people take a single course in archaeology and develop an active interest in the subject which endures through the rest of their lives. If you are one of these individuals, you can stay involved, at least tangentially, with archaeology in many ways.

Archaeology depends on informed amateur archaeologists (often called "avocationals"), who volunteer on excavations, in laboratories, and in museums. Many highly important contributions to archaeology come from amateur archaeologists, often members of local archaeological societies, who participate in digs and keep an eye out for new discoveries in their areas. There is a strong tradition of amateur scholarship in archaeology, especially in Europe, where some avocationals have become world authorities on specialized subjects such as ancient rabbit keeping or specific pottery forms— and they publish regularly in academic journals.

Archaeology could not function without volunteers, whether on Earthwatch-supported excavations or through quiet work behind the scenes cataloging artifacts or running lecture programs. If you have a serious interest in volunteering and pursuing archaeology on a regular basis as an amateur, there are many ways to become involved through local organizations such as colleges, museums, archaeological societies and chapters of the Archaeological Institute of America. The Arkansas Archaeological Survey has a long history of successful involvement with amateurs. In these days of highly specialized research and professional scholarship, it is easy to say that there is no place for amateurs. This arrogant statement is nonsense and misses the point. Amateurs bring an extraordinary range of skills to archaeology. During my career, I have worked with, among others, with an accountant (who straightened out my excavation books), an architect, a professional photographer and artist (who was a godsend in the field), a jeweler (who analyzed gold beads for me), and an expert on slash-and-burn agriculture (who had a passion for environmental history). Your talents are invaluable, and don't take no for an answer! I showed this passage to a colleague, who said that some of his students have gone on to highly successful and lucrative careers in business. Their quiet philanthropy has endowed professorships, paid for excavations, and supported students. Enough said!

Many people develop an interest in the past, which comes to the fore when they travel. Their background in archaeology obtained as an undergraduate enables them to visit famous sites all over the world as an informed observer and to enjoy the achievements of ancient peoples to the fullest. My files are full of postcards and letters from obscure places, like one mailed from Stonehenge: "Thank you for introducing me to archaeology," it reads. "I enjoyed Stonehenge so much more after taking your course." This postcard made my day, for archaeology cannot survive without the involvement and enthusiasm not just of professionals, but of everyone interested in the past. We are all stewards of a priceless and finite resource, which is vanishing before our eyes.

OUR RESPONSIBILITIES TO THE PAST

All of us, whether professional archaeologist, avocational fieldworker, casually interested traveler, or basically disinterested citizen, share a common responsibility for the past. It is our collective cultural heritage, whether the Parthenon, the Pyramids of Giza, Cahokia, or the tomb of Chinese emperor Shihuangdi. This past extends back deep into the Ice Age, for more than 2.5 million years, a precious legacy of cultural achievement that is unique to humanity and something that we must cherish and pass on to generations still unborn. The word *steward* is overused these days, but we are as much stewards of the past as we are of the oceans, forests, and every part of the natural environment. Archaeology is different in one important respect: Once destroyed, its archives can never be reconstructed. They are gone forever. Professional archaeologists subscribe to strict and explicit ethics in their dealings with the past, but, in the final analysis, preserving the past for the future is the responsibility of us all. (See Doing Archaeology box on p. 395.)

As I have emphasized many times in these pages, the world's archaeological sites are under attack from many sources: industrial development, mining, and agriculture, as well as treasure hunters, collectors, and professional tomb robbers. Demand far exceeds the supply, so even modest antiquities fetch high prices in international markets. No government can hope to free the necessary funds to protect its antiquities adequately. And such countries as Egypt, Guatemala, and Mexico, with rich archaeological heritages, have almost overwhelming problems protecting even their well-known sites. As long as there is a demand for antiquities among collectors and we maintain our materialistic values about personal possessions, destruction of archaeological sites will continue unabated. Even the necessary legal controls to prevent destruction of archaeological sites are just barely in force in most parts of the world. Yet, there is still hope, which stems from the enormous numbers of informed people who have gained an interest in archaeology from university and college courses or from chance encounters with archaeologists or the past. If sufficient numbers of laypeople can influence public behavior and attitudes toward archaeological sites and the morality of collecting, there is still hope that our descendants will have archaeological sites to study and enjoy.

I am very glad I became an archaeologist and that my passion for the past remains unabated after many years in the field, laboratory, and classroom. I

DOING ARCHAEOLOGY

A Simple Code of Archaeological Ethics for All

Is there a future for the past? Yes, but only if we all help, not only by influencing other people's attitudes toward archaeology but also by obeying this simple code of ethics:

- Treat all archaeological sites and artifacts as finite resources.
- Never dig an archaeological site.

- Never collect artifacts for yourself or buy and sell them for personal gain.
- Adhere to all federal, state, local, and tribal laws that affect the archaeological record.
- Report all accidental archaeological discoveries.
- Avoid disturbing any archaeological site, and respect the sanctity of all burial sites.

---

have met many extraordinary people and have been challenged by complex research problems that have taken my career in unexpected directions. But the moments I cherish most are those rare occasions when I stand on an archaeological site or among some deserted earthworks or weathered buildings, and the past suddenly comes to life. I am lucky to have experienced this many times: high in the Greek amphitheater at Epidauros, when Euripides' stanzas echoed with perfect acoustics; on cloud-mantled earthworks in Britain where you could almost hear the cries of Roman legionaries advancing into battle; and on a coastal shell midden in southern California where I could imagine planked canoes landing on a fine summer evening. These moments come without warning and are deeply emotional, triggered by evocative sunsets, effects of cloud and light, or even by a chance thought, but they are utterly precious.

The past is personal to us, however dedicated a scientist we are, or however casually we visit a site. If the archaeological record vanishes, with all its great achievements and moments of brilliant success and long-forgotten tragedy, our successors will never be able to learn from the experience of our forebears or enjoy the powerful and extraordinarily satisfying emotional pull of the past. We owe this legacy to our grandchildren.

SUMMARY

Chapter 13 summarizes the essential qualities of someone seeking to become an archaeologist and lays out some of the career opportunities. Career opportunities for professional archaeologists can be found in universities, colleges, museums, government service, and private businesses both in the United States and abroad. Most archaeological jobs require at least an M.A. and very often a Ph.D. Do not consider becoming a professional archaeologist unless you have an above-average academic record, some field experience, strong support from your professors, and a moral commitment not to collect artifacts for profit.

Even people who have no intention of becoming professional archaeologists can gain digging experience by attending a field school or by digging overseas. Archaeology can give you insight into the past and the potential for involvement as an informed layperson. It will also enable you to enjoy the major archaeological sites of the world in a unique way and to aid in archaeologists' attempts to preserve the past. All of us have ethical responsibilities to the past: not to collect artifacts; to report new finds; and to obey federal, state, and tribal laws that protect archaeological sites. Unless we all take our responsibility to the past seriously, the past has no future.

GUIDE TO FURTHER READING

Lynott, Mark J., and Alison Wylie. 1995. *Ethics in American Archaeology: Challenges for the 1990s*. Washington D.C.: Society for American Archaeology.
>Very much a working document, this important volume lays out the fundamentals of archaeological ethics as a basis for discussion in the profession.

Messenger, Phyllis M., ed. 1989. *The Ethics of Collecting Cultural Property*. Albuquerque: University of New Mexico Press.
>Invaluable essays on the international trade in antiquities and the ethics behind the controversy.

Vitelli, Karen, ed. 1997. *Archaelogical Ethics*. Walnut Creek, CA: AltaMira Press.
>A useful anthology of ethical issues in archaeology designed for students.

Zeitlin, Marilyn. 1997. *The American Archaeologist: A Profile*. Walnut Creek, CA: AltaMira Press.
>A study of American archaeologists based on the membership of the Society for American Archaeology, which gives valuable information on trends, careers, and so forth.

USEFUL ADDRESSES

Here are three addresses from which you can obtain information about archaeological activities and excavations that need volunteers:

Archaeological Institute of America
Box 1901, Kenmore Station
Boston, MA 02215
The Institute publishes the Archaeological Fieldwork Opportunities Bulletin. Members receive *Archaeology* magazine.
The Society for American Archaeology is the professional organization for all American archaeologists and many in other fields.

Society for American Archaeology
Railway Express Building
980 2nd Street NE Suite 12
Washington, D.C. 20002–3557
Society members receive a bulletin and *American Antiquity,* a more technical journal. You can contact the society at http://www.saa.org.

For excavation opportunities overseas, contact:
The Council for British Archaeology
Bowes Morrell House
111 Walmgate
York YO1 2UA
England

This admirable organization publishes a monthly *Calendar of Excavations,* which you can obtain by airmail subscription. It contains complete details of volunteer excavations in Britain and sometimes in other parts of the world. The council's guide is accessible on the World Wide Web at http://www.le.ac.uk/archaeology/adm3/wac/index.htm.

Information on archaeological field schools can be obtained from fliers posted on university department bulletin boards and also from the Society for American Archaeology. The American Anthropological Association publishes a summer field school list annually, too.

GLOSSARY OF TERMS

This glossary gives informal definitions of key words and ideas mentioned in the text. It is not a comprehensive dictionary of archaeology. Jargon is kept to a minimum, but a few technical expressions are inevitable. Terms such as *adaptation* and *mutation,* which are common in contexts other than archaeology, are not listed. A good dictionary will clarify these and other such terms.

absolute chronology Dating in calendar years before the present; chronometric dating.

accelerator mass spectrometry (AMS) dating A method of radiocarbon dating which counts actual 14C atoms. Requires much smaller samples for precise dates.

activity area An area identified as being devoted to a specific activity by artifact patternings.

activity set A set of artifacts that reveals the activities of an individual.

analogy A process of reasoning whereby two entities that share some similarities are assumed to share many others.

analysis A stage of archaeological research that involves describing and classifying artifactual and nonartifactual data.

anthropology The study of humanity in the widest possible sense. Anthropology studies humanity from the earliest times up to the present, and it includes cultural and physical anthropology and archaeology.

archaeological context *See* context.

archaeological culture A group of assemblages representing the surviving remains of an extinct culture.

archaeological data Material recognized as significant evidence by the archaeologist and collected and recorded as part of the research. The four main classes of archaeological data are artifacts, features, structures, and food remains.

archaeological record The material remains of the past, archaeological sites, artifacts, food remains, and so forth, which form the surviving database for the study of the human past.

archaeological theory A body of theoretical concepts providing both a framework and a means for archaeologists to look beyond the facts and material objects for explanations of events that took place in prehistory.

archaeological unit Arbitrary unit of classification set up by archaeologists to conveniently separate in time and space one grouping of artifacts from another.

archaeologist Someone who studies the past using scientific methods, with the motive of recording and interpreting ancient cultures rather than collecting artifacts for profit or display.

archaeology A special form of anthropology that uses material remains to study extinct human societies. The objectives of archaeology are to construct culture history, reconstruct past lifeways, and study cultural process.

Archaic In the New World, a period when hunter-gatherers were exploiting a broad spectrum of resources and may have been experimenting with agriculture.

area excavation Excavation of a large, horizontal area, usually used to uncover houses and prehistoric settlement patterns.

artifact Any object manufactured or modified by human beings.

assemblage All of the artifacts found at a site, including the sum of all subassemblages at the site.

association The relationship between an artifact and other archaeological finds and a site level or other artifact, structure, or feature in the site.

attribute A well-defined feature of an artifact that cannot be further subdivided. Archaeologists identify types of attributes, including form, style, and technology, in order to classify and interpret artifacts.

attritional age profile The distribution of ages in an animal population that results from selective hunting or predation.

Australopithecus Primates whose fossil remains have been found mainly in eastern and southern Africa. They are thought to be closely related to the first human beings, who may, indeed, have evolved among them.

band The simple form of human social organization that flourished for most of prehistory. Bands consist of a family or a series of families, usually ranging from 20 to 50 people.

battleship curve Shape on a seriation graph formed by plotted points representing, for instance, the rise in popularity of an artifact, its period of maximum popularity, and its eventual decline.

biosphere All of the earth's living organisms interacting with the physical environment.

blade In stone technology, a term applied to punch-struck flakes, usually removed from a cylindrical core. Often made by prehistoric societies after 35,000 years ago.

cambium A viscid substance under the bark of trees, in which the annual growth of wood and bark takes place.

carbon isotopic analysis The study of ancient diet using the ratio between stable carbon isotopes—carbon 12 and carbon 14—in animal tissue.

carrying capacity The number of people per square mile that a specified area of land can support, given a particular subsistence level.

catastrophic age profile Distribution of ages in an animal population as a result of death by natural causes.

causes In archaeology, events that force people to make decisions about how to deal with new situations.

ceramics Objects of fired clay.

characterization studies Methods of identifying the sources of prehistoric artifacts, especially those in clay, metal, and stone.

chiefdom A form of social organization more complex than a tribal society, which has evolved some form of leadership structure and some mechanisms for distributing goods and services throughout the society.

The chief who heads such a society and the specialists who work for the chief are supported by the voluntary contributions of the people.

chronological types Types defined by form that are time markers.

chronometric dating Dating in years before the present; absolute dating.

classical archaeologist A student of the classical civilizations of Greece and Rome.

classification The ordering of archaeological data into groups and classes, using various ordering systems.

cognitive archaeology *See* cognitive-processual archaeology.

cognitive-processual archaeology A theoretical approach to archaeology that combines processual approaches with other data to study religious beliefs and other intangibles.

community In archaeology, the tangible remains of the activities of the maximum number of people who together occupy a settlement at any one period.

component An association of all the artifacts from one occupation level at a site.

conchoidal fracture A type of fracture characteristic of crystalline rocks used for ancient stone tool manufacture.

context The position of an archaeological find in time and space, established by measuring and assessing its associations, matrix, and provenance. The assessment includes study of what has happened to the find since it was buried in the ground.

coprolite Excrement preserved by desiccation or fossilization.

core In archaeology, a lump of stone from which human-struck flakes have been removed.

crop mark Differential growth in crops and vegetational cover that reveals from the air the outlines of archaeological sites.

cross-dating Dating of sites by objects or artifact associations of known ages.

cultural ecology Study of the dynamic interactions between human societies and their environments. Under this approach, culture is the primary adaptive mechanism used by human societies.

cultural process A deductive approach to archaeological research that is designed to study the changes and interactions in cultural systems and the processes by which human cultures change throughout time. Processual archaeologists use both descriptive and explanatory models.

cultural resource management (CRM) The conservation and management of archaeological sites and artifacts as a means of protecting the past.

cultural selection The process that leads to the acceptance of some cultural traits and innovations that make a culture more adaptive to its environment; somewhat akin to natural selection in biological evolution.

cultural system A perspective on culture that thinks of culture and its environment as a number of linked systems in which change occurs through a series of minor, linked variations in one or more of these systems.

culture A theoretical concept used by archaeologists and anthropologists to describe humankind's external means of adapting to the natural environment. Human culture is a set of designs for living that help mold our responses to different situations. It is our primary means of adapting to our environment. A *culture* in archaeology is an arbitrary unit meaning similar assemblages of artifacts found at several sites, defined in a precise context of time and space.

culture area An arbitrary geographical area which shares a common human cultural tradition. For example, the Maori culture area occurs in New Zealand.

culture history An approach to archaeology assuming that artifacts can be used to build up a generalized picture of human culture and descriptive models in time and space, and that these can be interpreted.

cuneiform From the Greek word *cuneus,* meaning *a wedge.* The earliest known, wedgelike script from Mesopotamia.

debitage analysis The study of waste products resulting from tool manufacture to reconstruct stone technology; from the French word *debitage,* meaning *discarded waste.*

deductive reasoning A process of reasoning that involves testing generalizations by generating hypotheses and testing them with data. Deductive research is cumulative and involves constant refining of hypotheses. This contrasts with inductive approaches where one proceeds from specific observations to general conclusions.

dendrochronology Tree-ring chronology.

descriptive types Types based on the physical or external properties of an artifact.

diffusion The spread of a culture trait from one area to another by means of contact between people.

ecofact An object not modified by human manufacture brought into a site. An example: an unworked pebble brought into an early human occupation site.

ecosystem An environmental system maintained by the regulation of vertical food chains and patterns of energy flow.

Electronic spin resonance (ESR) A dating method that measures radiation-induced defects within a bone or shell sample up to a million years old.

endogamy A preference requiring marriage within a social or cultural unit.

epiphysis The articular end of a long bone, which fuses during adulthood.

ethnoarchaeology Living archaeology, a form of ethnography that deals mainly with material remains. Archaeologists carry out living archaeology to document the relationships between human behavior and the patterns of artifacts and food remains in the archaeological record.

ethnographic analogy *See* analogy.

ethnohistory Study of the past using non-Western, indigenous historical records, and especially oral traditions.

eustatic effect The effect of water locked up in ice sheets during glacial periods that melts in interglacials.

excavation The digging of archaeological sites, removal of the matrix, and observance of the provenance and context of the finds therein, and the recording of them in a three-dimensional way.

exchange system A system for exchanging goods and services between individuals and communities.

experimental archaeology The use of carefully controlled modern experiments to provide data to aid in interpretation of the archaeological record.

feature An artifact such as a house or storage pit, which cannot be removed from a site; normally, it is only recorded.

feces Excrement.

fission-track dating The observance of accumulations of radioactivity in glass and volcanic rocks to produce absolute dates.

flake tools Stone tools made of flakes removed from cores.

flotation In archaeology, recovering plant remains by using water to separate seeds from their surrounding deposit.

foot survey Archaeological reconnaissance on foot, often with a set interval between members of the survey team.

form The physical characteristics—size and shape or composition—of any archaeological find. Form is an essential part of attribute analysis.

formation processes *See* site-formation processes.

frequency seriation Artifact ordering using percentages of types or attributes.

function In an evolutionary context, the forms that directly affect the Darwinian fitness of the populations in which they occur.

functionalism The notion that a social institution within a society has a function in fulfilling the needs of a social organism.

functional type Type based on cultural use or function rather than on outward form or chronological position.

general systems theory The notion that any organism or organization can be studied as a system broken down into many interacting subsystems, or parts; sometimes called cybernetics.

geoarchaeology The study of archaeology using the methods and concepts of the earth sciences.

Geographic Information Systems (GIS) Computer-generated mapping systems that allow archaeologists to plot and analyze site distributions against environmental and other background data derived from remote sensing, digitized maps, and other sources.

half-life The time required for one-half of a radioactive isotope to decay into a stable element. Used as a basis for radiocarbon and other dating methods.

hieroglyphs Ancient writing form with pictographic or ideographic symbols; used in Egypt, Mesoamerica, and elsewhere.

historical archaeology The study of archaeological sites in conjunction with historical records. It is sometimes called historic sites archaeology.

history Study of the past through written records.

Holocene period Geological time since the Ice Age (Pleistocene) ended about 15,000 years ago.

hominid A member of the family Hominidae, represented today by one species, *Homo sapiens*.

Homo erectus Human beings who evolved from Lower Pleistocene hominids c. 1.9 million years ago. They possessed larger brains and made more elaborate stone tools than their predecessors and settled in much more extreme environments, as far apart as western Europe, Asia, and tropical Africa.

Homo habilis A toolmaking hominid form that flourished in tropical Africa about 2.5 million years ago, which is thought to be an ancestor of later humanity.

horizon A widely distributed set of culture traits and artifact assemblages whose distribution and chronology allow one to assume that they spread rapidly. Often, horizons are formed of artifacts that were associated with widespread, distinctive religious beliefs.

horizontal (area) excavation Archaeological excavation designed to uncover large areas of a site, especially settlement layouts.

household An arbitrary archaeological unit defining artifact patterns reflecting the activities that take place around a house and assumed to belong to one household.

human culture *See* culture.

ideology A set of political or religious beliefs.

ideology of domination A pervasive ideology which rationalizes the institutions of a state-organized society, notably divine kingship and social inequality.

inductive reasoning Reasoning by which one proceeds from specific observations to general conclusions.

inevitable variation The notion that cultures change and vary with time, cumulatively. The reasons for these changes are little understood.

intensive survey A systematic survey of a research area that attempts to find all possible sites.

interpretation The stage in research at which the results of archaeological analyses are synthesized and we attempt to explain their meaning.

invention The creation or evolution of a new idea.

isostatic effect The adjustment of the earth's crust to the weight of ice sheets.

landscape signature In archaeology, the material remains of human activities across the landscape.

lithic analysis The analysis of stone tools and stone tool technology.

loess Fine glacial dust transported by wind.

material culture Normally refers to technology and artifacts.

matriarchal Family authority resting with the woman's family.

matrix The physical substance that surrounds an archaeological find. It can be gravel, sand, mud, or water, or other such substances.

Mesoamerica That portion of Central America and Mexico where preindustrial civilizations developed.

midden In archaeology, an accumulation of food remains and other occupation debris. Often used to describe accumulations of shells and mollusks, hence "shell midden."

migration Movements of entire societies that decide to change their own sphere of influence.

multilinear cultural evolution A theory of cultural evolution that sees each human culture evolving in its own way by adaptation to diverse environments. Sometimes divided into four broad stages of evolution of social organization (band, tribe, chiefdom, and state-organized society).

natural type An archaeological type coinciding with an actual category recognized by the original toolmaker.

nonintrusive archaeology Archaeological research without excavation.

normative view A view of human culture arguing that one can identify the abstract rules regulating a particular culture; a com-monly used basis for studying archaeological cultures throughout time.

obsidian Volcanic glass.

offsite area Sites with low densities of artifacts.

oral traditions Cultural traditions transmitted from one generation to the next by word of mouth.

organic materials Materials such as bone, wood, horn, or hide that were once living organisms.

paleoethnobotany The study of the exploitation of ancient plants by humans.

palynology Pollen analysis.

periglacial Surrounding a glacial area.

phase An archaeological unit defined by characteristic groupings of culture traits that can be identified precisely in time and space. It lasts for a relatively short time and is found at one or more sites in a locality or region. Its culture traits are clear enough to distinguish it from other phases.

physical anthropologists Basically, those who study biological anthropology, which includes the study of fossil human beings, genetics, primates, and blood groups.

phytoliths Minute particles of silica from plant cells that provide a way of identifying ancient plants.

Pleistocene The last major geological epoch, extending from about 2.5 million years ago until about 11,000 B.C. It is sometimes called the the Great Ice Age and is part of the Quaternary with the Holocene.

postprocessual archaeology Theoretical approaches to archaeology that are critical of processual archaeology and that emphasize social factors in human societies.

potassium-argon dating An absolute dating technique based on the decay rate of potassium 40K, which becomes 40Ar.

potsherd A fragment of a clay vessel.

prehistorians Archaeologists who study the millennia of human history preceding written records. Prehistorians study prehistoric archaeology.

pre-state society A small-scale society characteristic of the community, band, or village.

primary context An undisturbed association, matrix, and provenance.

probabilistic sampling A means of relating small data samples in mathematical ways to much larger populations.

process In archaeology, the process of cultural change that takes place as a result of interactions between a cultural system's elements and the system and its environment.

processual archaeology An approach to archaeology that uses research design and the scientific method to analyze conditions of cultural change.

provenance (or provenience) The precise three-dimensional position of the find within the matrix as recorded by the archaeologist. It is derived from accurate records kept during excavations and site surveys, from evidence that is inevitably destroyed once a site is dug or artifacts are collected from a surface site.

public archaeology Basically archaeological education, informing the general public about archaeology and the past.

Quaternary *See* Pleistocene.

radiocarbon dating An absolute dating method based on measuring the decay rate of the carbon isotope, carbon 14, into stable nitrogen. The resulting dates are calibrated with tree-ring chronologies, from radiocarbon ages into dates in calendar years.

random sampling A sampling method using random choice of samples to obtain unbiased samples.

reciprocity In archaeology, the exchange of goods between two parties.

reconnaissance survey A provisional survey of an area to establish tentative site distributions.

redistribution The dispersal of goods from a central place throughout a society, a complex process that was a critical part of the evolution of civilization.

reductive technology A technology where an artisan acquires material, then shapes it by removing flakes or other fragments until it is fashioned into the finished product. A term normally applied to stone technology.

refitting (retrofitting) The reassembling of stone debitage and cores to reconstruct ancient lithic technologies.

region A geographically defined area in which ecological adaptations are basically similar.

relative chronology Time scale developed by the law of superposition or artifact ordering.

remote sensing Reconnaissance and site survey methods using such devices as aerial photography to detect subsurface features and sites.

research design A carefully formulated and systematic plan for executing archaeological research.

resistivity survey Measurement of differences in electrical conductivity in soils, used to detect buried features such as walls and ditches.

satellite sensor imagery A method of recording sites from the air using infrared radiation that is beyond the practical spectral response of photographic film. Useful for tracing prehistoric agricultural systems that have disturbed the topsoil over wide areas.

scientific method A disciplined and carefully ordered approach to acquiring knowledge about the real world using deductive reasoning combined with testing and retesting.

secondary context A context of an archaeological find that has been disturbed by subsequent human activity or natural phenomena.

selective excavation Archaeological excavation of parts of a site using sampling methods or carefully placed trenches that do not uncover the entire site.

seriation techniques Methods used to place artifacts in chronological order; artifacts closely similar in form or style are placed close to one another.

settlement archaeology The study of ancient settlements and settlement distributions in the context of their landscape.

settlement pattern (system) Distribution of human settlements on the landscape and within archaeological communities.

shovel unit or pit Trenching method used on archaeological survey as a form of test pit, employing a shallow cut made with a shovel.

site Any place where objects, features, or ecofacts manufactured or modified by human beings are found. A site can range from a living site to a quarry site, and it can be defined in functional and other ways.

site-formation processes The processes, natural and humanly caused, that modify the material remains of the past in the ground after their abandonment.

soil marks Marks in plowed land which reveal buried structures from the air.

sourcing *See* Characterization studies.

stratified sampling A probabilistic sampling technique used to cluster and isolate sample units when regular spacing is inappropriate for cultural reasons.

stratigraphy Observation of the superimposed layers in an archaeological site.

structures Houses, granaries, temples, and other buildings that can be identified from standing remains, patterns of postholes, and other features in the ground.

subassemblage Association of artifacts denoting a particular form of prehistoric activity practiced by a group of people.

superposition The principle, borrowed from geology, that states that a stratigraphic layer overlying another is younger than the one below it.

surface survey The collection of archaeological finds from sites, with the objective of gathering representative samples of artifacts from the surface. Surface survey also establishes the types of activity on the site, locates major structures, and gathers information on the most densely occupied areas of the site that could be most productive for total or sample excavation.

systematics In archaeology, procedures for creating sets of archaeological units derived from a logical system for a particular purpose.

systematic sampling An alternative form of random sampling in which one unit is chosen, then others at regular intervals from the first. Useful for studying artifact patterning.

taphonomy Study of the processes by which animal bones and other fossil remains are transformed after deposition.

taxonomy An ordered set of operations that results in the subdividing of objects into ordered classifications.

tell Arabic word for an occupation mound; a term referring to archaeological sites of this type in the Near East.

temper Coarse material such as sand or ground shell added to fine pot clay to make it bond during firing.

tempering A process for hardening iron blades, involving heating and rapid cooling. Also, material added to potters' clay.

test pit An excavation unit used to sample or probe a site before large-scale excavation or to check surface surveys.

thermoluminescence A chronometric dating method that measures the amount of light energy released by a baked clay object when heated rapidly. Gives an indication of the time elapsed since the object was last heated.

Three Age System A technological subdivision of the prehistoric past developed for Old World prehistory in 1806.

three-dimensional recording Establishing the exact position of an artifact, feature, or other archaeological find in time and space.

Total Data Station An electronic recording device used for surveying archaeological sites.

tool kit Basic set of tools used by a culture.

topographic maps Maps that can be used to relate archaeological sites to basic features of the natural landscape.

total excavation Complete excavation of an entire archaeological site.

trace element analysis A means of identifying the sources of artifacts and raw materials using X-ray spectrometry and other techniques which identify distinctive trace elements in stones and minerals. Trace element analysis is used to study the sources of obsidian and other materials traded over long distances.

tradition Persistent technological or cultural patterns identified by characteristic artifact forms. These persistent forms outlast a single phase and can occur over a wide area.

transformation processes Continuous, dynamic, and unique cultural or noncultural preocesses that affect archaeological sites after their abandonment.

tribe A larger group of bands unified by sodalities and governed by a council of representatives from the bands, kin groups, or sodalities within it.

type In archaeology, a grouping of artifacts created for comparison with other groups. This grouping may or may not coincide with the actual tool types designed by the original manufacturers.

typology   The classification of types.

underwater archaeology   Study of archaeological sites and shipwrecks beneath the surface of the water.

uranium-series dating   A dating method which measures the decay of uranium into various daughter elements inside calcium carbonate formations, such as limestone. Dates sites to between 50,000 and a million years old.

use-wear analysis   Microscopic analysis of artifacts such as stone tools to detect signs of wear through use on their working edges.

vertical excavation   Excavation undertaken to establish a chronological sequence, normally covering a limited area.

zooarchaeology   The study of animal remains in archaeology.

GLOSSARY OF SITES AND CULTURES

These brief descriptions give some background on prehistoric sites and cultures mentioned in the text; they are not meant to be precise definitions. Ask your instructor for more information and references if you need them. Some sites mentioned in passing are not included in this list. Numbers listed behind sites correspond to numbers on the endpaper map.

Abri Pataud, France (1) A large rockshelter near the Vezère River in the Dordogne region of southwestern France, occupied by Neanderthal and Cro-Magnon hunter-gatherers between about 50,000 and 19,000 years ago.

Abu Simbel, Egypt (2) Ancient Egyptian temple erected by Ramesses II in Nubia, c. 1250 B.C. The site with its seated figures of the pharaoh was moved to higher ground to prevent its flooding by Lake Nasser in 1968 at a cost of $40 million.

Abydos, Egypt (3) Site of many early ancient Egyptian burials including King Scorpion, c. 3150 B.C.

Acheulian A widespread early Stone Age culture named after the town of St. Acheul in northern France. The Acheulian flourished in Africa, western Europe, and southern Asia from before a million years ago until less than 100,000 years before present. The Acheulians made many types of stone artifacts, including multipurpose butchering hand axes and cleaving tools.

Adena, Ohio (4) A distinctive burial cult and village culture in the Ohio Valley of the Midwest. It flourished between about 700 B.C. and A.D. 200 and was remarkable for its long-distance trading and distinctive burial cults expressed in large earthworks and mounds.

'Ain Ghazal, Jordan (5) An early farming village in the Jordan valley, occupied c. 7500 B.C. It is remarkable for its clay female figurines, perhaps evidence of an early fertility cult.

Akrotiri, Greece A Bronze Age village on Santorini Island in the Aegean Sea destroyed by a huge volcanic explosion in about 1450 B.C.

Ali Kosh, Iran (6) Early farming site on the Deh Luran plain in Iran, where evidence for cereal cultivation was found with flotation techniques. The site dates to as early as 7500 B.C.

Angkor Wat, Cambodia (7) An elaborate mortuary temple built by Khmer King Suryavarman II in the twelfth century A.D. as a reproduction of the Hindu universe.

Apple Creek, Illinois (8) An Archaic site, where people engaged in intensive collecting of wild vegetable foods after 3000 B.C. They concentrated on hickory nuts, acorns, and other common species.

Aramis, Ethiopia (9) Early hominid site dating to c. 4.5 million years ago.

Avaris, Egypt (10) A palace and trading site in Lower Egypt celebrated for its Minoan (Cretan) wall paintings, evidence of trade between Egypt and Crete in about 1500 B.C.

Avebury, England (11) A spectacular stone circle and accompanying sacred landscape built c. 2500 B.C.

Benin, Nigeria (12) A West Africa state ruled from the city of Benin from before A.D. 1400 to modern times.

Betatakin, Arizona (13) An Anasazi pueblo dating to c. A.D. 1270.

Cahokia, Illinois (14) Mississippian ceremonial center at the height of its power in A.D. 1050 to 1250.

Carchemish, Syria (15) Hittite and Roman city on the Euphrates River. An important trading station and ferry point, especially in 1300 B.C.

Çatalhöyük, Turkey (44) Large farming village and obsidian trading center dating to c. 6000 B.C.

Céide Fields, Ireland (16) A Neolithic field system in northwestern Ireland dating to c. 5000 B.C.

Cerén, El Salvador (17) A Maya village buried by an unexpected volcanic eruption in A.D. 684. The ash mantled the village so completely that complete household inventories, even crops, are preserved in the archaeological record.

Cerro Palenque, Honduras (18) Terminal Classic Maya center dating to after A.D. 900.

Chaco Canyon, New Mexico Anasazi people built a series of "Great Houses," multiroom pueblos in this canyon between A.D. 950 and 1175.

Chauvet, Grotte de, France (19) Cave in southeastern France famous for its rock art, dating to c. 31,000 to 24,000 years ago.

Chichén Itzá, Mexico (20) A Postclassic Maya ceremonial center in the northern Yucatán dating to c. A.D. 1100.

Chinchorro culture, Chile (21) A coastal forager culture in northern Chile, famous for its mummies, dating to c. 2500 B.C.

Clovis (22) Paleo-Indian culture that flourished in North America, and perhaps further afield, about 8950 B.C. and somewhat earlier.

Colonial Williamsburg, Virginia (23) Reconstruction of Virginia's first capital city, carried out partly with the aid of archaeological research.

Copán, Honduras (24) A Classic Maya city, A.D. 435 to 900.

Diospolis Parva, Egypt (25) A Predynastic cemetery site, c. 3500 B.C., famous for Petrie's sequence dating.

Dirst, Arkansas (26) A site in the Buffalo River Valley occupied intermittently during the past 10,000 years, and intensively during Late Woodland times, between A.D. 600 and 900.

Easton Down, England (27) A Stone Age communal burial mound, built in about 3200 B.C. (*See also* Avebury.)

Epidauros, Greece (28) Greek amphitheater first dedicated in the fifth century B.C. and subsequently restored by the Romans.

Eridu, Iraq (29) An early city in the Mesopotamia delta that boasted of a major temple as early as 4000 B.C. One of the earliest cities in the world.

Flag Fen, England (30) A Late Bronze Age field system and ceremonial center in eastern England dating to c.1350 B.C. and later, famous for its wooden artifacts and timber posts and trackways.

Folsom (31) Paleo-Indian culture that flourished on the North American Plains after 9000 B.C.

Fort Mose, Florida (32) The first free African-American settlement in North America, 1738–1762.

Galatea Bay, New Zealand (33) An important shell midden site, about 500 years old, on New Zealand's North Island, famous for exemplary excavation methods and data recovery.

Garnsey, New Mexico A bison kill site of the fifteenth century A.D.

Giza, Egypt (34) The Pyramids at Giza were built in the desert near Cairo during Egypt's Old Kingdom, around 2550 B.C. The Great Pyramid is 481 feet (146.6 m) high and covers 13.1 acres (21 ha).

Godin Tepe, Iran (35) A trading settlement dating to c. 4000 B.C.

Gournia, Crete (36) A small Minoan town, c. 1500 B.C.

Grasshopper Pueblo, Arizona (37) An important Pueblo site occupied in the fourteenth and fifteenth centuries A.D.

Great Zimbabwe, Zimbabwe A complex of stone buildings in Central Africa associated with Shona chieftains and cattle groups dating to between A.D. 900 and 1500.

Hadar, Ethiopia (38) A region of Ethiopia where hominid fossils dating to as early as 4 million years ago have been found.

Hadrian's Wall, England (39) A wall built across northern England by the Roman emperor Hadrian in the second century A.D. to keep out the Scots.

Halieis, Greece (40) A Classical town of the fourth century B.C. Famous for its olive oil.

Harappan civilization, Pakistan (41) An urban civilization based on the Indus Valley, which flourished from before 2500 B.C. to 1500.

Head-Smashed-In, Canada Bison kill site in western Canada used by Plains hunters for over 5,000 years and intensively after A.D. 150 as a mass killing site.

Herculaneum, Italy (42) A Roman town destroyed by an eruption of Mount Vesuvius in A.D. 79.

Hissarlik, Turkey (43) The site of Homeric Troy in northwestern Turkey, which was an important Bronze Age city during the second millennium B.C.

Hogup Cave, Utah (45) A dry cave in the Great Basin occupied from c. 9000 B.C. until recent times, famous for its excellent dry preservation of organic artifacts such as fiber sandals.

Hohokam, Arizona A Southwestern cultural tradition that originated as early as 300 B.C. and lasted until A.D. 1500. The Hohokam people were farmers who occupied much of what is now Arizona. Their cultural heirs are the Pima and Tohono O'odham Indians of today.

Hopewell, Ohio (46) Between 200 B.C. and A.D. 600, the "Hopewell Interaction Sphere" flourished in the Midwest. Hopewell religious cults and distinctive burial customs were associated with an art tradition that spread far and wide through long-distance trading connections.

Ingombe Ilede, Zambia (47) Trading village in the middle Zambezi valley, dating to the fifteenth century A.D.

Inyan Ceyaka Atonwan, Minnesota (48) A historic Dakota Indian settlement occupied in the early nineteenth century A.D.

Jericho, Jordan (88) Long-lived city, with roots in early farming towns dating to the eighth millennium B.C.

Jomon tradition, Japan (49) A Japanese cultural tradition dating from before 8000 B.C. until about 300 B.C., remarkable for its early manufacturing of pottery and complex hunter-gatherer culture.

Kanesh, Turkey (50) An important Hittite trading town of 1900 B.C., famous for its Assyrian colony outside the community.

Karnak, Egypt (51) Site of the Temple of the ancient Egyptian sun god Amun, which reached the height of its glory in the New Kingdom c. 1500 B.C.

Keatley Creek, Canada (52) An important fishing and trading site near the Fraser River in interior British Columbia, dating to between 3,500 and 200 years ago.

Khok Phanom Di, Thailand A village and burial ground dating to 2000 to 1400 B.C.

Khorsabad, Iraq (53) Palace of Assyrian King Sargon, eighth century B.C.

Klasies River Cave, South Africa (54) A Middle Stone Age cave, occupied c. 120,000 to 100,000 years ago, which yielded fossil and cultural evidence for very early modern humans.

Knossos, Crete (55) Palace and shrine complex in northern Crete, which started life as a small village in about 6000 B.C. and became the major center of Minoan civilization. It was abandoned in the late second millennium B.C.

Koobi Fora, Kenya (56) A location on the eastern shores of Lake Turkana in northern Kenya, where the earliest traces of human culture have been found, dating to more than 2.5 milion years ago.

Koster, Illinois (57) From before 7000 B.C. until less than 1,000 years ago, huntergatherers and later farmers settled at this location on the Illinois River to exploit the fertile river bottom. The site is unusual for its long stratigraphic sequence of Archaic and Woodland settlements and abundant food remains.

Kourion, Cyprus (58) A small Roman port in southwestern Cyprus in the eastern Mediterranean overwhelmed by a great earthquake early on the morning of July 21, A.D. 365. Excavations at the village have revealed many details of a long-forgotten disaster.

Laetoli, Tanzania (59) This East African site yielded the earliest hominid footprints, potassium-argon dated to more than 3.5 million years ago.

Lascaux Cave, France (60) A painted cave of the Magdalenian culture of southwestern France dating to about 15,000 years ago.

Lovelock Cave, Nevada (61) A desert site in the far West occupied as early as 7000 B.C. Located near a desert marsh, it has yielded minute details of prehistoric desert adaptations over a long period.

Maiden Castle, England (62) An Iron Age hillfort in southern England attacked by the Romans in A.D. 43.

Martin's Hundred, Virginia (63) A Colonial American village dating to A.D. 1620–1623. (*See also* Colonial Williamsburg, Virginia.)

Meer, Belgium (64) Stone Age site of 7000 B.C., famous for its stone tool research.

Mesa Verde, Colorado (65) An area famous for its Anasazi pueblos, notably the Cliff Palace, which reached its heyday in the twelfth century A.D.

Mezhirich, Ukraine A settlement of mammoth-bone framed houses near the Dnepr river, occupied by Stone Age big-game hunters about 18,000 years ago.

Mississippian A widespread cultural tradition in the souhteastern United States from the eleventh to fifteenth centuries A.D. and more recently.

Minoan civilization, Crete Bronze Age civilization based on trading of olive oil and wine, c. 2000 to 1450 B.C.

Moche civilization (68) A coastal state in northern coastal Peru, which reached its height after A.D. 400.

Modjokerto, Indonesia (67) *Homo erectus* site dating to 1.8 million years ago.

Monte Alban, Mexico (69) Ancient Zapotec capital of the Valley of Oaxaca, Mexico, in its heyday in the late to mid first millennium A.D.

Moundville, Alabama (70) Mississippian ceremonial center of the early first millennium A.D.

Naranjo, Guatemala (71) Maya center dating to c. A.D. 900. (*See also* Tikal.)

Neanderthal, Germany (72) Cave which yielded the first Neanderthal skull (named after the site) in 1856.

Nelson's Bay, South Africa (73) Late–Stone Age coastal cave in southeastern Africa occupied c. 5000 B.C.

Nevado Ampato, Peru (74) Site of an Inca ceremonial burial, c. A.D. 1490.

Nimrud, Iraq (75) Assyrian city, the biblical Calah. (*See also* Khorsabad, Iraq.)

Nineveh, Iraq (76) Assyrian capital, famous for the palace of King Assurbanipal in the seventh century B.C. (*See also* Khorsabad, Iraq.)

Nippur, Iraq (77) A Sumerian city in southern Iraq, c. 2800 B.C., celebrated in archaeological circles for its clay tablet archives.

Olduvai Gorge, Tanzania (78) Stratified lake beds with associated artifact scatters and kill sites, also early hominids, dating from slightly before 1.75 million years ago up to 100,000 years before present.

Olmec Olmec culture flourished in lowland Mexico from around 1200 B.C. to 500 B.C. Olmec people traded widely, had a distinctive art tradition that depicted humanlike jaguars and both natural and supernatural beings, and developed many of the basic patterns that were to sustain the Maya and other Mesoamerican civilizations such as Teotihuacán.

Olsen-Chubbuck, Colorado (79) An 8,000-year-old bison kill site on the North American plains that revealed many details of Paleo-Indian hunting and butchering techniques.

Olympia, Greece (80) Site of the Olympic Games in the northern Peloponnese c. 400 B.C.

Ozette, Washington (81) A coastal settlement in Washington state occupied for at least 1,000 years by ancestors of the present-day Makah Indians. Ozette suffered disaster two centuries ago when houses were buried by mudslides and preserved in perfect condition for archaeologists to investigate in the 1970s.

Palenque, Mexico (82) Classic Maya city and ceremonial center, which reached its height in the mid first millennium A.D.

Paleo-Indian A generic term used by American archaeologists to describe the earliest cultural traditions of the New World.

Paracas, Peru Cemeteries along the dry Peruvian coast used by ancient Andeans between 600 and 150 B.C.

Pecos, New Mexico (83) An Anasazi pueblo in the Southwest that was occupied for much of the past 2,000 years and provided the first stratigraphic sequence for Southwestern prehistory as a result of A. V. Kidder's excavations.

Pompeii, Italy (84) Roman town destroyed by an eruption of Mount Vesuvius in A.D. 79.

Port Royal, Jamaica (85) A waterside settlement in Jamaica partially submerged by an earthquake on June 7, 1692, that was once famous for its pirates and freebooters.

Pueblo Bonito, New Mexico (86) Anasazi pueblo first constructed about A.D. 850 and in its heyday in the twelfth century A.D.

Pulltrouser Swamp, Belize (87) Maya raised and wet field systems dating to between 200 B.C. and A.D. 850.

Qafzeh, Israel (89) A rock shelter that has yielded Neanderthal burials, thermoluminescence-dated to about 90,000 years ago.

Sand Canyon, Colorado (90) Anasazi pueblo in the Four Corners region of the Southwest occupied in the twelfth century A.D. (*See also* Mesa Verde, Colorado.)

Schoningen, Germany Site where 400,000-year-old wooden spears were discovered, probably manufactured by *Homo erectus*.

Shang Civilization Early Chinese civilization that flourished from as early as 2700 B.C. when the Xia dynasty arose in the north. The Shang dynasty rose to power around 1766 B.C. and ruled until 1122 B.C. Its rulers occupied a series of capitals near the Yellow River, the most famous being Anyang, occupied around 1400 B.C.

Sipán, Peru (91) Site of four spectacularly adorned warrior-priest graves of the Moche civilization, C. A.D. 400.

Similaun, Italy (92) The Similaun glacier high in the European Alps yielded the well-preserved corpse of a Bronze Age man, dating to about 3350 to 3300 B.C.

Snaketown, Arizona (93) A Hohokam pueblo in Arizona, occupied about 850 to 500 years ago and famous for its ball court and platform mounds. The Snaketown people probably maintained trading contacts with Mexican communities to the south.

Sounion, Greece (94) Classical Greek temple of the fifth century B.C. dedicated to the sea god Poseidon.

Star Carr, England (95) A postglacial hunting site in northeast England dating to about 9200 B.C., remarkable for the bone and wooden artifacts recovered from a small birchbark platform at the edge of a small lake.

Stonehenge (96) Stone circles in southern Britain that formed a sacred precinct as early as 2700 B.C. and remained in use until about 1600 B.C. Some authorities believe Stonehenge was an astronomical observa-

tory, but this viewpoint is controversial. (*See also* Avebury, England.)

Sumerians Creators of the civilization that flourished in southern Iraq between about 2900 and 2200 B.C. Sumerians lived in small city-states that perennially quarreled with one another. They depended on irrigation agriculture.

Tehuacán Valley, Mexico (97) A valley in which evidence for a gradual shift from hunting and gathering to deliberate cultivation of squashes and other minor crops, then maize, has been documented. Tehuacán was occupied as early as 10,000 B.C., with maize agriculture appearing before 2700 B.C.

Telloh, Iraq (98) Sumerian city where the civilization of that name was first recognized in the 1870s. (*See also* Eridu, Iraq.)

Tenochtitlán, Mexico (99) The spectacular capital of the Aztec civilization in the Valley of Mexico, founded in A.D. 1325 and destroyed by Spanish conquistador Hernan Cortés in 1521.

Teotihuacán, Mexico (100) A vast pre-Columbian city in highland Mexico that flourished from as early as 200 B.C. until it declined around A.D. 750. Teotihuacán maintained extensive political and trade contacts with lowland Mexico and is famed for its enormous public buildings and pyramids.

Tikal, Guatemala (101) Classic Maya city in the Guatemalan lowlands, which reached its height in about A.D. 600.

Tiwanaku, Bolivia (102) An Andean state and major ceremonial complex near Lake Titicaca at the height of its powers during the first millennium A.D.

Tollund, Denmark (103) Site of a bog corpse dating to the Danish Iron Age, C. 2000 years ago.

Ubar, Saudi Arabia (104) Desert city of the first millennium A.D. Celebrated for its spice trading.

Uluburun, Turkey (105) Spectacular Bronze Age shipwreck dating to 1305 B.C. with cargo from all over the eastern Mediterranean.

Ur, Iraq (106) Biblical city in southern Iraq that grew from a tiny farming hamlet founded as early as 4700 B.C. Known for its Early Dynastic Sumerian burials, where a ruler's entire retinue committed institutionalized suicide. (*See also* Eridu, Iraq.)

Uxmal, Mexico (107) Late Classic Maya city and ceremonial center in the northern Yucatán.

Valley of Kings, Egypt (108) Narrow, dry valley where Egypt's New Kingdom pharaohs were buried, including Tutankhamun.

Wadi Kubbaniyah, Egypt A hunter-gatherer site by the banks of the Nile river, occupied about 18,000 years ago.

Walpi Pueblo, Arizona (109) Hopi pueblo dating to c. A.D. 1400.

Wroxeter, England (110) Roman city in west-central England dating to the first few centuries after Christ.

REFERENCES

Anderson, Arthur O., and Charles E. Dibble. 1955. *Florentine Codex: General History of the Things of New Spain*. Vol. 7. Salt Lake City: University of Utah Press.

Belzoni, Giovanni Battista. 1820. *Narrative of the Recent Operations in Egypt and Nubia*. London: John Murray.

Binford, L. R., and Sally Binford, eds. *An Archaeological Perspective*. Chicago: Aldine.

Chauvet, Jean-Marie, Éliette Brunel Deschamps, and Christian Hillaire. 1996. *Dawn of Art: The Chauvet Cave*. New York: Abrams.

Clendinnen, Inga. 1991. *Aztecs*. Cambridge, Eng.: Cambridge University Press.

Deetz, James. 1967. *Invitation to Archaeology*. Garden City, NY: Natural History Press.

Fagan, Brian M. 1998. *From Black Land to Fifth Sun*. Reading, MA: Helix.

Flannery, Kent V., and Joyce Marcus. 1993. "Cognitive Archaeology." *Cambridge Journal of Archaeology* 3(2):260–267.

Kürten, Björn. 1986. *How to Deep-Freeze a Mammoth*. New York: Columbia University Press.

Nöel Hume, Ivor. 1983. *Martin's Hundred*. New York: Alfred Knopf.

Petrie, Flinders. 1904. *Methods and Aims in Archaeology*. London: John Murray.

Spector, Janet. 1993. *What This Awl Means* St. Paul: University of Minnesota Press.

Stephens, John Lloyd. 1841. *Incidents of Travel in Chiaspas and Yucatan*. New York: Harpers.

Swann, Brian, ed. 1994. *Coming to Light*. New York: Random House.

Tedlock, Dennis. 1996. *Popol Vub*. New York: Simon and Schuster.

Tylor, Edward. 1972. *Anthropology*. London: Macmillan.

Wheeler, Mortimer. 1943. *Maiden Castle*. London: Society of Antiquaries.

Woolley, Leonard. 1982. *Ur of the Chaldees*. New York: Barnes and Noble.

Worsaae, J. J. A. 1843. *Denmarks Oldtid*. Copenhagen: Neilson.

INDEX